IX

STORY BY YUU KAMIYA & TSUBAKI HIMANA
MANGA BY KURO
CHARACTER DESIGN BY SINO

ClockWork Planet
CONTENTS

IX

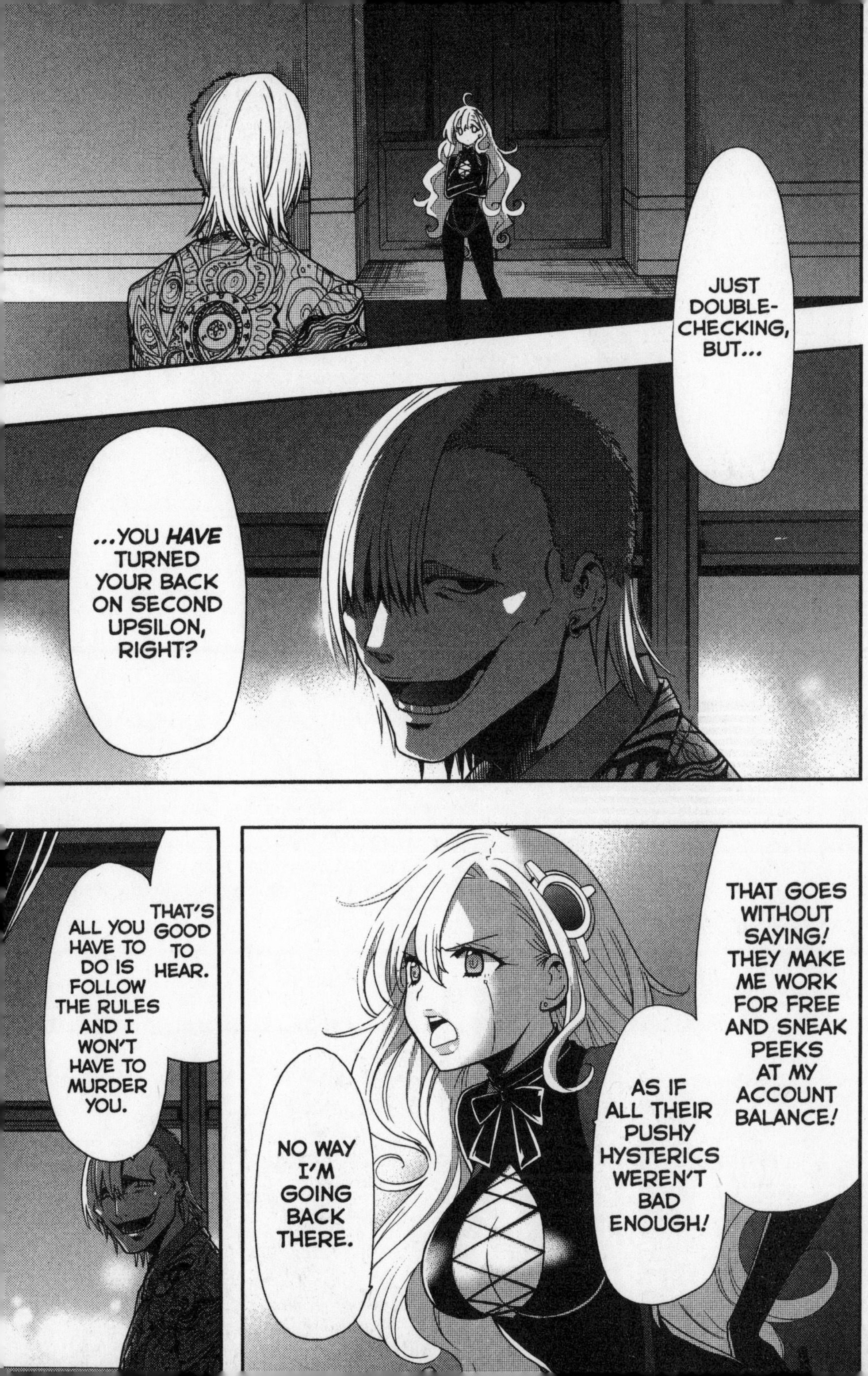
JUST DOUBLE-CHECKING, BUT...
...YOU *HAVE* TURNED YOUR BACK ON SECOND UPSILON, RIGHT?
THAT GOES WITHOUT SAYING! THEY MAKE ME WORK FOR FREE AND SNEAK PEEKS AT MY ACCOUNT BALANCE!
AS IF ALL THEIR PUSHY HYSTERICS WEREN'T BAD ENOUGH!
NO WAY I'M GOING BACK THERE.
THAT'S GOOD TO HEAR.
ALL YOU HAVE TO DO IS FOLLOW THE RULES AND I WON'T HAVE TO MURDER YOU.

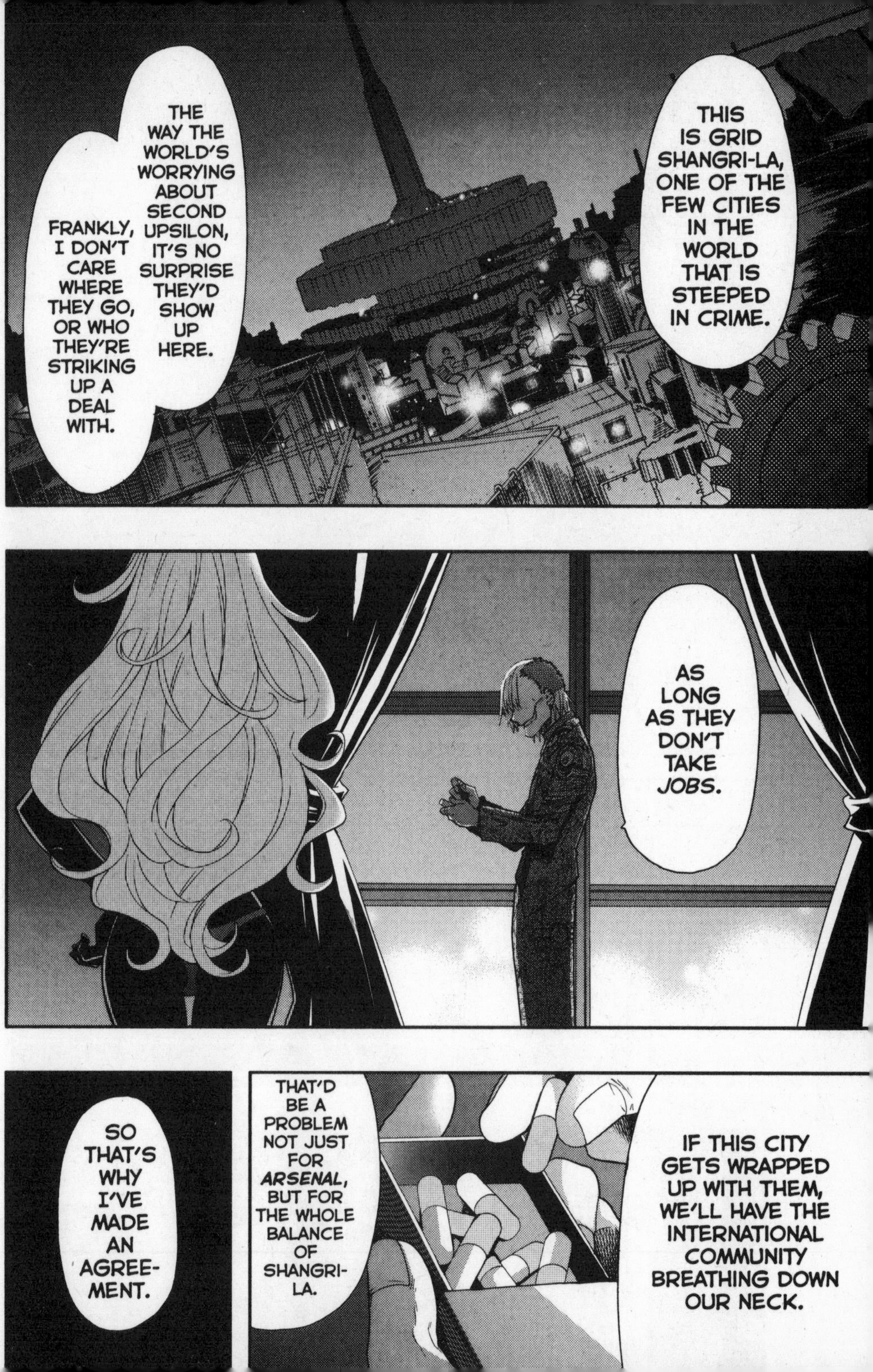
THIS IS GRID SHANGRI-LA, ONE OF THE FEW CITIES IN THE WORLD THAT IS STEEPED IN CRIME.
THE WAY THE WORLD'S WORRYING ABOUT SECOND UPSILON, IT'S NO SURPRISE THEY'D SHOW UP HERE.
FRANKLY, I DON'T CARE WHERE THEY GO, OR WHO THEY'RE STRIKING UP A DEAL WITH.
AS LONG AS THEY DON'T TAKE *JOBS*.
IF THIS CITY GETS WRAPPED UP WITH THEM, WE'LL HAVE THE INTERNATIONAL COMMUNITY BREATHING DOWN OUR NECK.
THAT'D BE A PROBLEM NOT JUST FOR *ARSENAL*, BUT FOR THE WHOLE BALANCE OF SHANGRI-LA.
SO THAT'S WHY I'VE MADE AN AGREE-MENT.

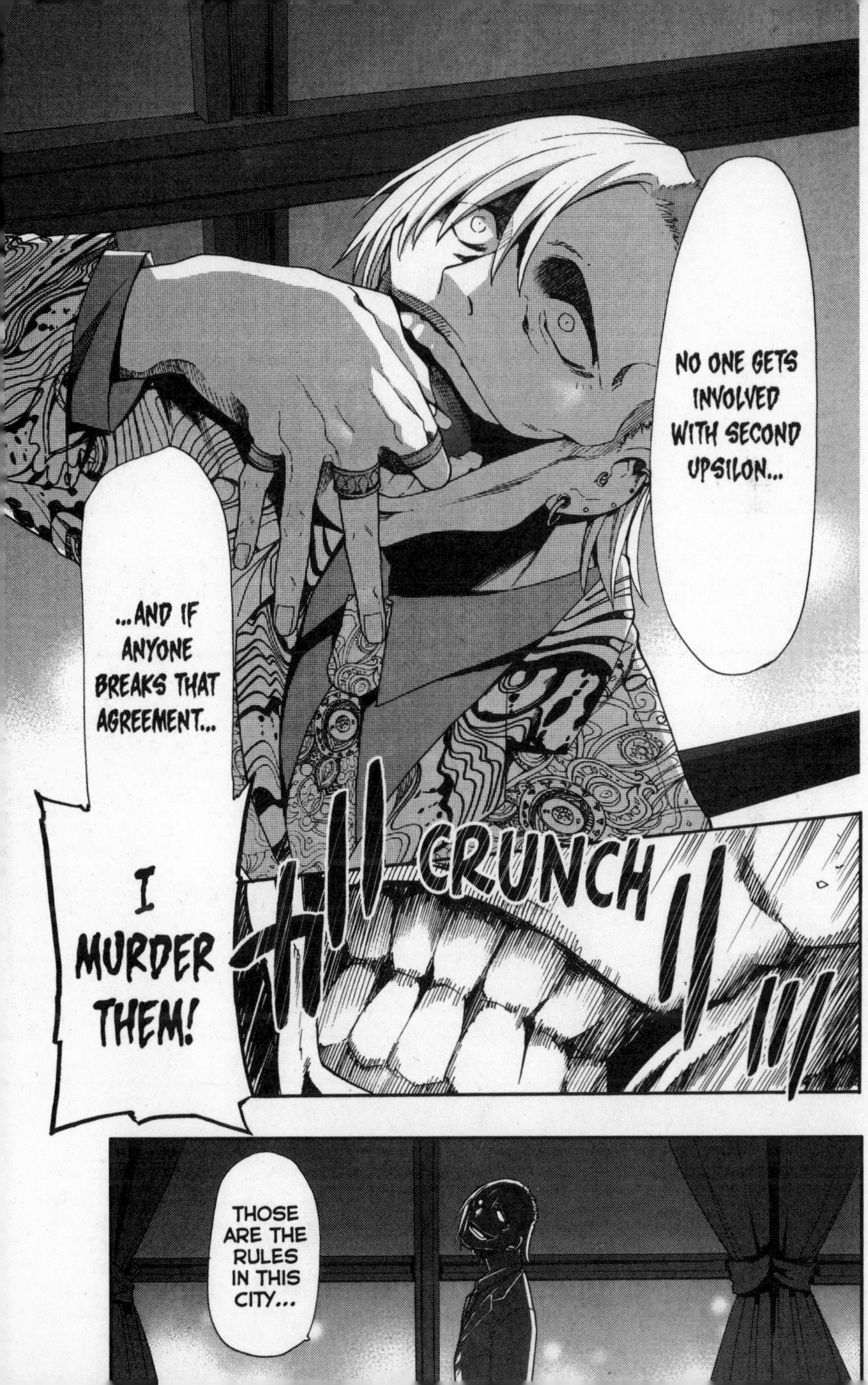
NO ONE GETS INVOLVED WITH SECOND UPSILON...
...AND IF ANYONE BREAKS THAT AGREEMENT...
I MURDER THEM!
CRUNCH
THOSE ARE THE RULES IN THIS CITY...

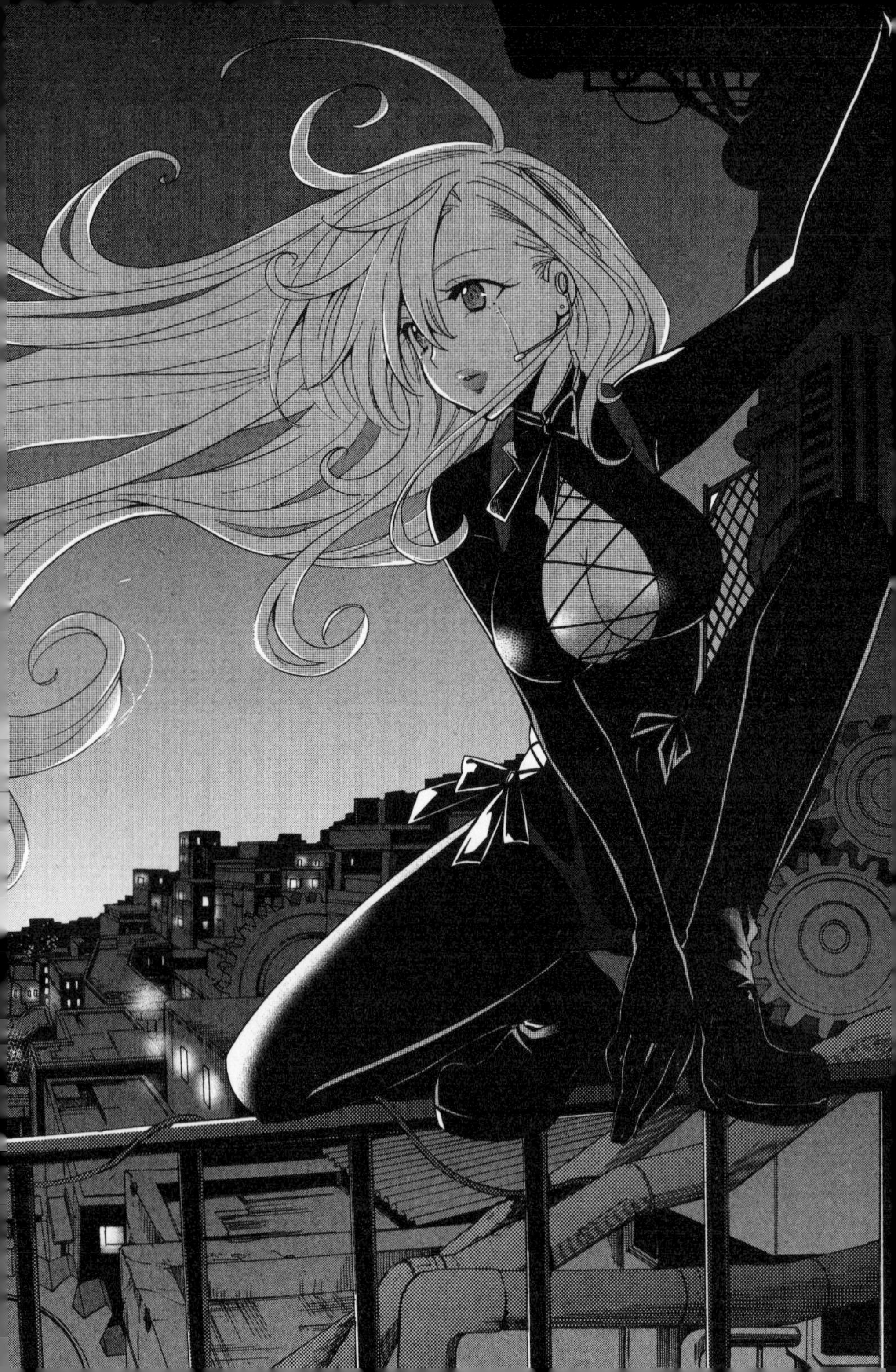

Clock 41: Giovanni Artigiano

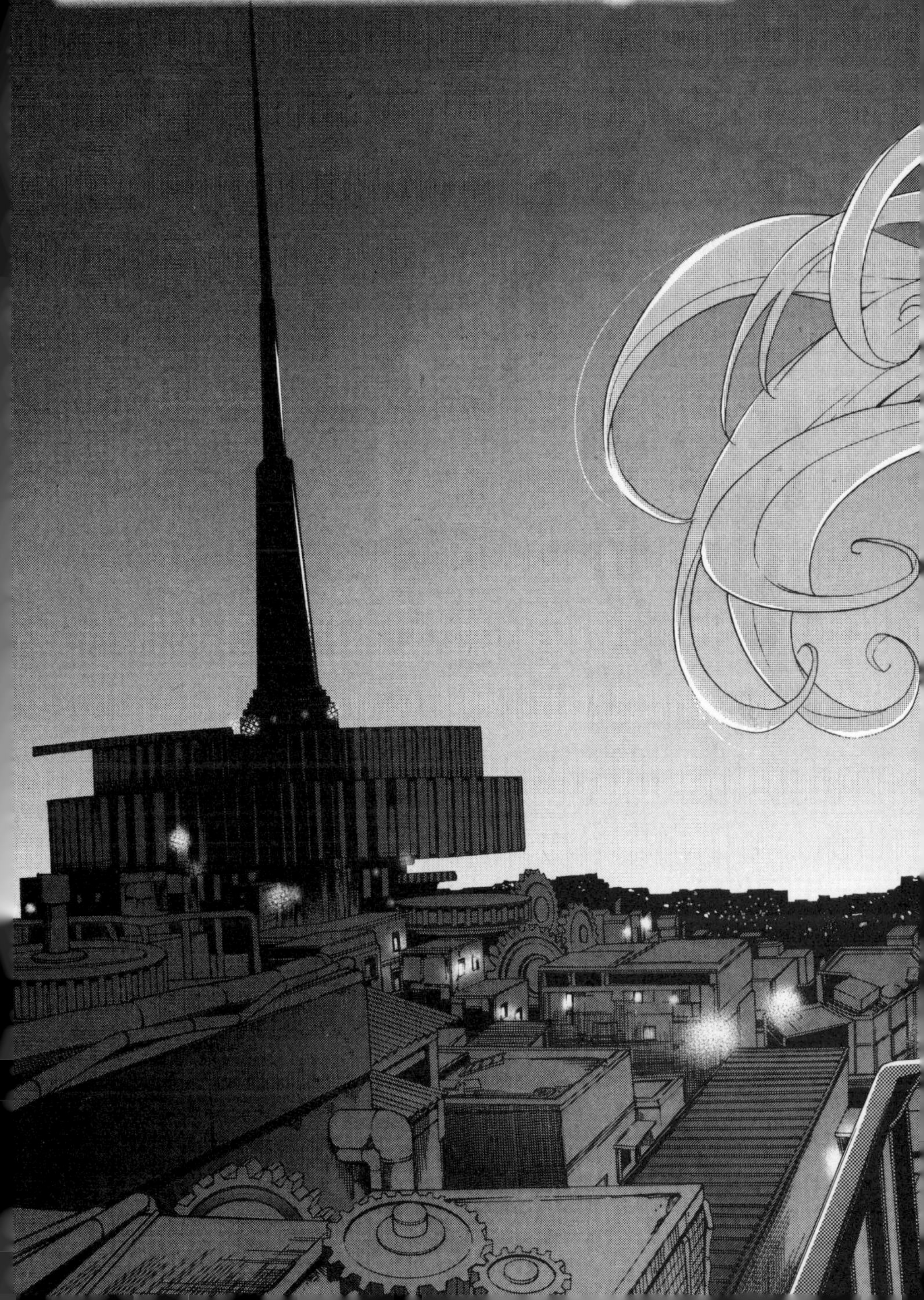

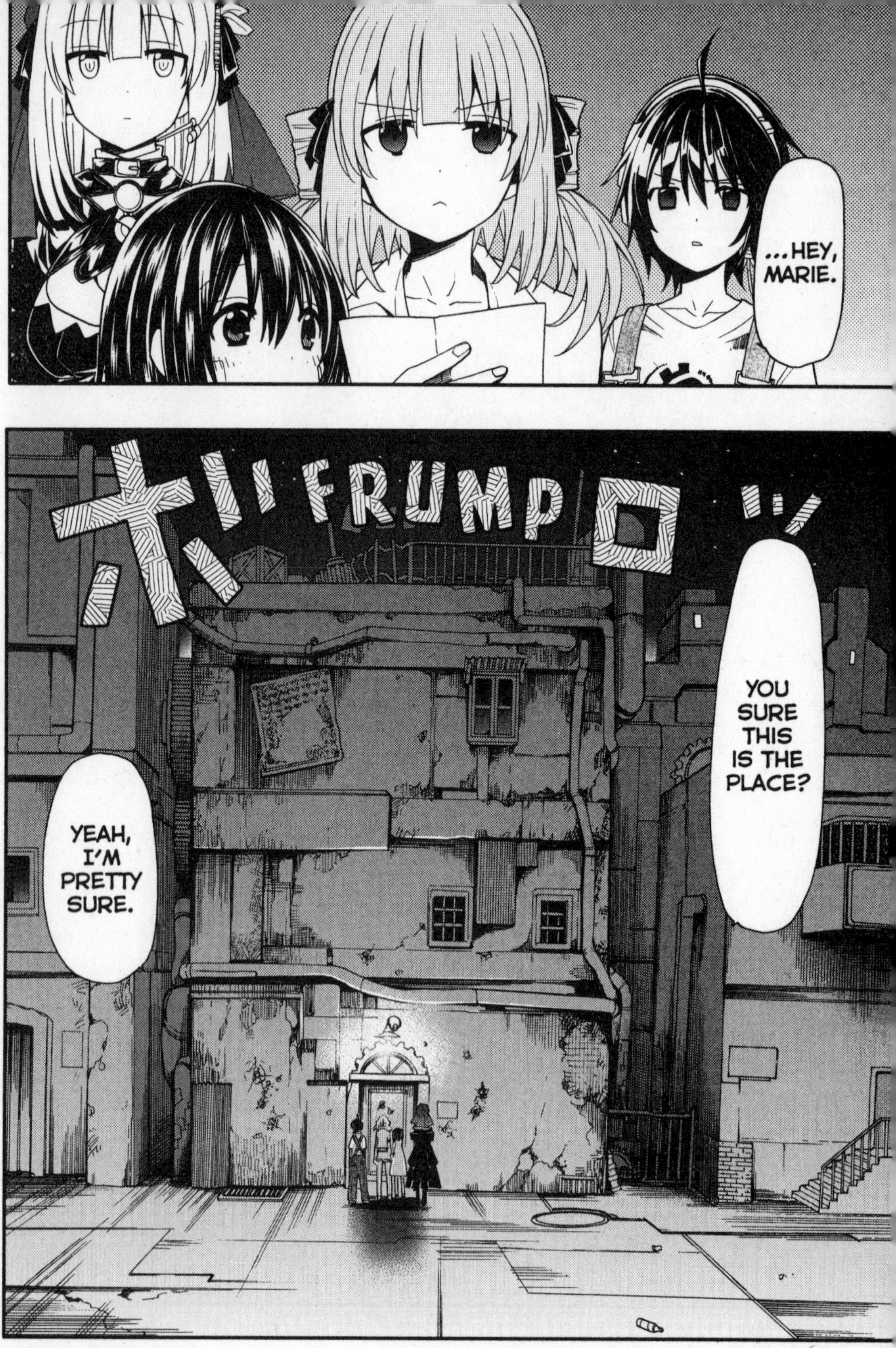
...HEY, MARIE.
FRUMP
YOU SURE THIS IS THE PLACE?
YEAH, I'M PRETTY SURE.

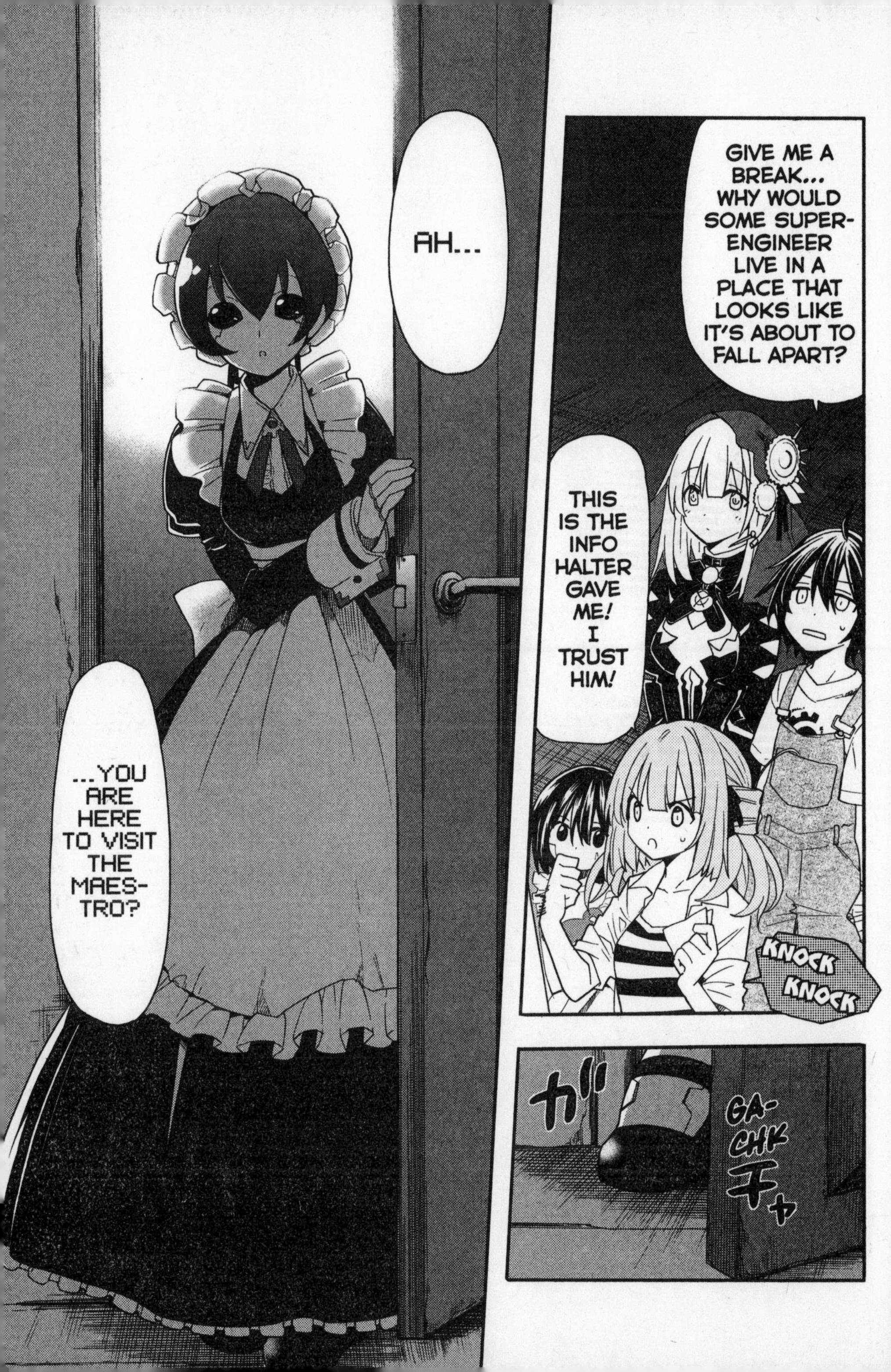
GIVE ME A BREAK... WHY WOULD SOME SUPER-ENGINEER LIVE IN A PLACE THAT LOOKS LIKE IT'S ABOUT TO FALL APART?
THIS IS THE INFO HALTER GAVE ME! I TRUST HIM!
KNOCK KNOCK
GA-CHK
AH...
...YOU ARE HERE TO VISIT THE MAES-TRO?

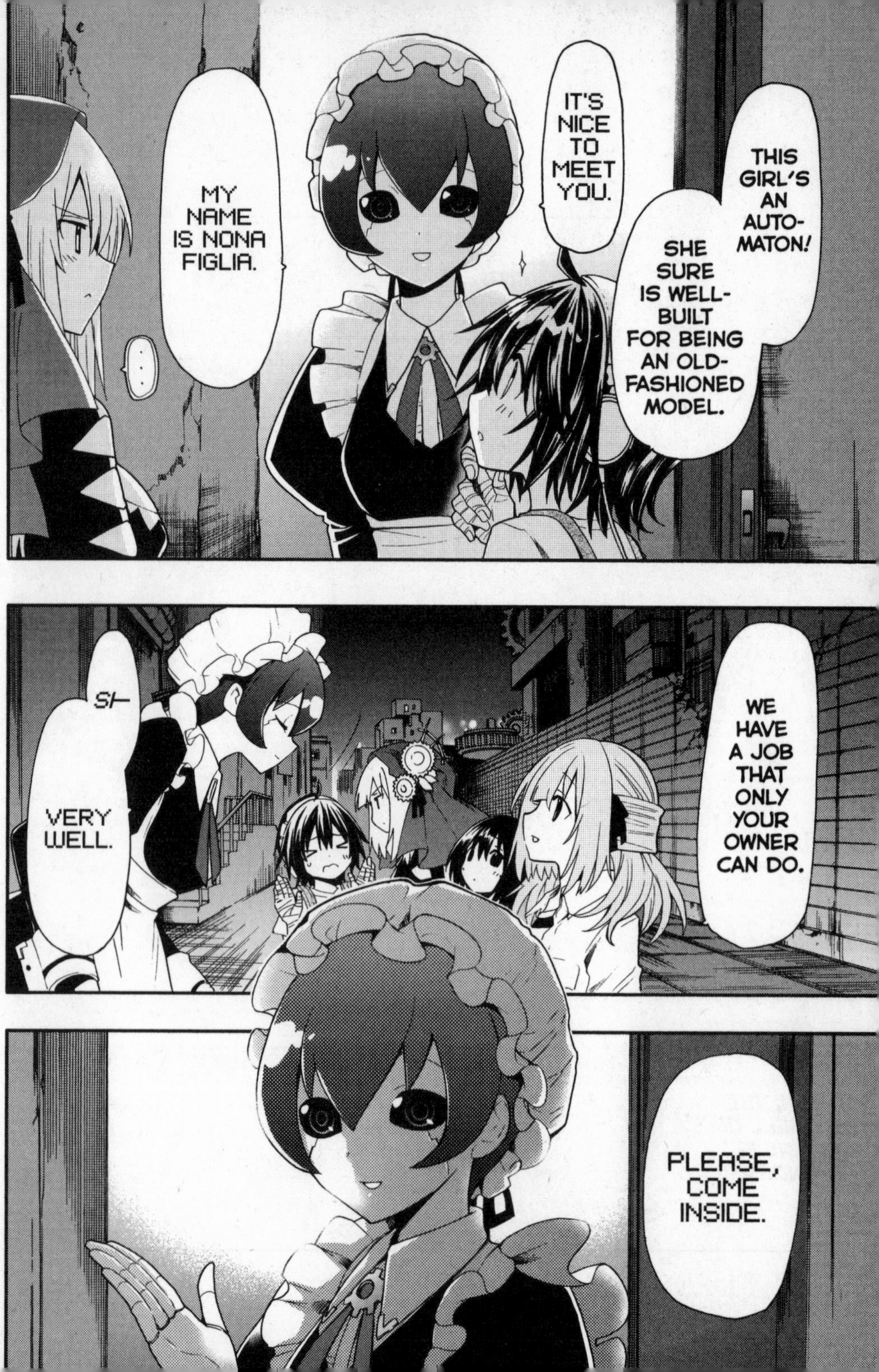
THIS GIRL'S AN AUTO-MATON!
SHE SURE IS WELL-BUILT FOR BEING AN OLD-FASHIONED MODEL.
IT'S NICE TO MEET YOU.
MY NAME IS NONA FIGLIA.
...
WE HAVE A JOB THAT ONLY YOUR OWNER CAN DO.
SI— VERY WELL.
PLEASE, COME INSIDE.

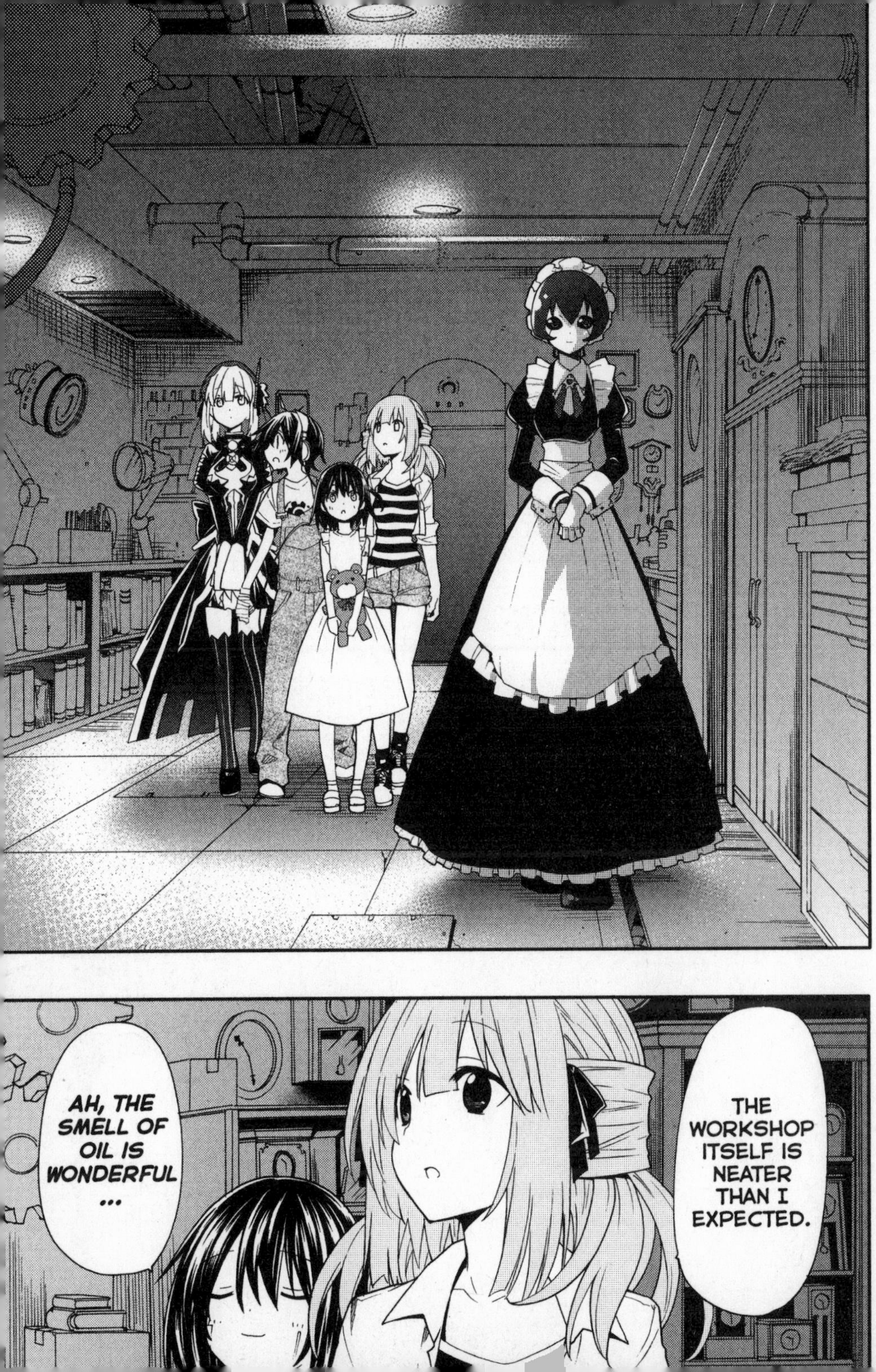
THE WORKSHOP ITSELF IS NEATER THAN I EXPECTED.
AH, THE SMELL OF OIL IS WONDERFUL ...

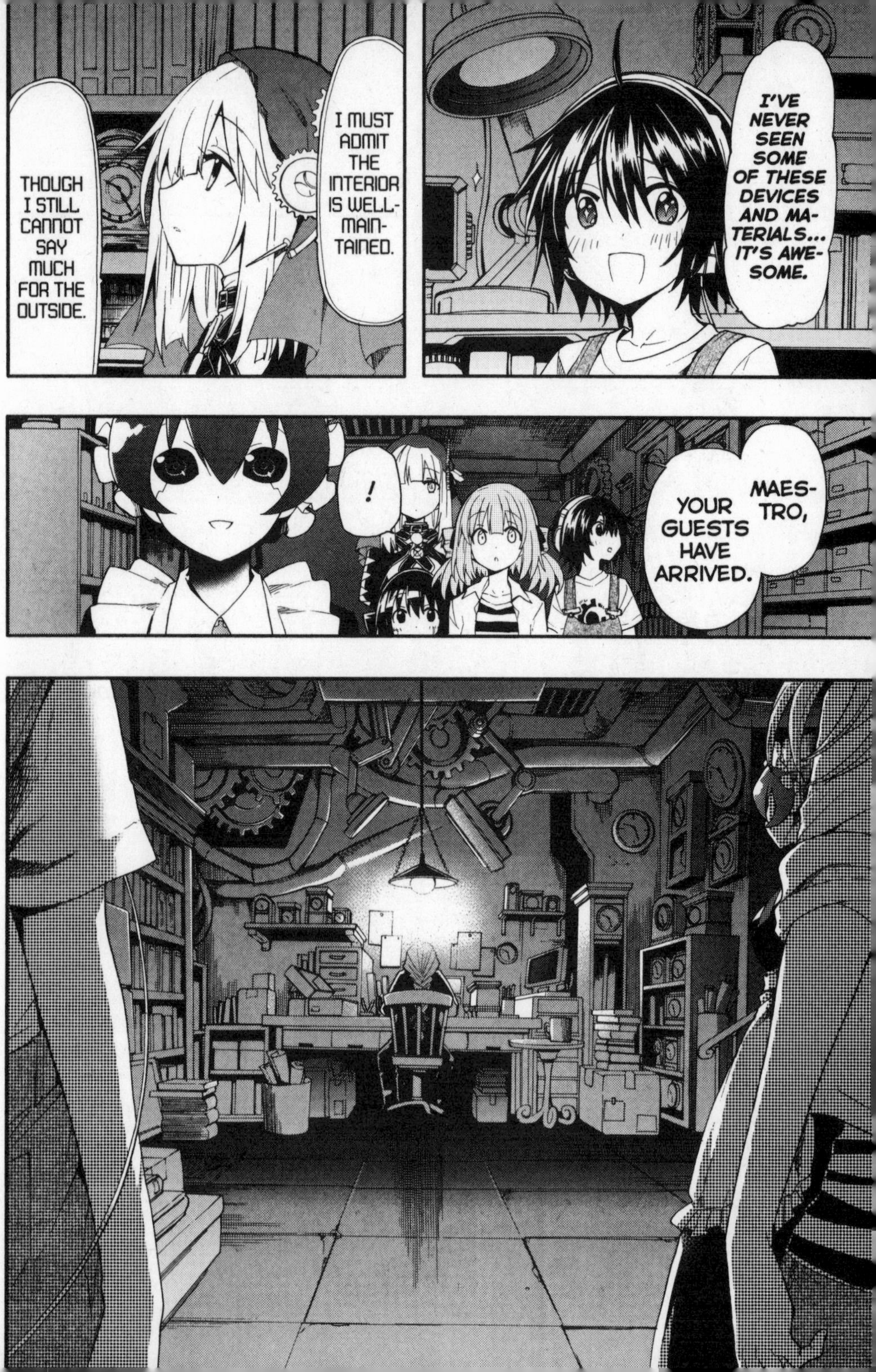
I'VE NEVER SEEN SOME OF THESE DEVICES AND MATERIALS... IT'S AWESOME.
I MUST ADMIT THE INTERIOR IS WELL-MAINTAINED.
THOUGH I STILL CANNOT SAY MUCH FOR THE OUTSIDE.
MAESTRO, YOUR GUESTS HAVE ARRIVED.
!

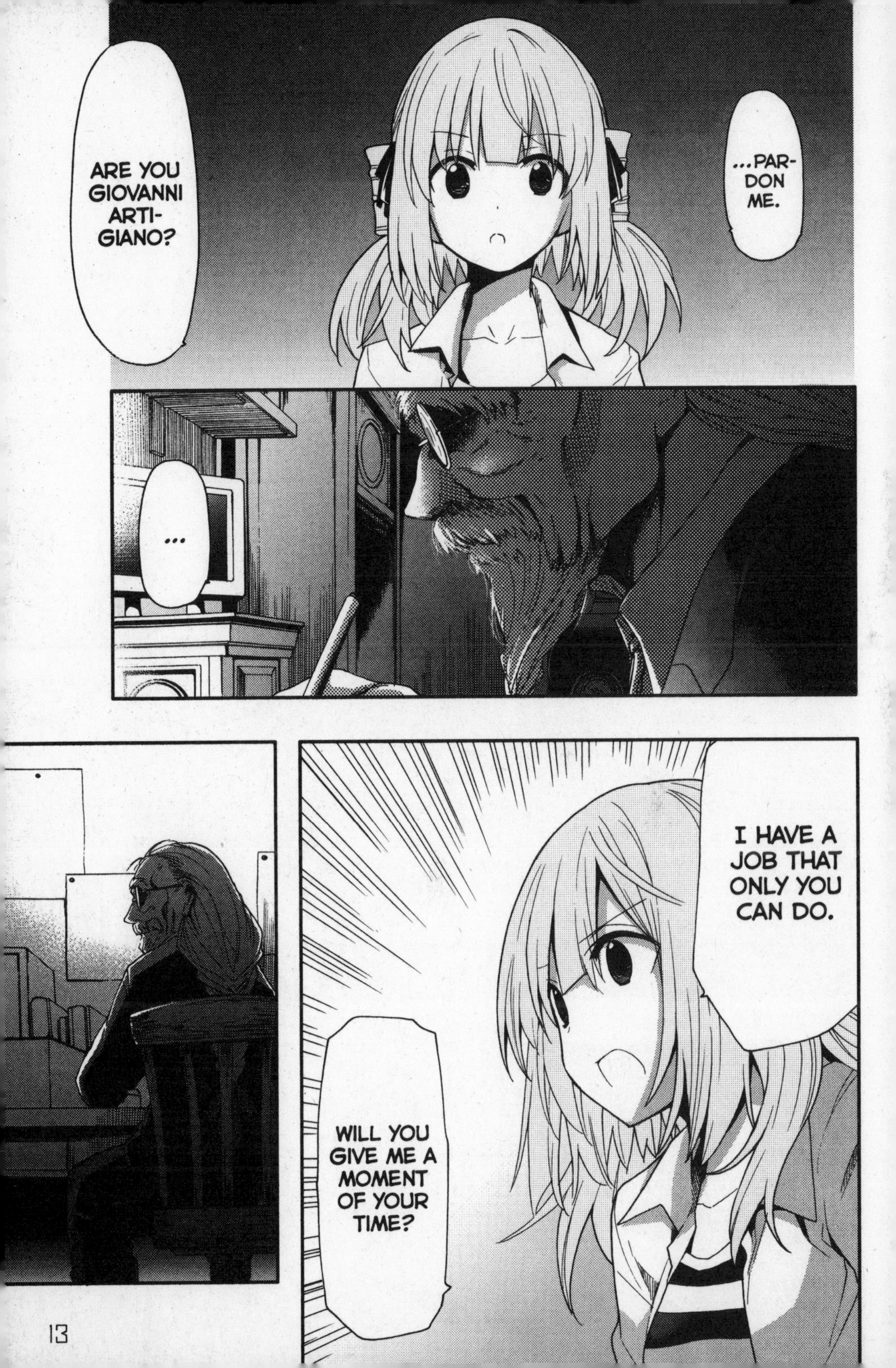
...PARDON ME.
ARE YOU GIOVANNI ARTIGIANO?
...
I HAVE A JOB THAT ONLY YOU CAN DO.
WILL YOU GIVE ME A MOMENT OF YOUR TIME?

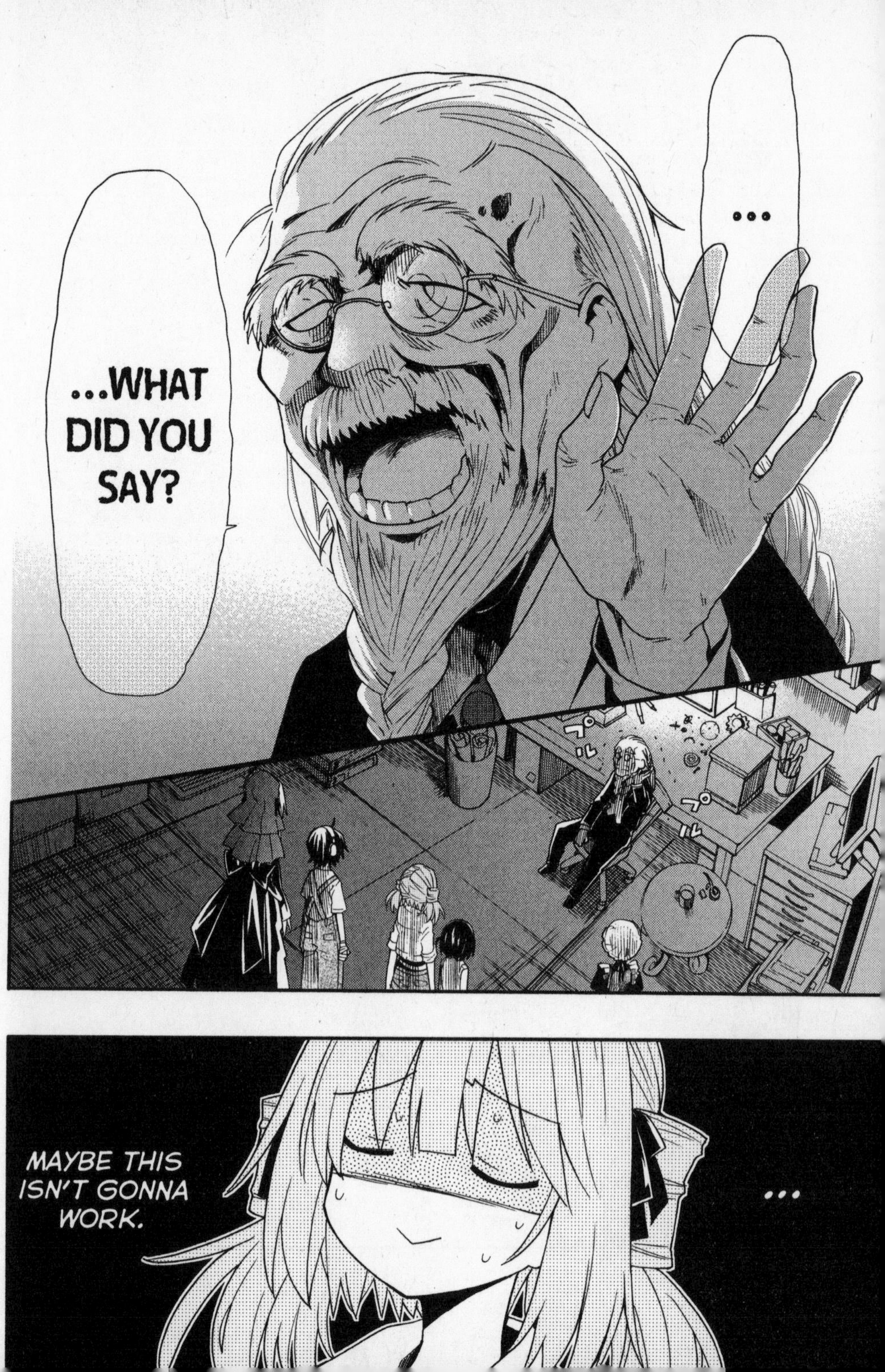
...
...WHAT DID YOU SAY?
...
MAYBE THIS ISN'T GONNA WORK.

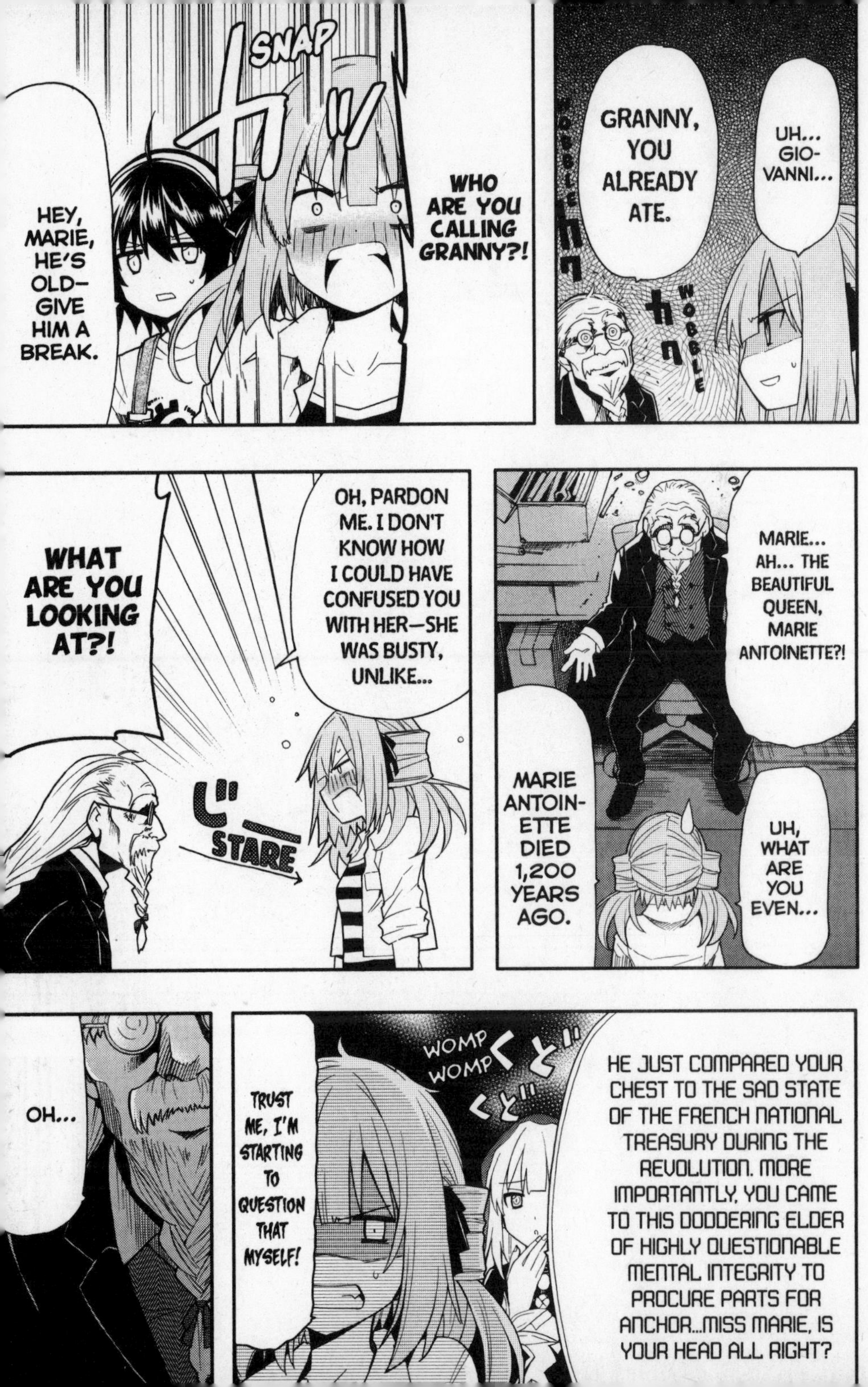
UH... GIO-VANNI...
GRANNY, YOU ALREADY ATE.
WOBBLE WOBBLE
SNAP
WHO ARE YOU CALLING GRANNY?!
HEY, MARIE, HE'S OLD–GIVE HIM A BREAK.
MARIE... AH... THE BEAUTIFUL QUEEN, MARIE ANTOINETTE?!
UH, WHAT ARE YOU EVEN...
MARIE ANTOIN-ETTE DIED 1,200 YEARS AGO.
OH, PARDON ME. I DON'T KNOW HOW I COULD HAVE CONFUSED YOU WITH HER—SHE WAS BUSTY, UNLIKE...
WHAT ARE YOU LOOKING AT?!
STARE
HE JUST COMPARED YOUR CHEST TO THE SAD STATE OF THE FRENCH NATIONAL TREASURY DURING THE REVOLUTION. MORE IMPORTANTLY, YOU CAME TO THIS DODDERING ELDER OF HIGHLY QUESTIONABLE MENTAL INTEGRITY TO PROCURE PARTS FOR ANCHOR...MISS MARIE, IS YOUR HEAD ALL RIGHT?
WOMP WOMP
TRUST ME, I'M STARTING TO QUESTION THAT MYSELF!
OH...

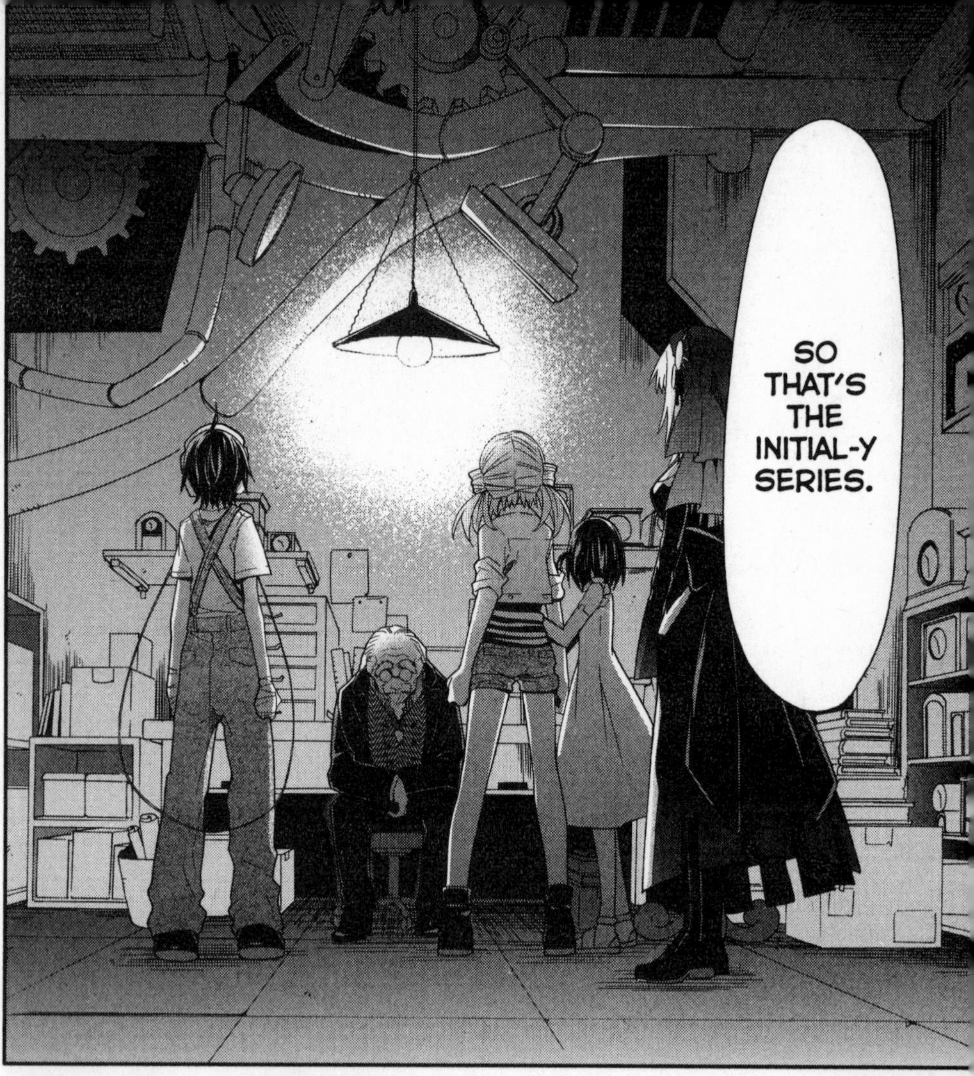
SO THAT'S THE INITIAL-Y SERIES.

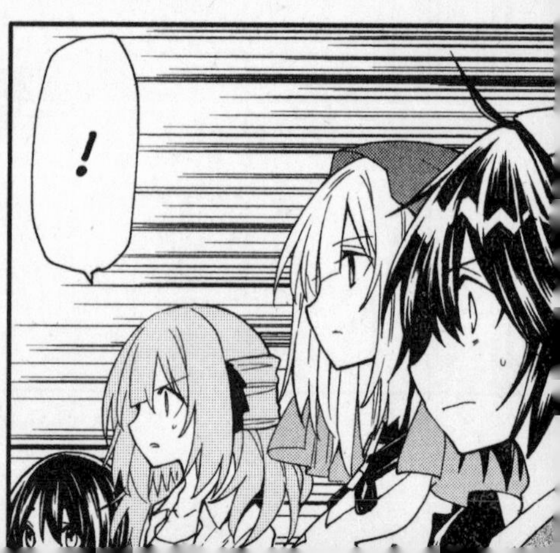
!

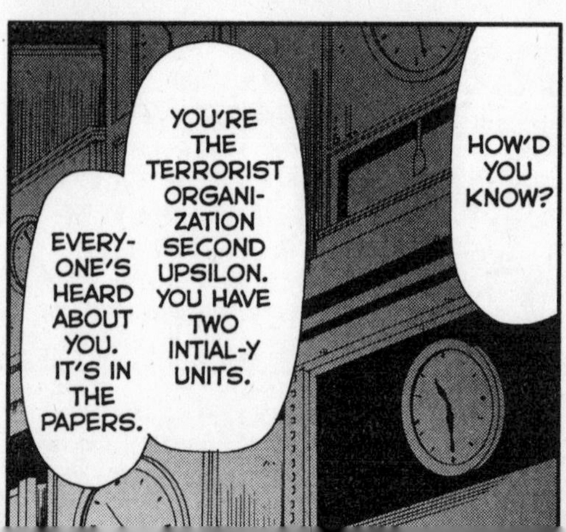
HOW'D YOU KNOW?
YOU'RE THE TERRORIST ORGANI-ZATION SECOND UPSILON. YOU HAVE TWO INTIAL-Y UNITS.
EVERY-ONE'S HEARD ABOUT YOU. IT'S IN THE PAPERS.

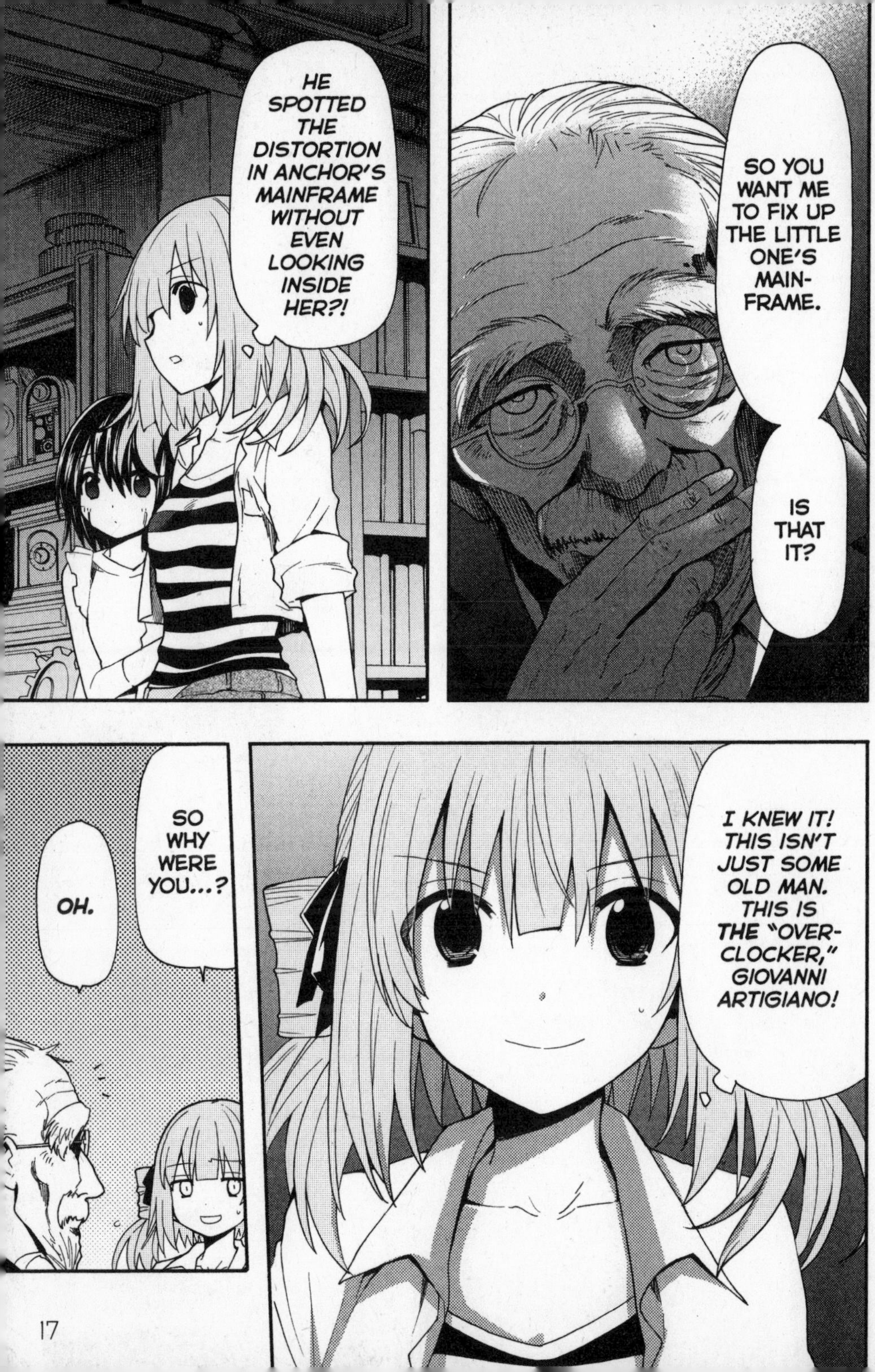
SO YOU WANT ME TO FIX UP THE LITTLE ONE'S MAIN-FRAME.
IS THAT IT?
HE SPOTTED THE DISTORTION IN ANCHOR'S MAINFRAME WITHOUT EVEN LOOKING INSIDE HER?!
I KNEW IT! THIS ISN'T JUST SOME OLD MAN. THIS IS THE "OVER-CLOCKER," GIOVANNI ARTIGIANO!
SO WHY WERE YOU...?
OH.

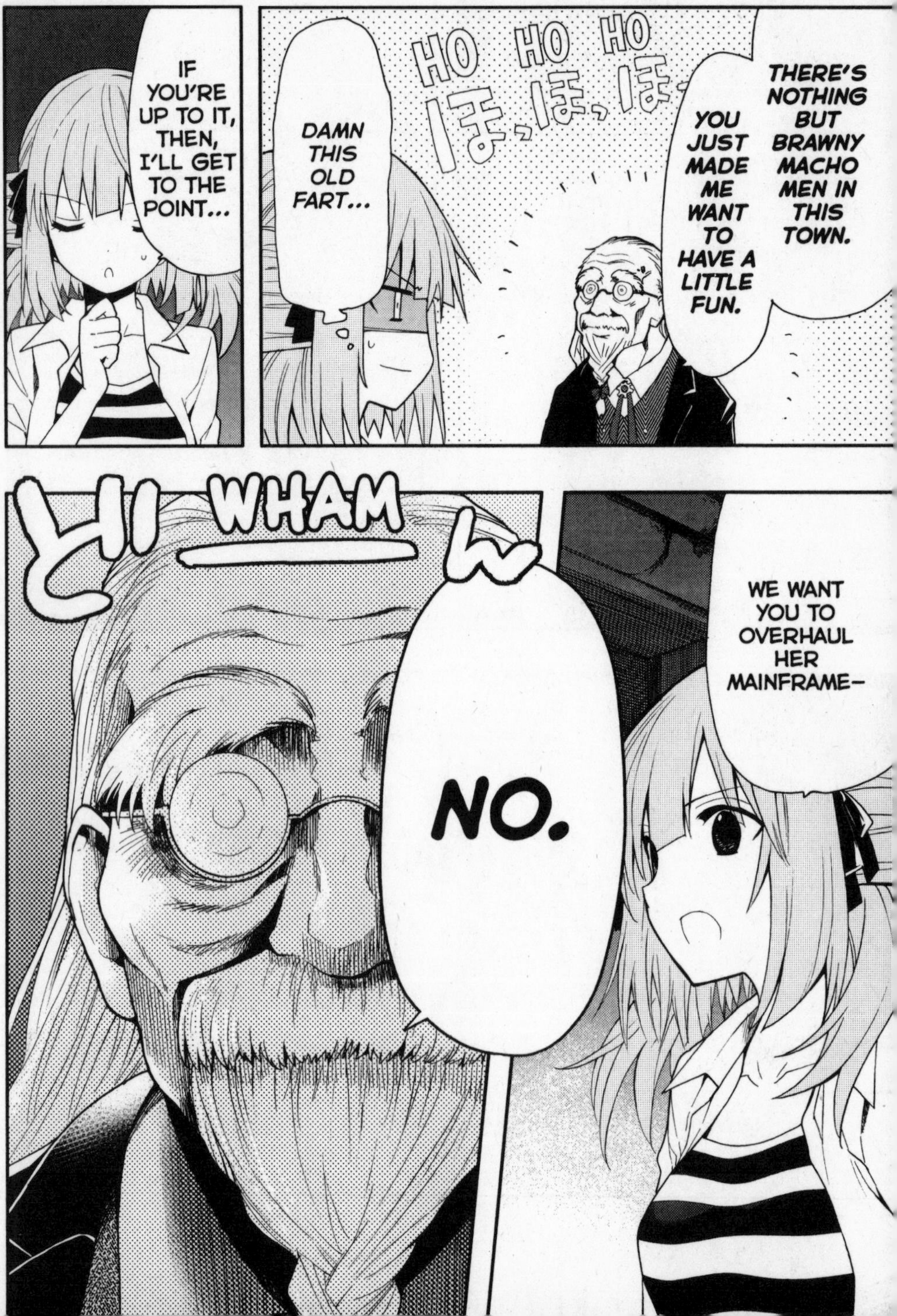
THERE'S NOTHING BUT BRAWNY MACHO MEN IN THIS TOWN.
YOU JUST MADE ME WANT TO HAVE A LITTLE FUN.
HO HO HO
ほっほっほっ
DAMN THIS OLD FART...
IF YOU'RE UP TO IT, THEN, I'LL GET TO THE POINT...
WE WANT YOU TO OVERHAUL HER MAINFRAME–
どーん
WHAM
NO.

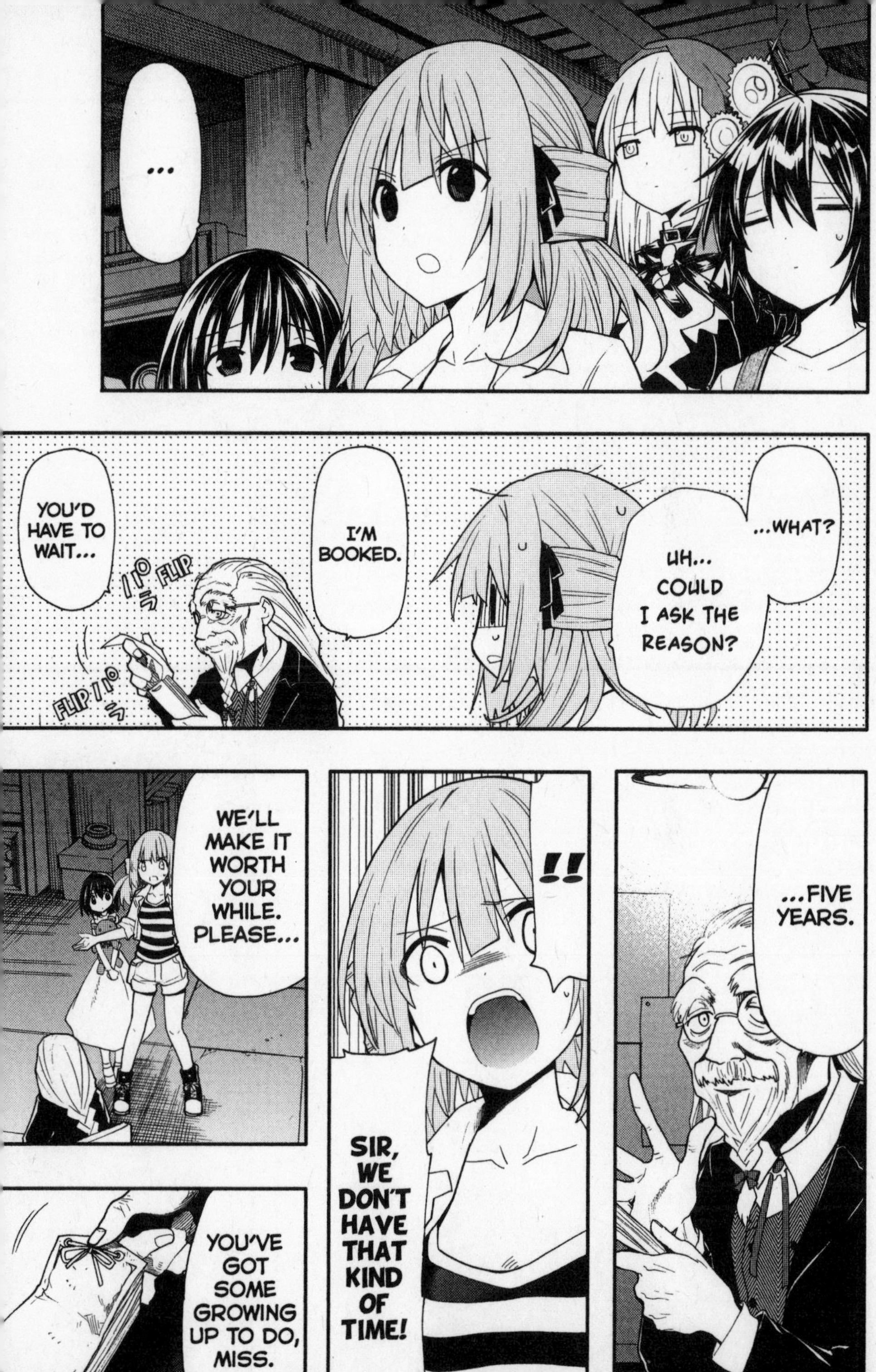
...
...WHAT?
UH... COULD I ASK THE REASON?
I'M BOOKED.
YOU'D HAVE TO WAIT...
パラ FLIP
パラ FLIP
...FIVE YEARS.
!!
SIR, WE DON'T HAVE THAT KIND OF TIME!
WE'LL MAKE IT WORTH YOUR WHILE. PLEASE...
YOU'VE GOT SOME GROWING UP TO DO, MISS.

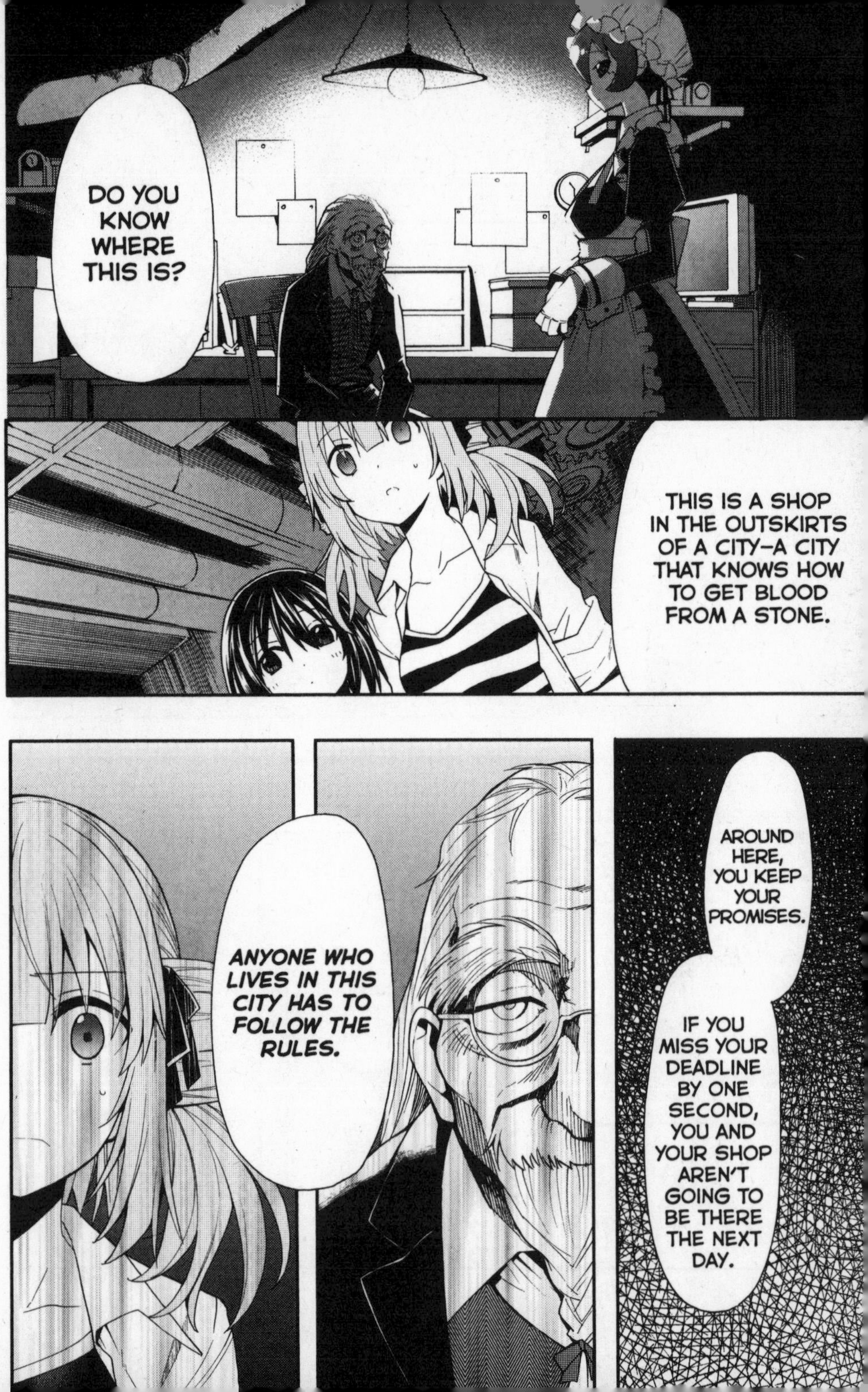
DO YOU KNOW WHERE THIS IS?
THIS IS A SHOP IN THE OUTSKIRTS OF A CITY—A CITY THAT KNOWS HOW TO GET BLOOD FROM A STONE.
AROUND HERE, YOU KEEP YOUR PROMISES.
IF YOU MISS YOUR DEADLINE BY ONE SECOND, YOU AND YOUR SHOP AREN'T GOING TO BE THERE THE NEXT DAY.
ANYONE WHO LIVES IN THIS CITY HAS TO FOLLOW THE RULES.

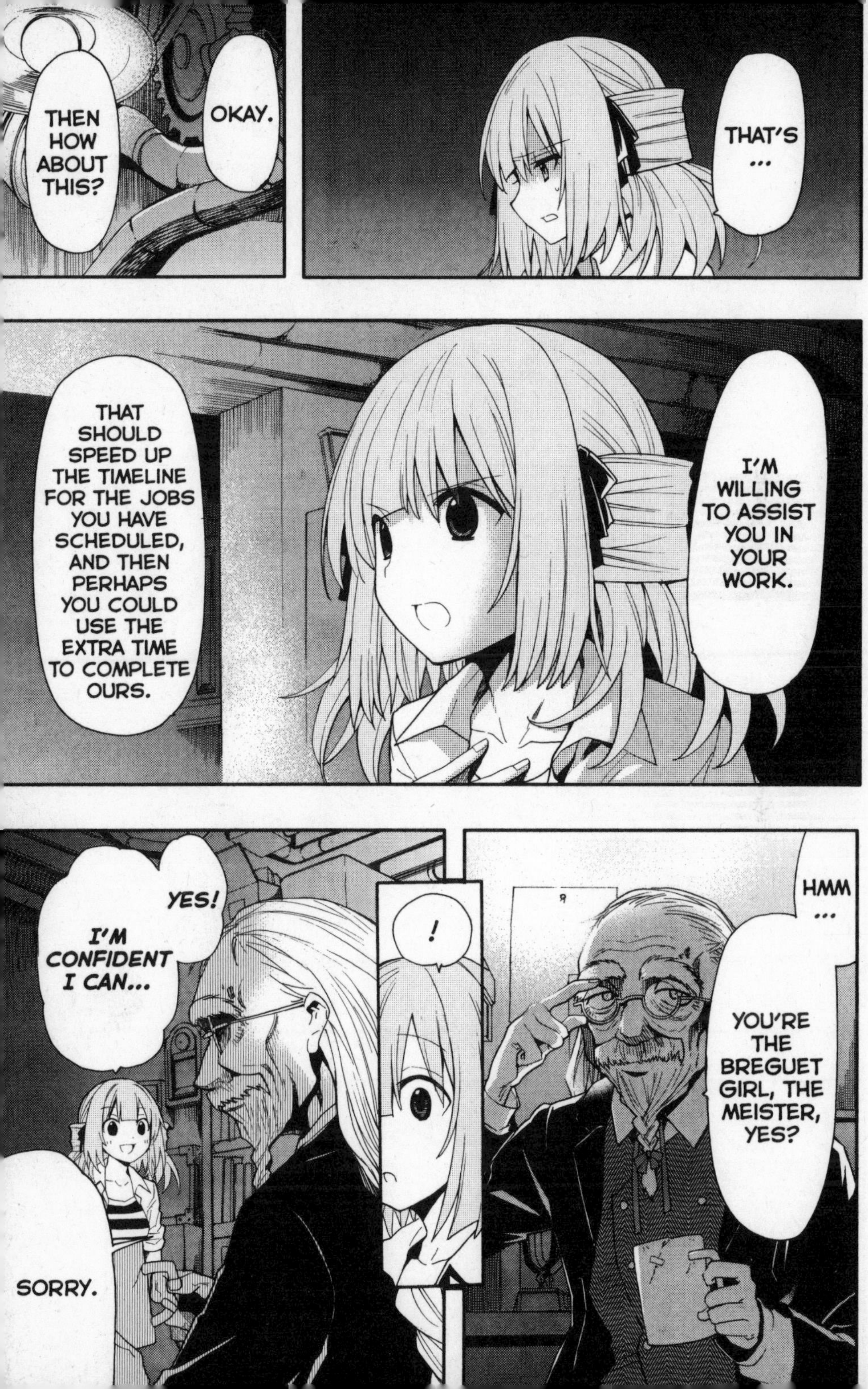
THAT'S ...
OKAY.
THEN HOW ABOUT THIS?
I'M WILLING TO ASSIST YOU IN YOUR WORK.
THAT SHOULD SPEED UP THE TIMELINE FOR THE JOBS YOU HAVE SCHEDULED, AND THEN PERHAPS YOU COULD USE THE EXTRA TIME TO COMPLETE OURS.
HMM ...
YOU'RE THE BREGUET GIRL, THE MEISTER, YES?
!
YES!
I'M CONFIDENT I CAN...
SORRY.

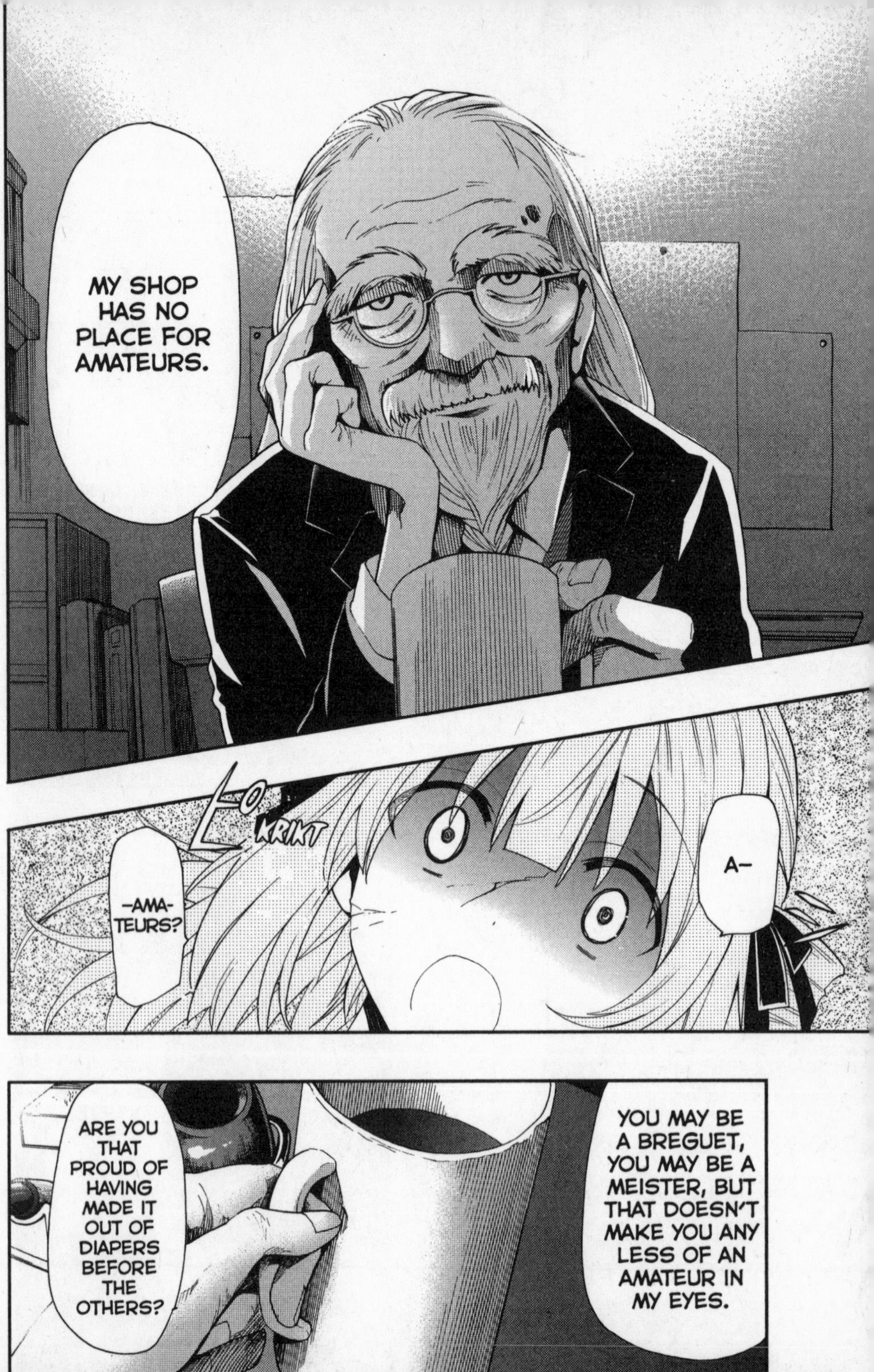
MY SHOP HAS NO PLACE FOR AMATEURS.
A–
KRIKT
–AMA-TEURS?
YOU MAY BE A BREGUET, YOU MAY BE A MEISTER, BUT THAT DOESN'T MAKE YOU ANY LESS OF AN AMATEUR IN MY EYES.
ARE YOU THAT PROUD OF HAVING MADE IT OUT OF DIAPERS BEFORE THE OTHERS?

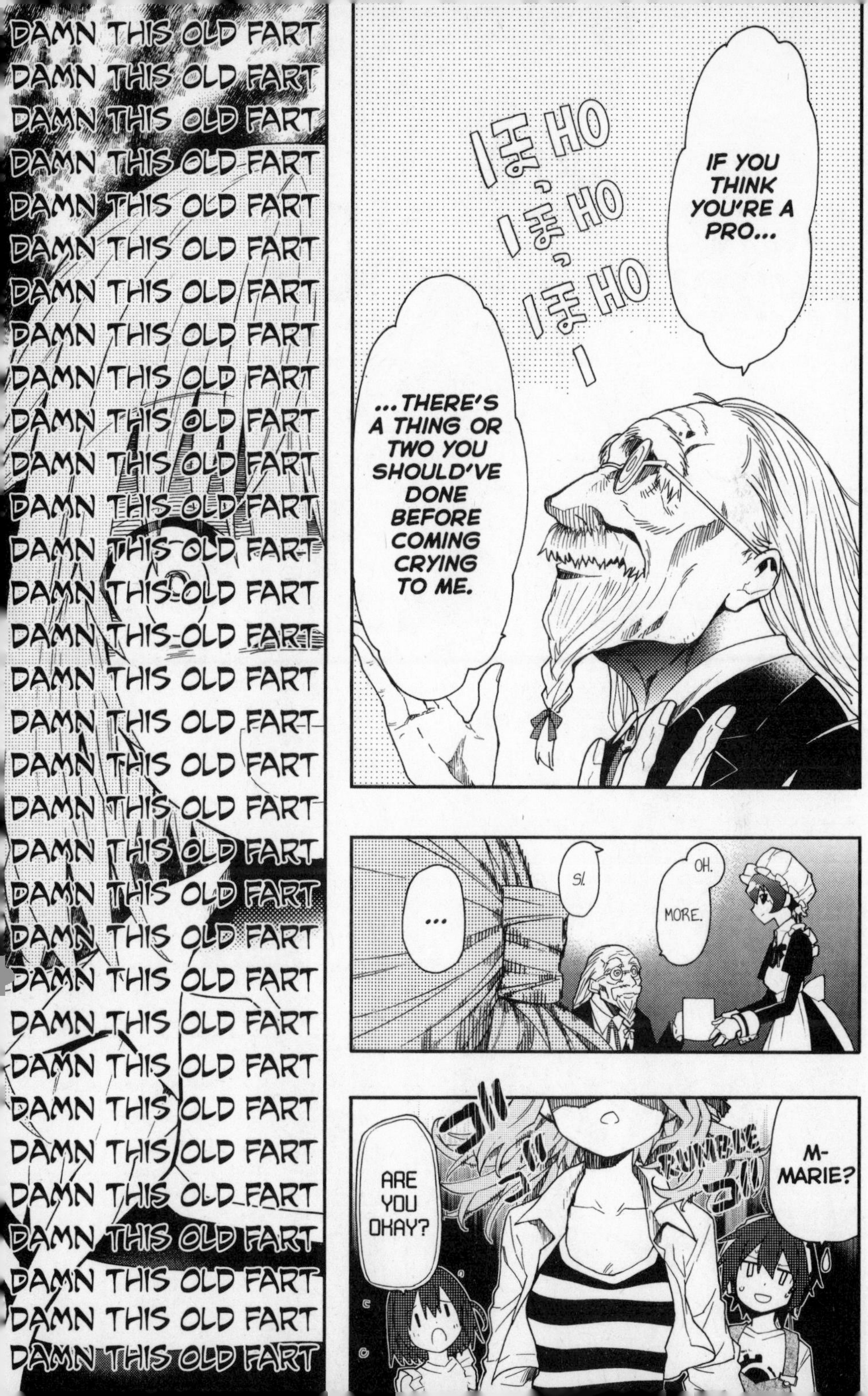
IF YOU THINK YOU'RE A PRO...
ほっ HO ほっ HO ほー HO
...THERE'S A THING OR TWO YOU SHOULD'VE DONE BEFORE COMING CRYING TO ME.
OH. MORE.
SI.
...
M-MARIE?
RUMBLE
ARE YOU OKAY?
DAMN THIS OLD FART
DAMN THIS OLD FART
DAMN THIS OLD FART
DAMN THIS OLD FART
DAMN THIS OLD FART
DAMN THIS OLD FART
DAMN THIS OLD FART
DAMN THIS OLD FART
DAMN THIS OLD FART
DAMN THIS OLD FART
DAMN THIS OLD FART
DAMN THIS OLD FART
DAMN THIS OLD FART
DAMN THIS OLD FART
DAMN THIS OLD FART
DAMN THIS OLD FART
DAMN THIS OLD FART
DAMN THIS OLD FART
DAMN THIS OLD FART
DAMN THIS OLD FART
DAMN THIS OLD FART
DAMN THIS OLD FART
DAMN THIS OLD FART
DAMN THIS OLD FART
DAMN THIS OLD FART
DAMN THIS OLD FART
DAMN THIS OLD FART
DAMN THIS OLD FART
DAMN THIS OLD FART
DAMN THIS OLD FART
DAMN THIS OLD FART
DAMN THIS OLD FART

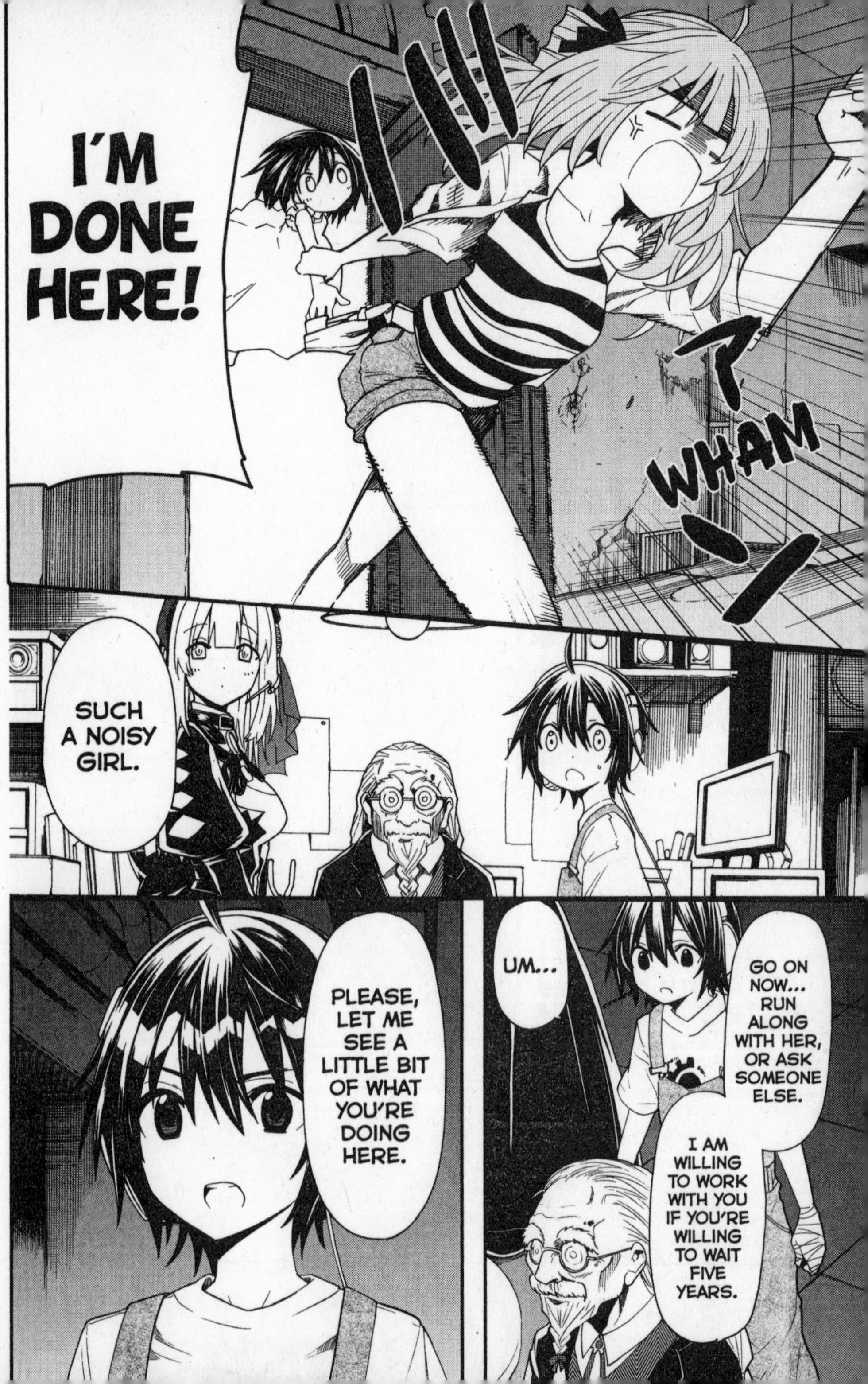

I'M DONE HERE!
WHAM
SUCH A NOISY GIRL.
UM...
GO ON NOW... RUN ALONG WITH HER, OR ASK SOMEONE ELSE.
I AM WILLING TO WORK WITH YOU IF YOU'RE WILLING TO WAIT FIVE YEARS.
PLEASE, LET ME SEE A LITTLE BIT OF WHAT YOU'RE DOING HERE.

...BUT I SIMPLY DO NOT HAVE THE TIME TO INSTRUCT A THIRD-RATE APPRENTICE.

I'M SORRY, BOY...

SHIK

RYUZU, HE'S RIGHT. I AM.

WELL, YOU DARE TO CALL MASTER NAOTO THIRD-RATE.

I COULD SEE IT IN HIS EYES... WHAT HE WAS TRYING TO SAY...

SURE HE COULD. HE NEVER SAID HE CAN'T.

NO, MASTER NAOTO, YOU ARE SUPERIOR TO HIM.

I DO NOT BELIEVE THIS MAN CAN FIX ANCHOR...

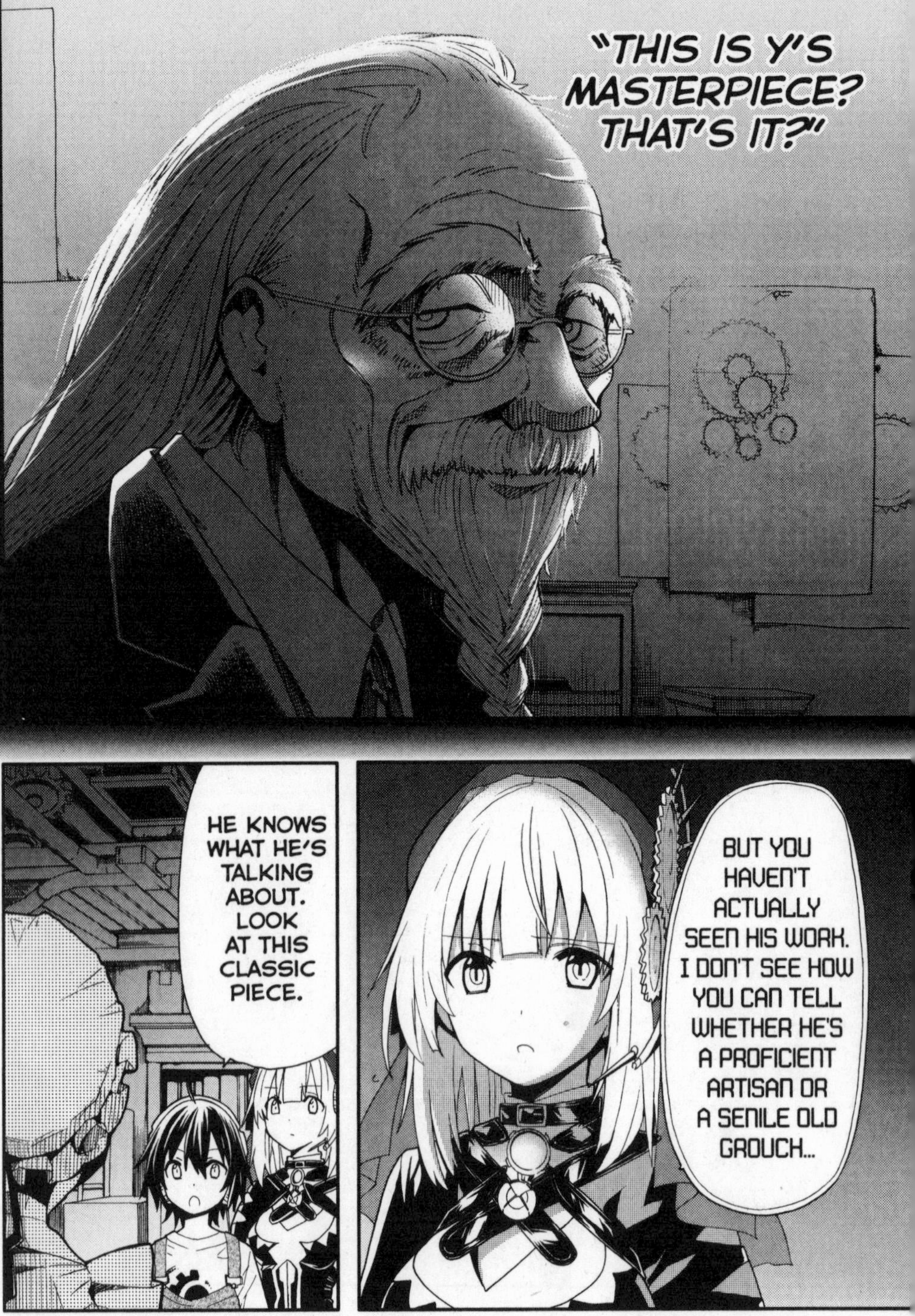
"THIS IS Y'S MASTERPIECE? THAT'S IT?"
BUT YOU HAVEN'T ACTUALLY SEEN HIS WORK. I DON'T SEE HOW YOU CAN TELL WHETHER HE'S A PROFICIENT ARTISAN OR A SENILE OLD GROUCH...
HE KNOWS WHAT HE'S TALKING ABOUT. LOOK AT THIS CLASSIC PIECE.

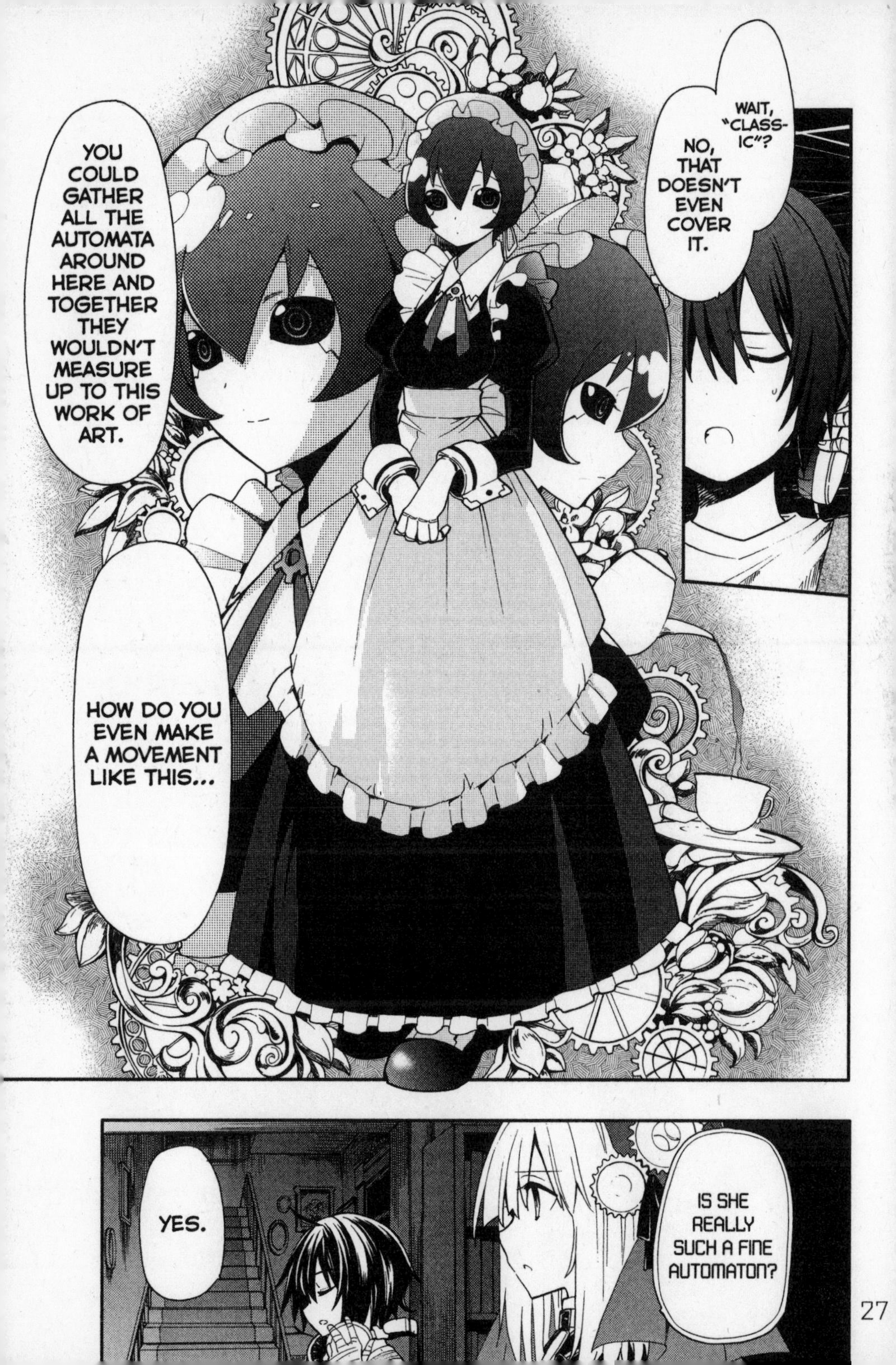
WAIT, "CLASSIC"?
NO, THAT DOESN'T EVEN COVER IT.
YOU COULD GATHER ALL THE AUTOMATA AROUND HERE AND TOGETHER THEY WOULDN'T MEASURE UP TO THIS WORK OF ART.
HOW DO YOU EVEN MAKE A MOVEMENT LIKE THIS...
IS SHE REALLY SUCH A FINE AUTOMATON?
YES.

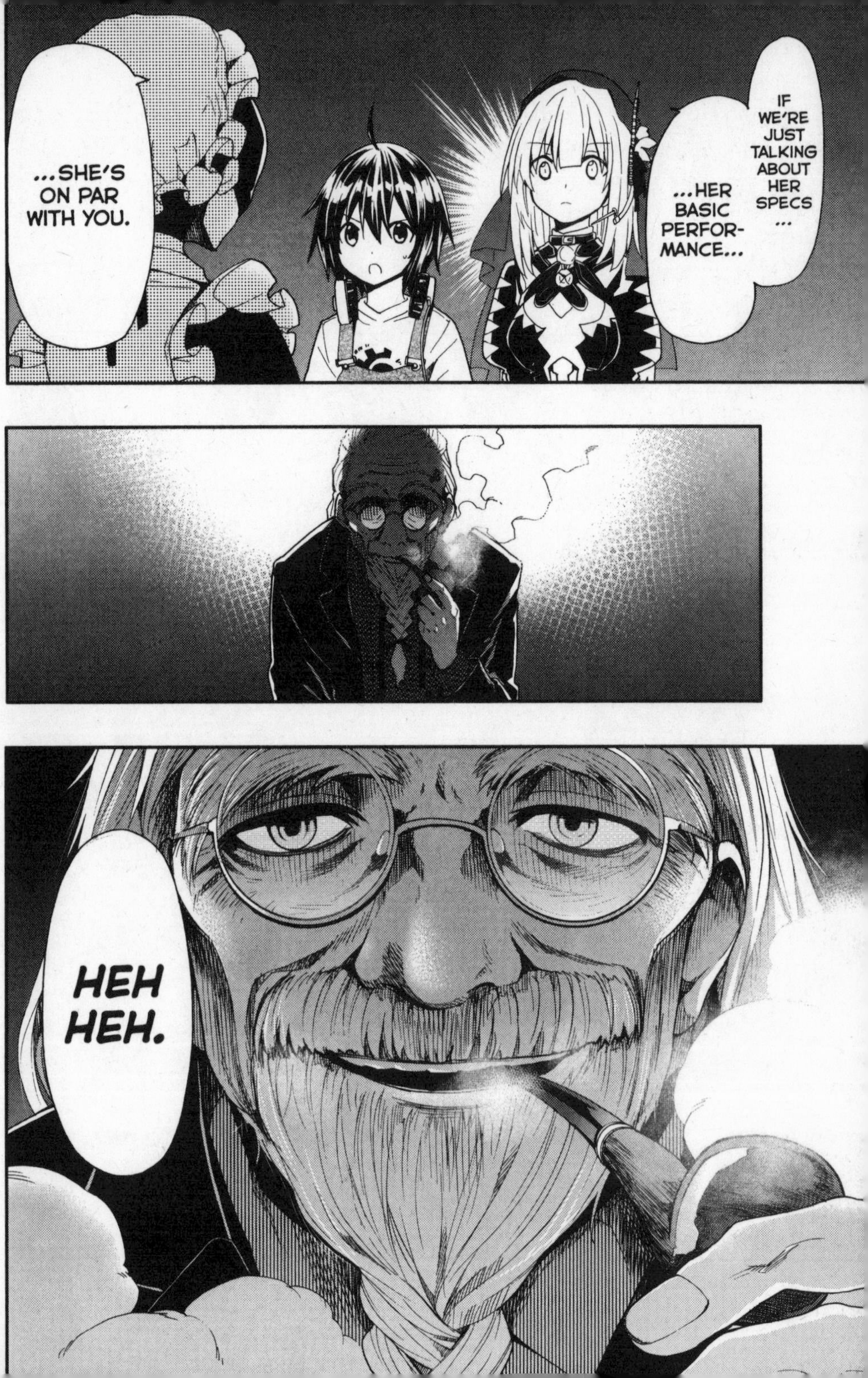
IF WE'RE JUST TALKING ABOUT HER SPECS ...
...HER BASIC PERFORMANCE...
...SHE'S ON PAR WITH YOU.
HEH HEH.

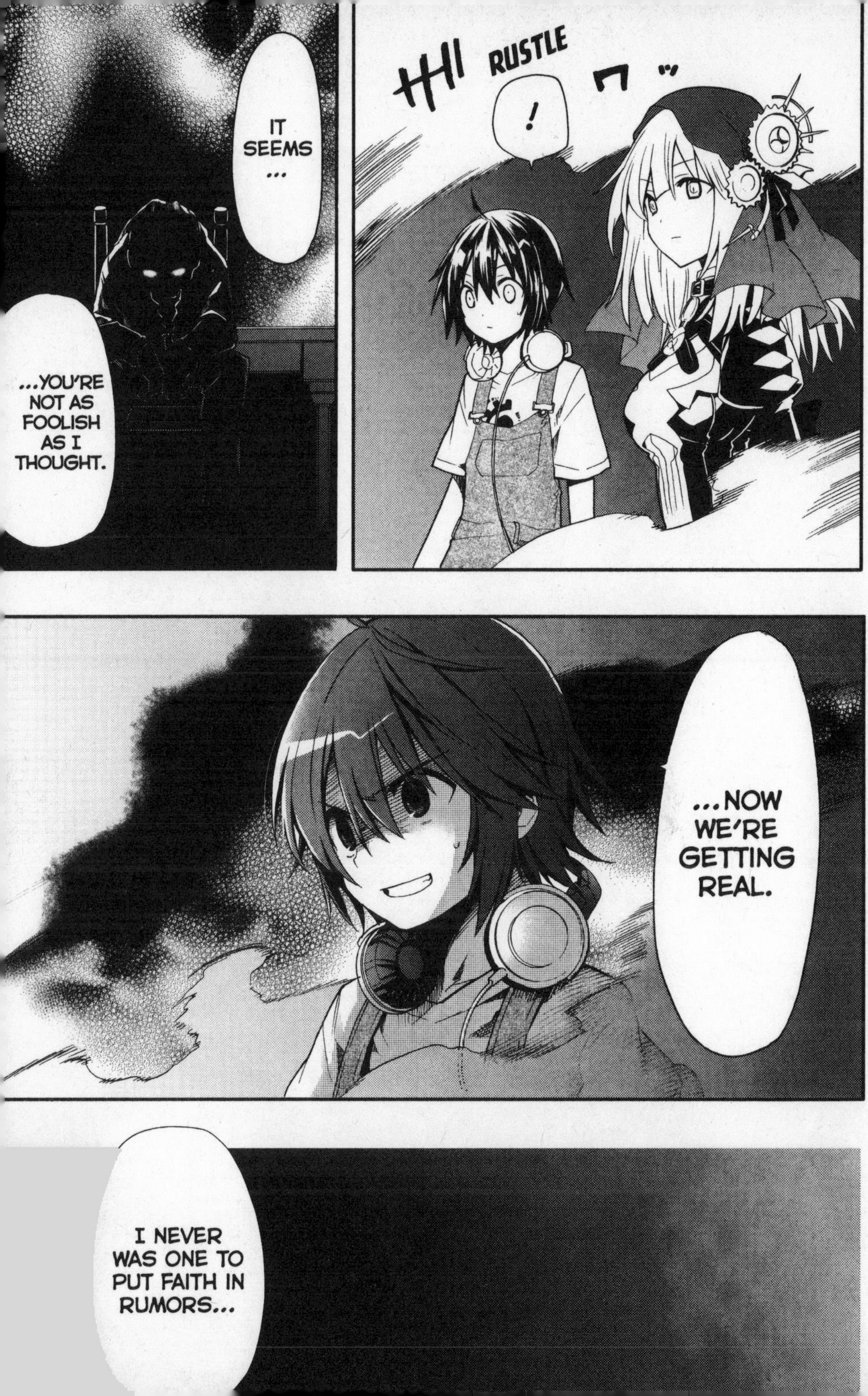
RUSTLE
!
IT SEEMS...
...YOU'RE NOT AS FOOLISH AS I THOUGHT.
...NOW WE'RE GETTING REAL.
I NEVER WAS ONE TO PUT FAITH IN RUMORS...

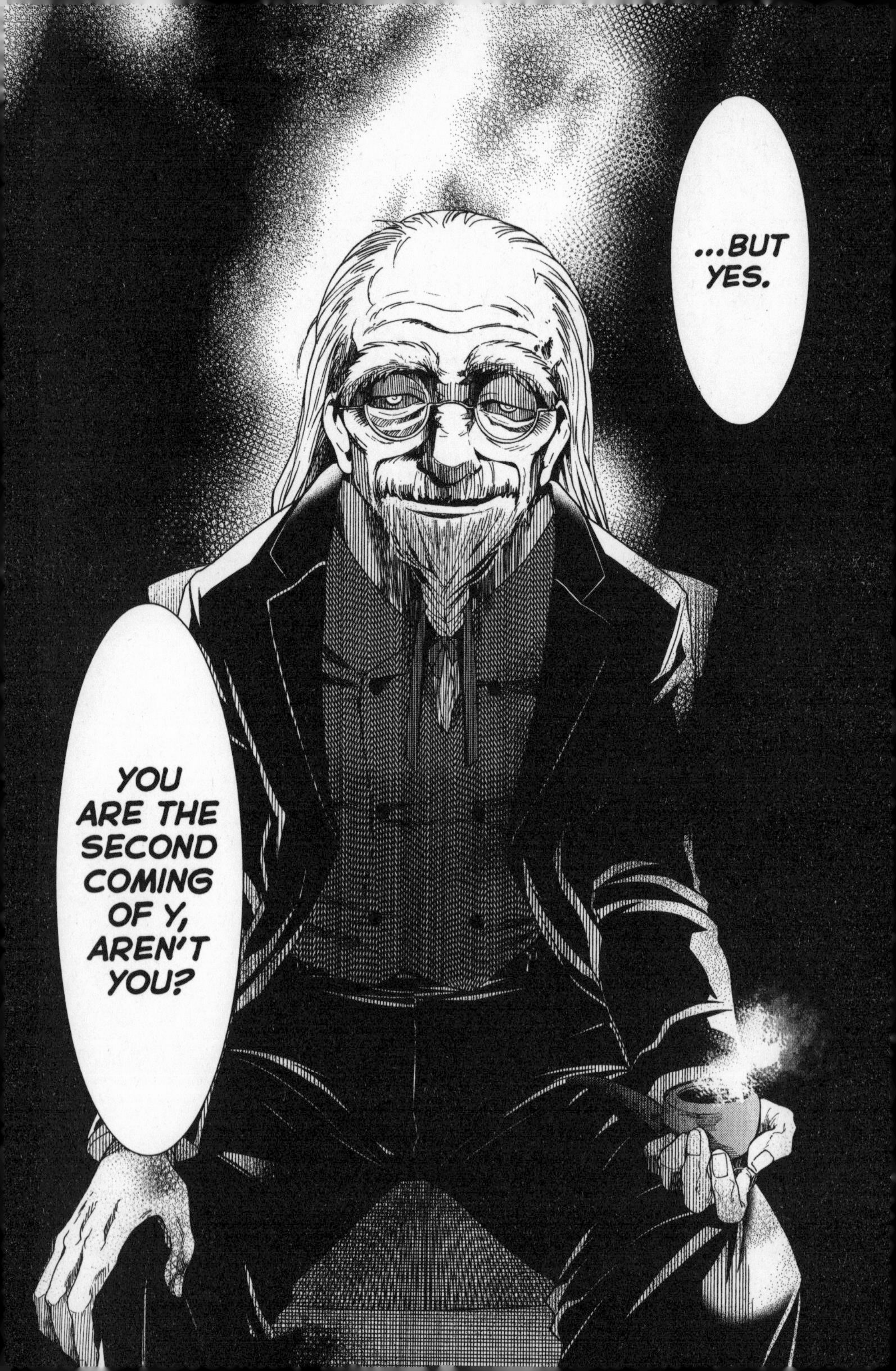
...BUT YES.
YOU ARE THE SECOND COMING OF Y, AREN'T YOU?

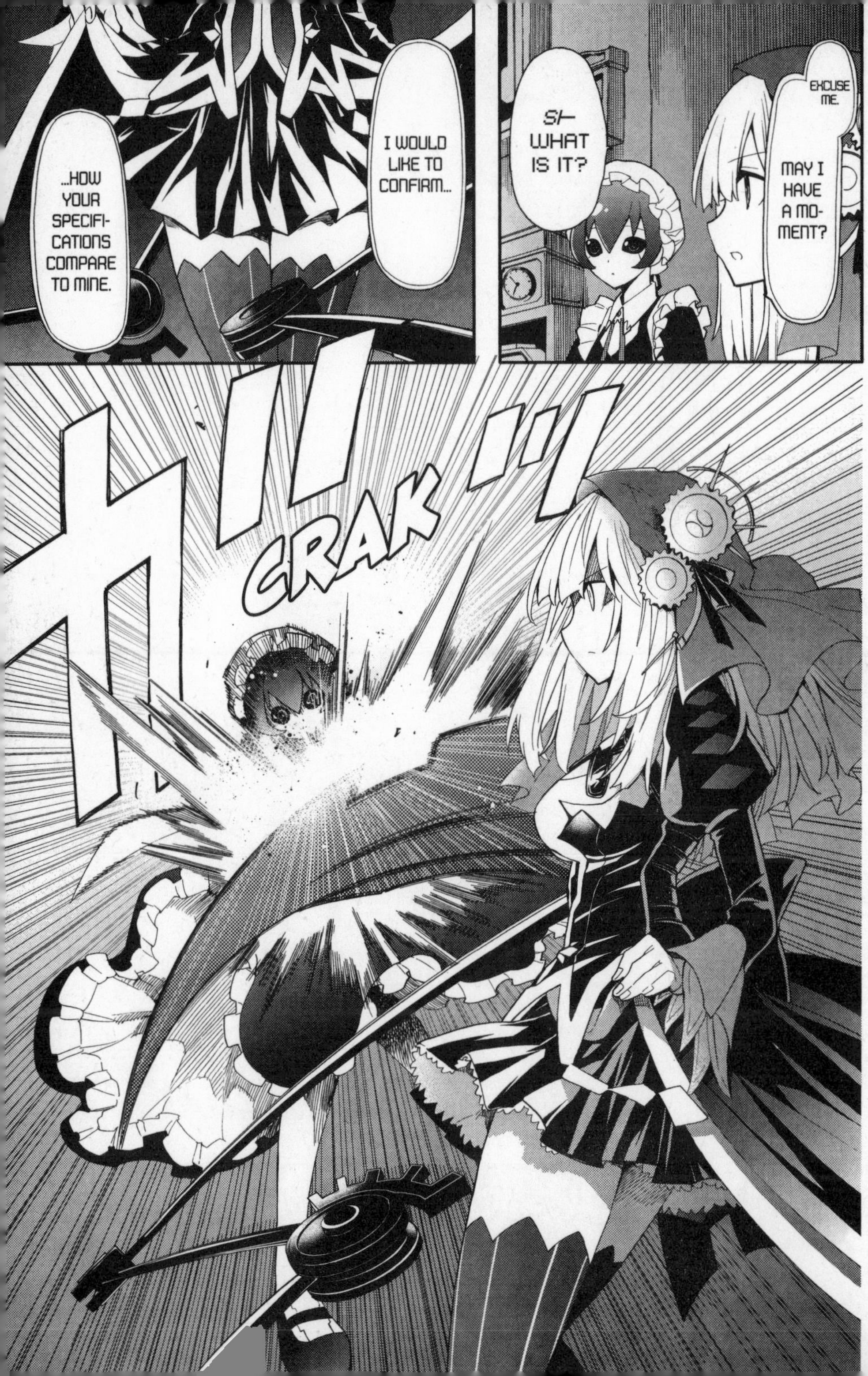
EXCUSE ME.
MAY I HAVE A MO-MENT?
S!— WHAT IS IT?
I WOULD LIKE TO CONFIRM...
...HOW YOUR SPECIFI-CATIONS COMPARE TO MINE.
CRAK

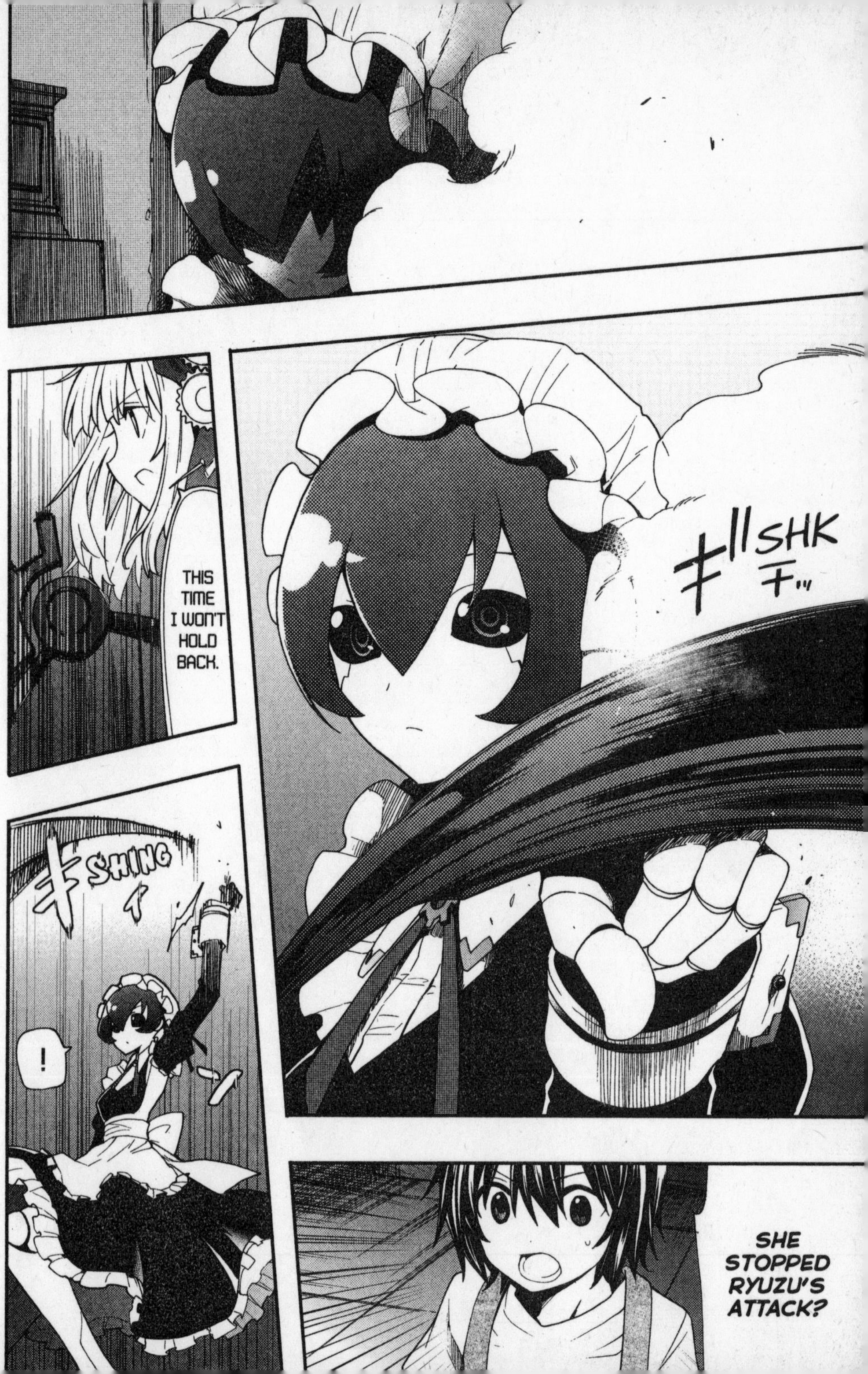
SHK
THIS TIME I WON'T HOLD BACK.
SHING
!
SHE STOPPED RYUZU'S ATTACK?

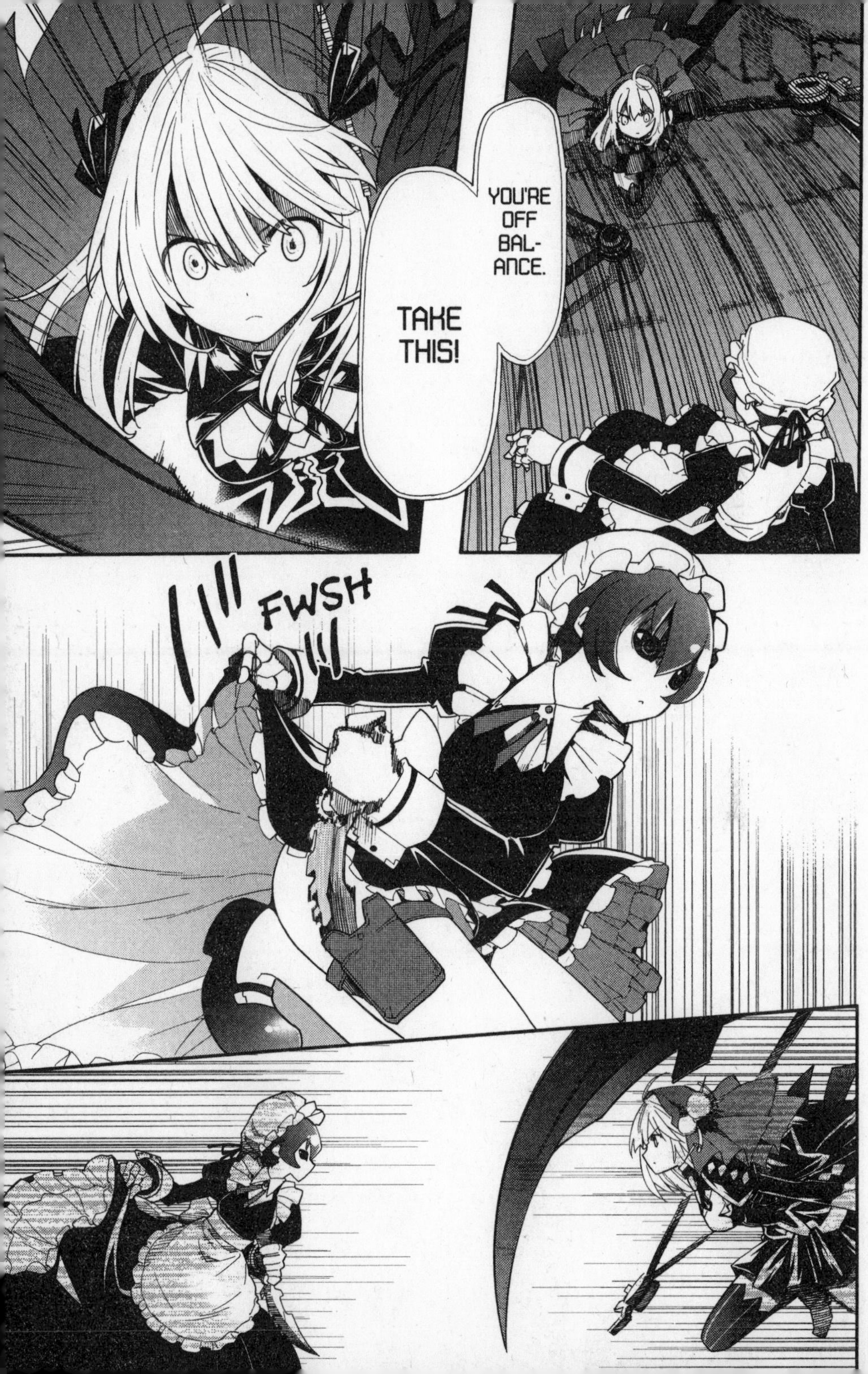
YOU'RE OFF BAL-ANCE.
TAKE THIS!
FWSH

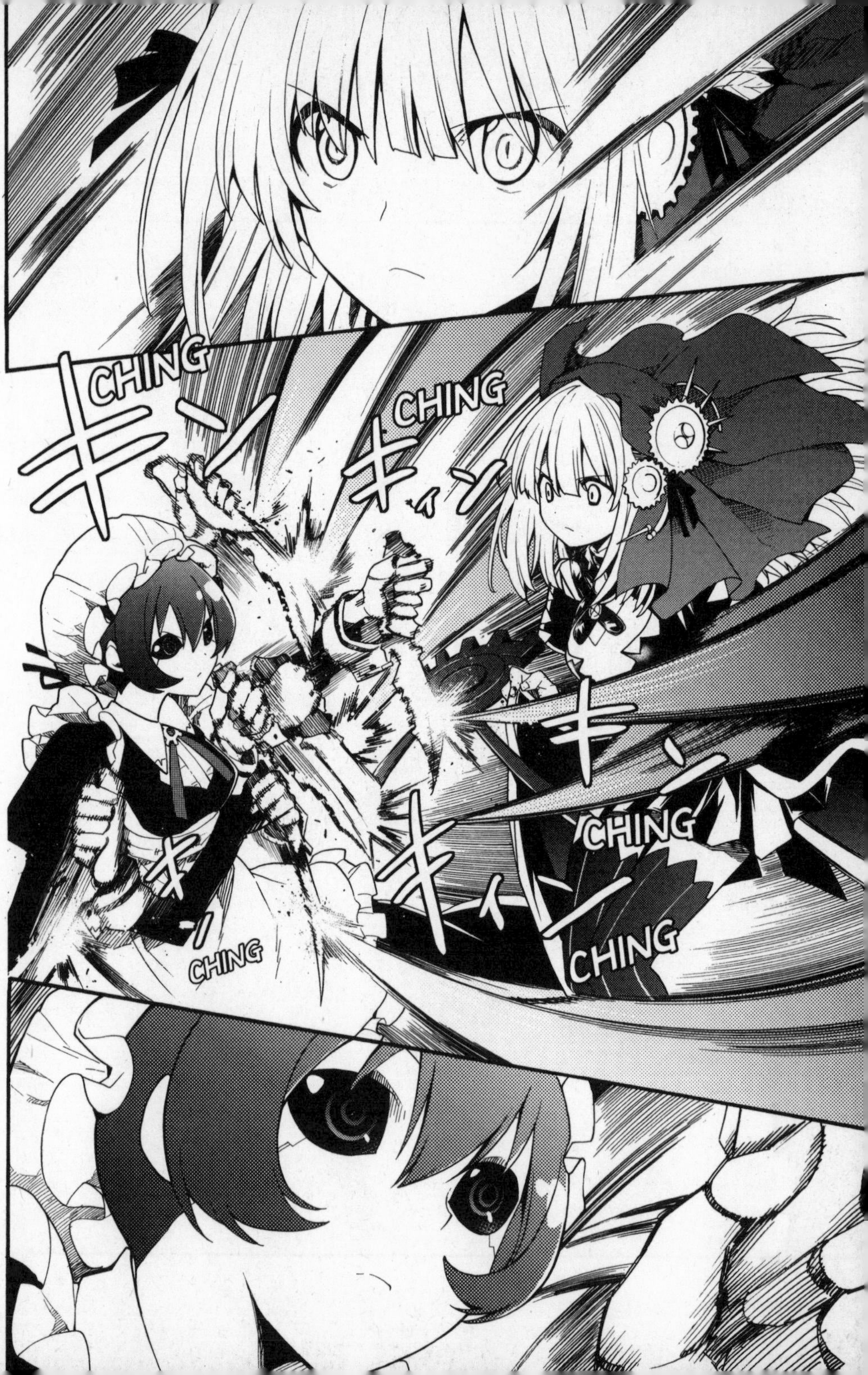
CHING
CHING
CHING
CHING
CHING

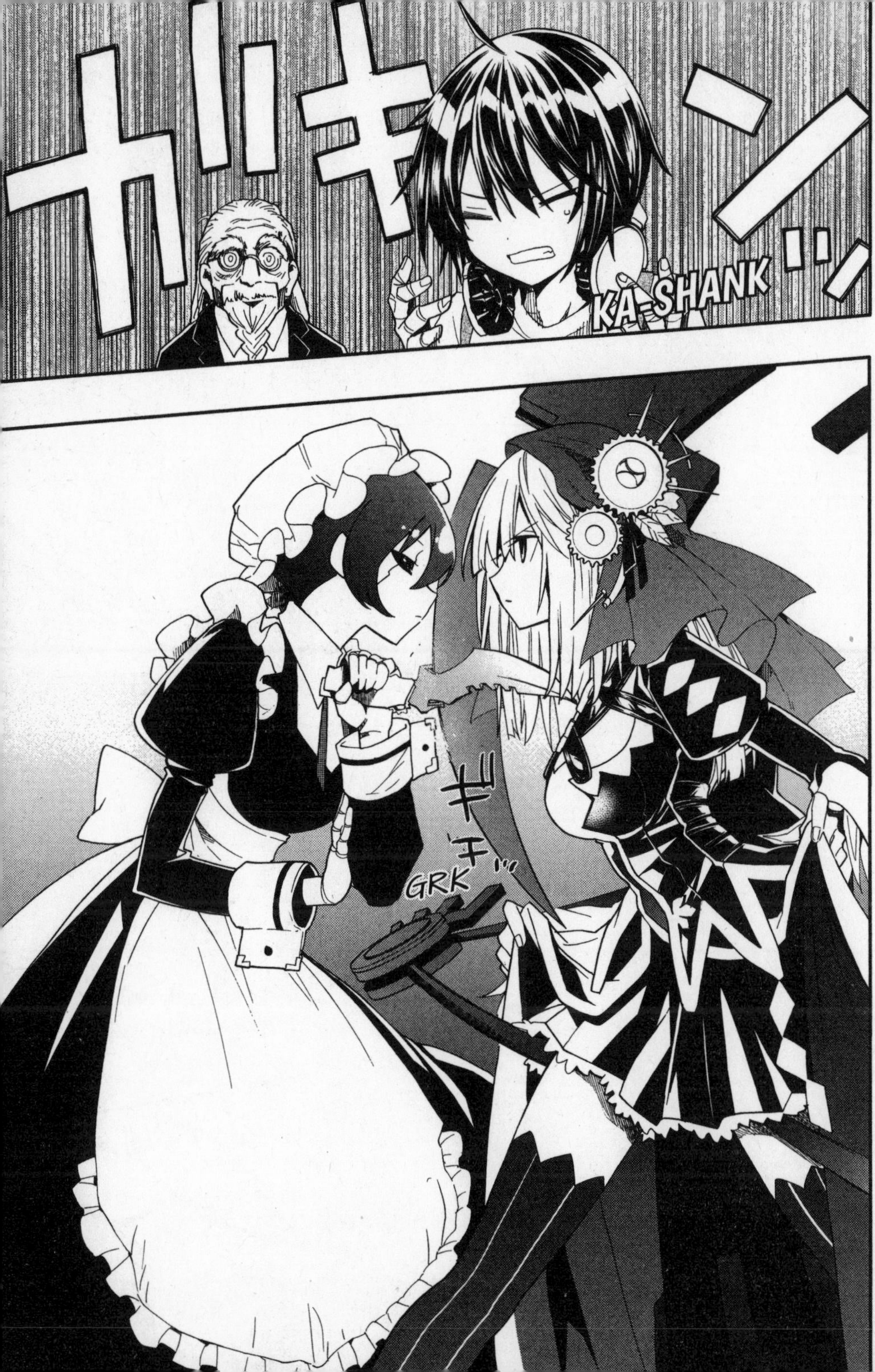
カリキーン
KA-SHANK
ギチ…
GRK

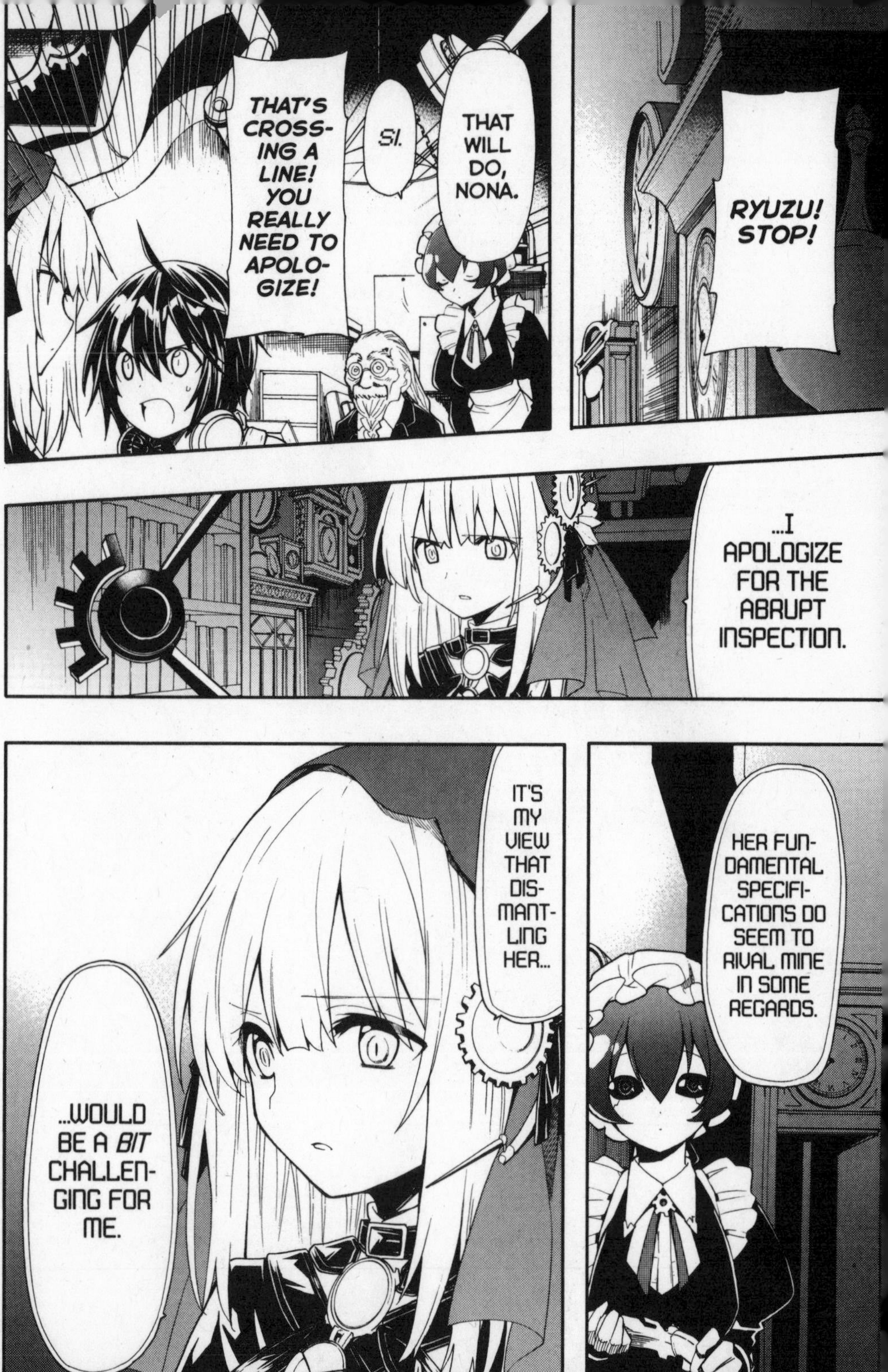
RYUZU! STOP!
THAT WILL DO, NONA.
SI.
THAT'S CROSSING A LINE! YOU REALLY NEED TO APOLOGIZE!
...I APOLOGIZE FOR THE ABRUPT INSPECTION.
HER FUNDAMENTAL SPECIFICATIONS DO SEEM TO RIVAL MINE IN SOME REGARDS.
IT'S MY VIEW THAT DISMANTLING HER...
...WOULD BE A *BIT* CHALLENGING FOR ME.

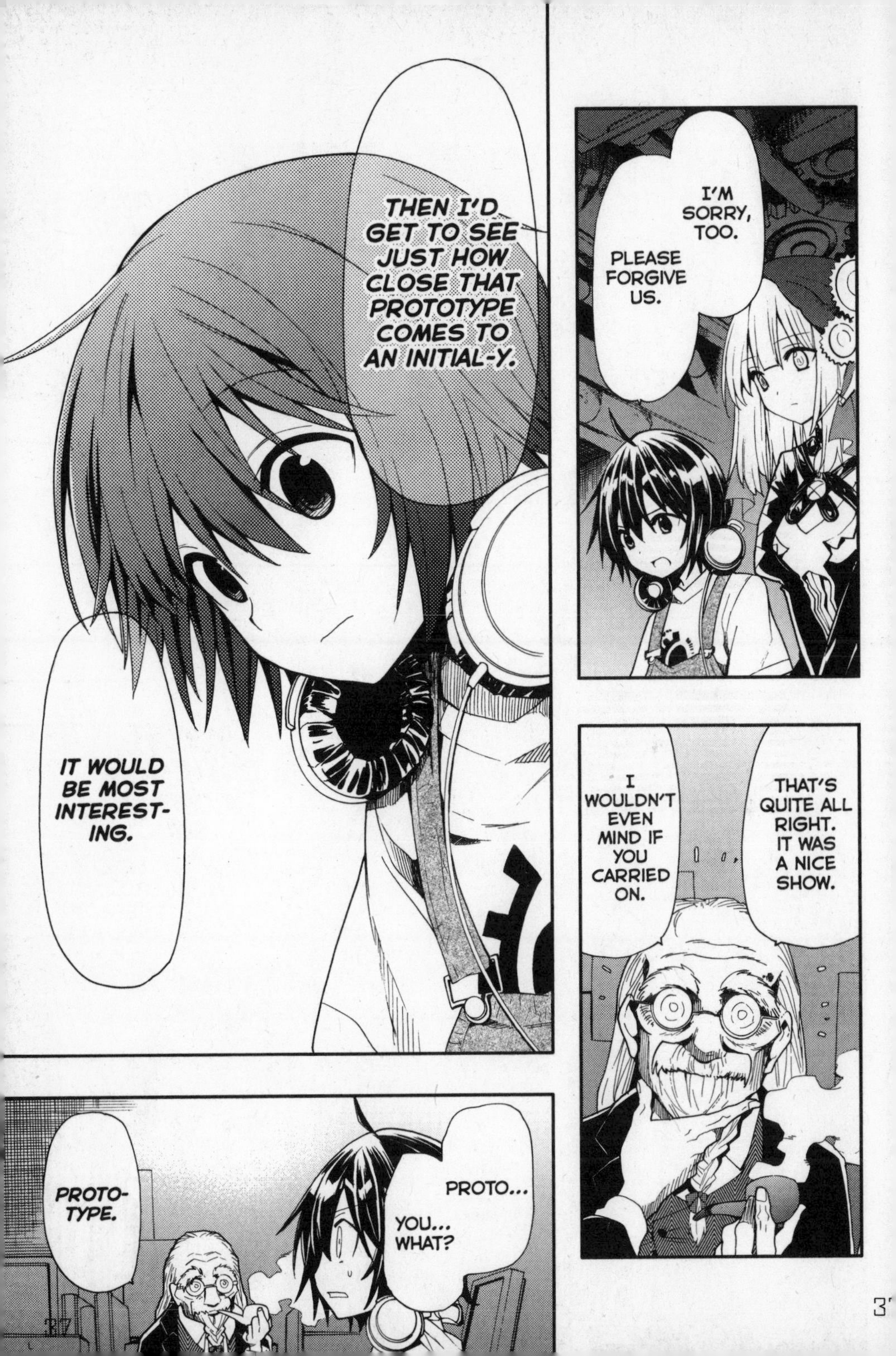
I'M SORRY, TOO.
PLEASE FORGIVE US.
THAT'S QUITE ALL RIGHT. IT WAS A NICE SHOW.
I WOULDN'T EVEN MIND IF YOU CARRIED ON.
THEN I'D GET TO SEE JUST HOW CLOSE THAT PROTOTYPE COMES TO AN INITIAL-Y.
IT WOULD BE MOST INTEREST-ING.
PROTO...
YOU... WHAT?
PROTO-TYPE.

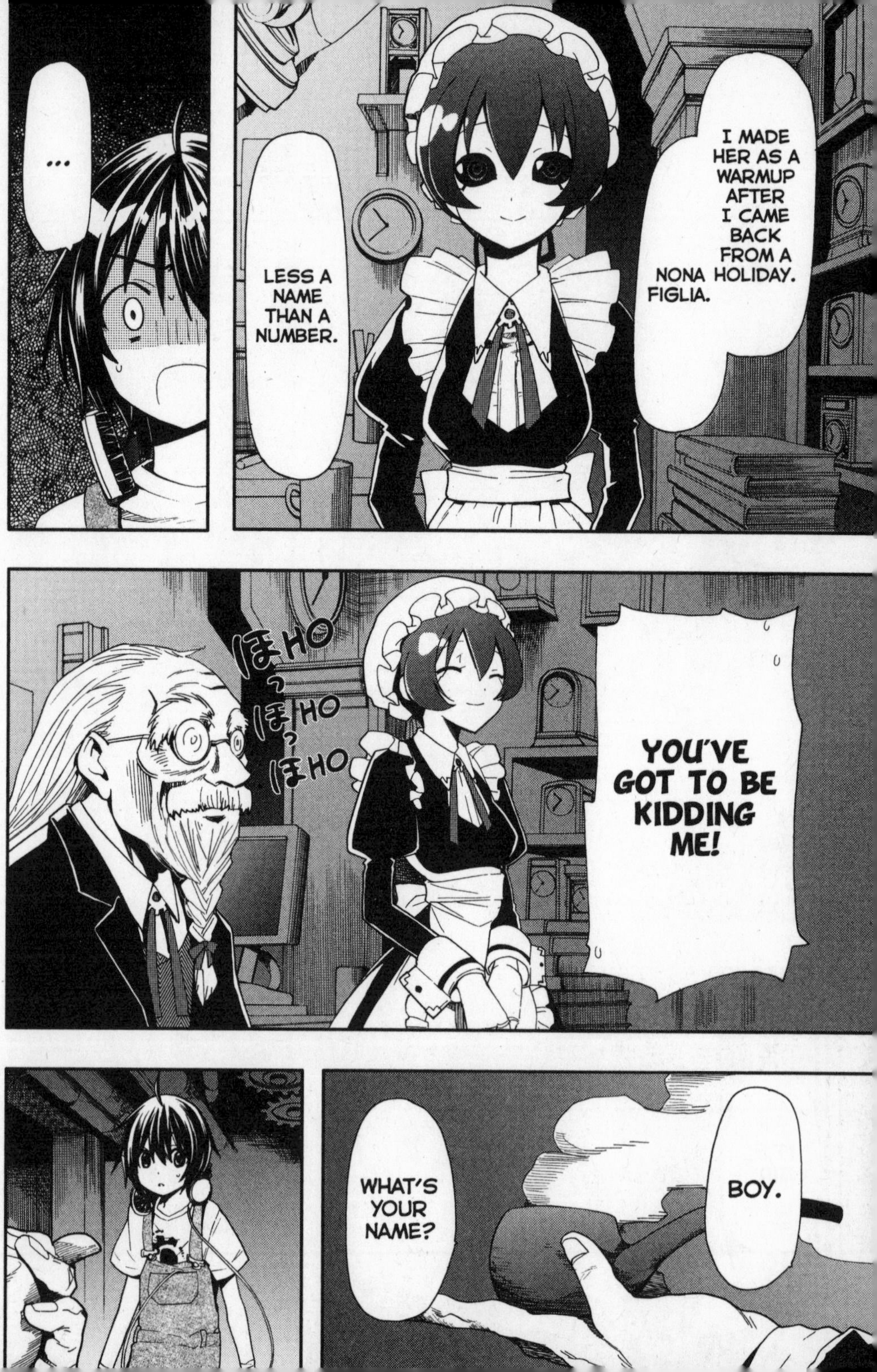

I MADE HER AS A WARMUP AFTER I CAME BACK FROM A HOLIDAY. NONA FIGLIA.
LESS A NAME THAN A NUMBER.
...
YOU'VE GOT TO BE KIDDING ME!
ほっHO ほっHO ほHO
BOY.
WHAT'S YOUR NAME?

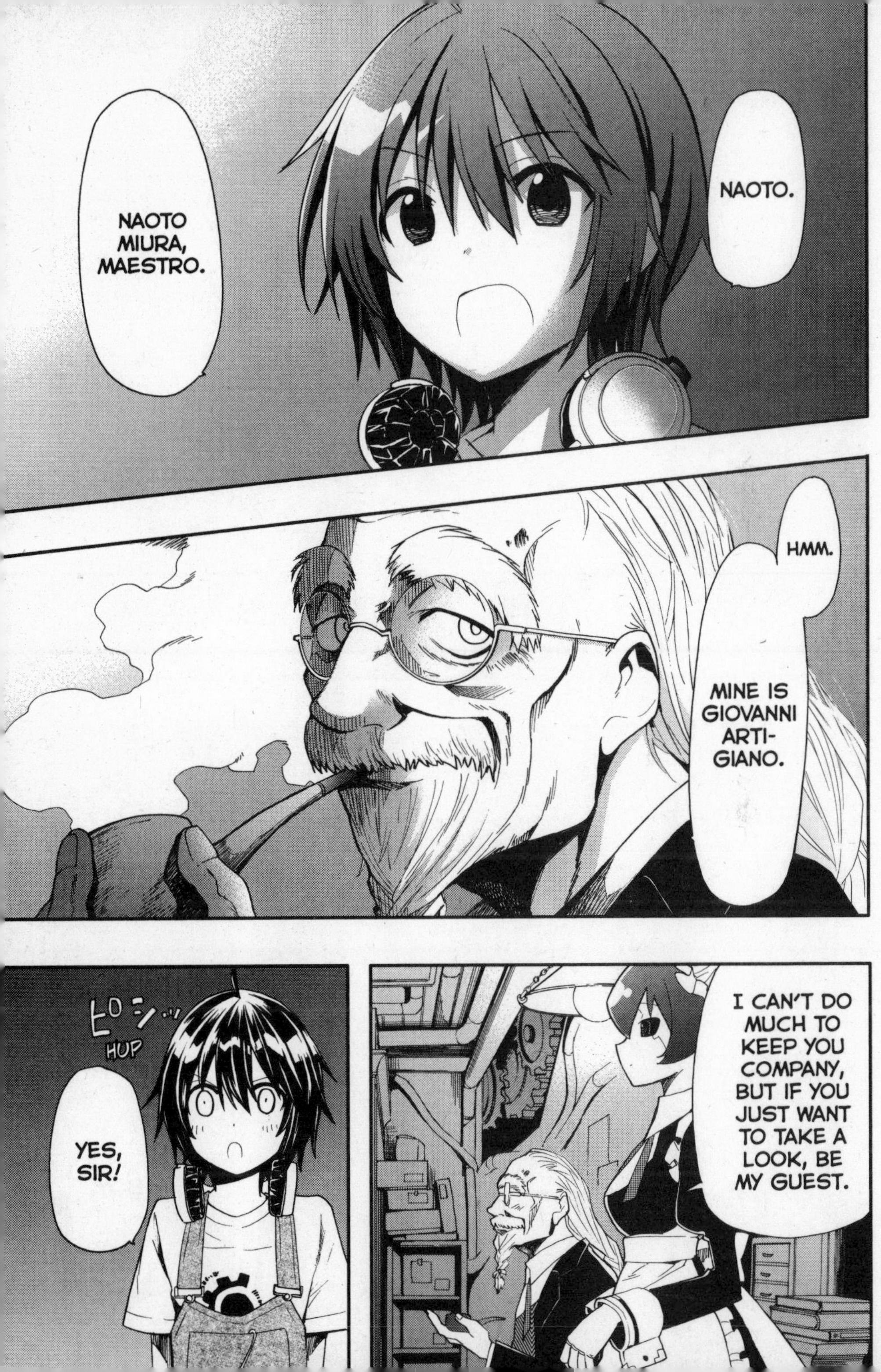
NAOTO.
NAOTO MIURA, MAESTRO.
HMM.
MINE IS GIOVANNI ARTI-GIANO.
I CAN'T DO MUCH TO KEEP YOU COMPANY, BUT IF YOU JUST WANT TO TAKE A LOOK, BE MY GUEST.
HUP
YES, SIR!

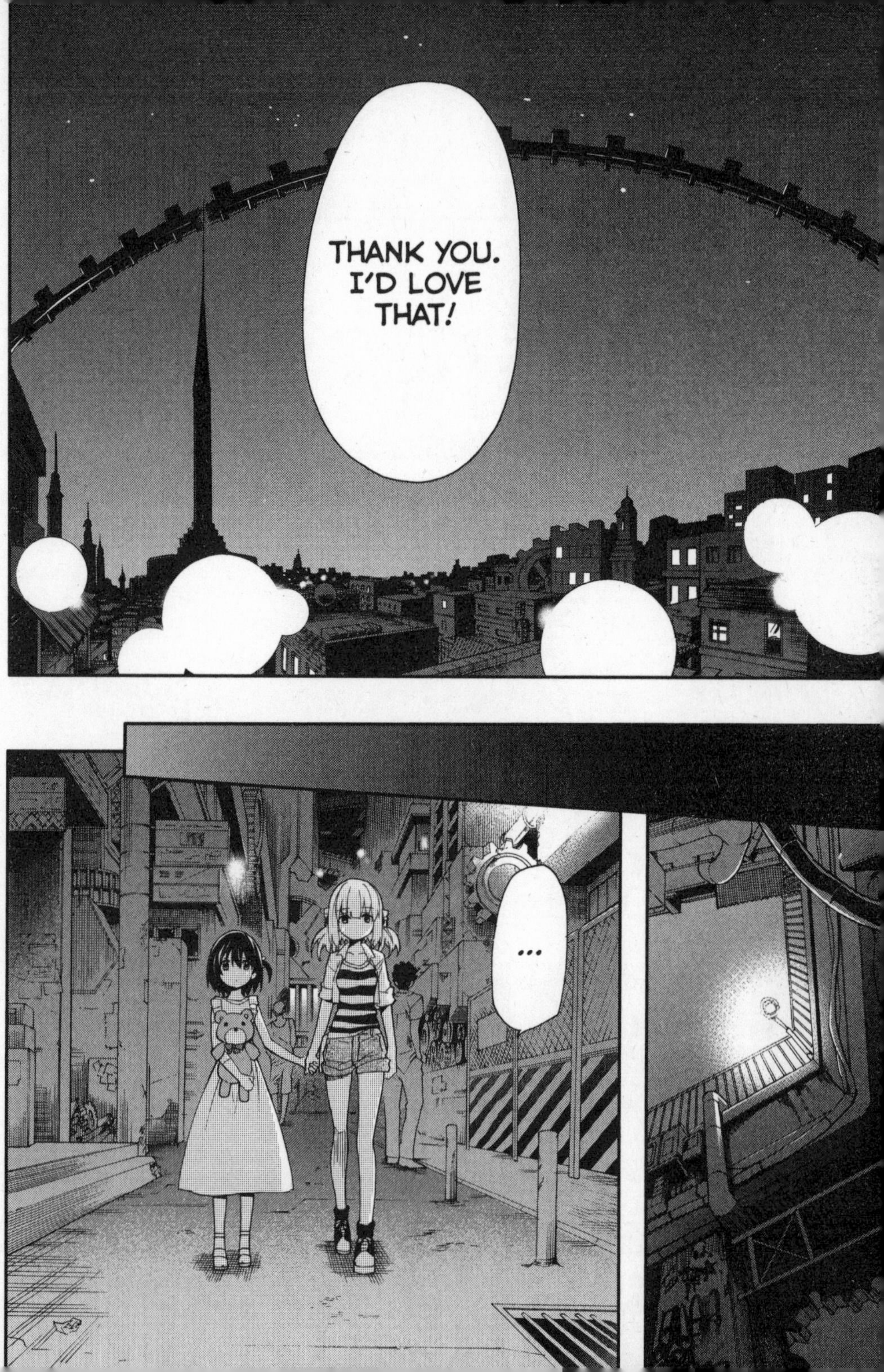
THANK YOU. I'D LOVE THAT!
...

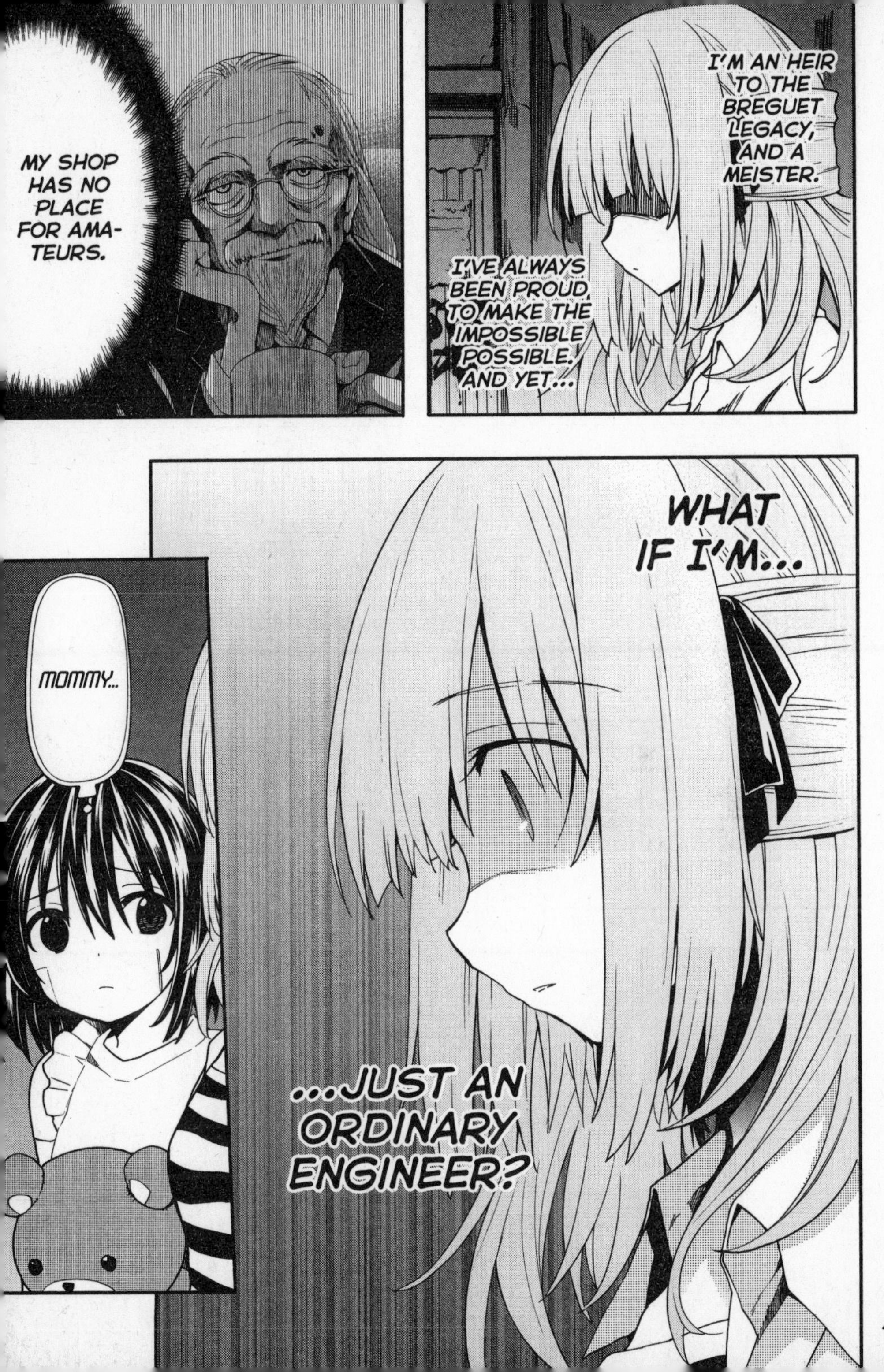

I'M AN HEIR TO THE BREGUET LEGACY, AND A MEISTER.
I'VE ALWAYS BEEN PROUD TO MAKE THE IMPOSSIBLE POSSIBLE. AND YET...
MY SHOP HAS NO PLACE FOR AMA-TEURS.
WHAT IF I'M...
...JUST AN ORDINARY ENGINEER?
MOMMY...

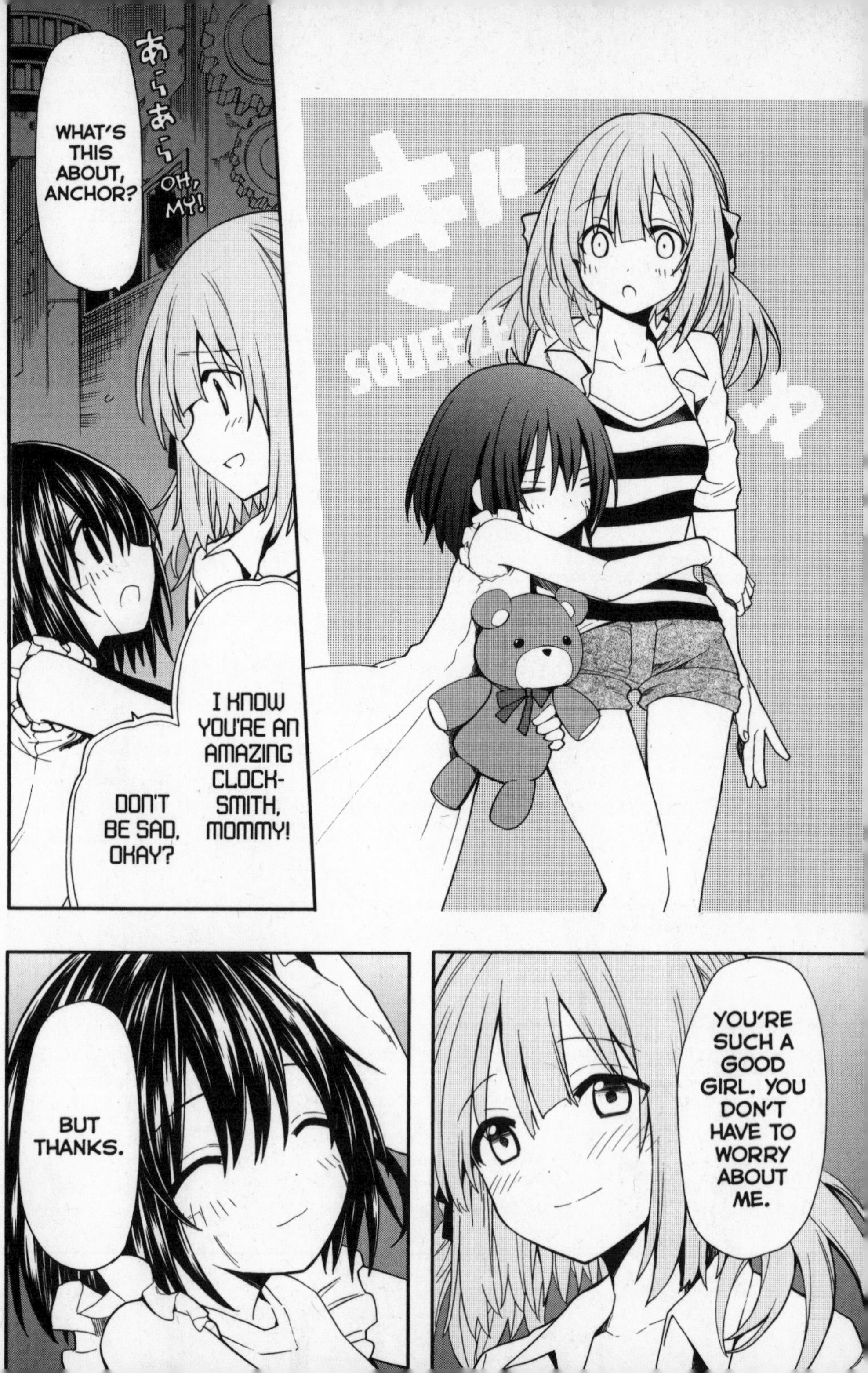

SQUEEZE
I KNOW YOU'RE AN AMAZING CLOCK-SMITH, MOMMY!
DON'T BE SAD, OKAY?
WHAT'S THIS ABOUT, ANCHOR?
あらあら
OH, MY!
YOU'RE SUCH A GOOD GIRL. YOU DON'T HAVE TO WORRY ABOUT ME.
BUT THANKS.

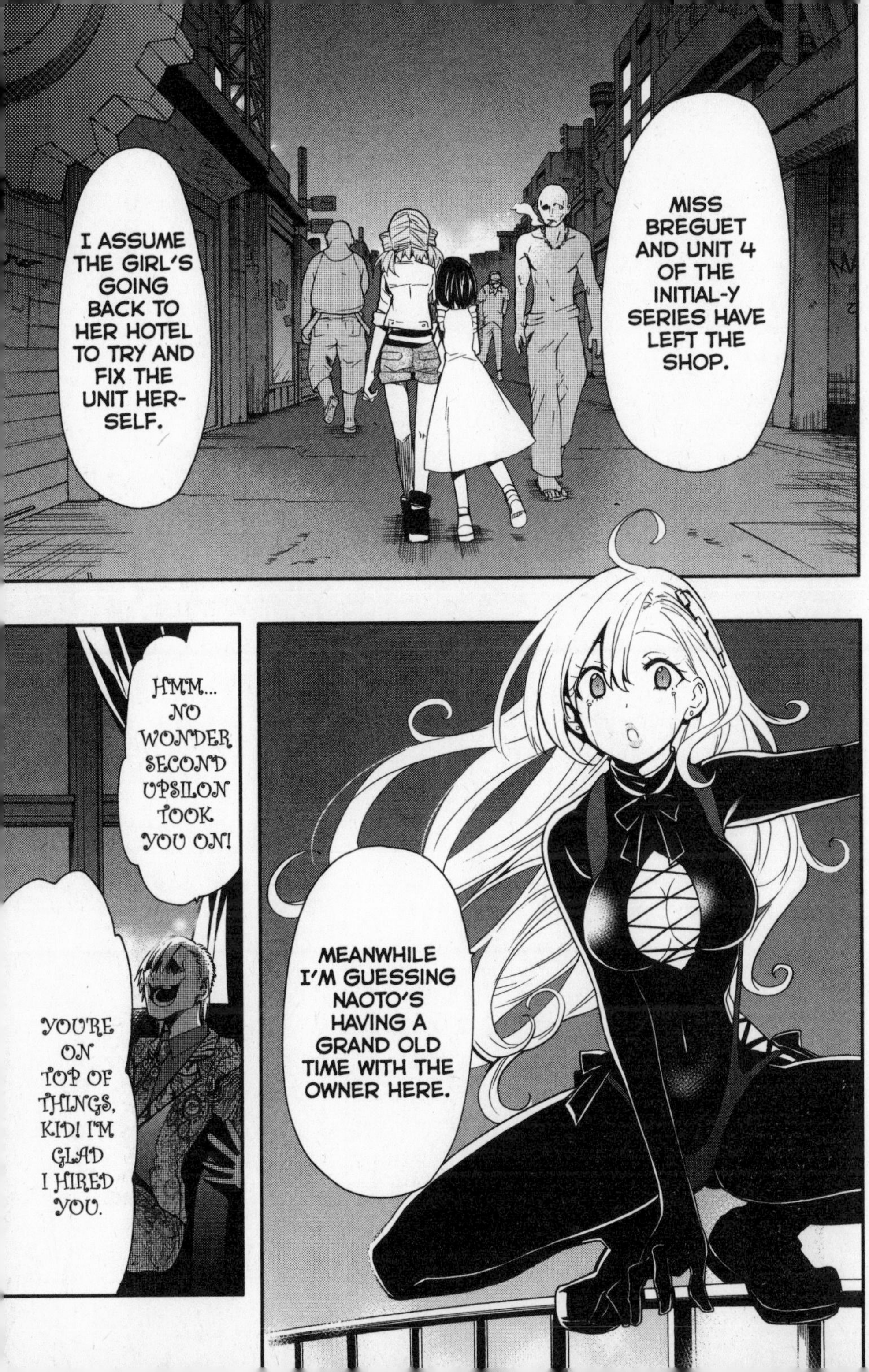
MISS BREGUET AND UNIT 4 OF THE INITIAL-Y SERIES HAVE LEFT THE SHOP.
I ASSUME THE GIRL'S GOING BACK TO HER HOTEL TO TRY AND FIX THE UNIT HER-SELF.
MEANWHILE I'M GUESSING NAOTO'S HAVING A GRAND OLD TIME WITH THE OWNER HERE.
HMM... NO WONDER SECOND UPSILON TOOK YOU ON!
YOU'RE ON TOP OF THINGS, KID! I'M GLAD I HIRED YOU.

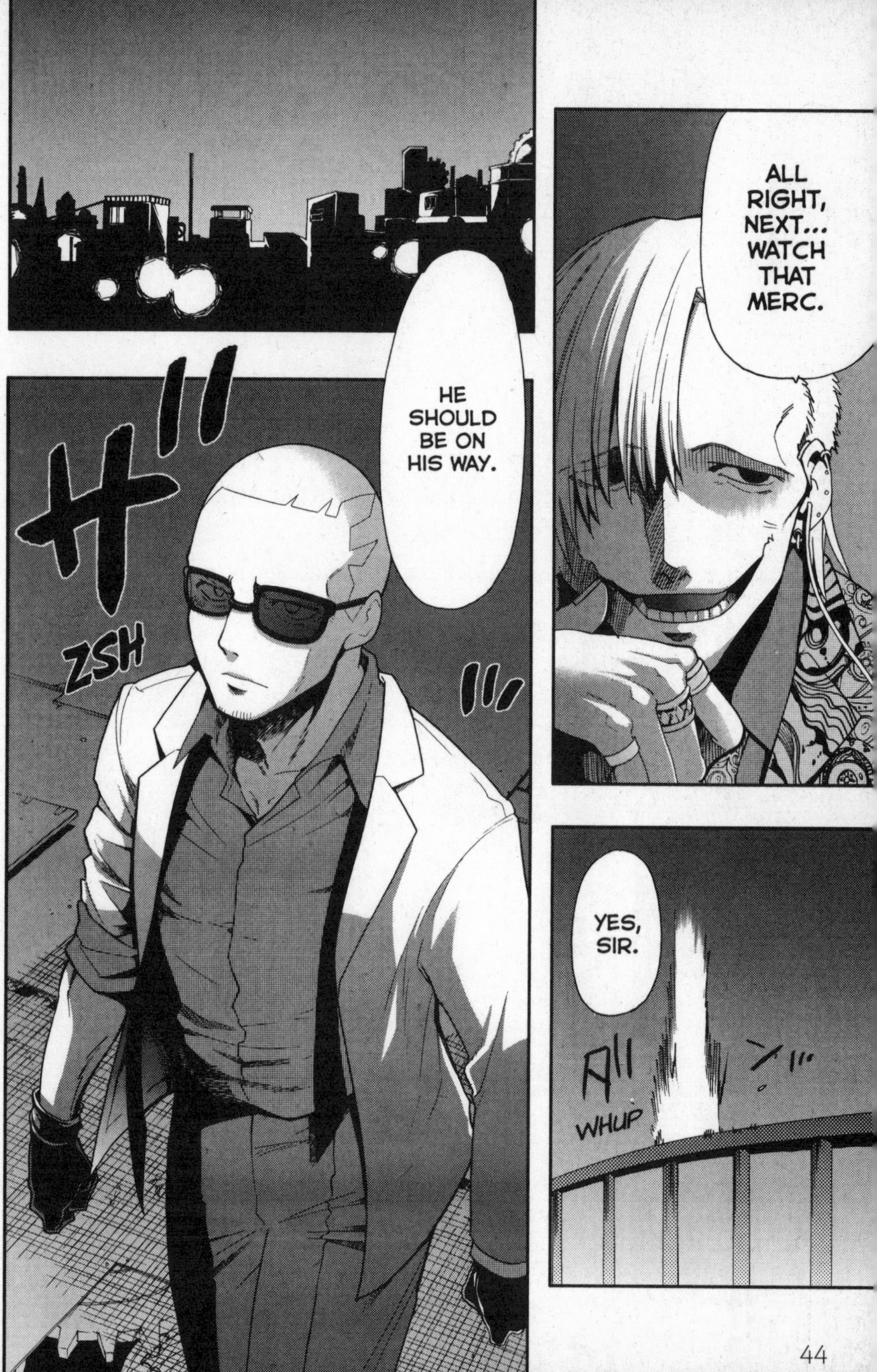
ALL RIGHT, NEXT... WATCH THAT MERC.
HE SHOULD BE ON HIS WAY.
YES, SIR.
WHUP
ZSH

CLOCKWORK PLANET

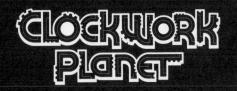

Clockwork Planet

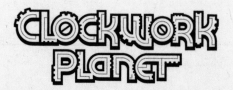

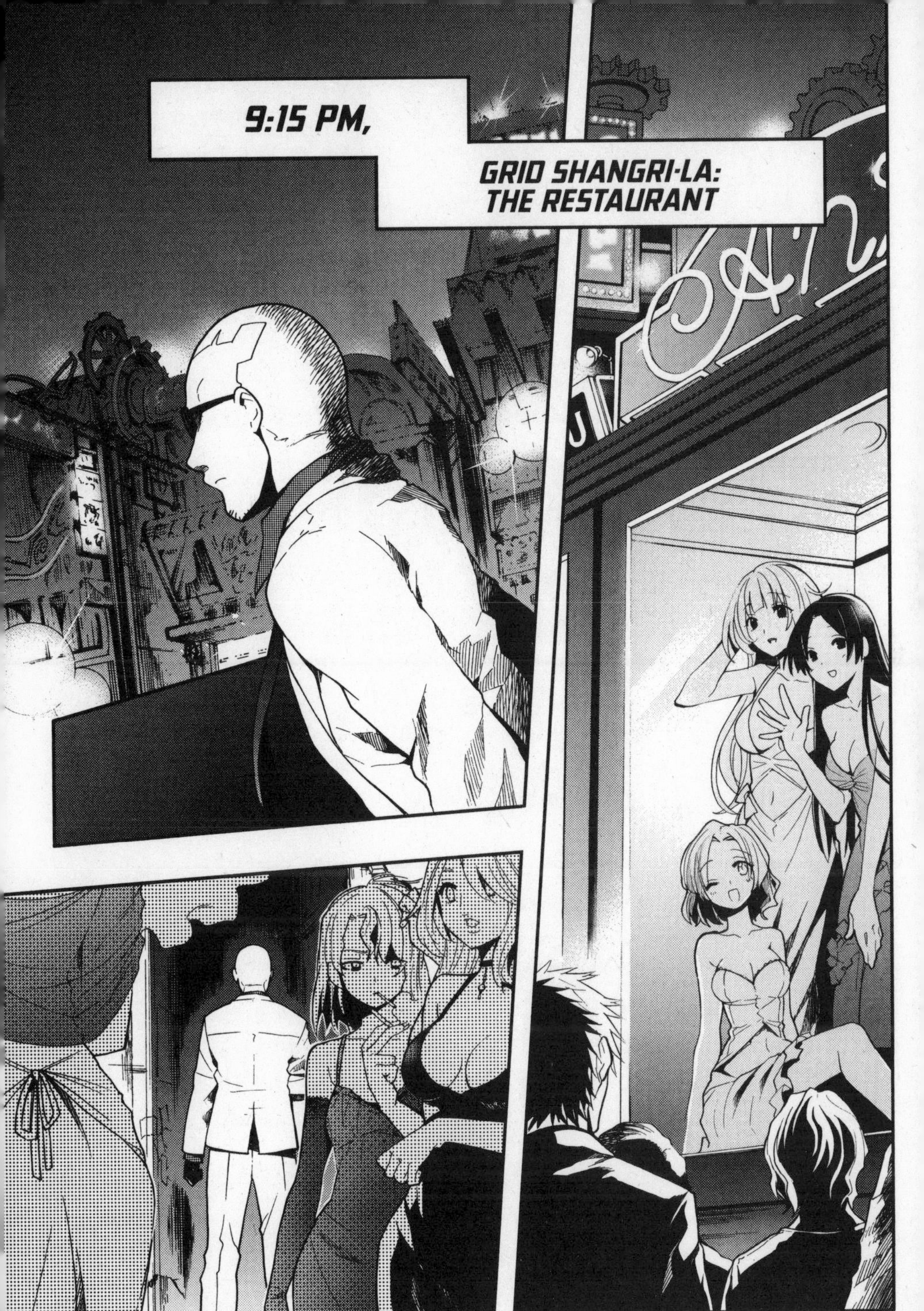
9:15 PM,
GRID SHANGRI-LA: THE RESTAURANT

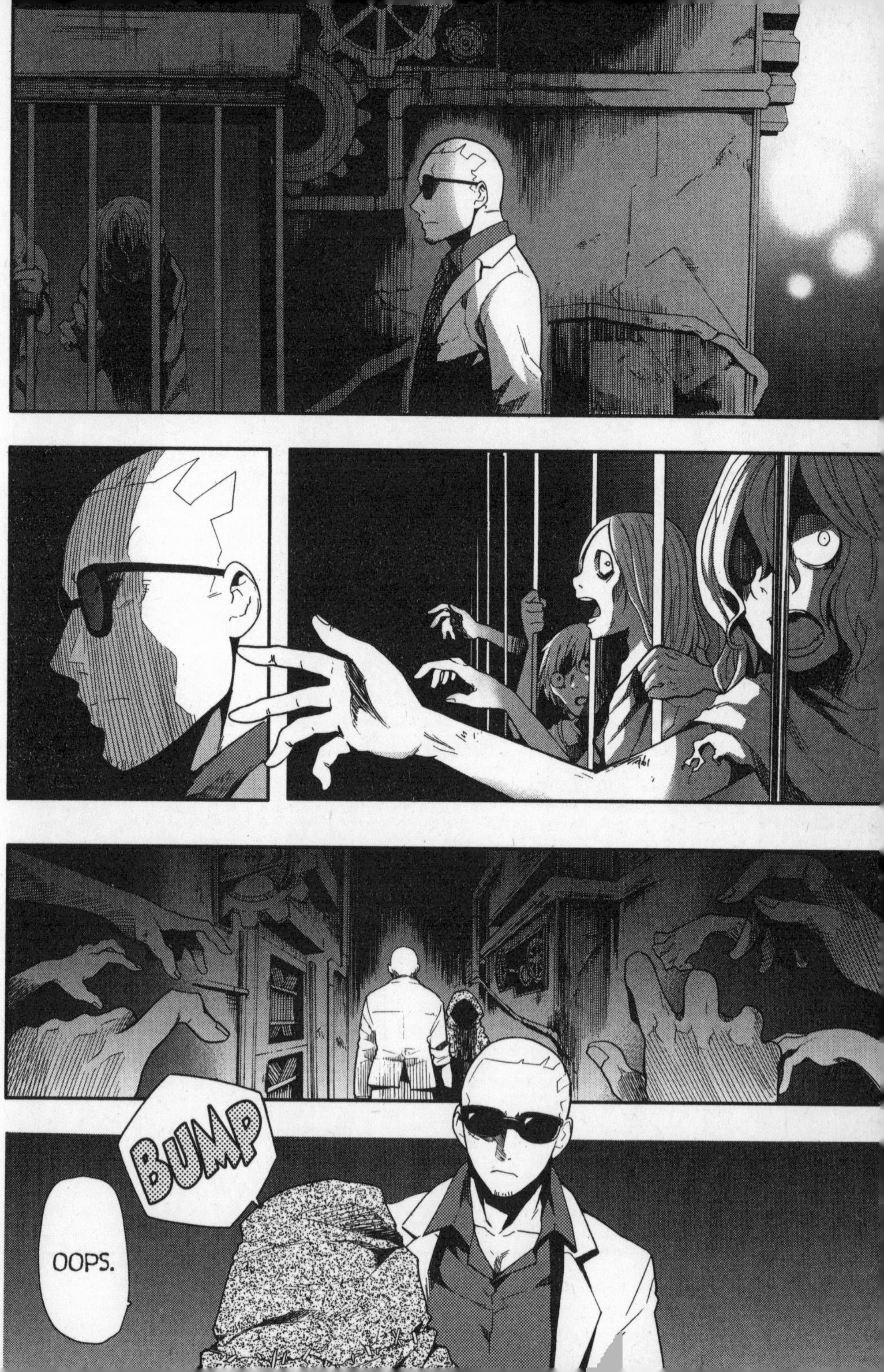
BUMP
OOPS.

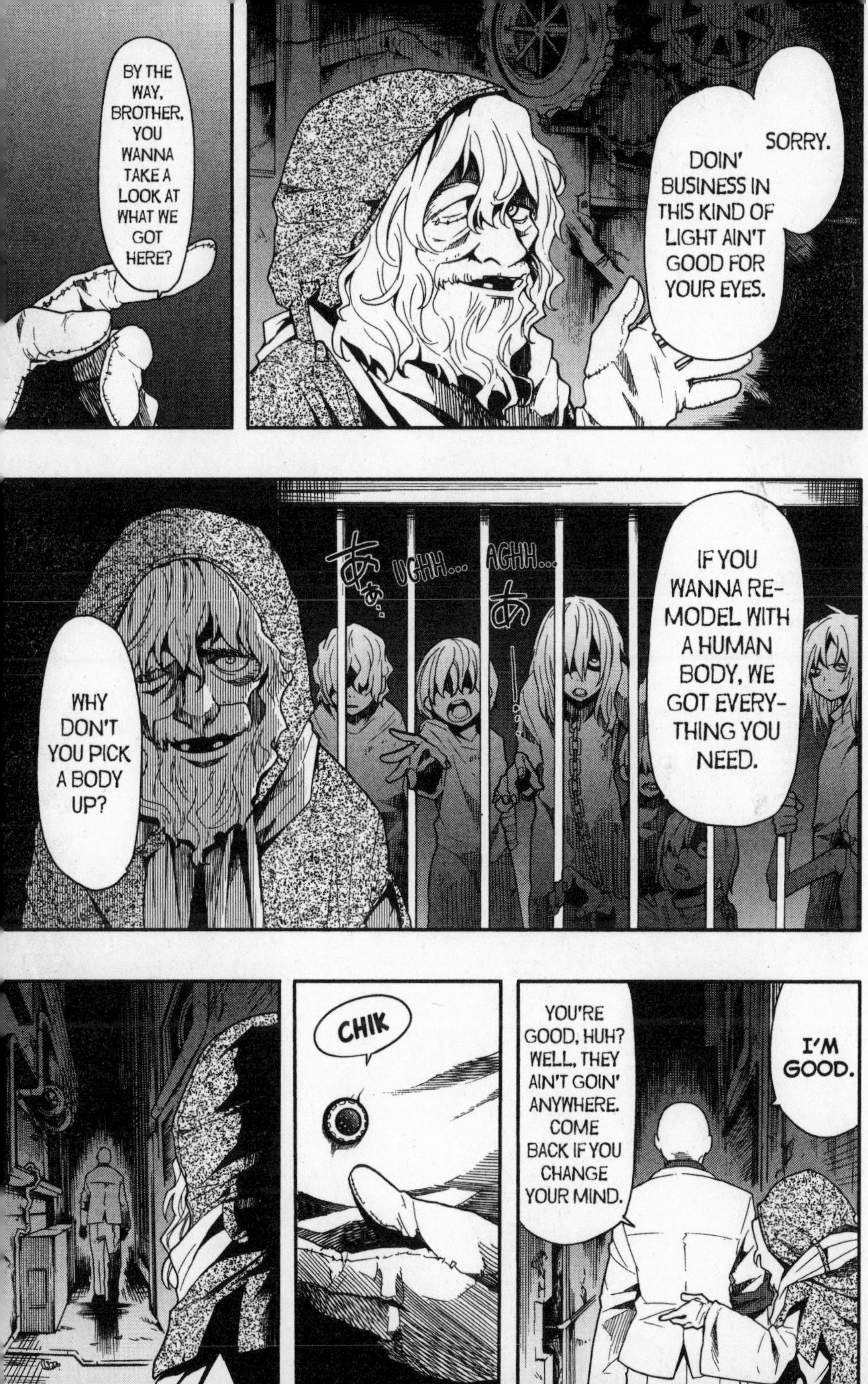
SORRY.
DOIN' BUSINESS IN THIS KIND OF LIGHT AIN'T GOOD FOR YOUR EYES.
BY THE WAY, BROTHER, YOU WANNA TAKE A LOOK AT WHAT WE GOT HERE?
IF YOU WANNA RE-MODEL WITH A HUMAN BODY, WE GOT EVERY-THING YOU NEED.
AGHH...
UGHH...
WHY DON'T YOU PICK A BODY UP?
I'M GOOD.
YOU'RE GOOD, HUH? WELL, THEY AIN'T GOIN' ANYWHERE. COME BACK IF YOU CHANGE YOUR MIND.
CHIK

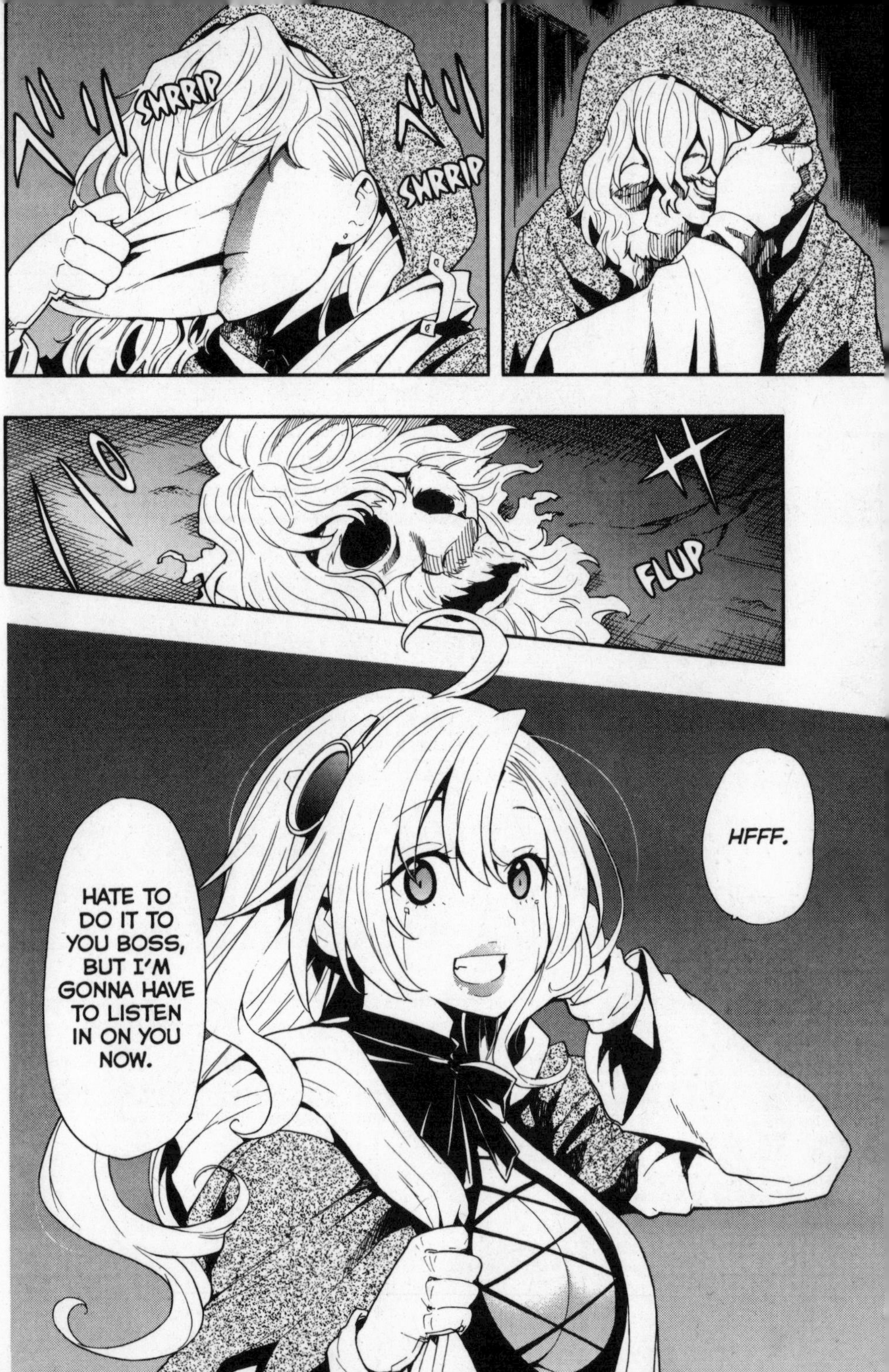
SHRRIP
SHRRIP
FLUP
HFFF.
HATE TO DO IT TO YOU BOSS, BUT I'M GONNA HAVE TO LISTEN IN ON YOU NOW.

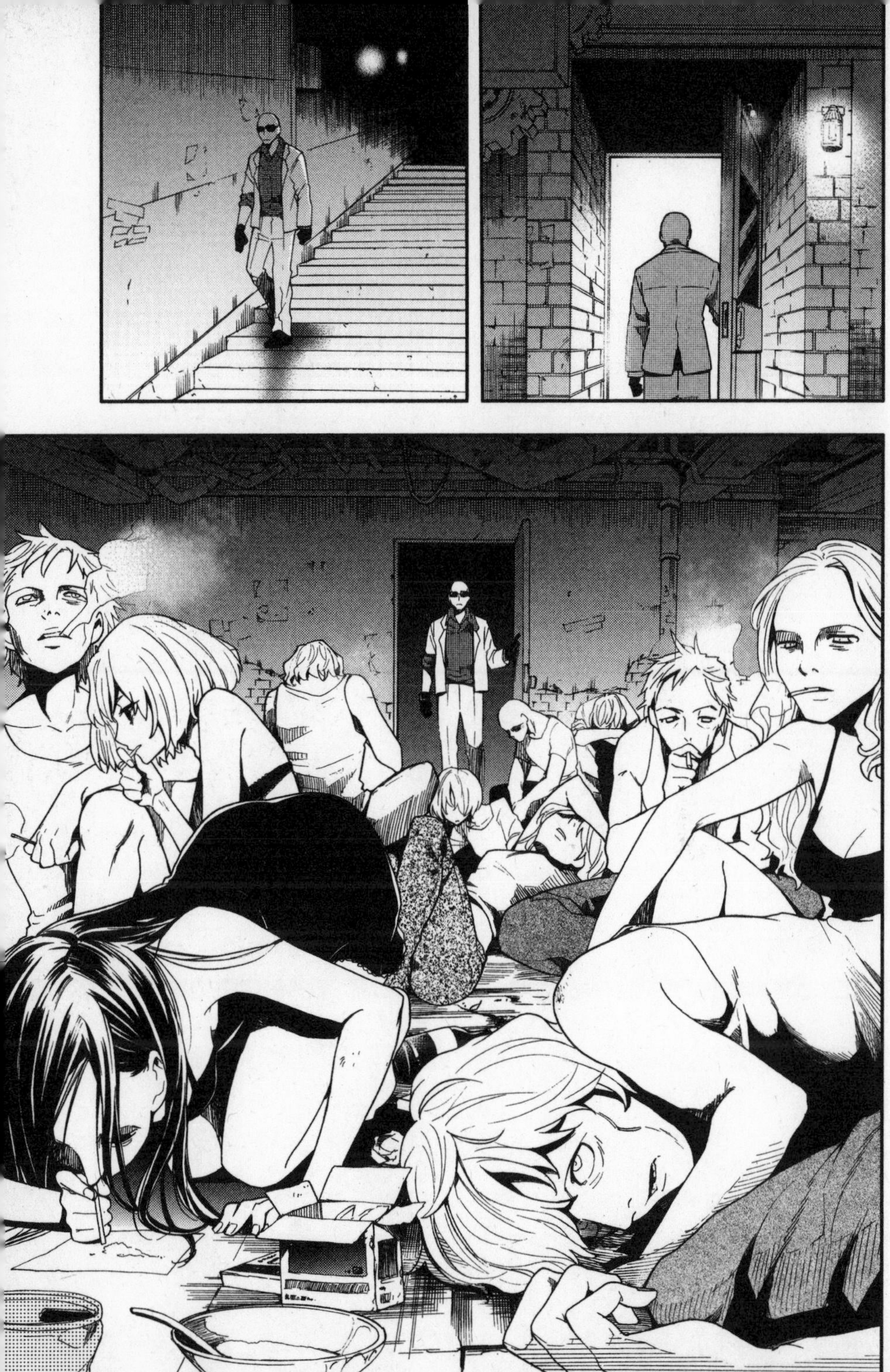

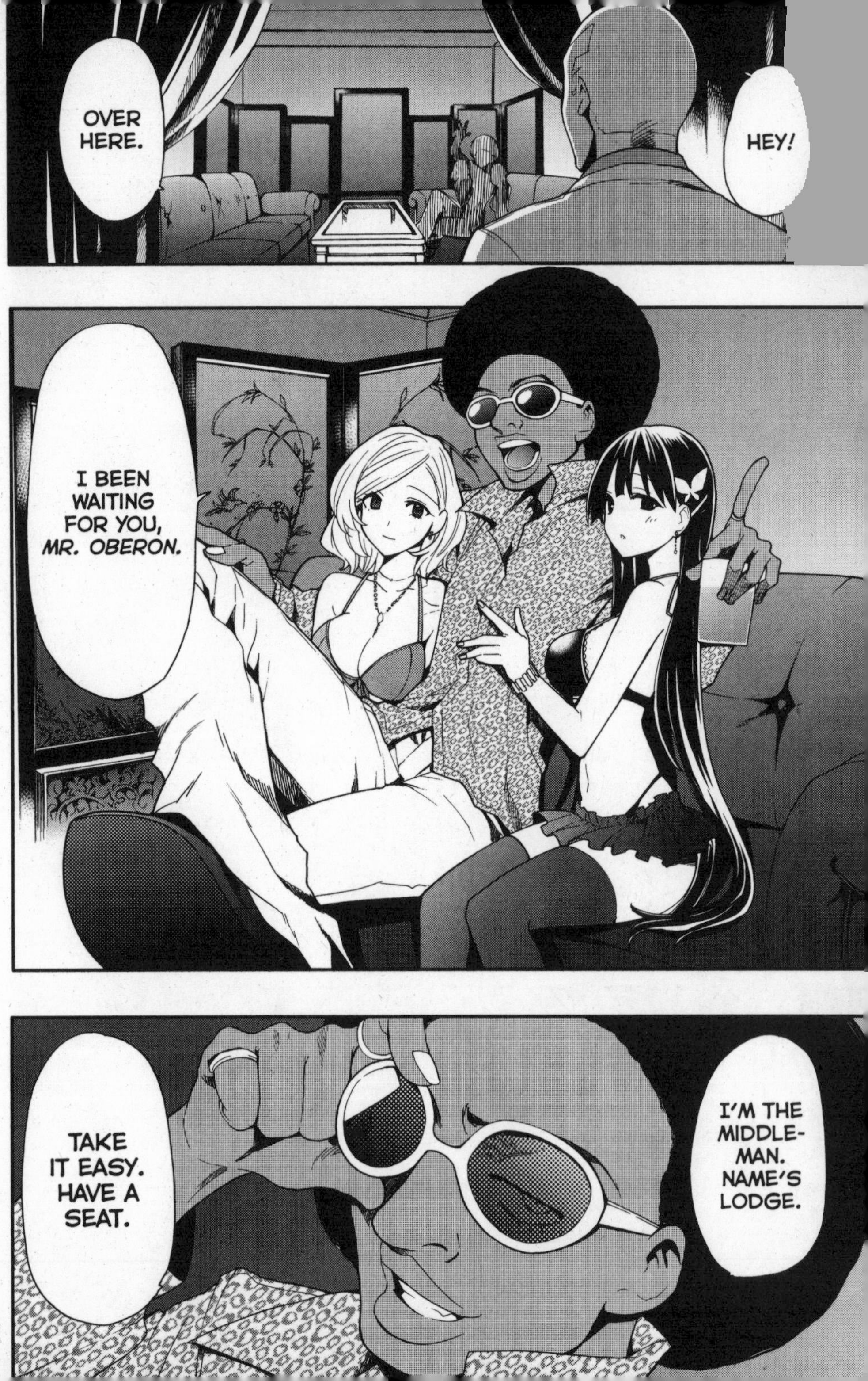
HEY!
OVER HERE.
I BEEN WAITING FOR YOU, *MR. OBERON.*
I'M THE MIDDLE-MAN. NAME'S LODGE.
TAKE IT EASY. HAVE A SEAT.

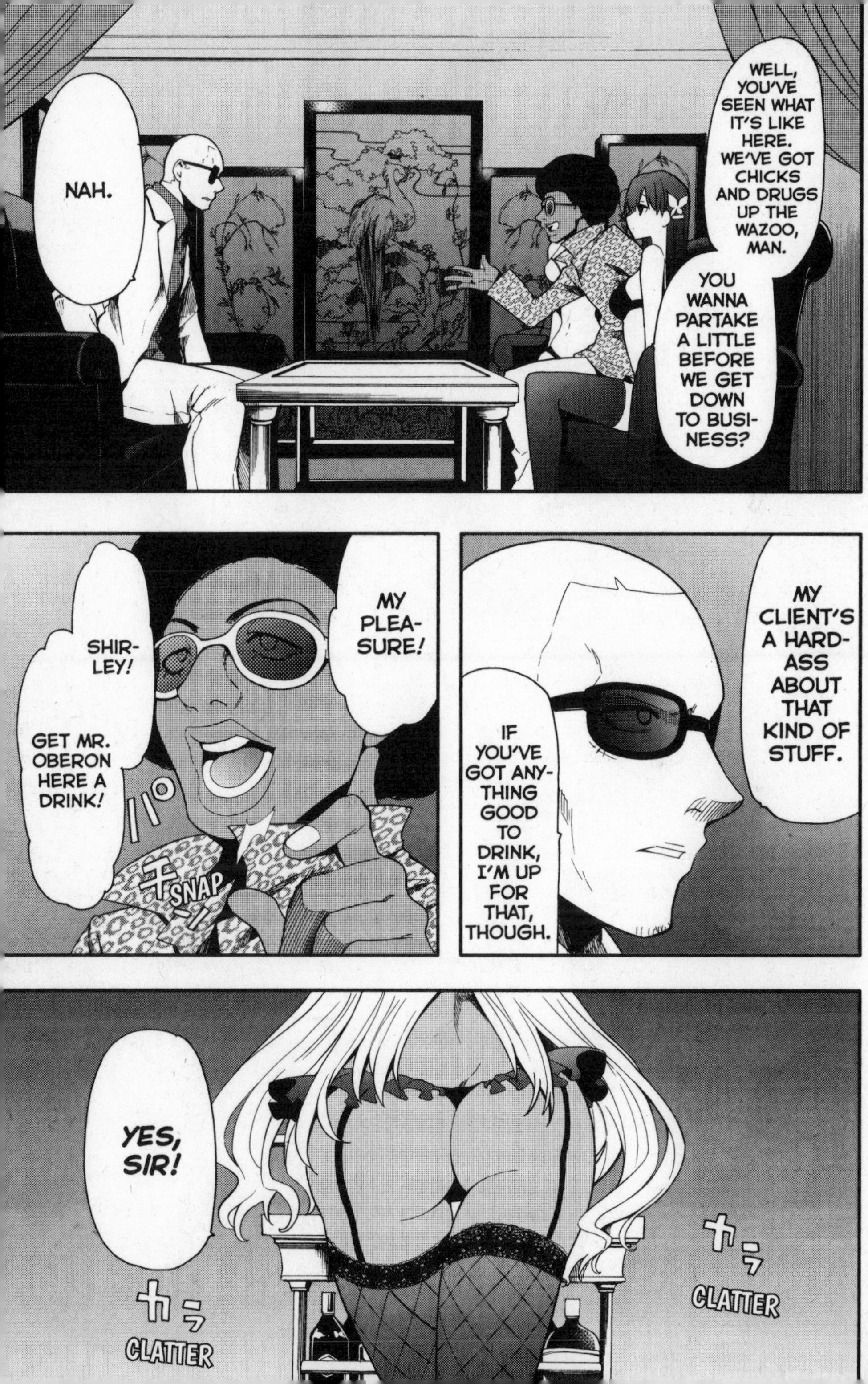
WELL, YOU'VE SEEN WHAT IT'S LIKE HERE. WE'VE GOT CHICKS AND DRUGS UP THE WAZOO, MAN.
YOU WANNA PARTAKE A LITTLE BEFORE WE GET DOWN TO BUSI-NESS?
NAH.
MY CLIENT'S A HARD-ASS ABOUT THAT KIND OF STUFF.
IF YOU'VE GOT ANY-THING GOOD TO DRINK, I'M UP FOR THAT, THOUGH.
MY PLEA-SURE!
SHIR-LEY!
GET MR. OBERON HERE A DRINK!
パ
チー
SNAP
YES, SIR!
カラ
CLATTER
カラ
CLATTER

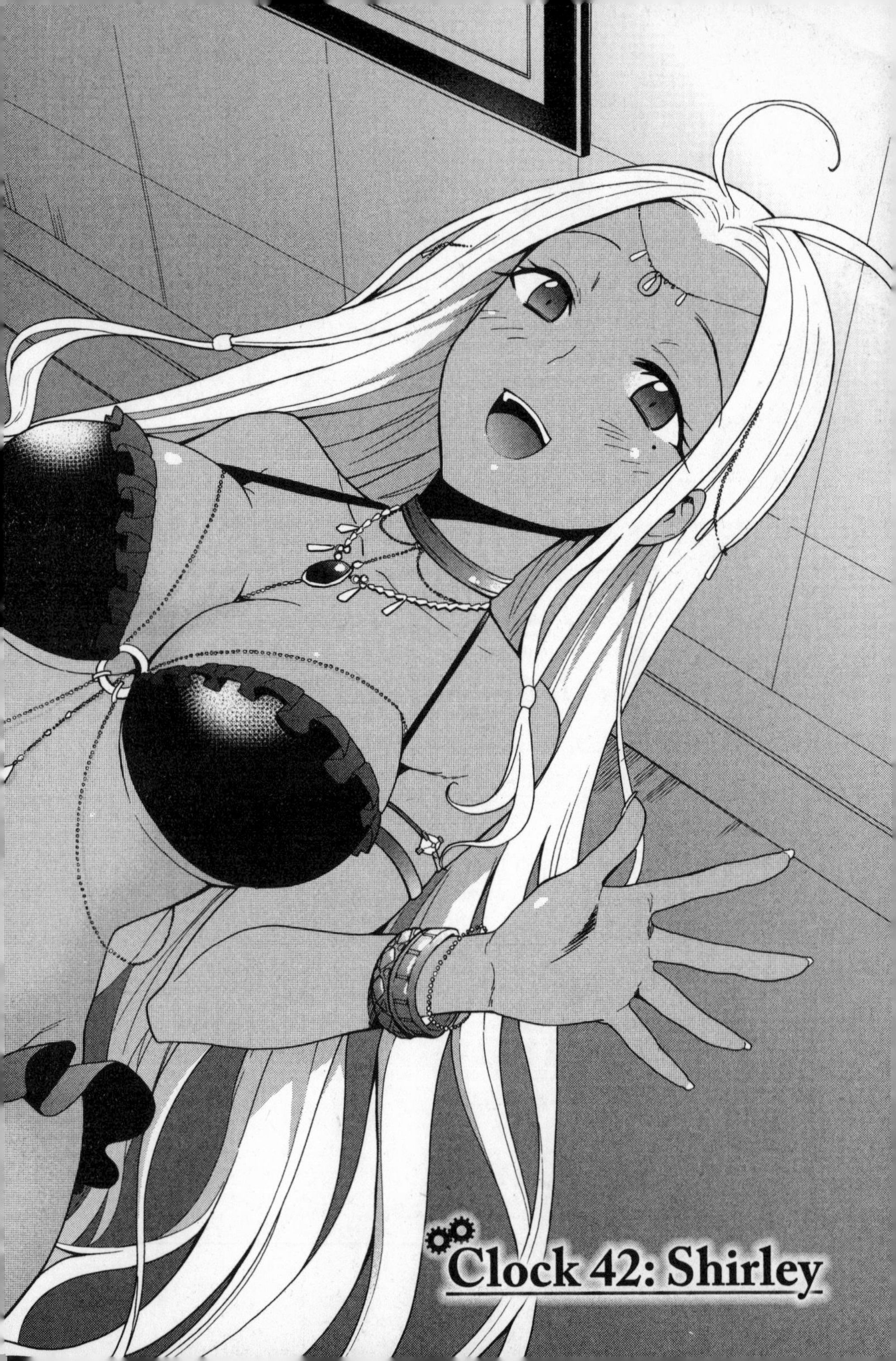
Clock 42: Shirley

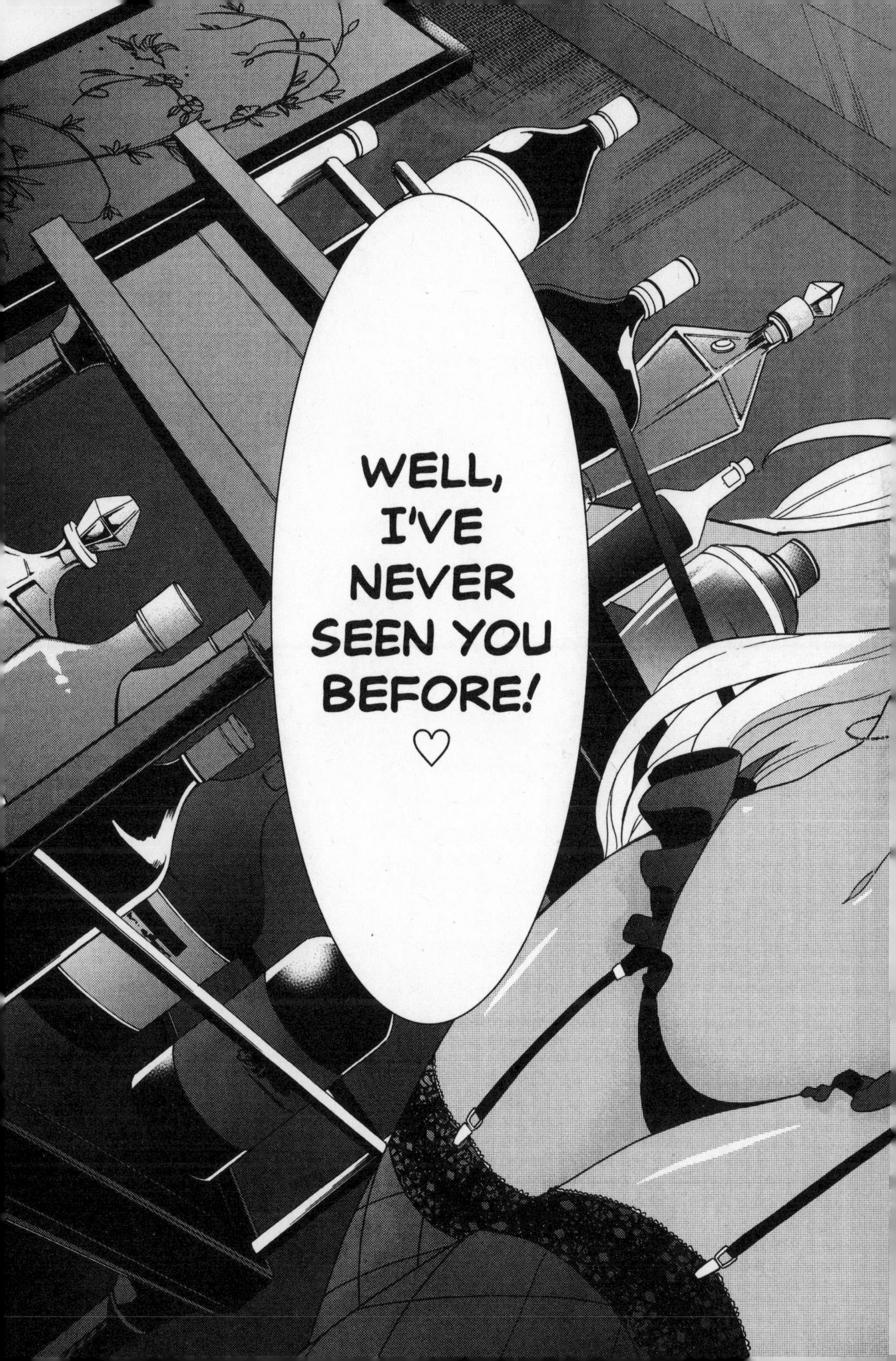
WELL, I'VE NEVER SEEN YOU BEFORE! ♡

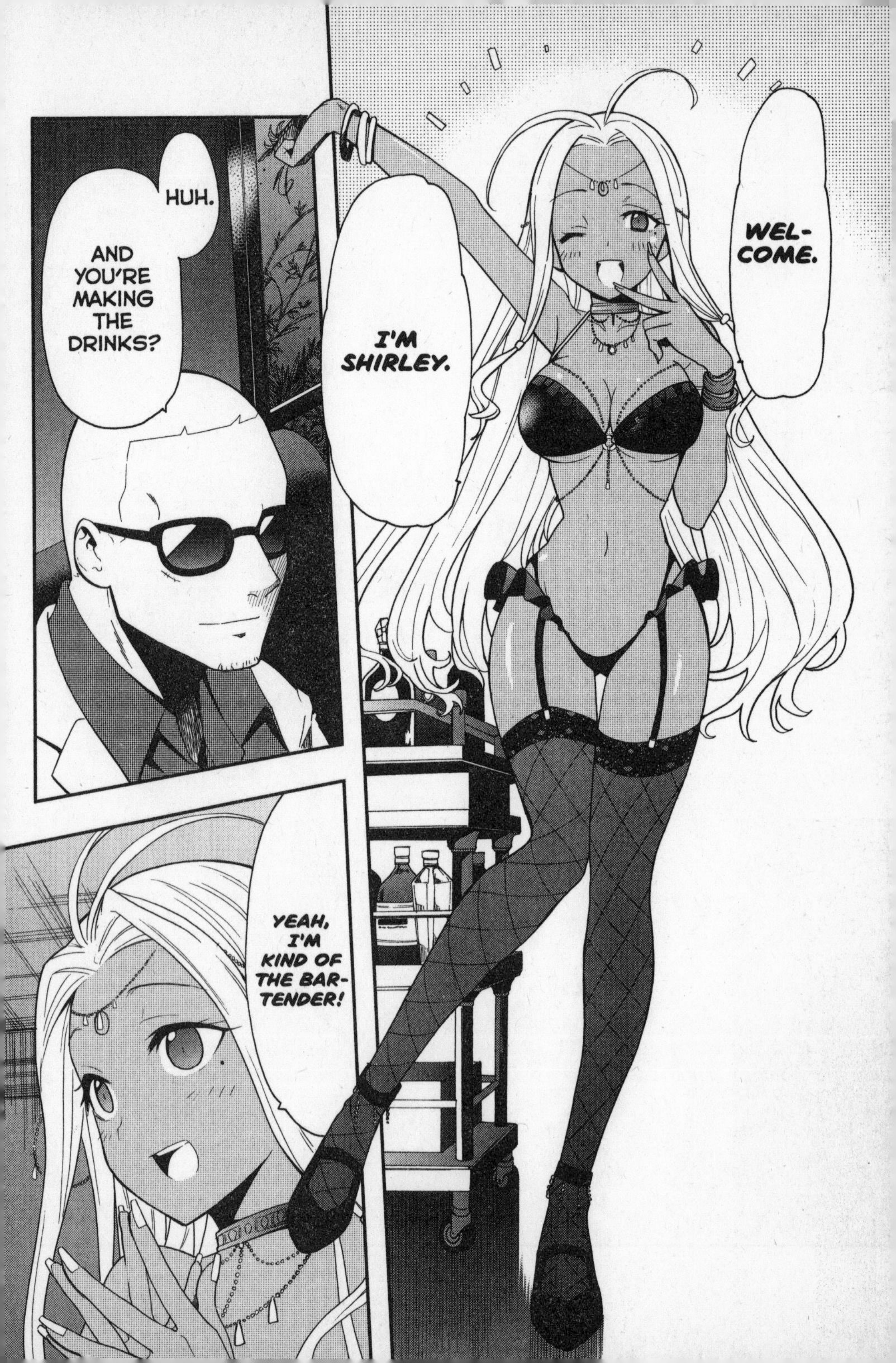
WEL-COME.
I'M SHIRLEY.
HUH.
AND YOU'RE MAKING THE DRINKS?
YEAH, I'M KIND OF THE BAR-TENDER!

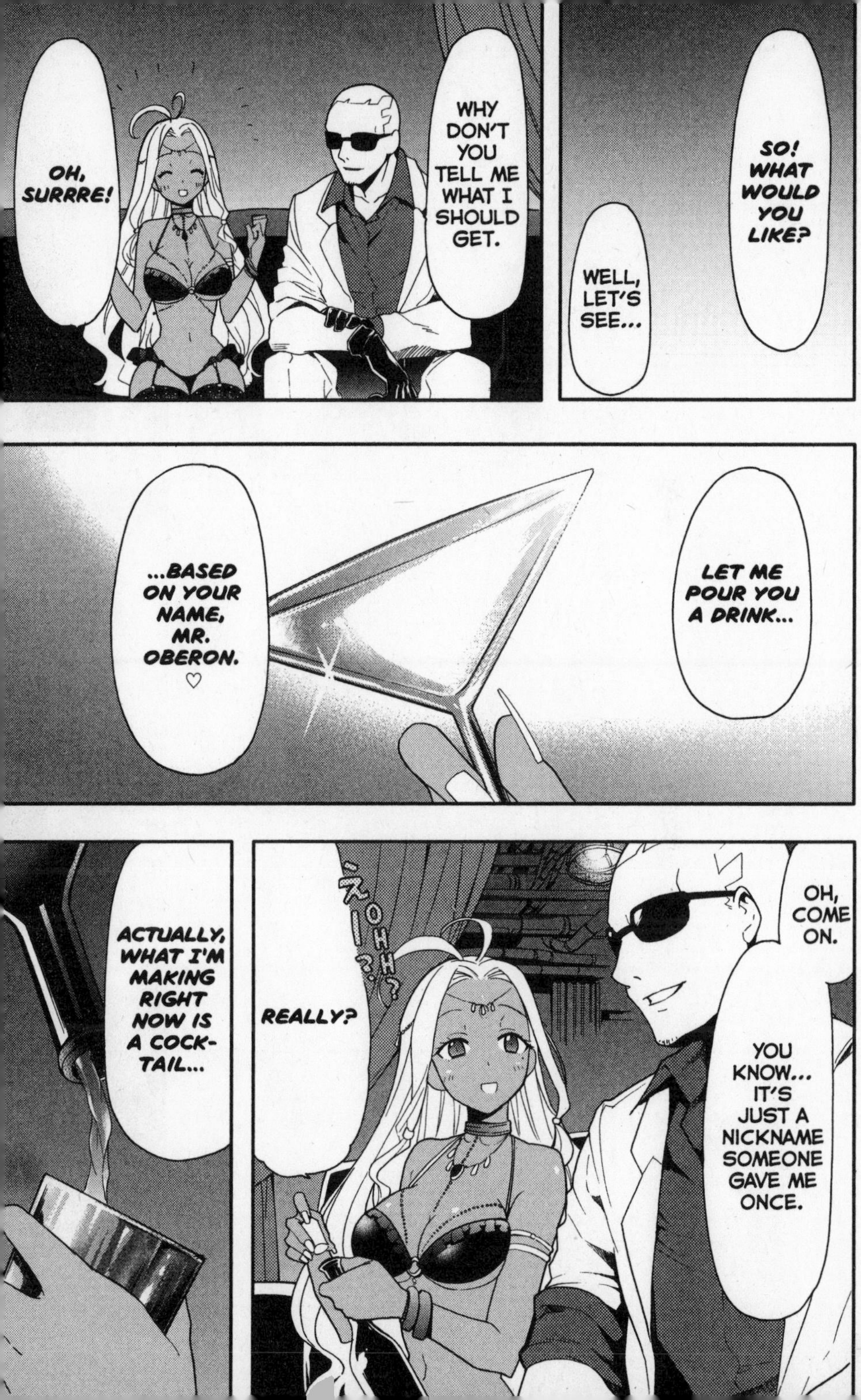
SO! WHAT WOULD YOU LIKE?
WELL, LET'S SEE...
WHY DON'T YOU TELL ME WHAT I SHOULD GET.
OH, SURRRE!
LET ME POUR YOU A DRINK...
...BASED ON YOUR NAME, MR. OBERON. ♡
OH, COME ON.
YOU KNOW... IT'S JUST A NICKNAME SOMEONE GAVE ME ONCE.
REALLY?
ACTUALLY, WHAT I'M MAKING RIGHT NOW IS A COCKTAIL...

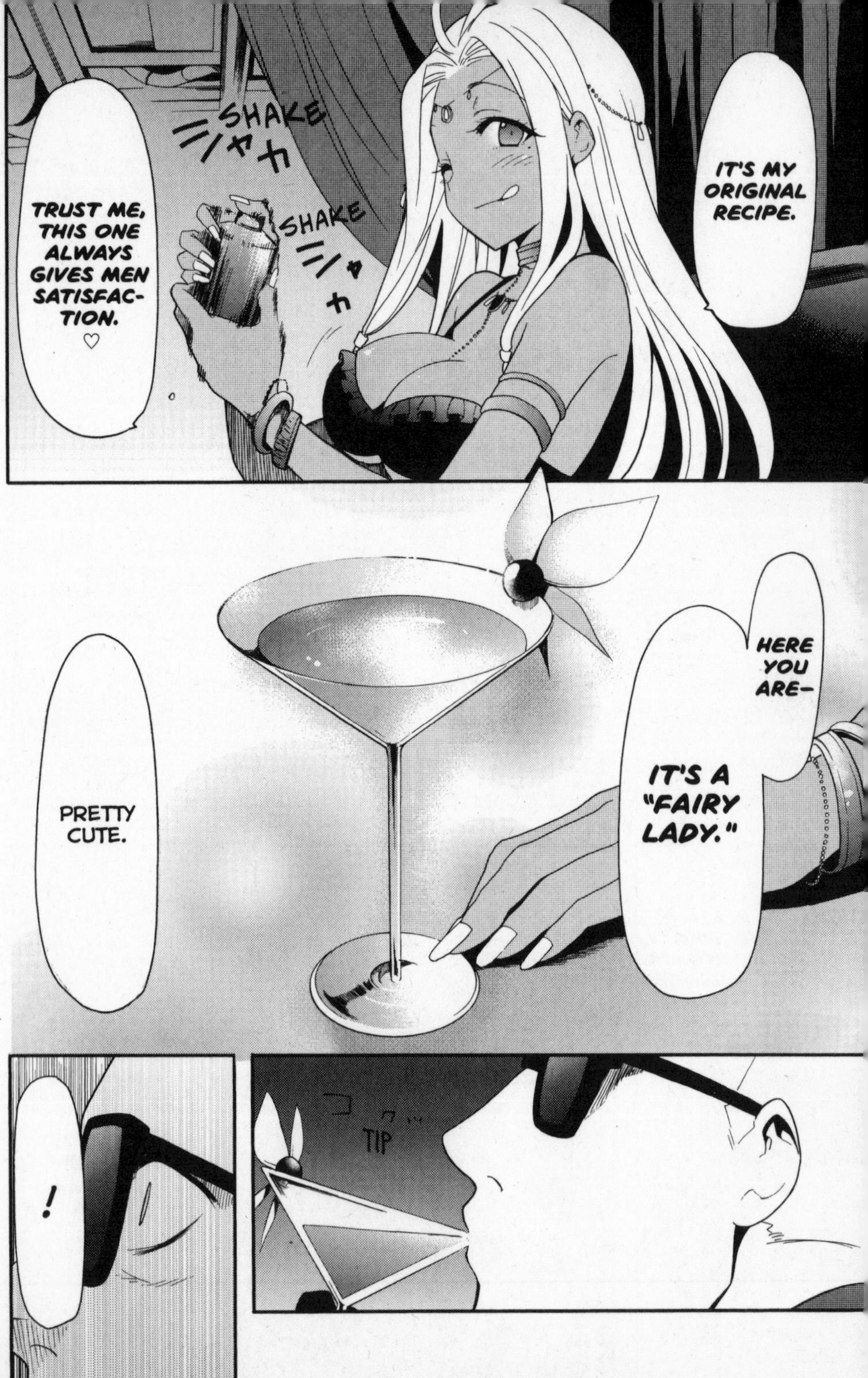

IT'S MY ORIGINAL RECIPE.
SHAKE
シャカ
SHAKE
シャカ
TRUST ME, THIS ONE ALWAYS GIVES MEN SATISFACTION. ♡
HERE YOU ARE—
IT'S A "FAIRY LADY."
PRETTY CUTE.
TIP
!

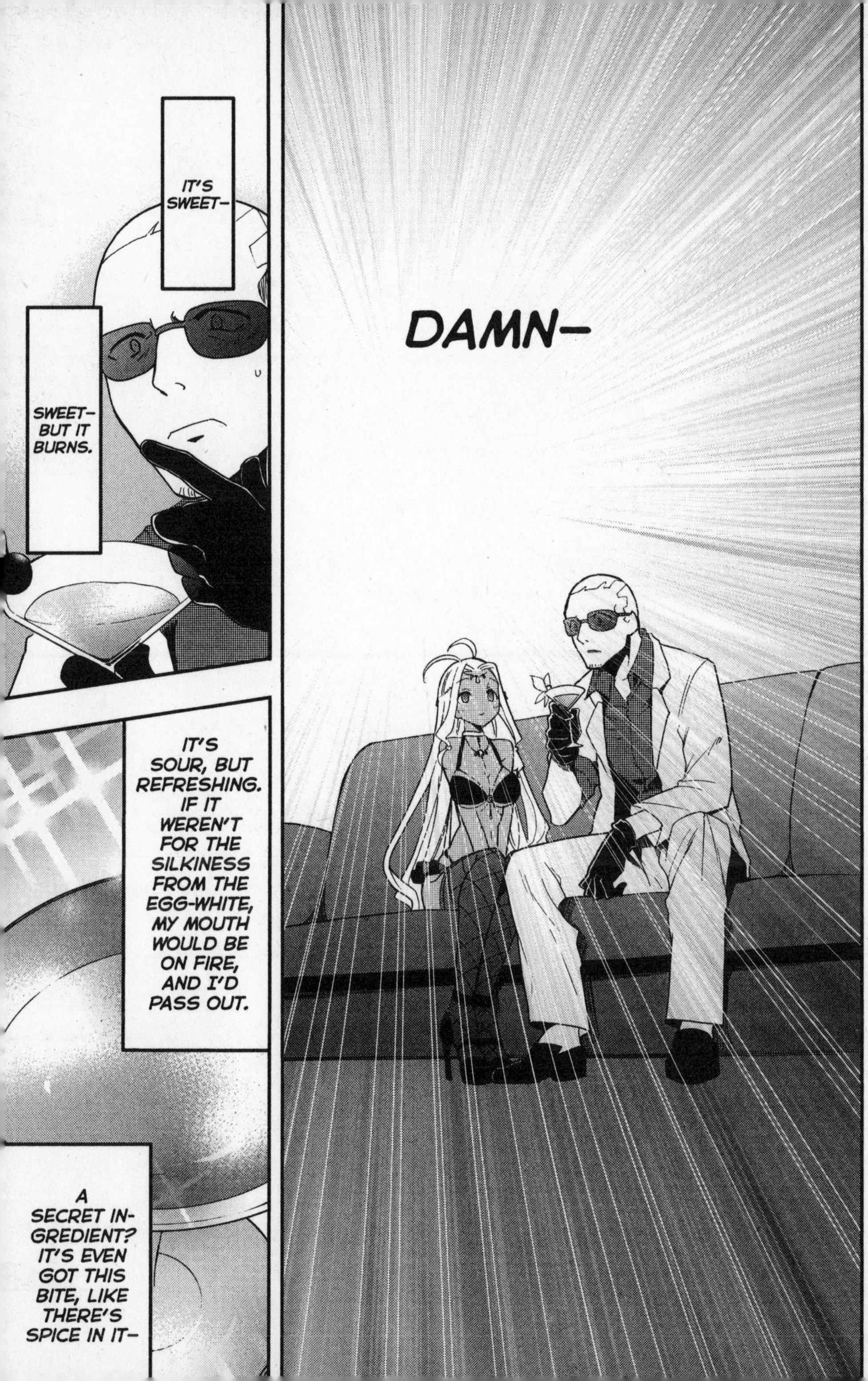
DAMN-
IT'S SWEET-
SWEET- BUT IT BURNS.
IT'S SOUR, BUT REFRESHING. IF IT WEREN'T FOR THE SILKINESS FROM THE EGG-WHITE, MY MOUTH WOULD BE ON FIRE, AND I'D PASS OUT.
A SECRET IN-GREDIENT? IT'S EVEN GOT THIS BITE, LIKE THERE'S SPICE IN IT-

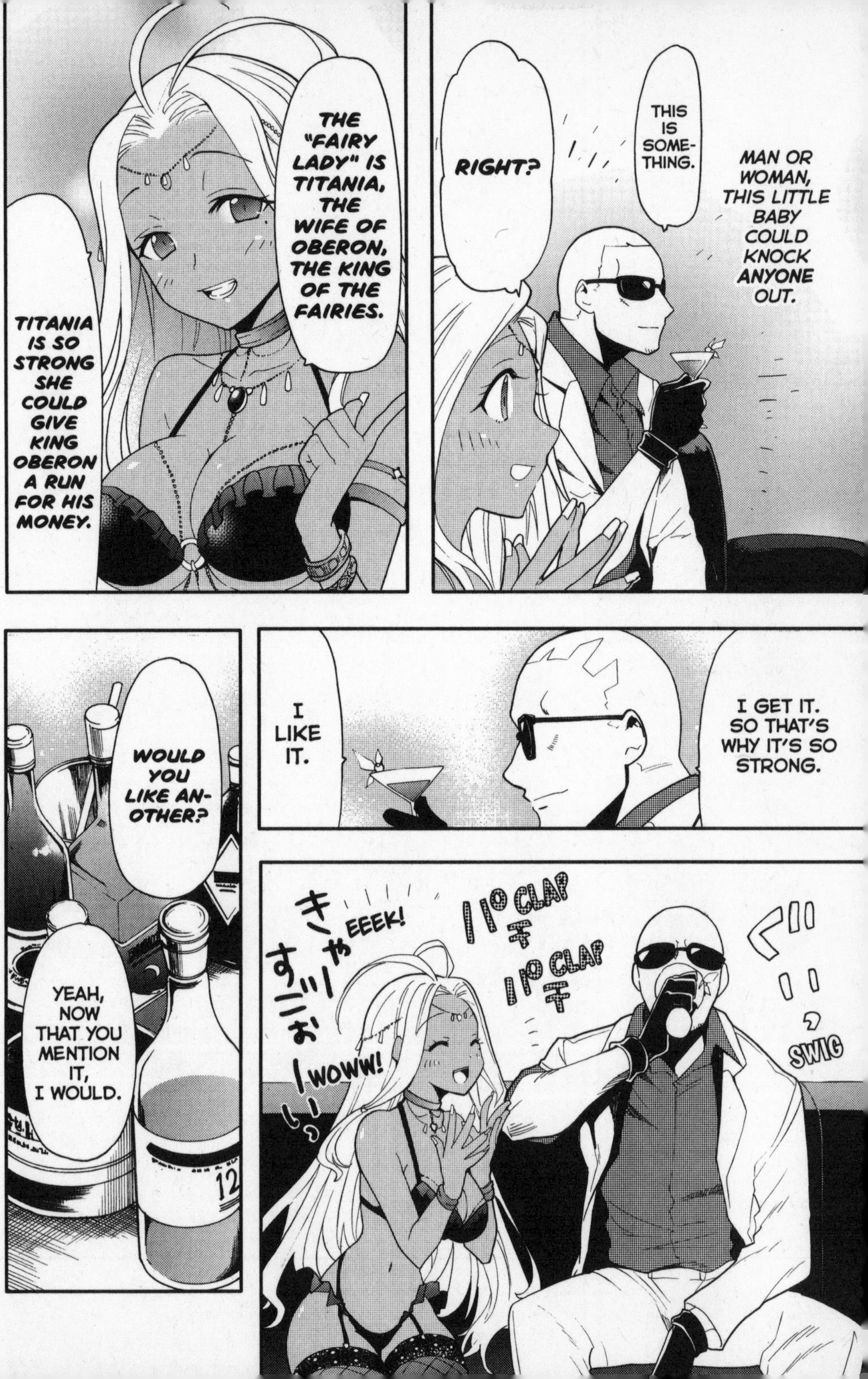
MAN OR WOMAN, THIS LITTLE BABY COULD KNOCK ANYONE OUT.
THIS IS SOME-THING.
RIGHT?
THE "FAIRY LADY" IS TITANIA, THE WIFE OF OBERON, THE KING OF THE FAIRIES.
TITANIA IS SO STRONG SHE COULD GIVE KING OBERON A RUN FOR HIS MONEY.
I GET IT. SO THAT'S WHY IT'S SO STRONG.
I LIKE IT.
ぐいっ
SWIG
パチ CLAP
パチ CLAP
きゃー EEEK!
すごぉい WOWW!
WOULD YOU LIKE AN-OTHER?
YEAH, NOW THAT YOU MENTION IT, I WOULD.

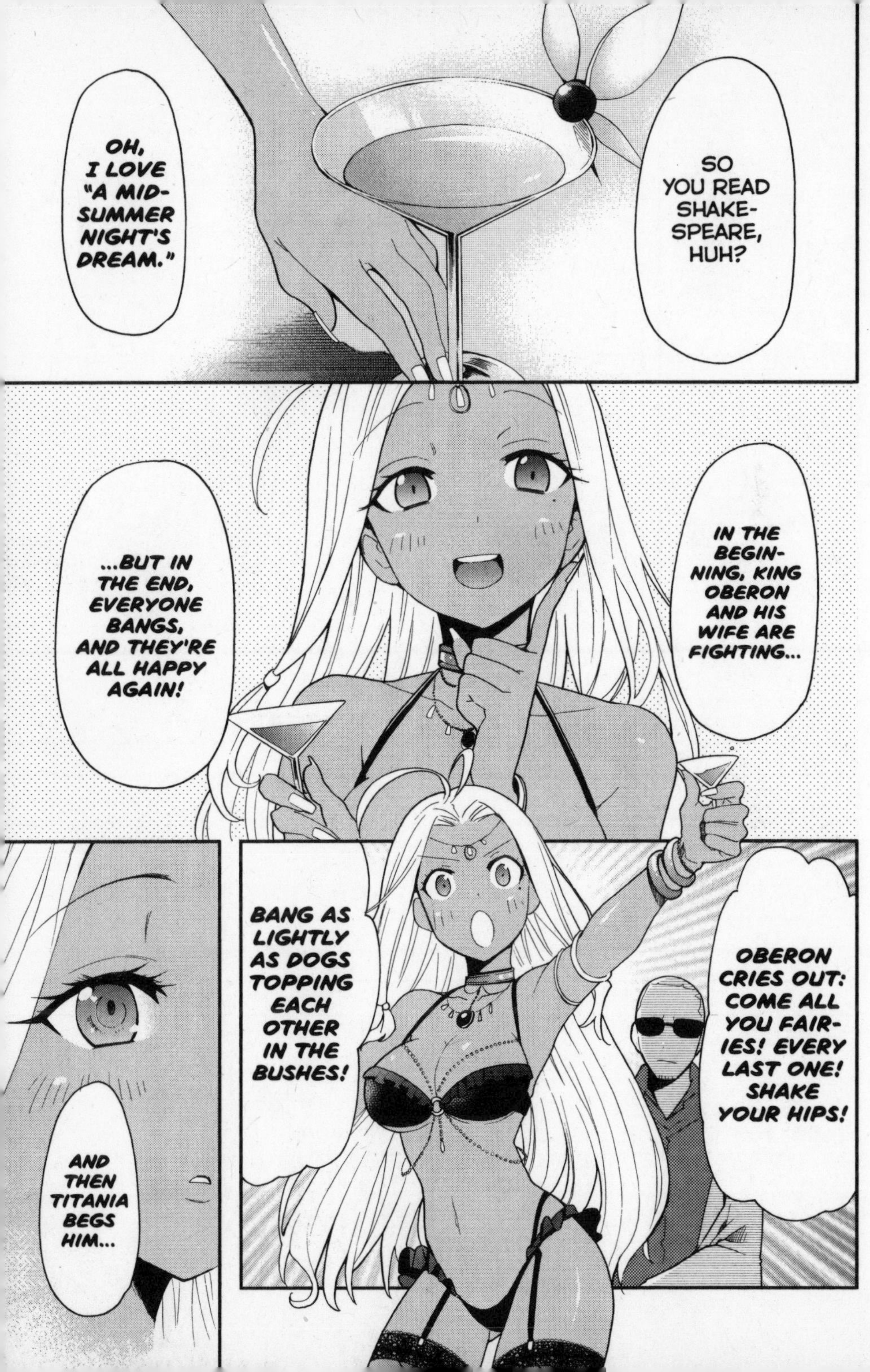
SO YOU READ SHAKE-SPEARE, HUH?
OH, I LOVE "A MID-SUMMER NIGHT'S DREAM."
IN THE BEGIN-NING, KING OBERON AND HIS WIFE ARE FIGHTING...
...BUT IN THE END, EVERYONE BANGS, AND THEY'RE ALL HAPPY AGAIN!
OBERON CRIES OUT: COME ALL YOU FAIR-IES! EVERY LAST ONE! SHAKE YOUR HIPS!
BANG AS LIGHTLY AS DOGS TOPPING EACH OTHER IN THE BUSHES!
AND THEN TITANIA BEGS HIM...

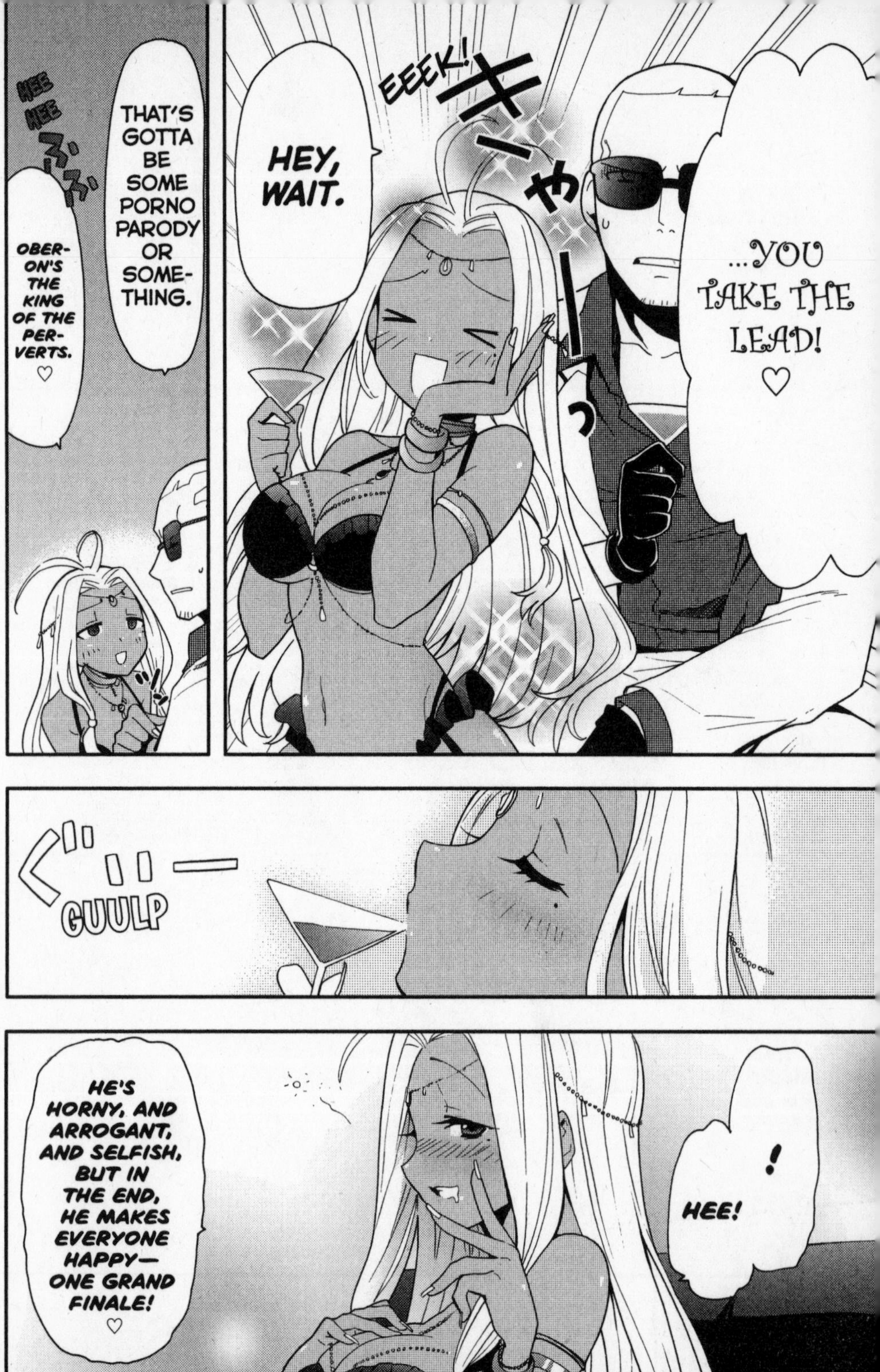
...YOU TAKE THE LEAD! ♡
キャーッ
EEEK!
HEY, WAIT.
THAT'S GOTTA BE SOME PORNO PARODY OR SOMETHING.
ふふ
HEE HEE
OBERON'S THE KING OF THE PERVERTS. ♡
ぐいーー
GUULP
!
HEE!
HE'S HORNY, AND ARROGANT, AND SELFISH, BUT IN THE END, HE MAKES EVERYONE HAPPY— ONE GRAND FINALE! ♡

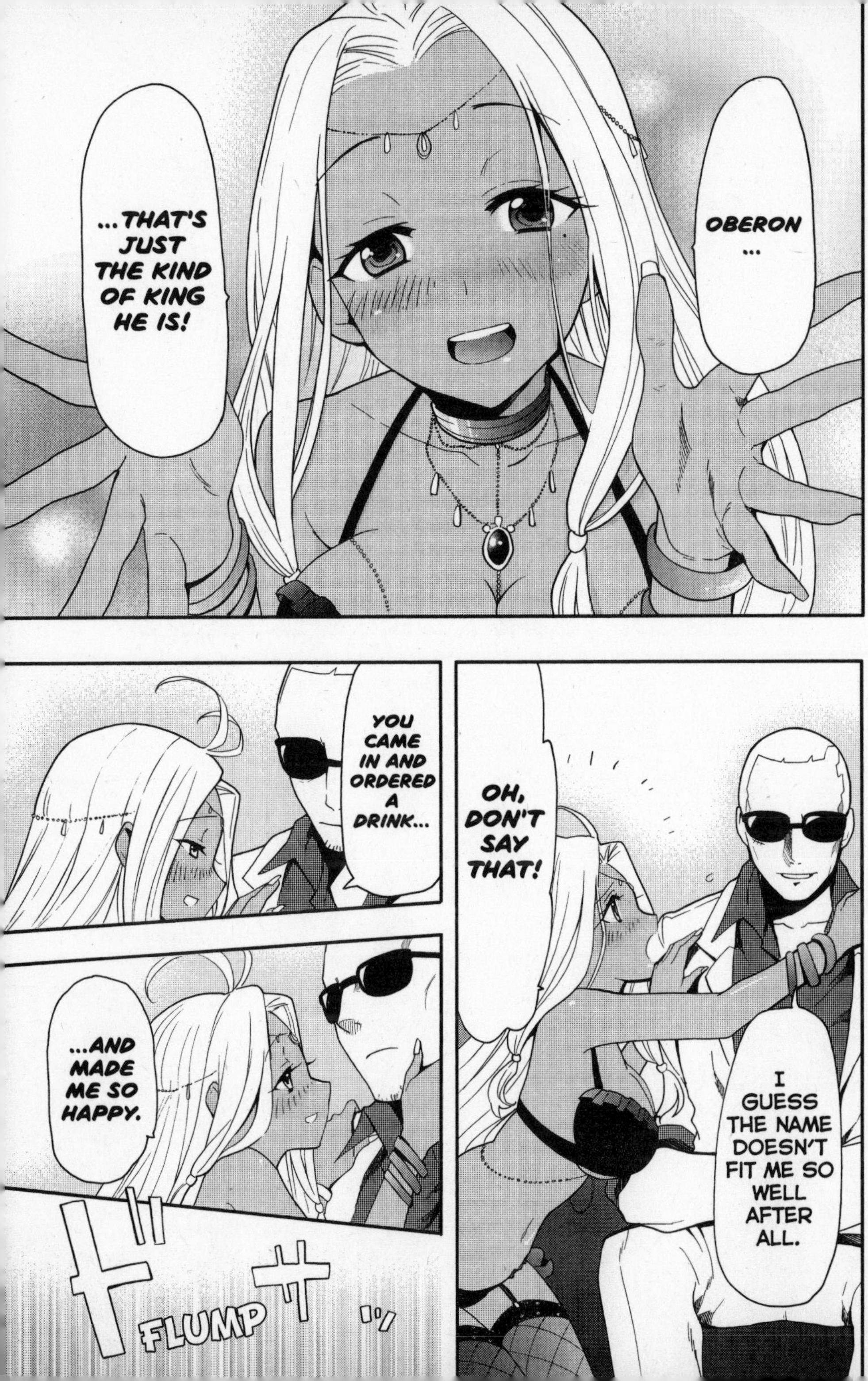
OBERON ...
...THAT'S JUST THE KIND OF KING HE IS!
OH, DON'T SAY THAT!
I GUESS THE NAME DOESN'T FIT ME SO WELL AFTER ALL.
YOU CAME IN AND ORDERED A DRINK...
...AND MADE ME SO HAPPY.
FLUMP

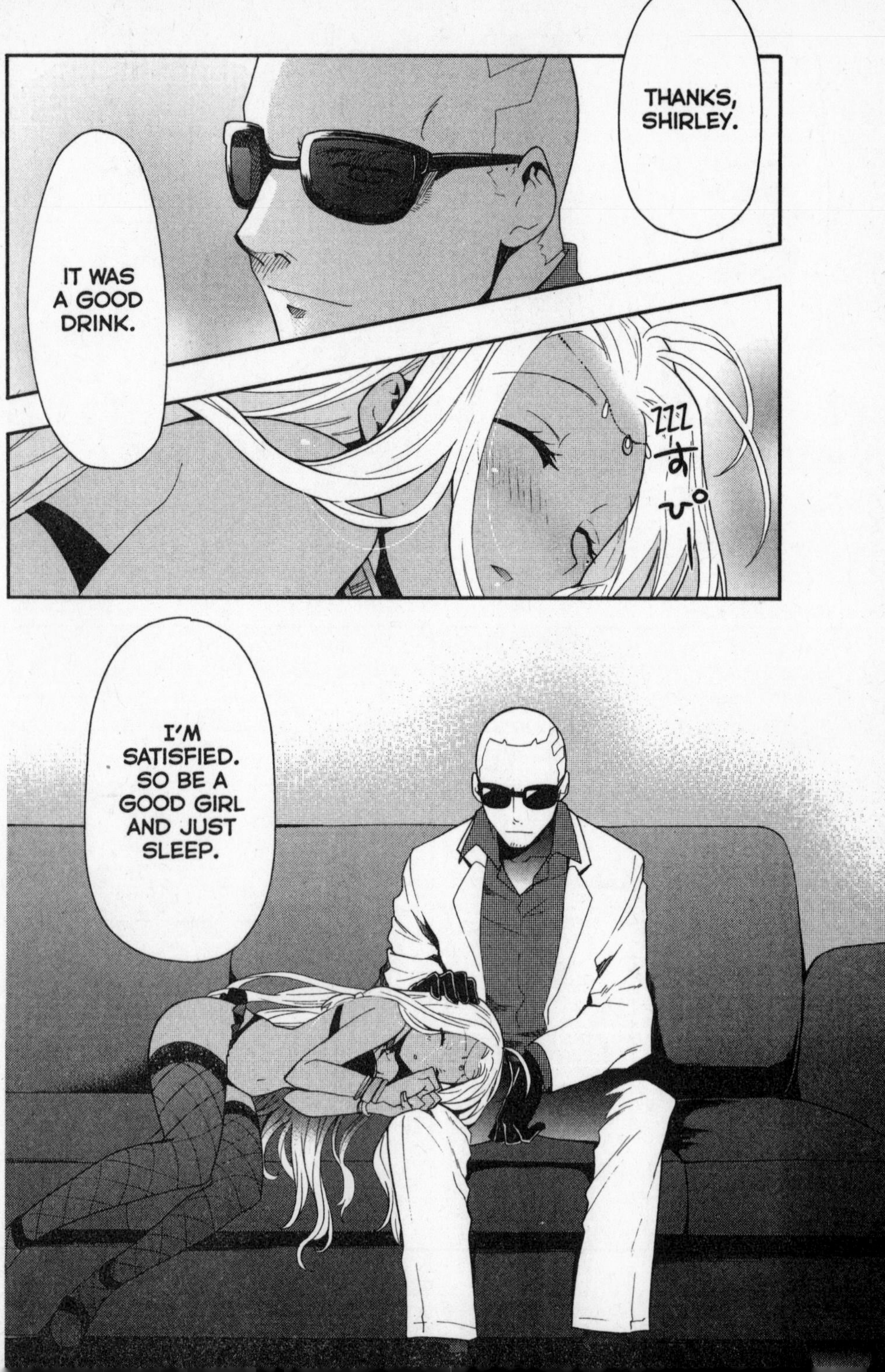
THANKS, SHIRLEY.
IT WAS A GOOD DRINK.
ZZZ
すぴー
I'M SATISFIED. SO BE A GOOD GIRL AND JUST SLEEP.

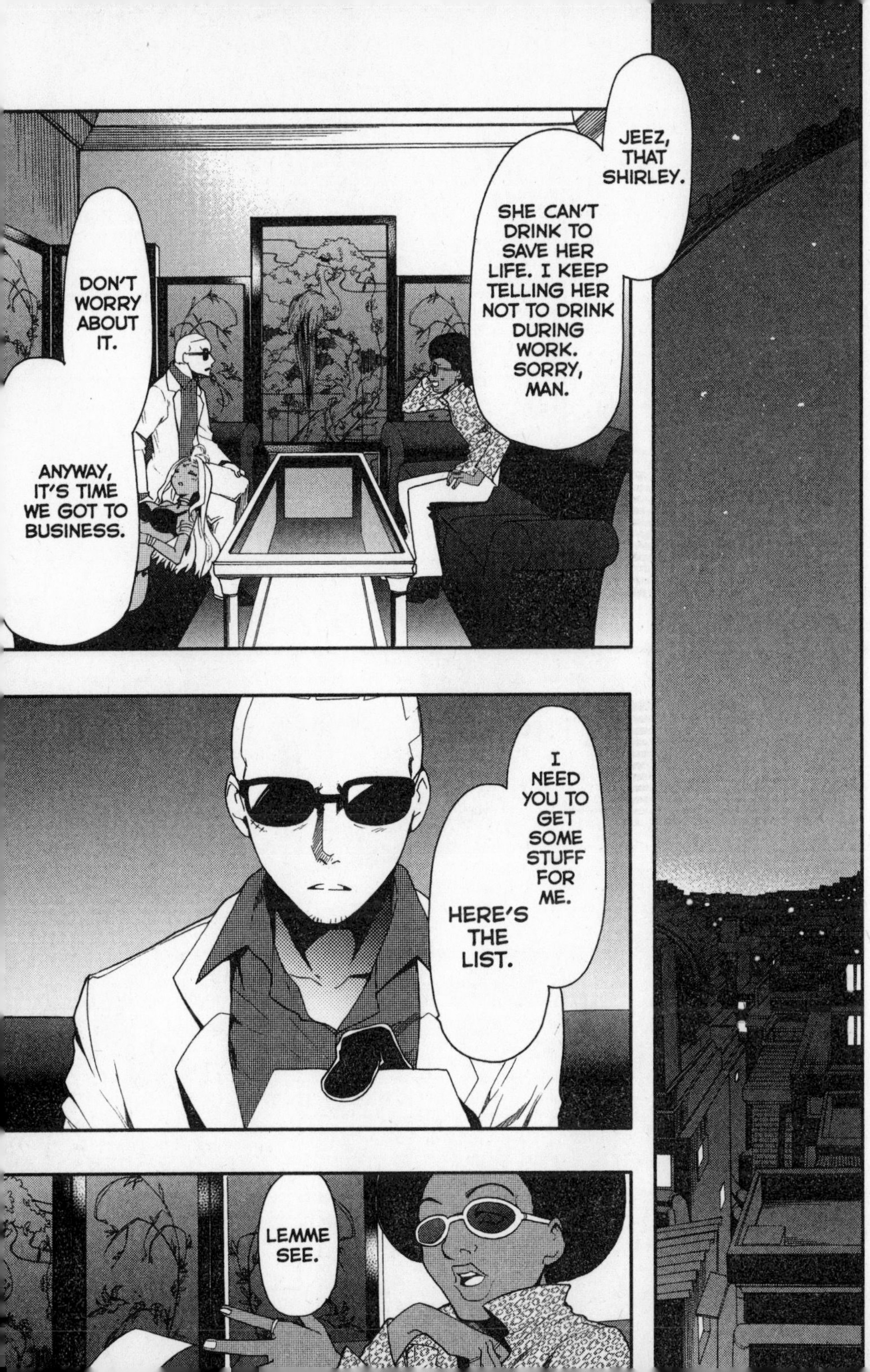
JEEZ, THAT SHIRLEY.
SHE CAN'T DRINK TO SAVE HER LIFE. I KEEP TELLING HER NOT TO DRINK DURING WORK. SORRY, MAN.
DON'T WORRY ABOUT IT.
ANYWAY, IT'S TIME WE GOT TO BUSINESS.
I NEED YOU TO GET SOME STUFF FOR ME.
HERE'S THE LIST.
LEMME SEE.

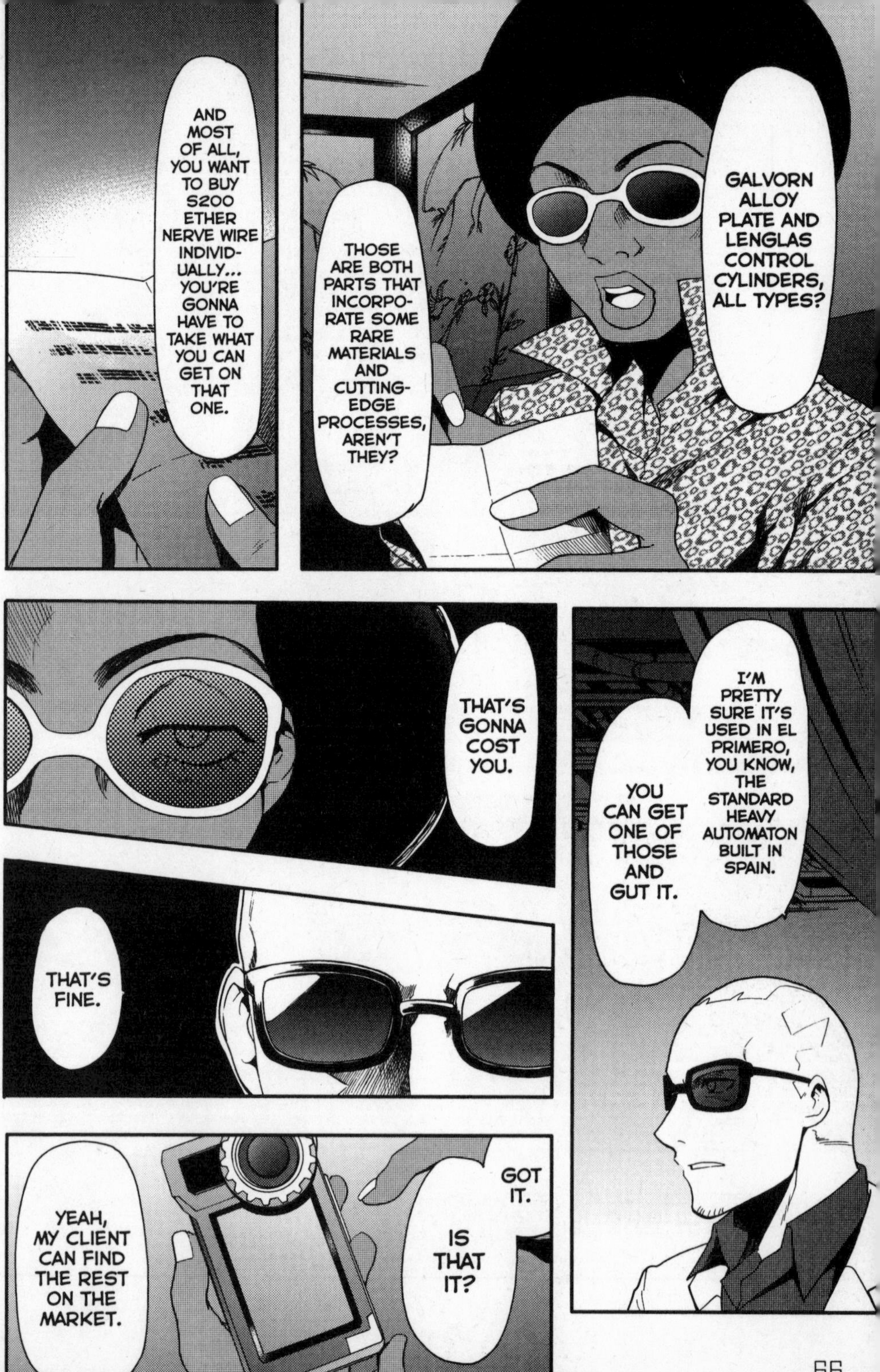
GALVORN ALLOY PLATE AND LENGLAS CONTROL CYLINDERS, ALL TYPES?
THOSE ARE BOTH PARTS THAT INCORPORATE SOME RARE MATERIALS AND CUTTING-EDGE PROCESSES, AREN'T THEY?
AND MOST OF ALL, YOU WANT TO BUY S200 ETHER NERVE WIRE INDIVIDUALLY... YOU'RE GONNA HAVE TO TAKE WHAT YOU CAN GET ON THAT ONE.
I'M PRETTY SURE IT'S USED IN EL PRIMERO, YOU KNOW, THE STANDARD HEAVY AUTOMATON BUILT IN SPAIN.
YOU CAN GET ONE OF THOSE AND GUT IT.
THAT'S GONNA COST YOU.
THAT'S FINE.
GOT IT.
IS THAT IT?
YEAH, MY CLIENT CAN FIND THE REST ON THE MARKET.

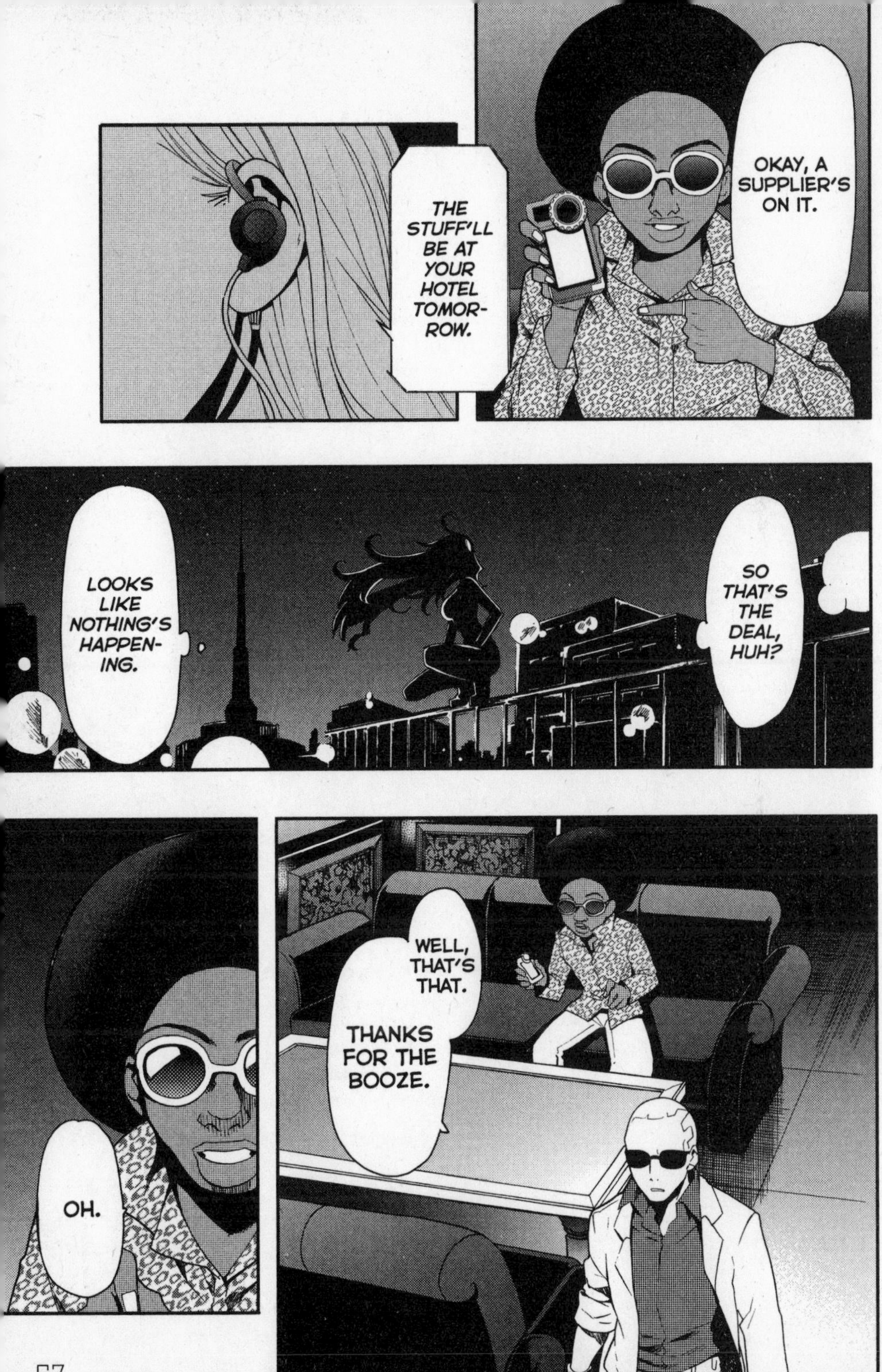
OKAY, A SUPPLIER'S ON IT.
THE STUFF'LL BE AT YOUR HOTEL TOMORROW.
SO THAT'S THE DEAL, HUH?
LOOKS LIKE NOTHING'S HAPPENING.
WELL, THAT'S THAT.
THANKS FOR THE BOOZE.
OH.

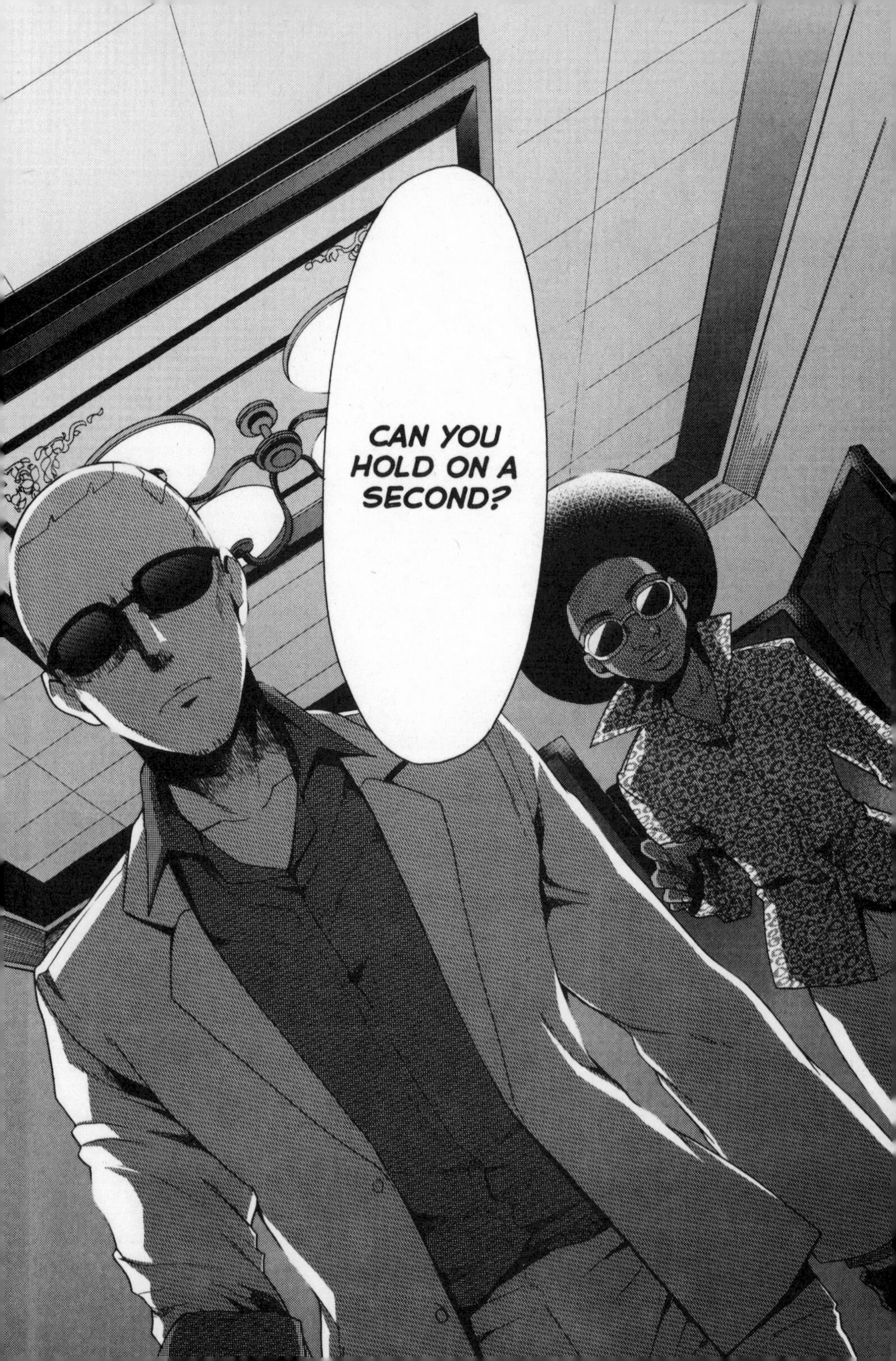
CAN YOU HOLD ON A SECOND?

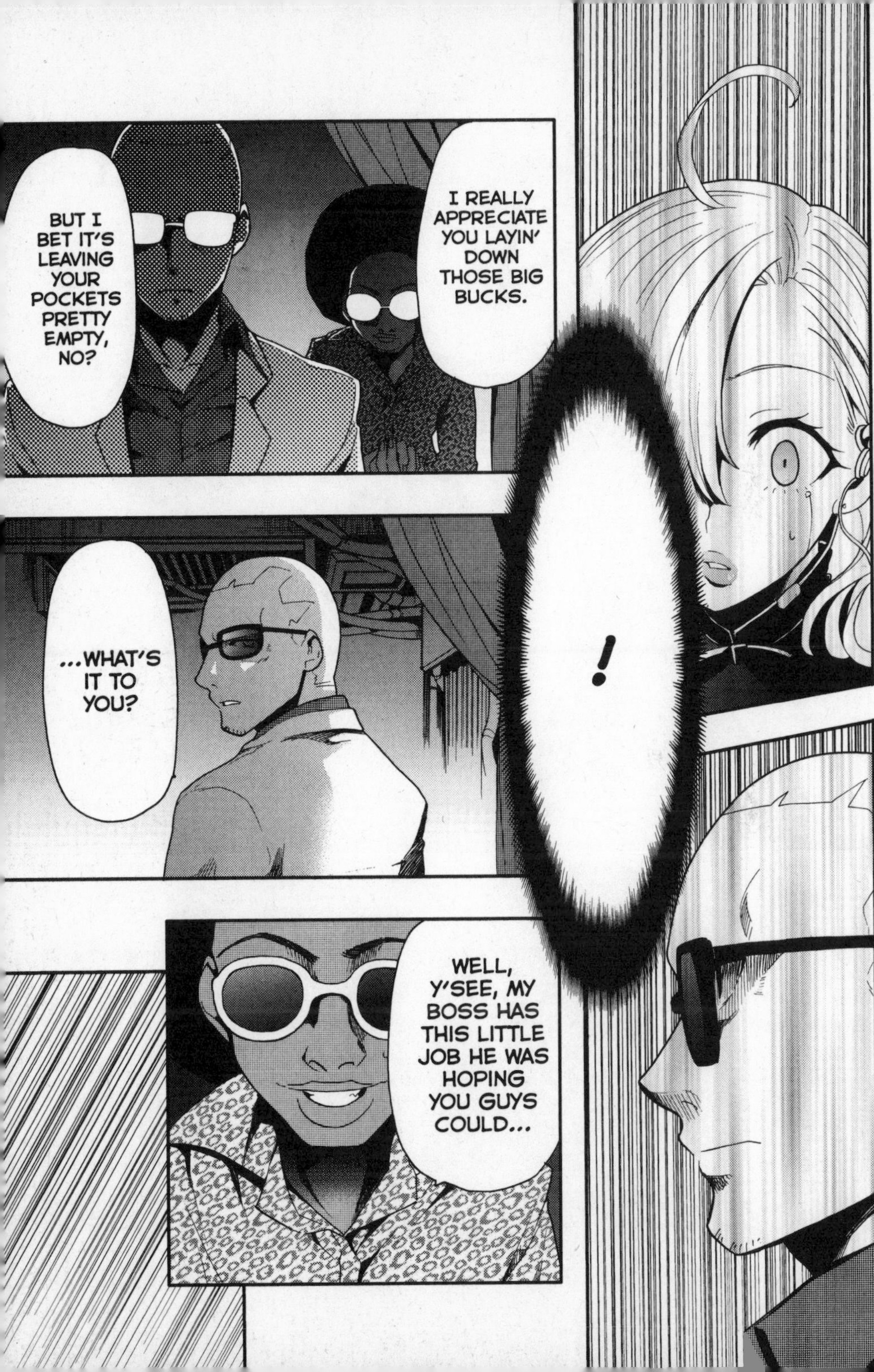
!
I REALLY APPRECIATE YOU LAYIN' DOWN THOSE BIG BUCKS.
BUT I BET IT'S LEAVING YOUR POCKETS PRETTY EMPTY, NO?
...WHAT'S IT TO YOU?
WELL, Y'SEE, MY BOSS HAS THIS LITTLE JOB HE WAS HOPING YOU GUYS COULD...

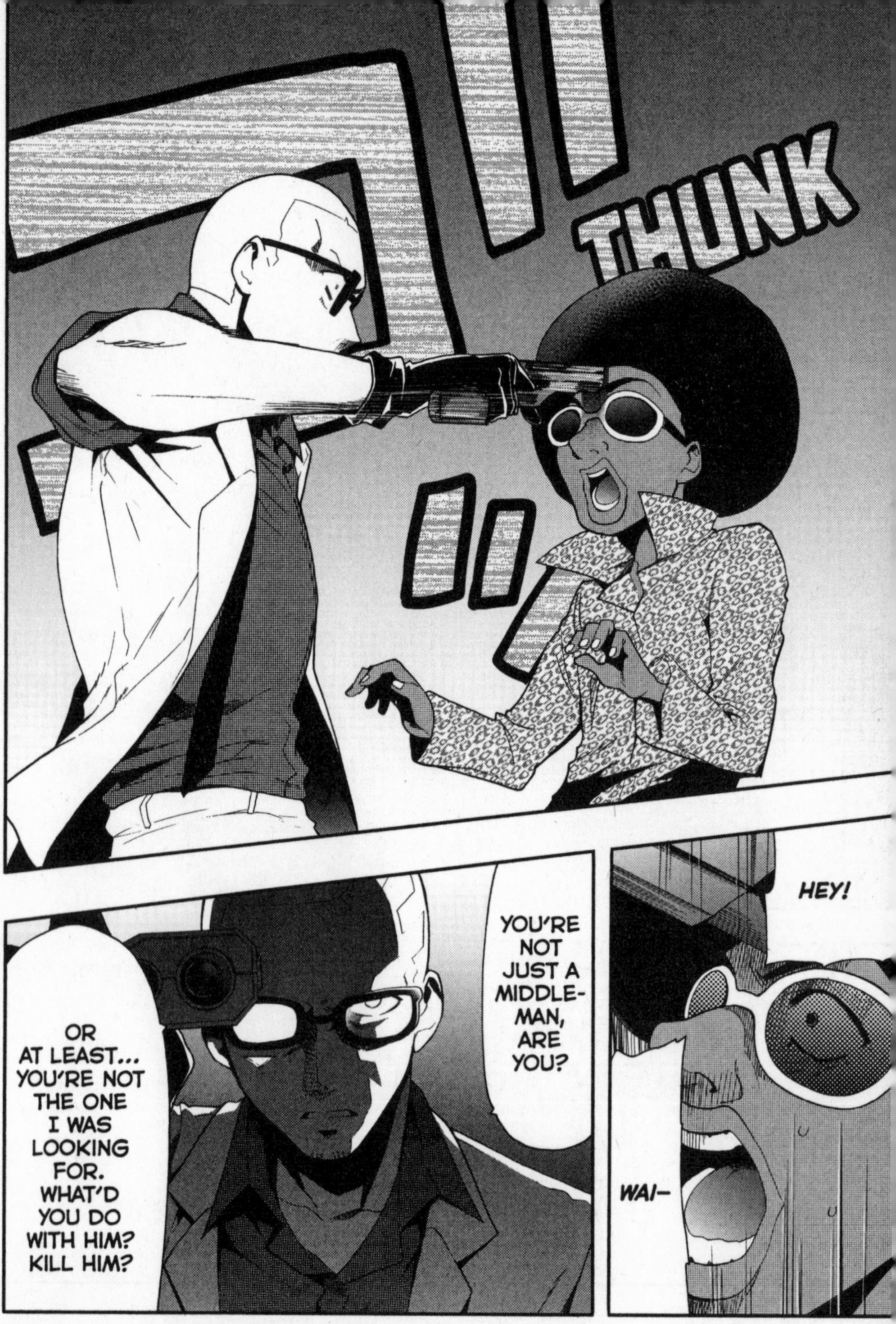
THUNK
HEY!
WAI–
YOU'RE NOT JUST A MIDDLE-MAN, ARE YOU?
OR AT LEAST... YOU'RE NOT THE ONE I WAS LOOKING FOR. WHAT'D YOU DO WITH HIM? KILL HIM?

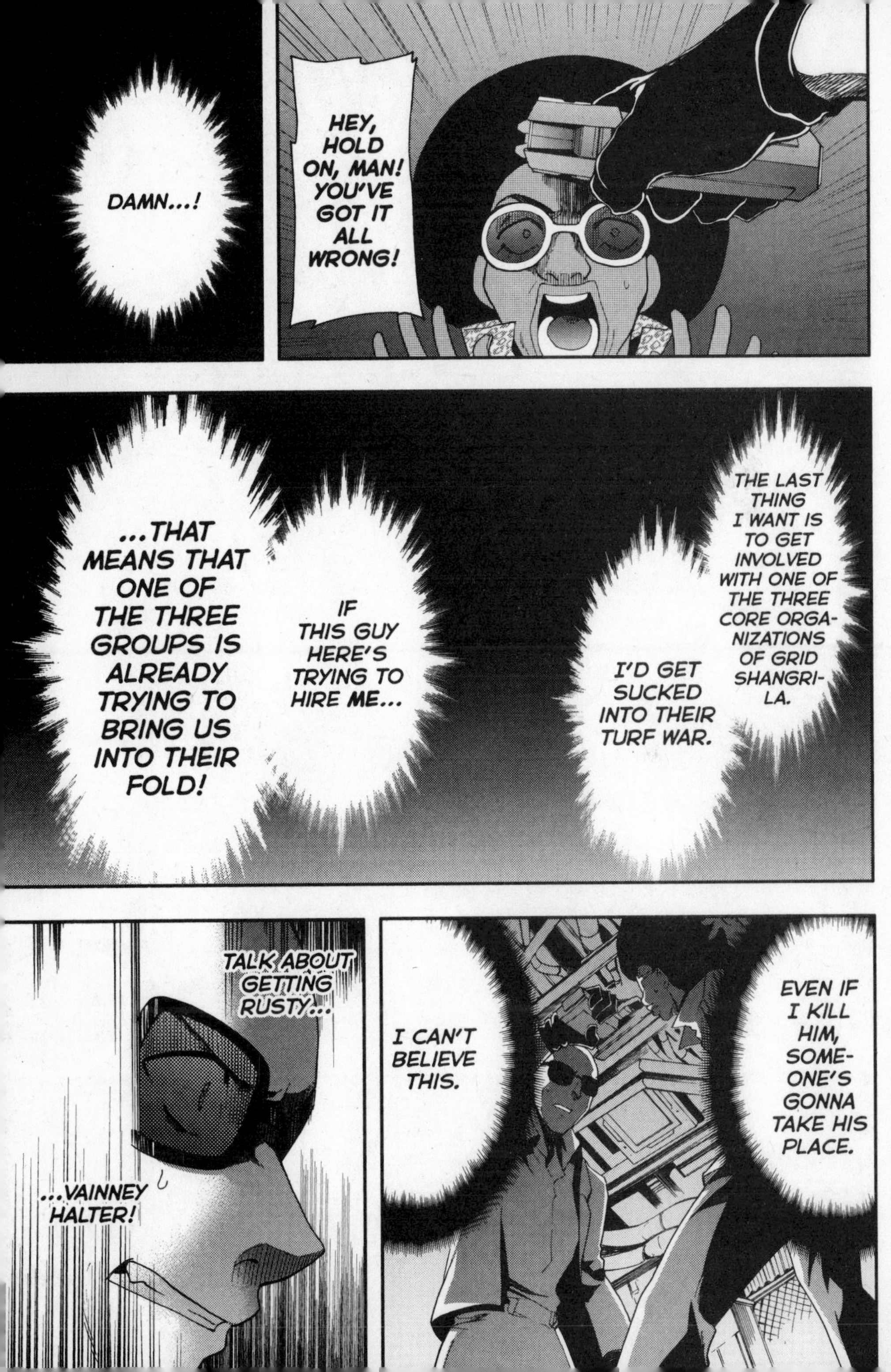
HEY, HOLD ON, MAN! YOU'VE GOT IT ALL WRONG!
DAMN...!
THE LAST THING I WANT IS TO GET INVOLVED WITH ONE OF THE THREE CORE ORGA-NIZATIONS OF GRID SHANGRI-LA.
I'D GET SUCKED INTO THEIR TURF WAR.
IF THIS GUY HERE'S TRYING TO HIRE ME...
...THAT MEANS THAT ONE OF THE THREE GROUPS IS ALREADY TRYING TO BRING US INTO THEIR FOLD!
EVEN IF I KILL HIM, SOME-ONE'S GONNA TAKE HIS PLACE.
I CAN'T BELIEVE THIS.
TALK ABOUT GETTING RUSTY...
...VAINNEY HALTER!

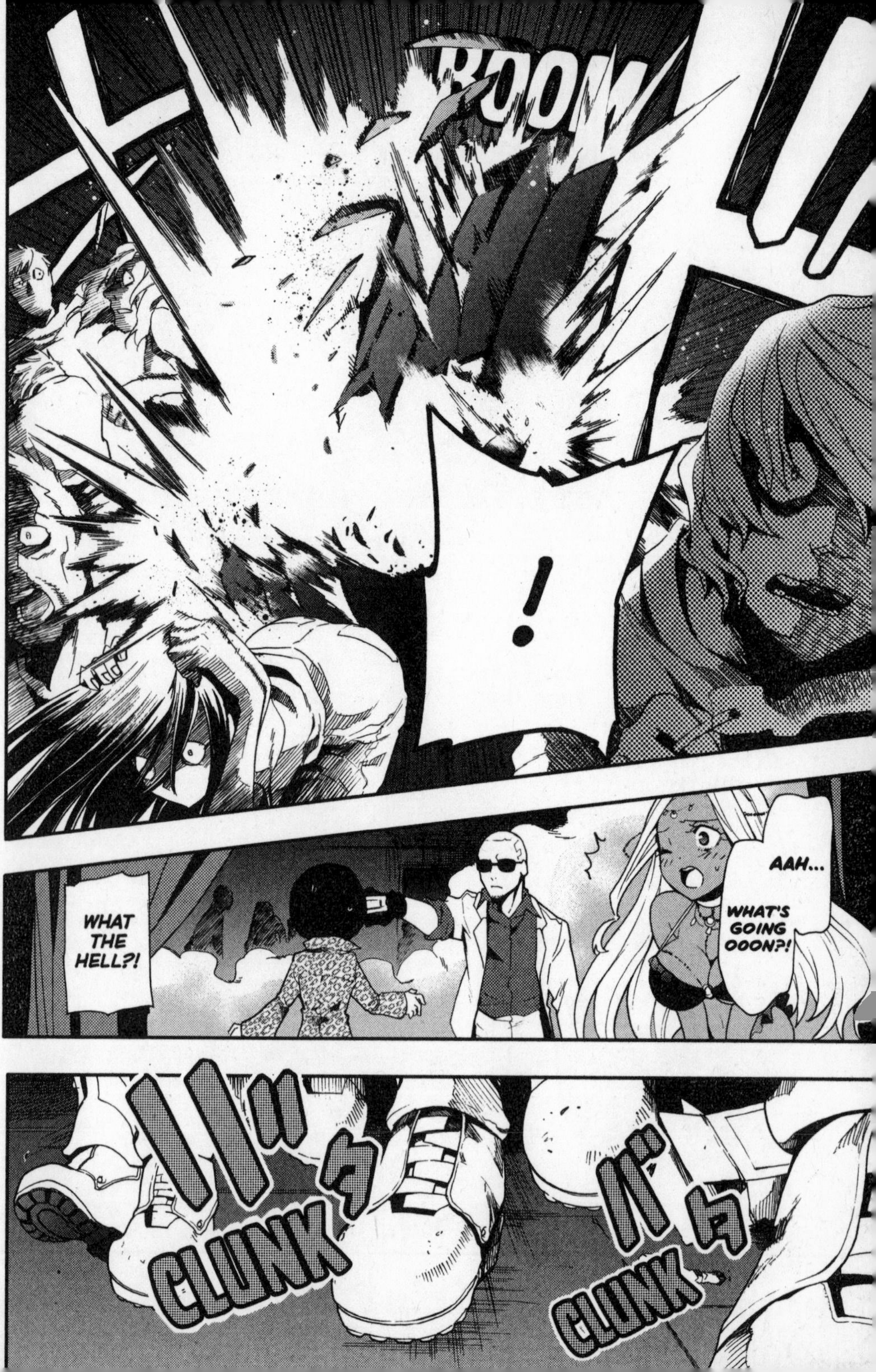
BOOM
!
AAH...
WHAT'S GOING OOON?!
WHAT THE HELL?!
CLUNK
CLUNK

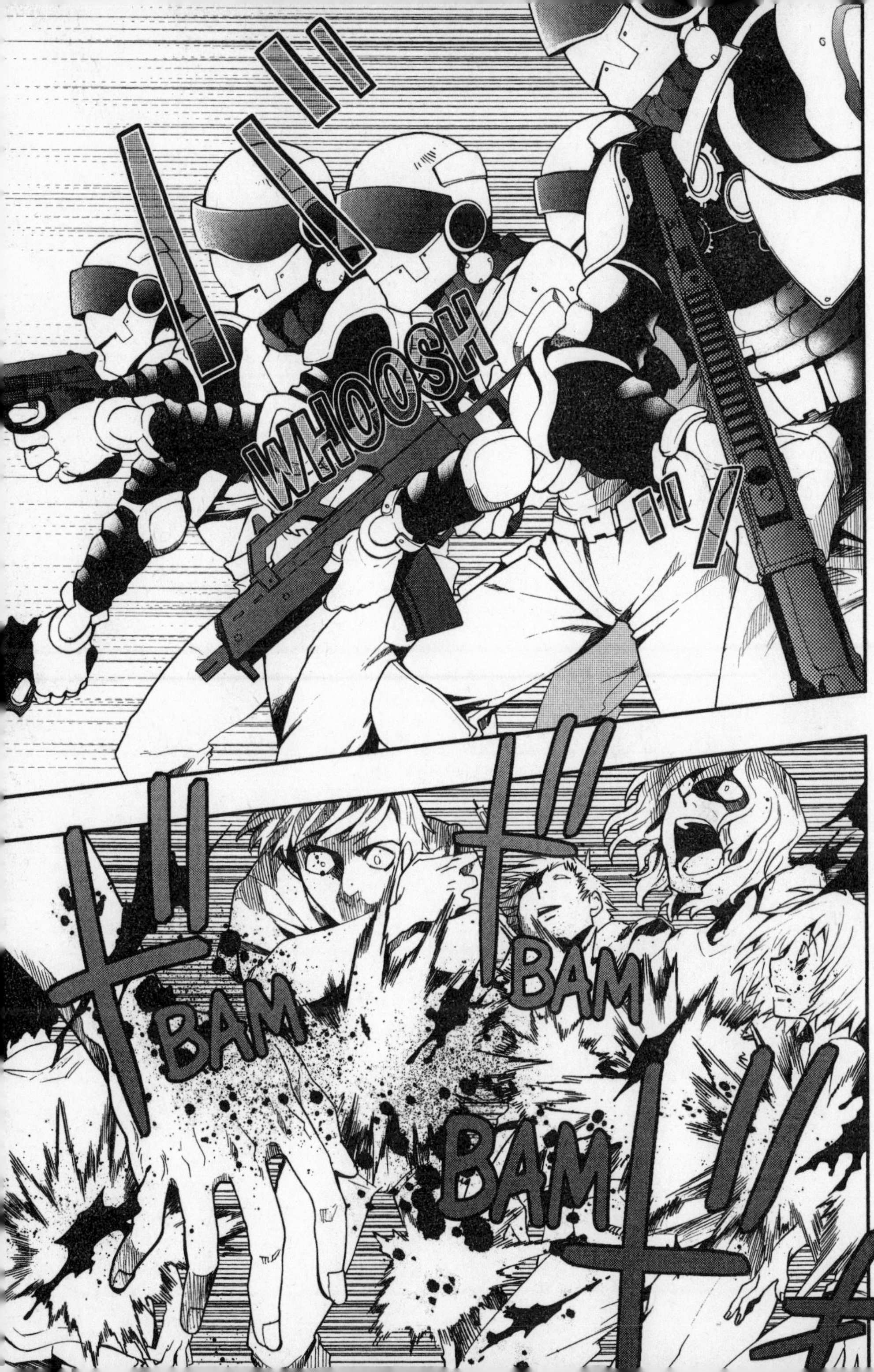
WHOOSH
BAM
BAM
BAM

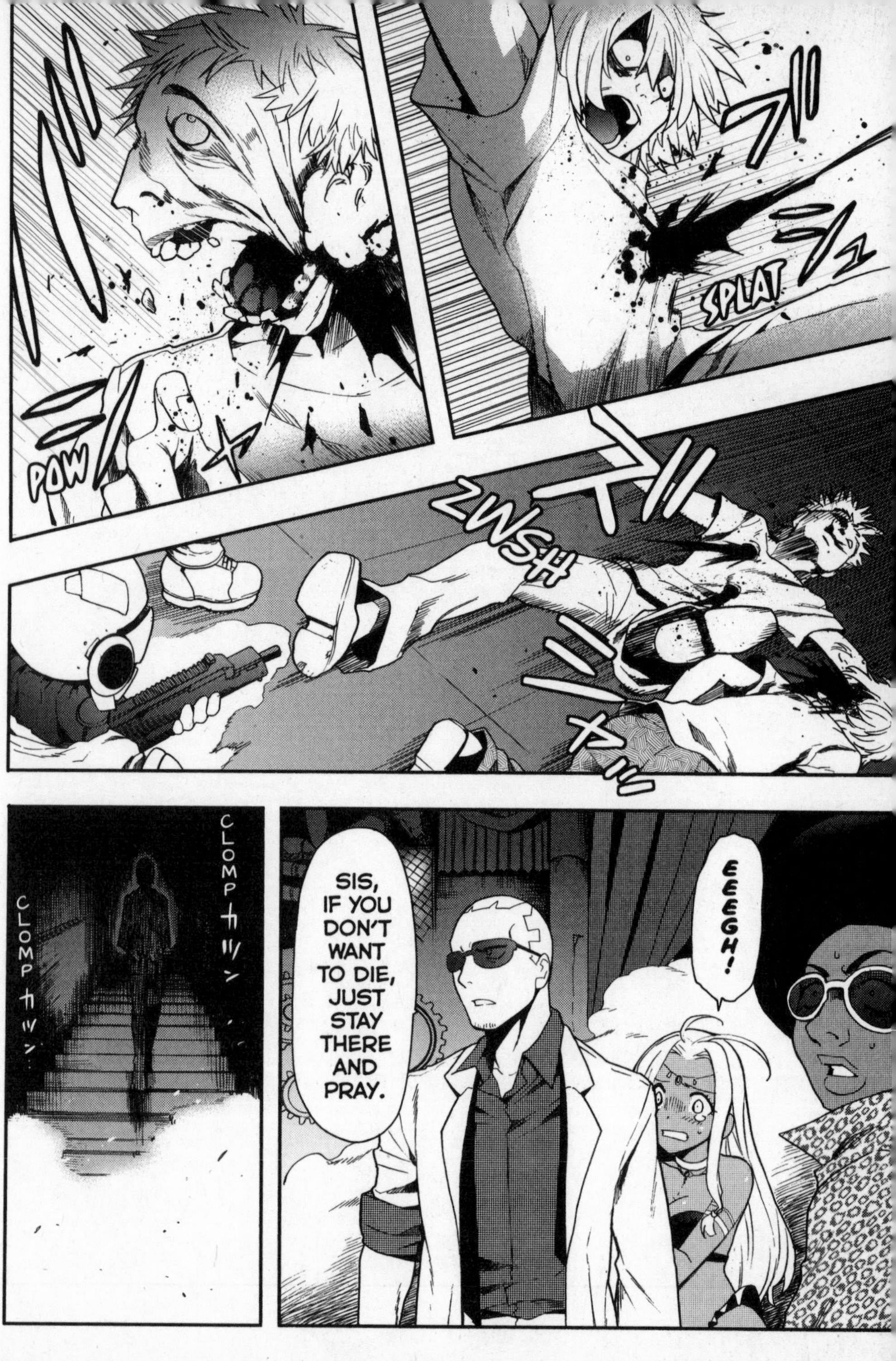
SPLAT
POW
ZWSH
EEEGH!
SIS, IF YOU DON'T WANT TO DIE, JUST STAY THERE AND PRAY.
CLOMP カツン
CLOMP カツン

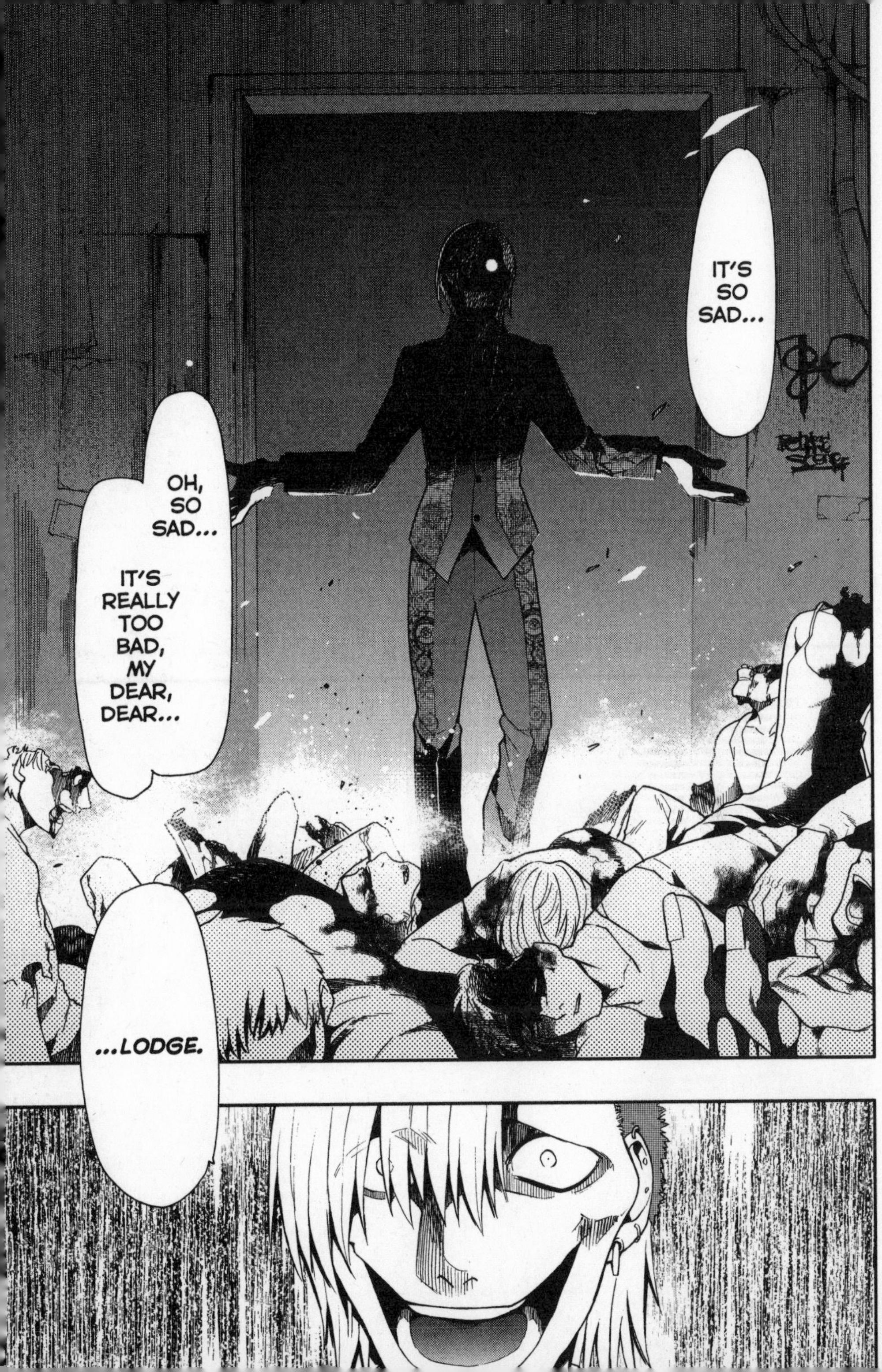
IT'S SO SAD...
OH, SO SAD...
IT'S REALLY TOO BAD, MY DEAR, DEAR...
...LODGE.

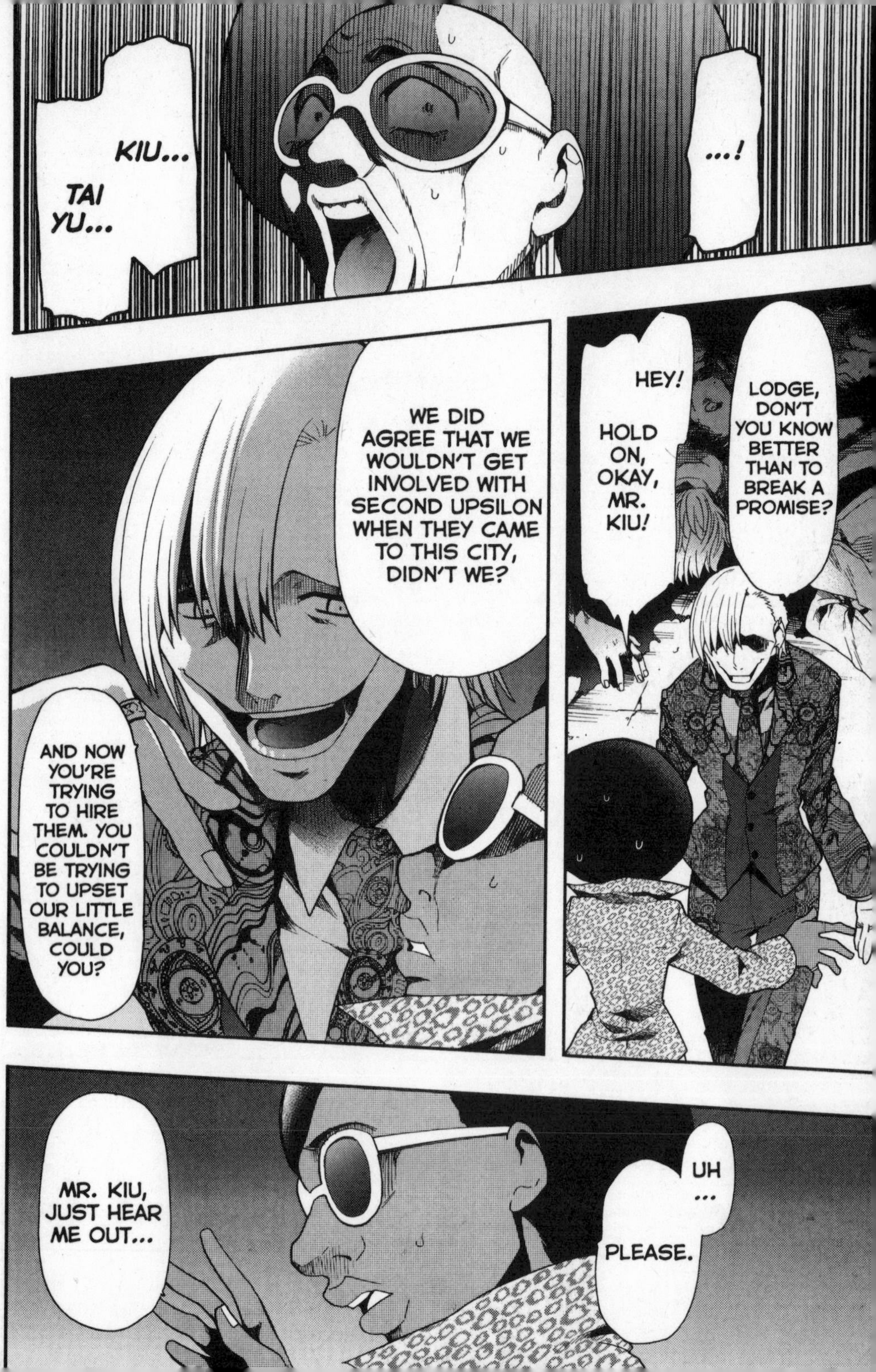
...!
KIU... TAI YU...
LODGE, DON'T YOU KNOW BETTER THAN TO BREAK A PROMISE?
HEY! HOLD ON, OKAY, MR. KIU!
WE DID AGREE THAT WE WOULDN'T GET INVOLVED WITH SECOND UPSILON WHEN THEY CAME TO THIS CITY, DIDN'T WE?
AND NOW YOU'RE TRYING TO HIRE THEM. YOU COULDN'T BE TRYING TO UPSET OUR LITTLE BALANCE, COULD YOU?
UH... PLEASE.
MR. KIU, JUST HEAR ME OUT...

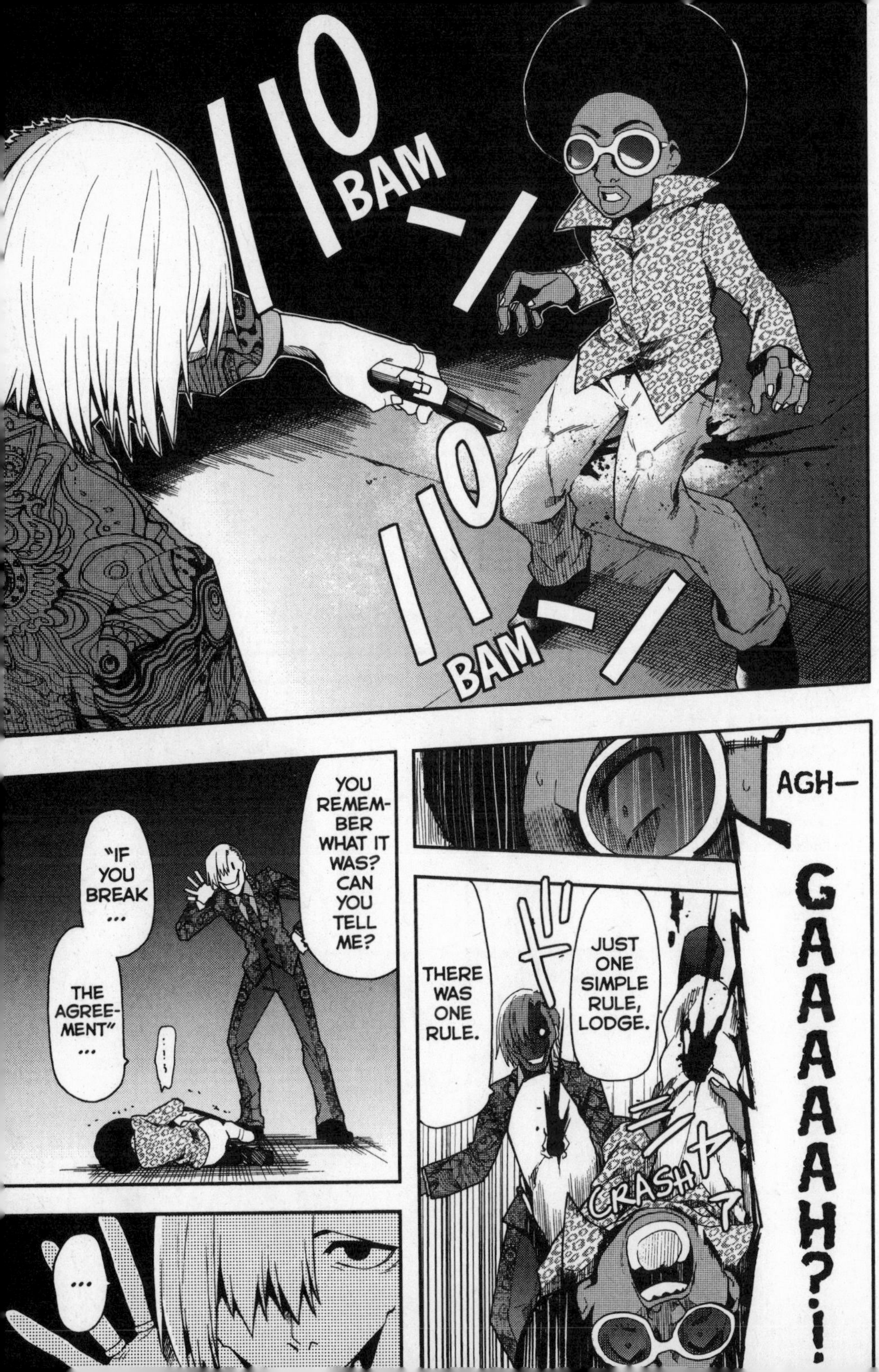
BAM
BAM
AGH—
GAAAAAH?!
JUST ONE SIMPLE RULE, LODGE.
THERE WAS ONE RULE.
CRASH
YOU REMEMBER WHAT IT WAS? CAN YOU TELL ME?
"IF YOU BREAK ...
THE AGREEMENT" ...
...

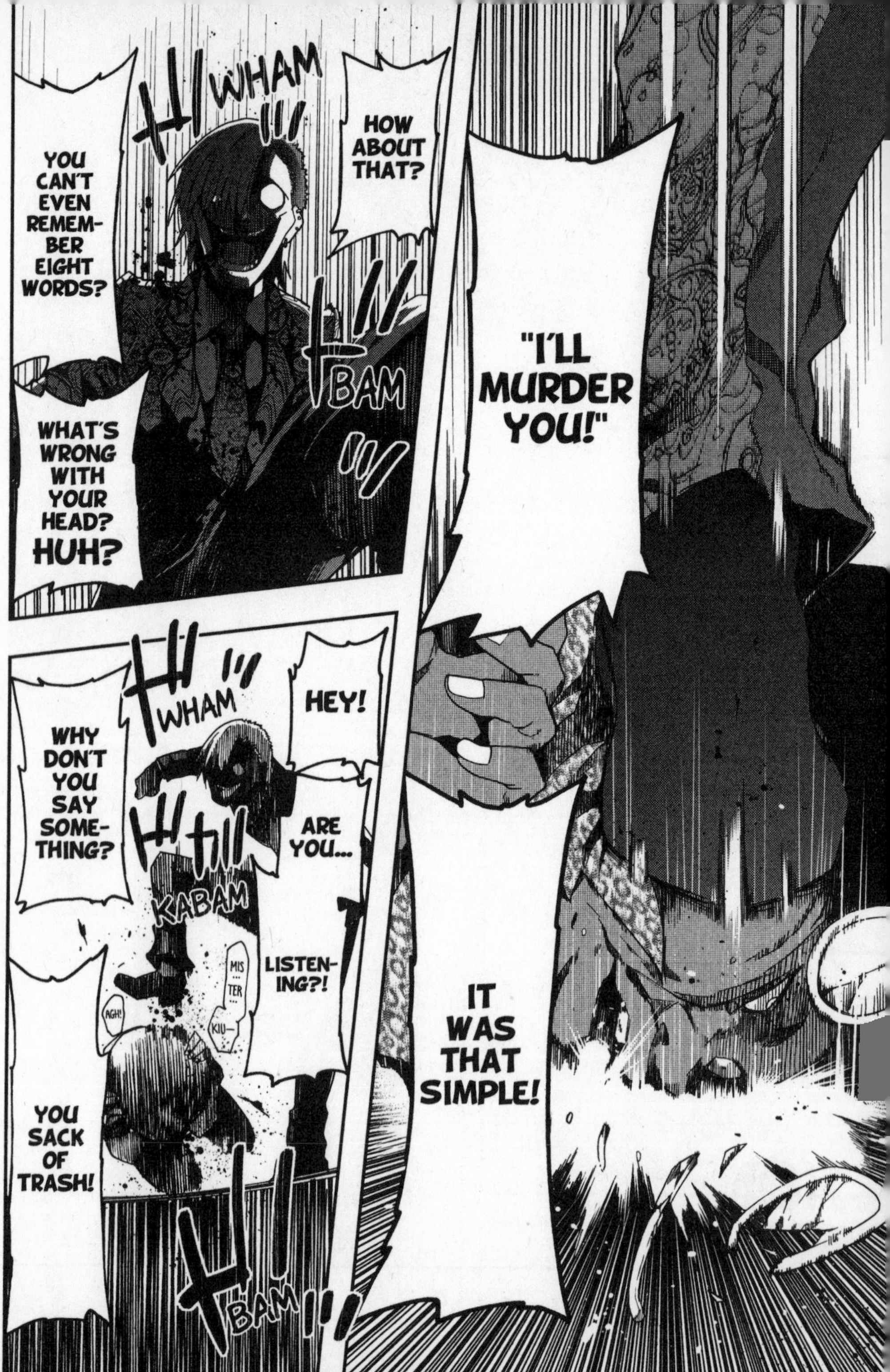
"I'LL MURDER YOU!"
IT WAS THAT SIMPLE!
HOW ABOUT THAT?
WHAM
YOU CAN'T EVEN REMEMBER EIGHT WORDS?
BAM
WHAT'S WRONG WITH YOUR HEAD? HUH?
HEY!
WHAM
WHY DON'T YOU SAY SOMETHING?
ARE YOU...
KABAM
LISTENING?!
MIS... TER... KIU-
AGH!
YOU SACK OF TRASH!
BAM

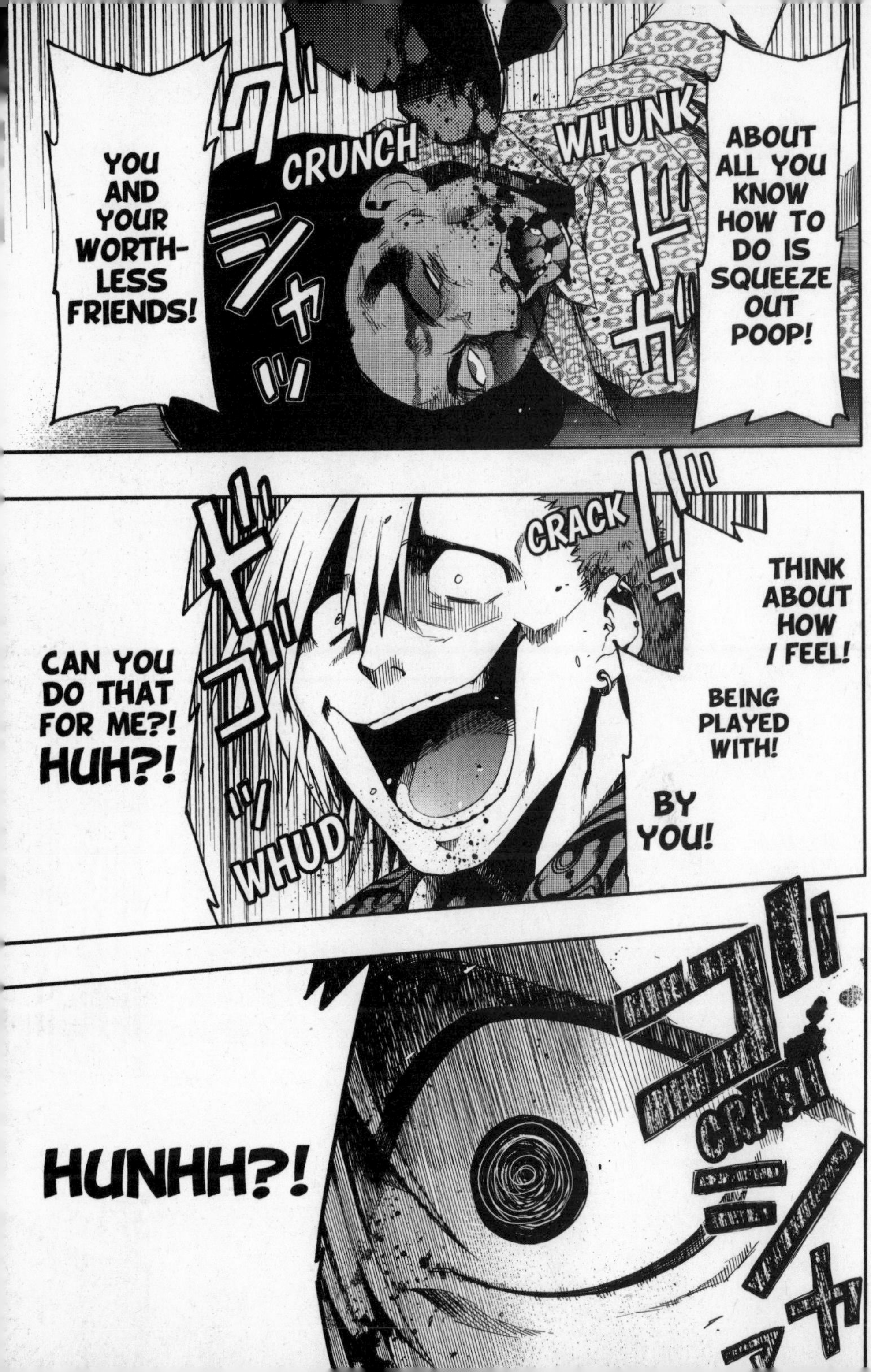
ABOUT ALL YOU KNOW HOW TO DO IS SQUEEZE OUT POOP!
WHUNK
CRUNCH
YOU AND YOUR WORTH-LESS FRIENDS!
CRACK
THINK ABOUT HOW I FEEL!
BEING PLAYED WITH!
BY YOU!
CAN YOU DO THAT FOR ME?! HUH?!
WHUD
CRASH
HUNHH?!

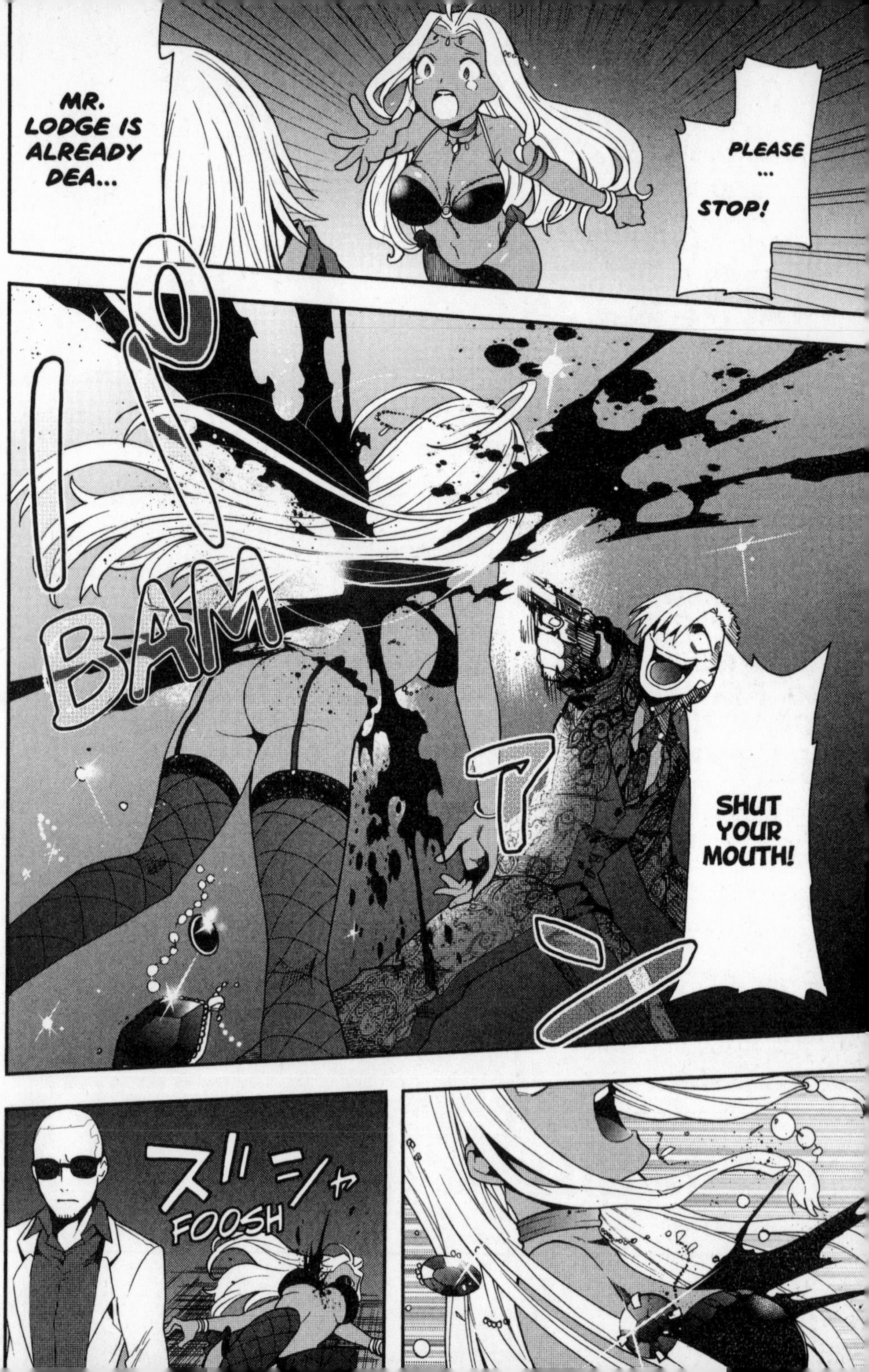
PLEASE ... STOP!
MR. LODGE IS ALREADY DEA...
SHUT YOUR MOUTH!
BAM
FOOSH

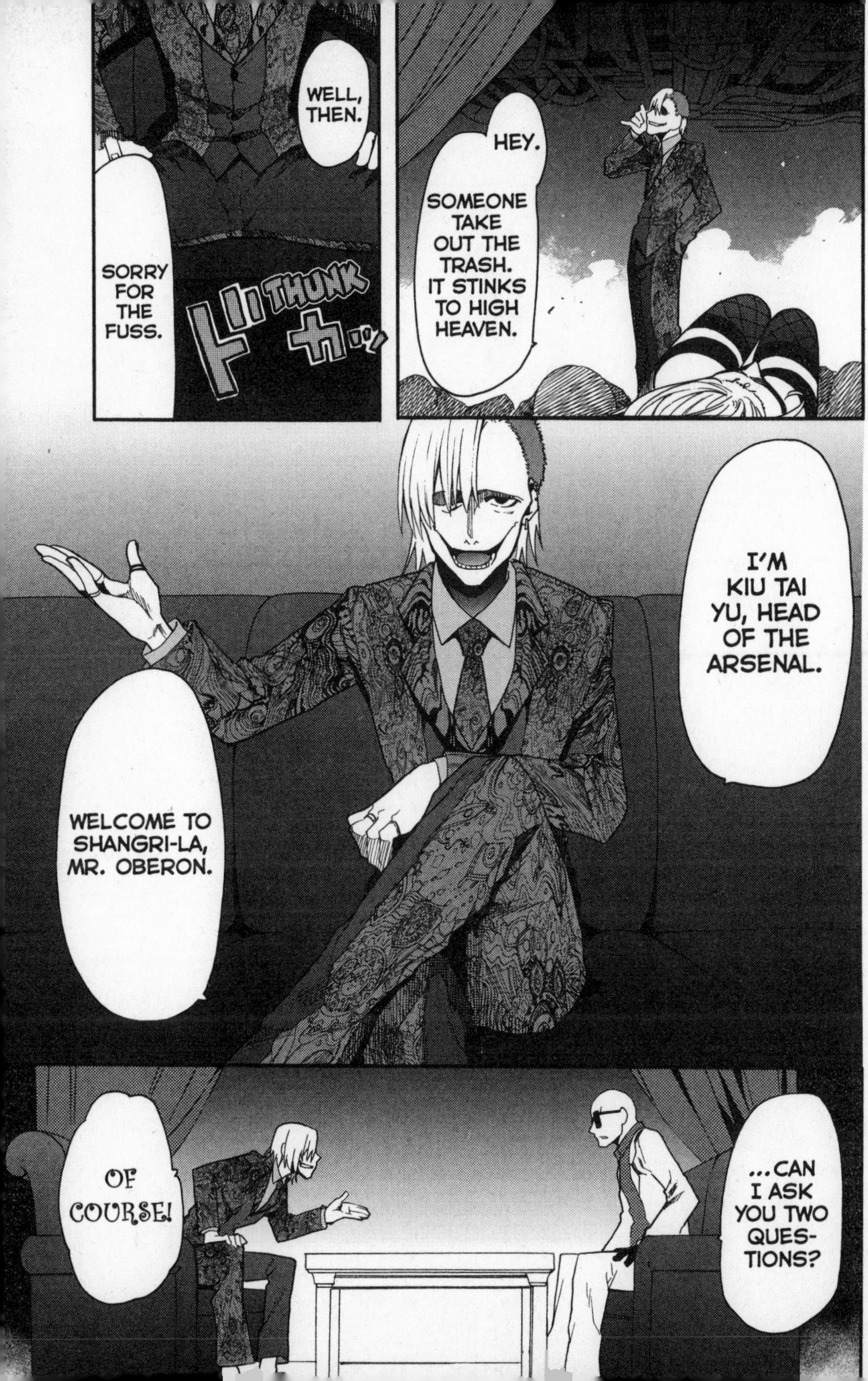
HEY.
SOMEONE TAKE OUT THE TRASH. IT STINKS TO HIGH HEAVEN.
WELL, THEN.
SORRY FOR THE FUSS.
THUNK
I'M KIU TAI YU, HEAD OF THE ARSENAL.
WELCOME TO SHANGRI-LA, MR. OBERON.
...CAN I ASK YOU TWO QUESTIONS?
OF COURSE!

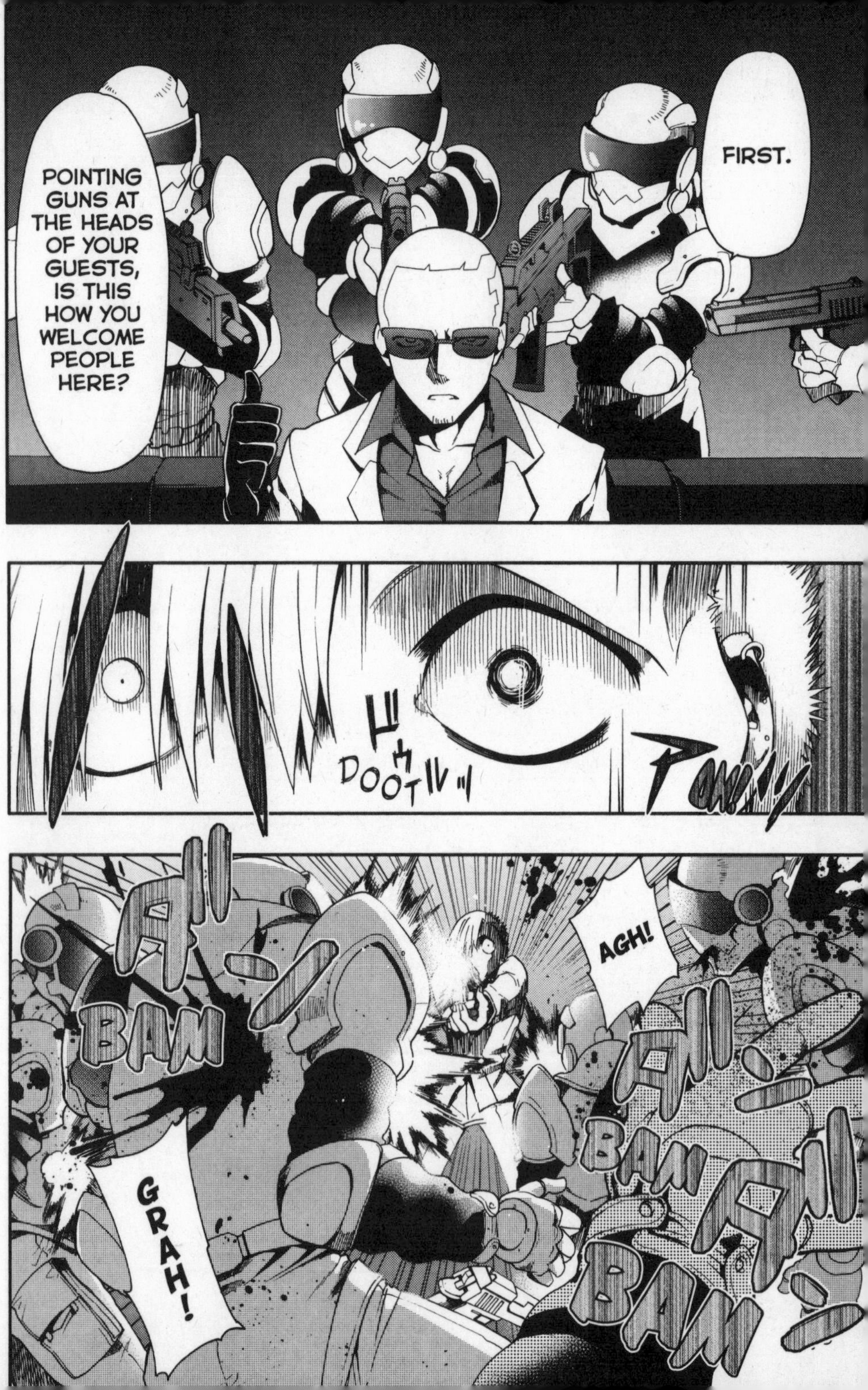
FIRST.
POINTING GUNS AT THE HEADS OF YOUR GUESTS, IS THIS HOW YOU WELCOME PEOPLE HERE?
POW!!
DOOT
AGH!
BAM
BAM
BAM
GRAH!
BAM

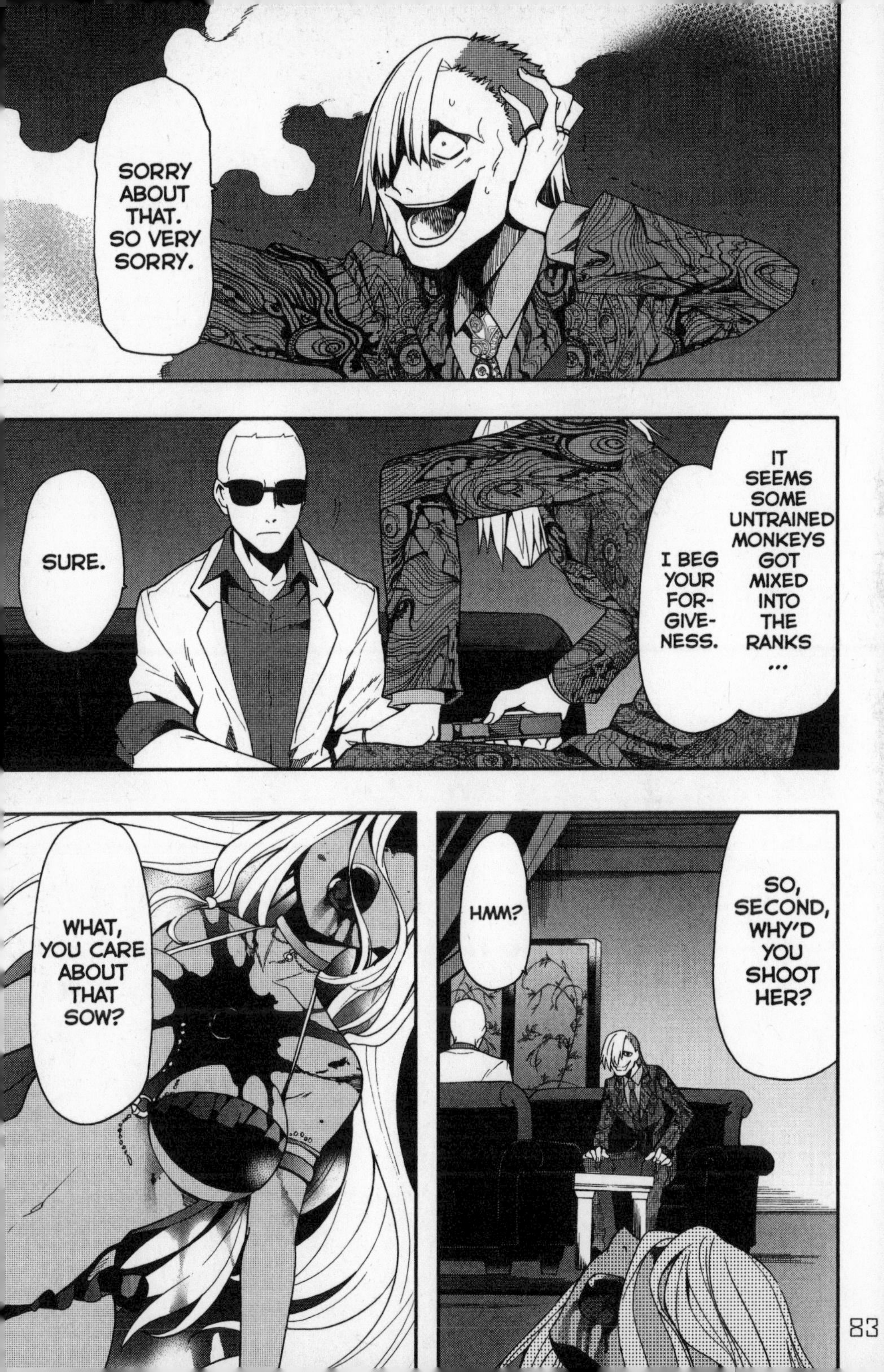
SORRY ABOUT THAT. SO VERY SORRY.
IT SEEMS SOME UNTRAINED MONKEYS GOT MIXED INTO THE RANKS...
I BEG YOUR FOR-GIVE-NESS.
SURE.
SO, SECOND, WHY'D YOU SHOOT HER?
HMM?
WHAT, YOU CARE ABOUT THAT SOW?

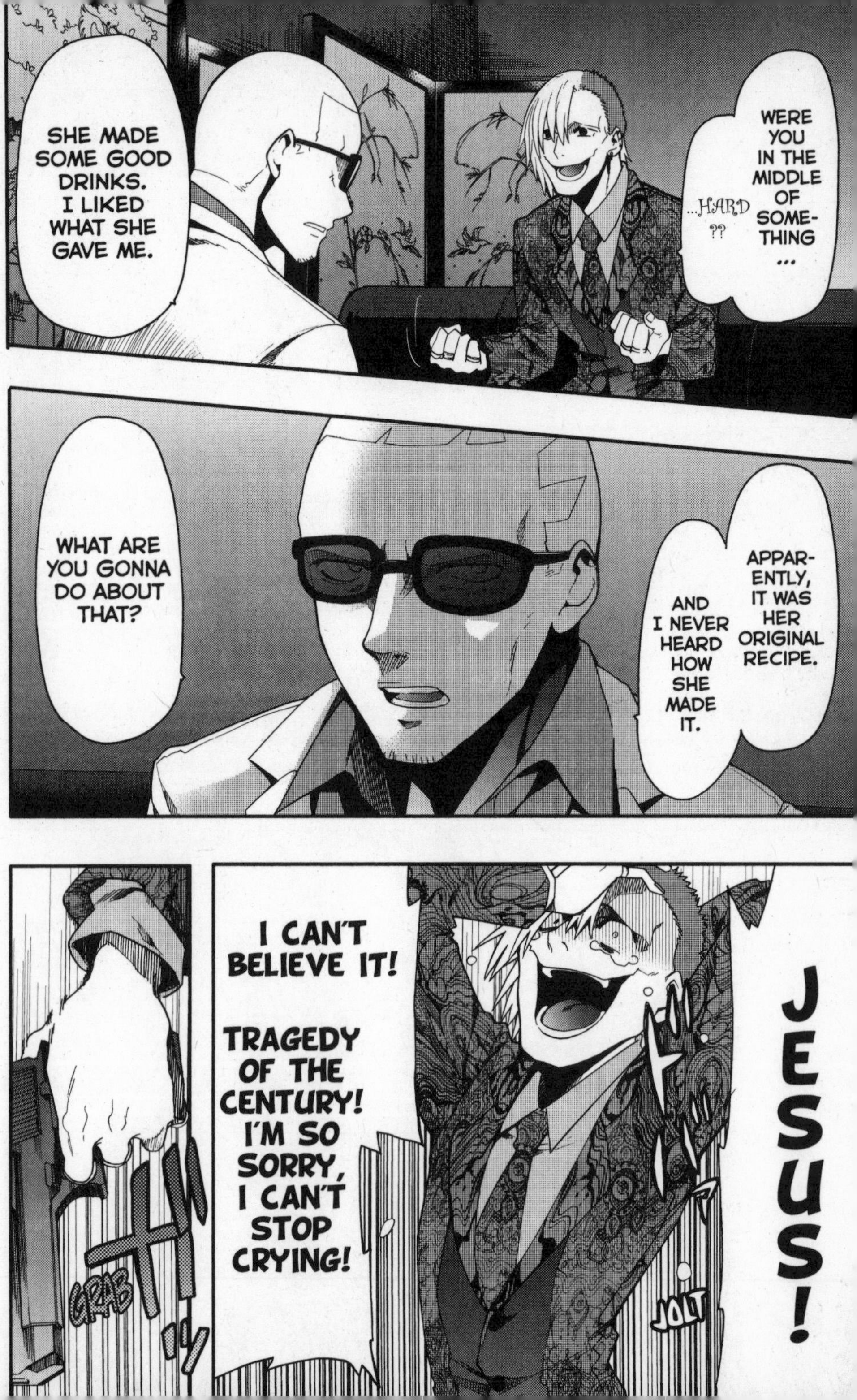
WERE YOU IN THE MIDDLE OF SOMETHING...
...HARD ??
SHE MADE SOME GOOD DRINKS. I LIKED WHAT SHE GAVE ME.
APPARENTLY, IT WAS HER ORIGINAL RECIPE.
AND I NEVER HEARD HOW SHE MADE IT.
WHAT ARE YOU GONNA DO ABOUT THAT?
JESUS!
JOLT
I CAN'T BELIEVE IT!
TRAGEDY OF THE CENTURY! I'M SO SORRY, I CAN'T STOP CRYING!
GRAB

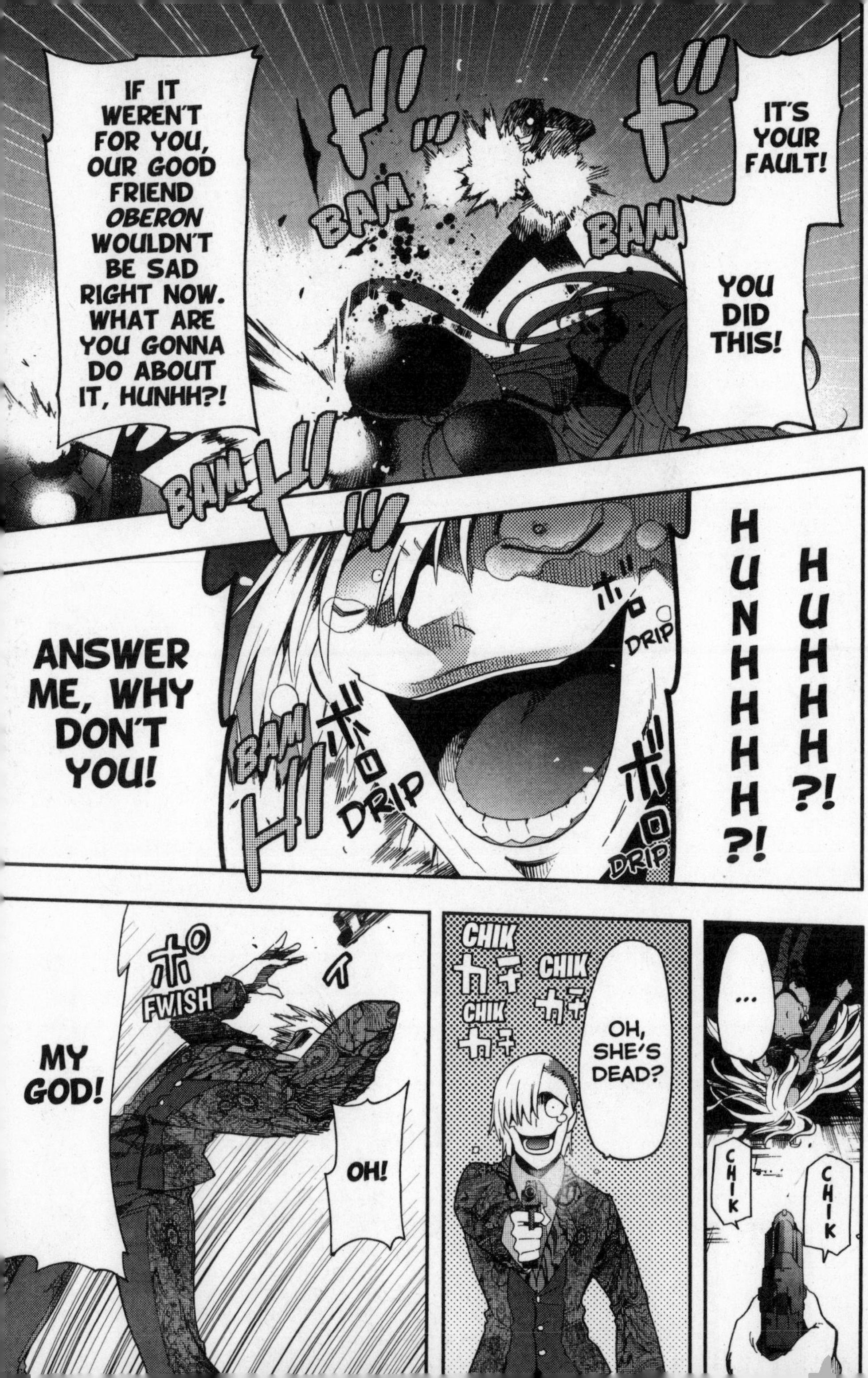
IT'S YOUR FAULT!
YOU DID THIS!
BAM
BAM
IF IT WEREN'T FOR YOU, OUR GOOD FRIEND *OBERON* WOULDN'T BE SAD RIGHT NOW. WHAT ARE YOU GONNA DO ABOUT IT, HUNHH?!
BAM
HUHHHH?!
HUNHHHHH?!
DRIP
DRIP
DRIP
BAM
ANSWER ME, WHY DON'T YOU!
...
CHIK
CHIK
CHIK
CHIK
CHIK
OH, SHE'S DEAD?
FWISH
OH!
MY GOD!

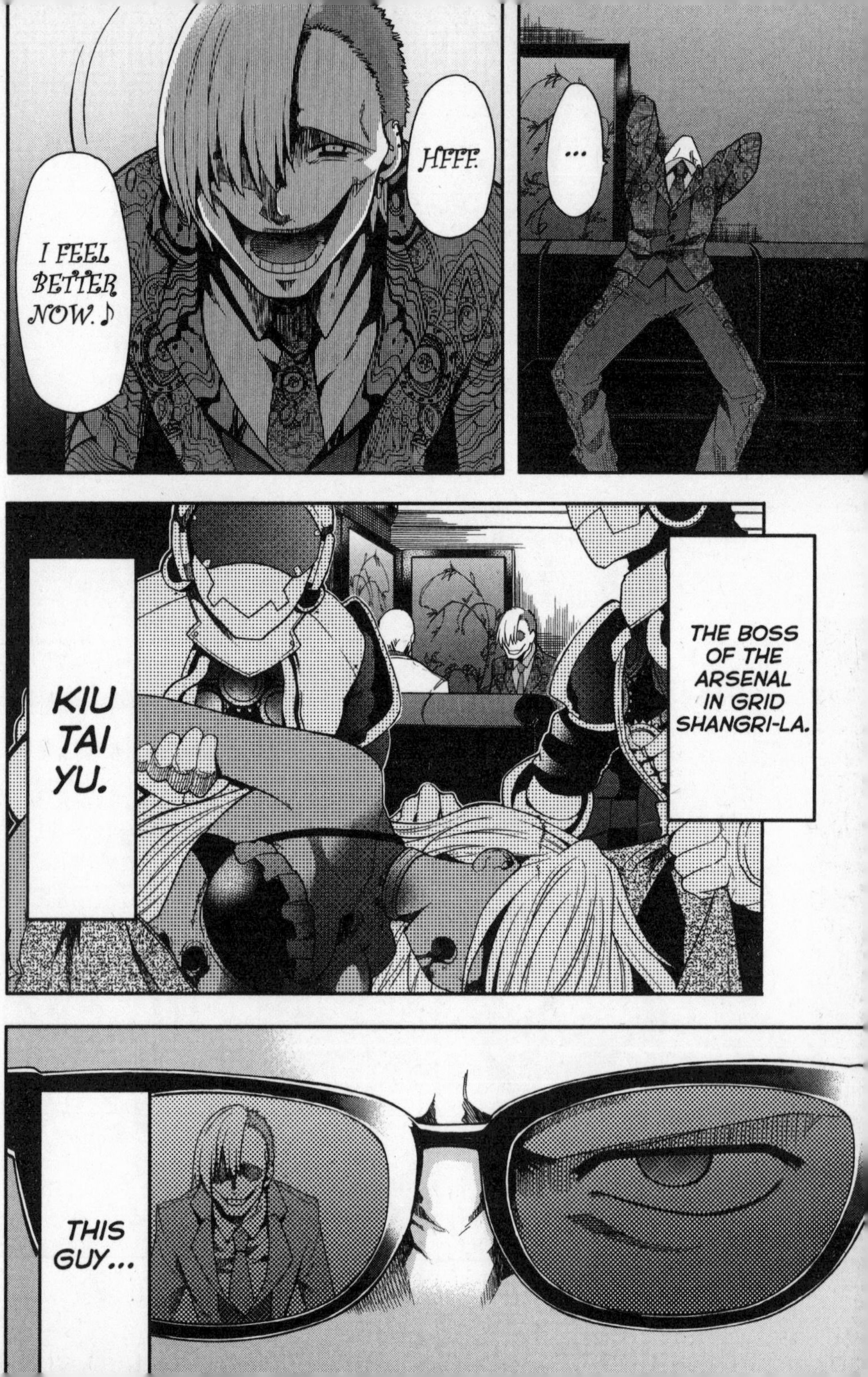
...
HFFF.
I FEEL BETTER NOW.♪
THE BOSS OF THE ARSENAL IN GRID SHANGRI-LA.
KIU TAI YU.
THIS GUY...

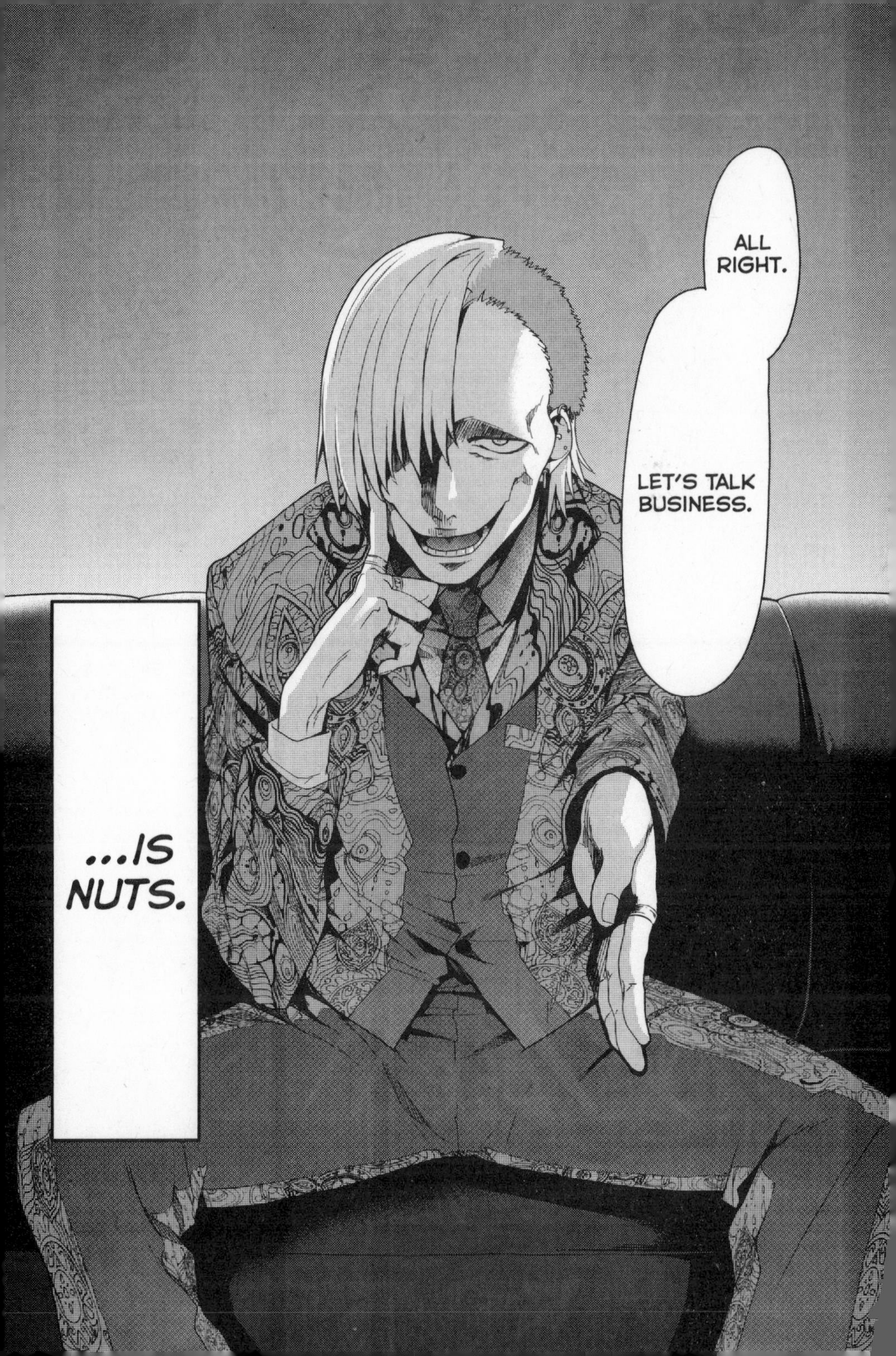
ALL RIGHT.
LET'S TALK BUSINESS.
...IS NUTS.

Clockwork Planet

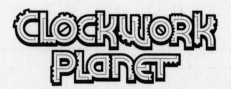

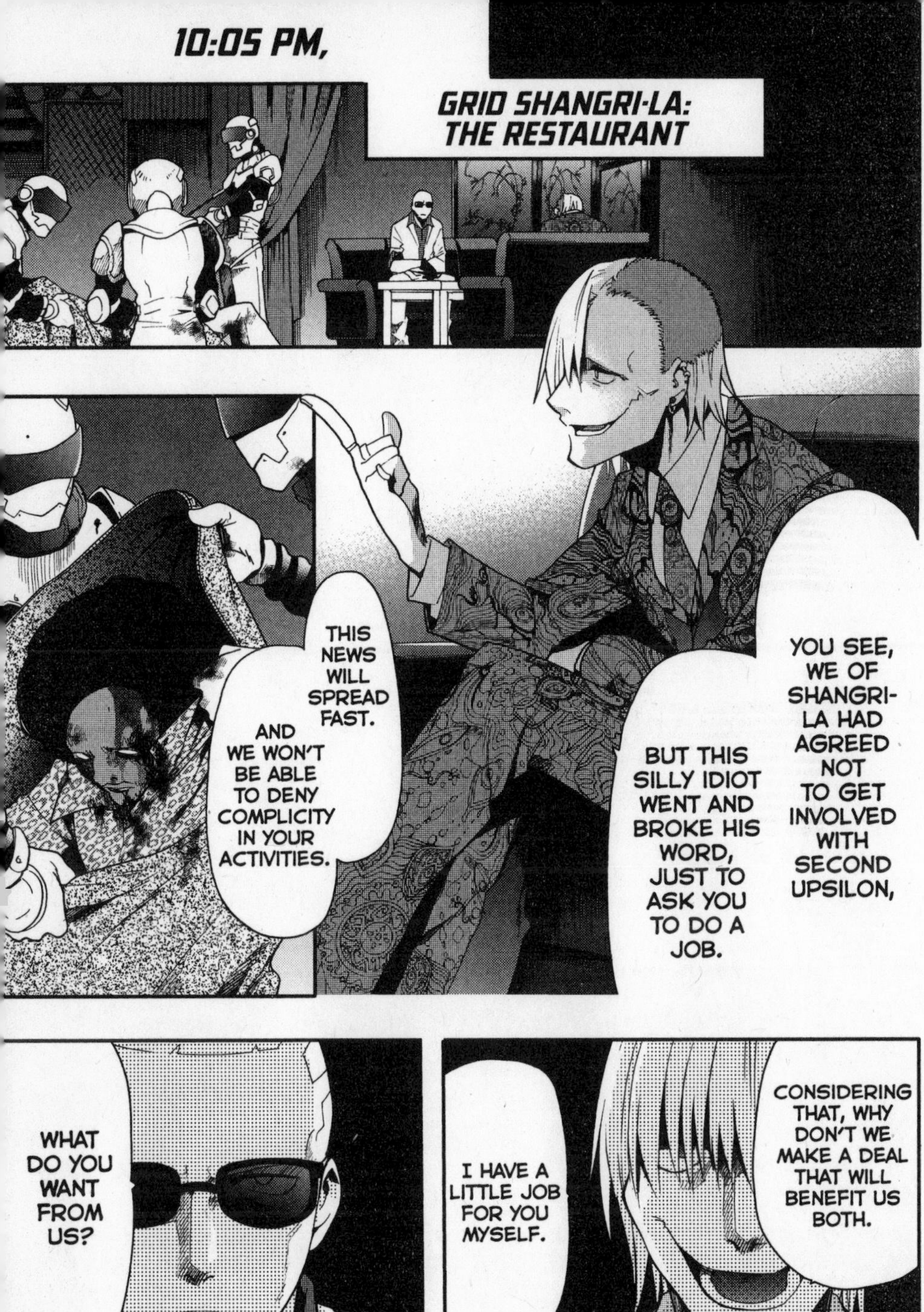
10:05 PM,
GRID SHANGRI-LA: THE RESTAURANT
YOU SEE, WE OF SHANGRI-LA HAD AGREED NOT TO GET INVOLVED WITH SECOND UPSILON,
BUT THIS SILLY IDIOT WENT AND BROKE HIS WORD, JUST TO ASK YOU TO DO A JOB.
THIS NEWS WILL SPREAD FAST.
AND WE WON'T BE ABLE TO DENY COMPLICITY IN YOUR ACTIVITIES.
CONSIDERING THAT, WHY DON'T WE MAKE A DEAL THAT WILL BENEFIT US BOTH.
I HAVE A LITTLE JOB FOR YOU MYSELF.
WHAT DO YOU WANT FROM US?

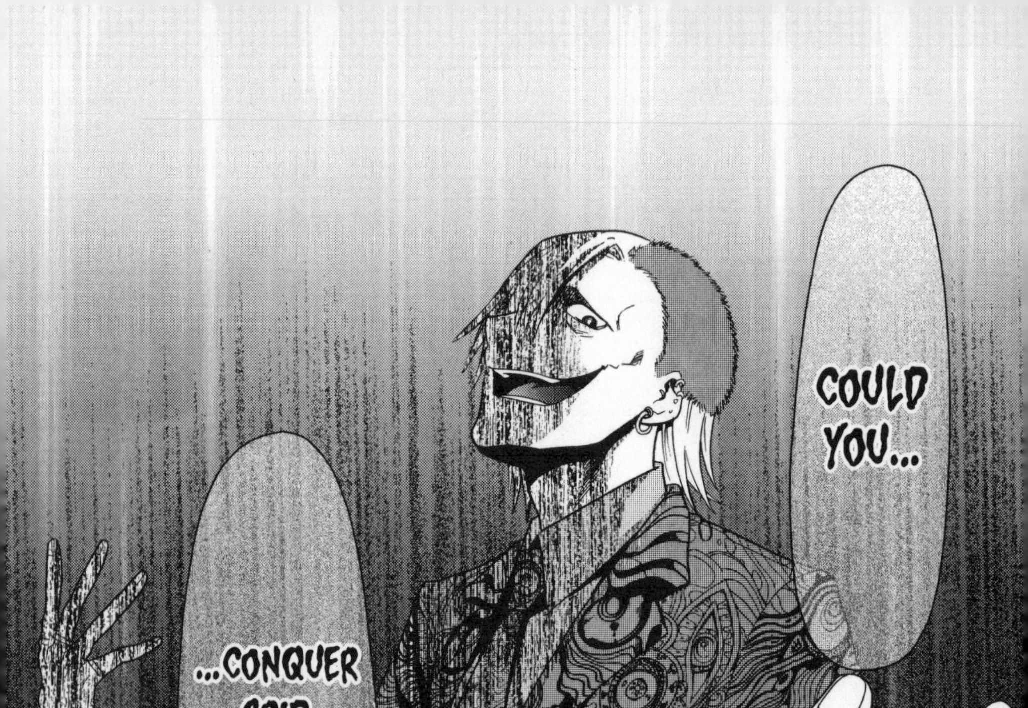
COULD YOU...
...CONQUER GRID SHANGRI-LA FOR ME?
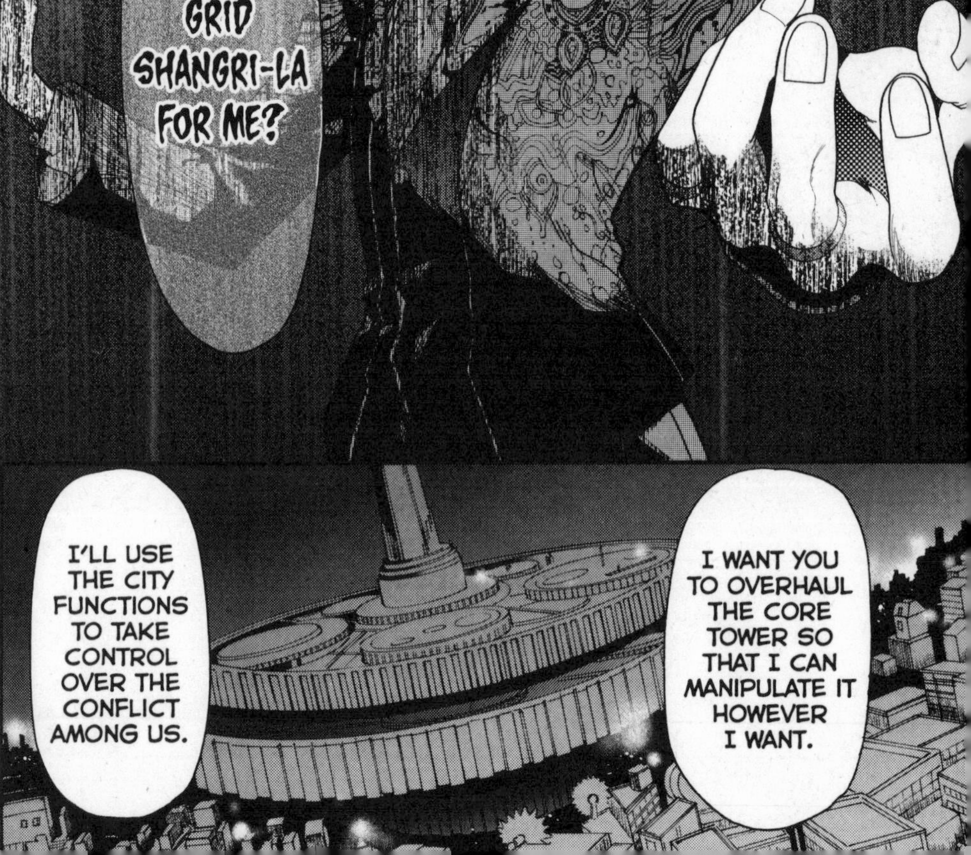
I WANT YOU TO OVERHAUL THE CORE TOWER SO THAT I CAN MANIPULATE IT HOWEVER I WANT.
I'LL USE THE CITY FUNCTIONS TO TAKE CONTROL OVER THE CONFLICT AMONG US.

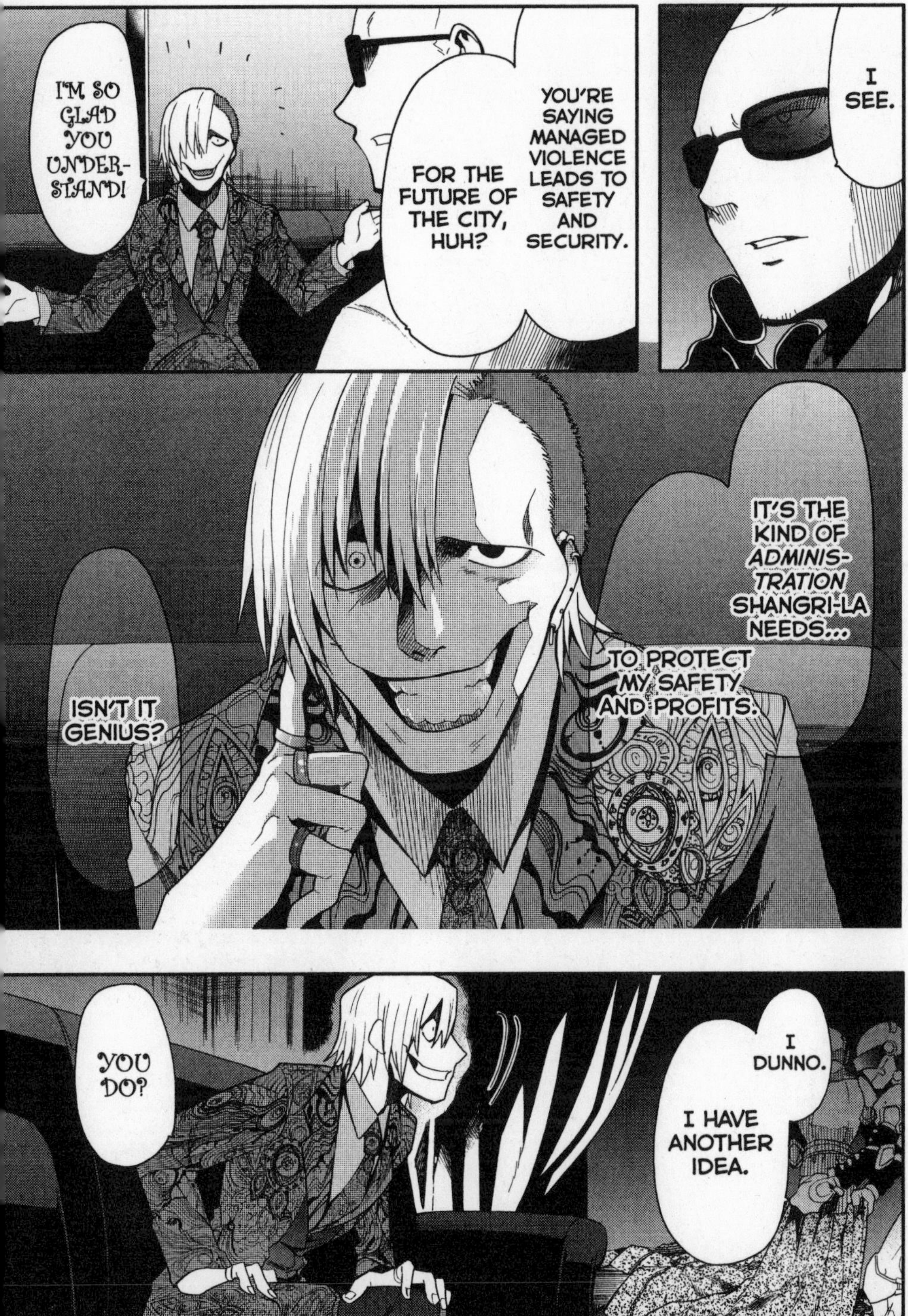
I SEE.
YOU'RE SAYING MANAGED VIOLENCE LEADS TO SAFETY AND SECURITY.
FOR THE FUTURE OF THE CITY, HUH?
I'M SO GLAD YOU UNDER-STAND!
IT'S THE KIND OF *ADMINIS-TRATION* SHANGRI-LA NEEDS...
TO PROTECT MY SAFETY AND PROFITS.
ISN'T IT GENIUS?
I DUNNO.
I HAVE ANOTHER IDEA.
YOU DO?

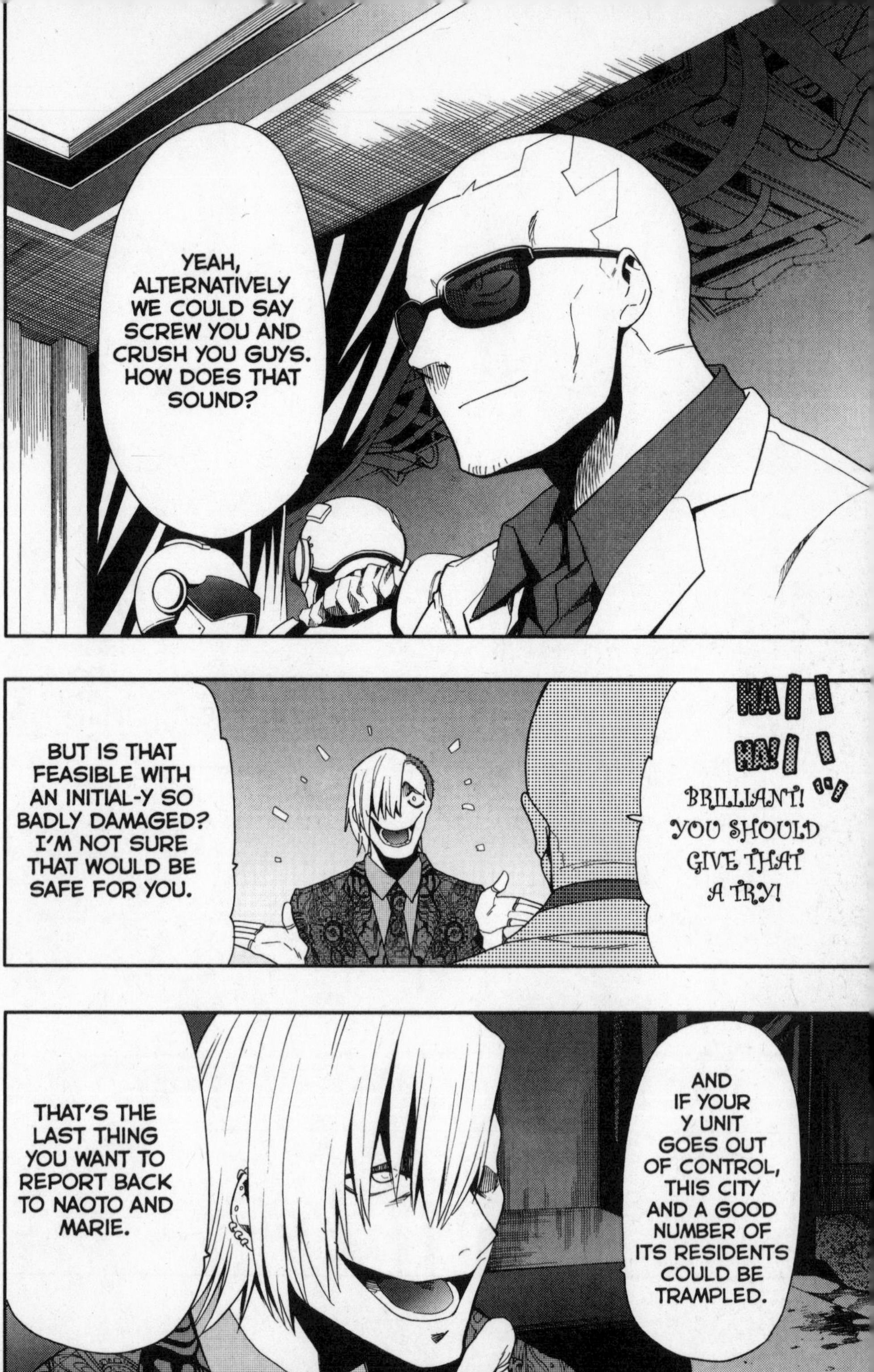
YEAH, ALTERNATIVELY WE COULD SAY SCREW YOU AND CRUSH YOU GUYS. HOW DOES THAT SOUND?
HA! HA!
BRILLIANT! YOU SHOULD GIVE THAT A TRY!
BUT IS THAT FEASIBLE WITH AN INITIAL-Y SO BADLY DAMAGED? I'M NOT SURE THAT WOULD BE SAFE FOR YOU.
AND IF YOUR Y UNIT GOES OUT OF CONTROL, THIS CITY AND A GOOD NUMBER OF ITS RESIDENTS COULD BE TRAMPLED.
THAT'S THE LAST THING YOU WANT TO REPORT BACK TO NAOTO AND MARIE.

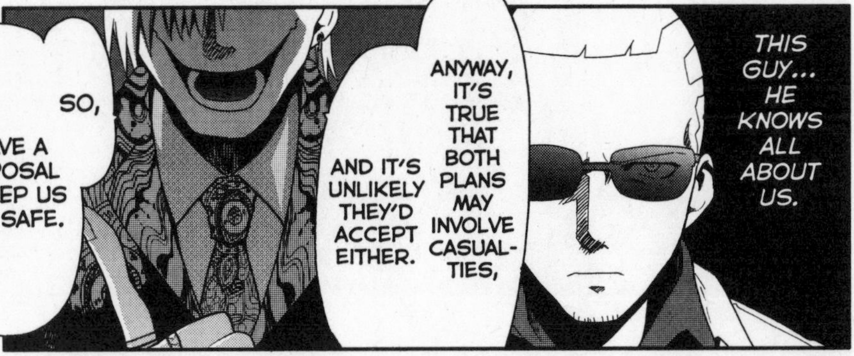
THIS GUY... HE KNOWS ALL ABOUT US.
ANYWAY, IT'S TRUE THAT BOTH PLANS MAY INVOLVE CASUAL-TIES,
AND IT'S UNLIKELY THEY'D ACCEPT EITHER.
SO,
I HAVE A PROPOSAL TO KEEP US BOTH SAFE.

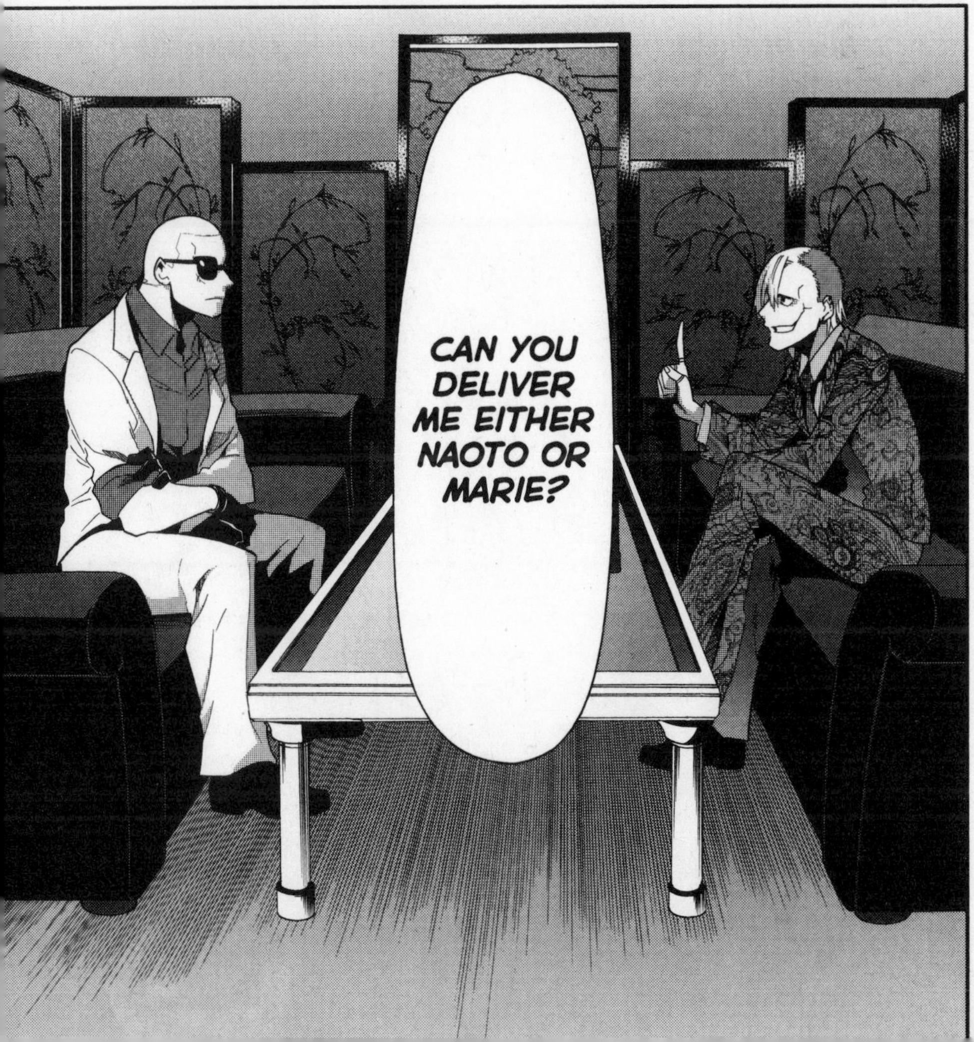
CAN YOU DELIVER ME EITHER NAOTO OR MARIE?

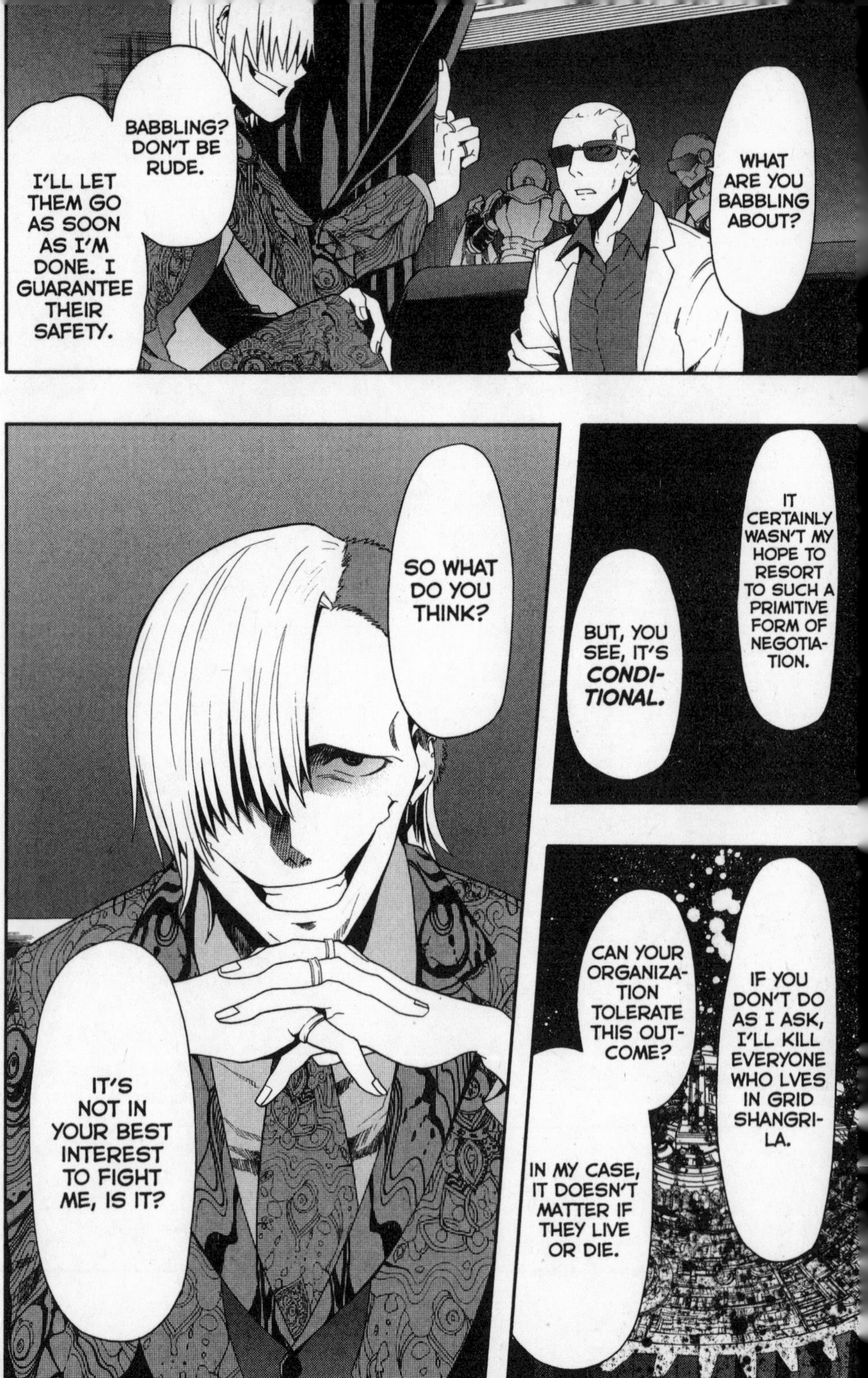
WHAT ARE YOU BABBLING ABOUT?
BABBLING? DON'T BE RUDE.
I'LL LET THEM GO AS SOON AS I'M DONE. I GUARANTEE THEIR SAFETY.
IT CERTAINLY WASN'T MY HOPE TO RESORT TO SUCH A PRIMITIVE FORM OF NEGOTIATION.
BUT, YOU SEE, IT'S *CONDITIONAL.*
IF YOU DON'T DO AS I ASK, I'LL KILL EVERYONE WHO LVES IN GRID SHANGRI-LA.
CAN YOUR ORGANIZATION TOLERATE THIS OUTCOME?
IN MY CASE, IT DOESN'T MATTER IF THEY LIVE OR DIE.
SO WHAT DO YOU THINK?
IT'S NOT IN YOUR BEST INTEREST TO FIGHT ME, IS IT?

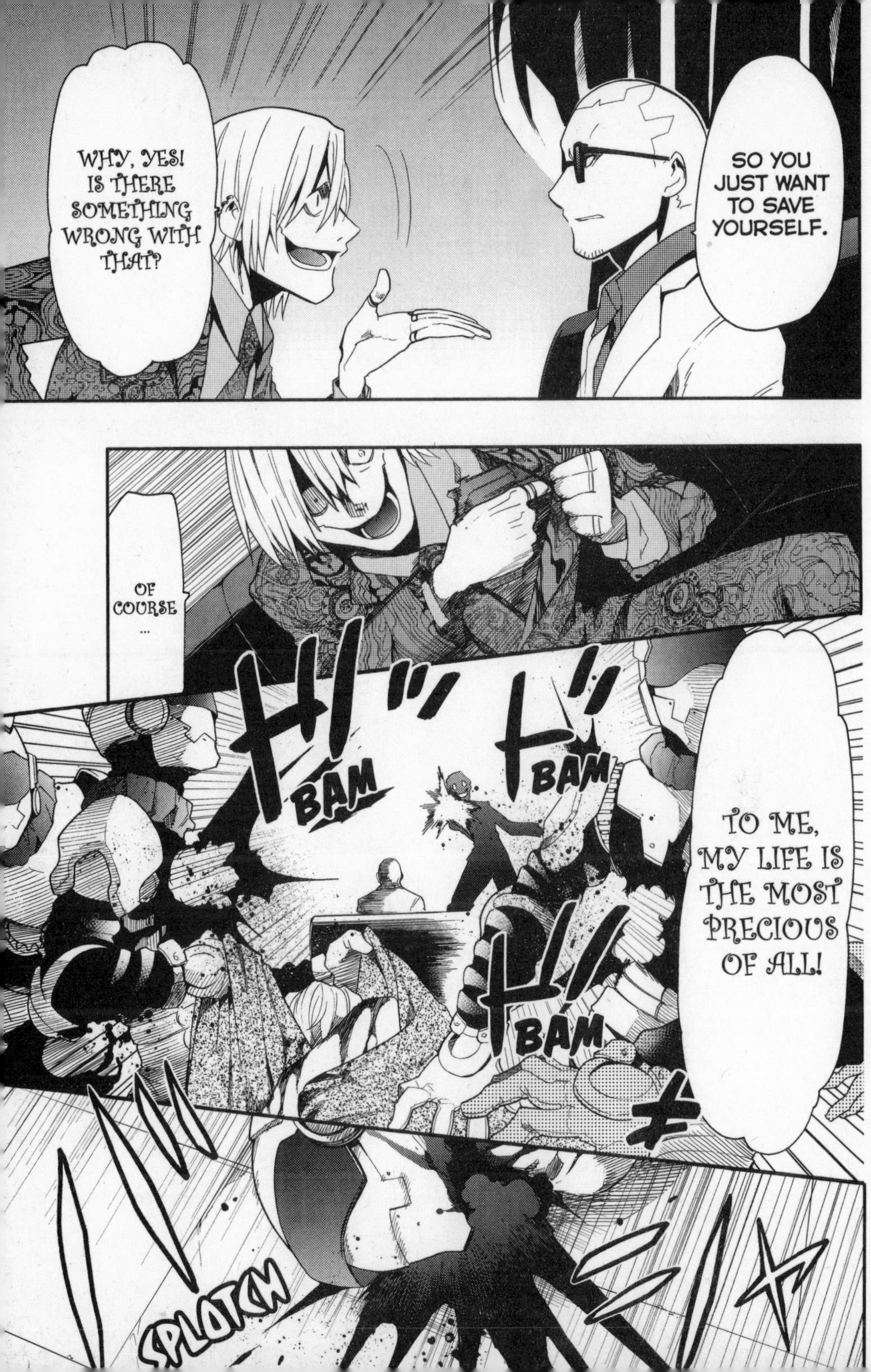
SO YOU JUST WANT TO SAVE YOURSELF.
WHY, YES! IS THERE SOMETHING WRONG WITH THAT?
OF COURSE ...
TO ME, MY LIFE IS THE MOST PRECIOUS OF ALL!
BAM
BAM
BAM
SPLOTCH

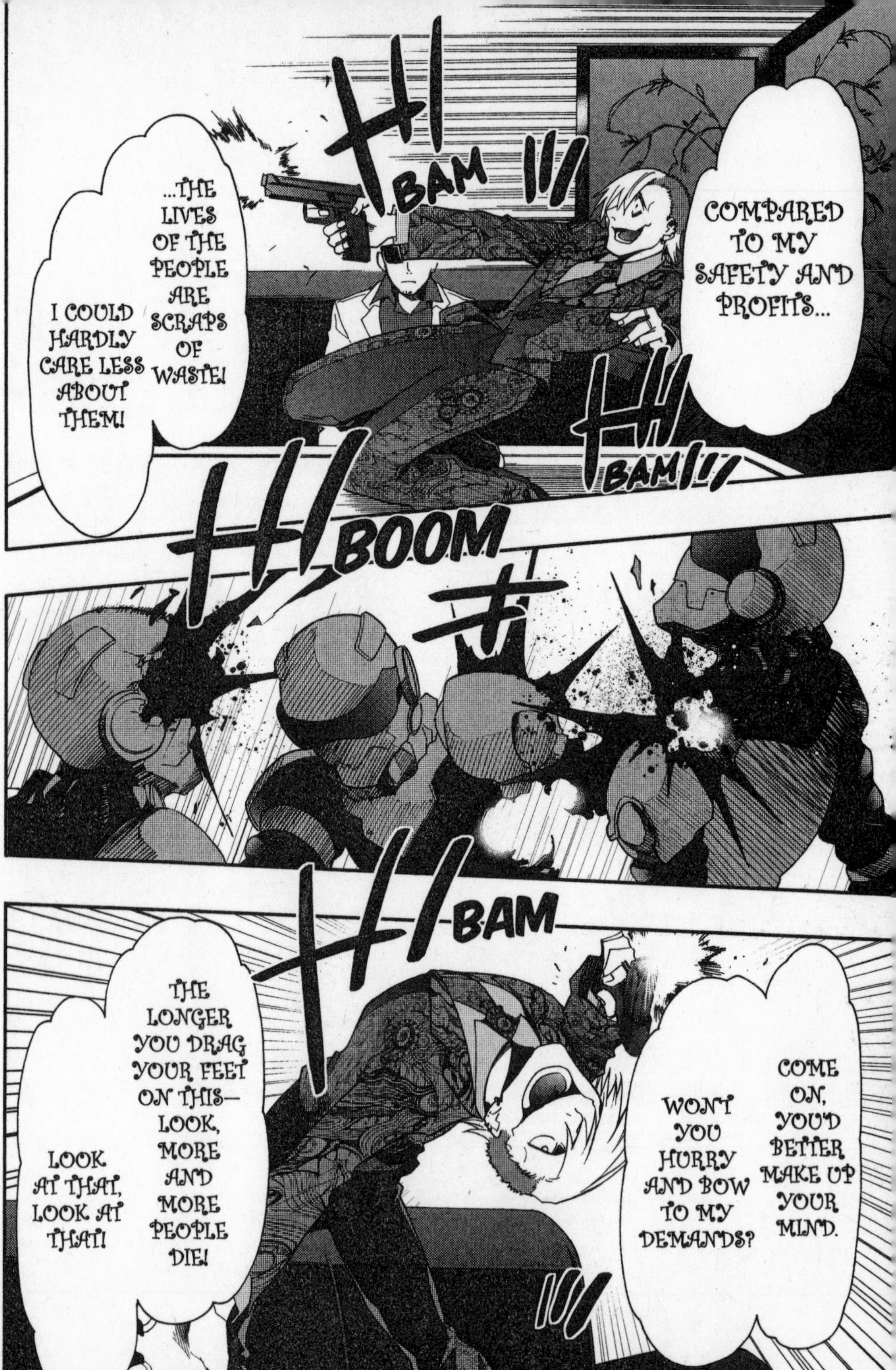
COMPARED TO MY SAFETY AND PROFITS...
BAM
...THE LIVES OF THE PEOPLE ARE SCRAPS OF WASTE!
I COULD HARDLY CARE LESS ABOUT THEM!
BAM
BOOM
BAM
COME ON, YOU'D BETTER MAKE UP YOUR MIND.
WON'T YOU HURRY AND BOW TO MY DEMANDS?
THE LONGER YOU DRAG YOUR FEET ON THIS— LOOK, MORE AND MORE PEOPLE DIE!
LOOK AT THAT, LOOK AT THAT!

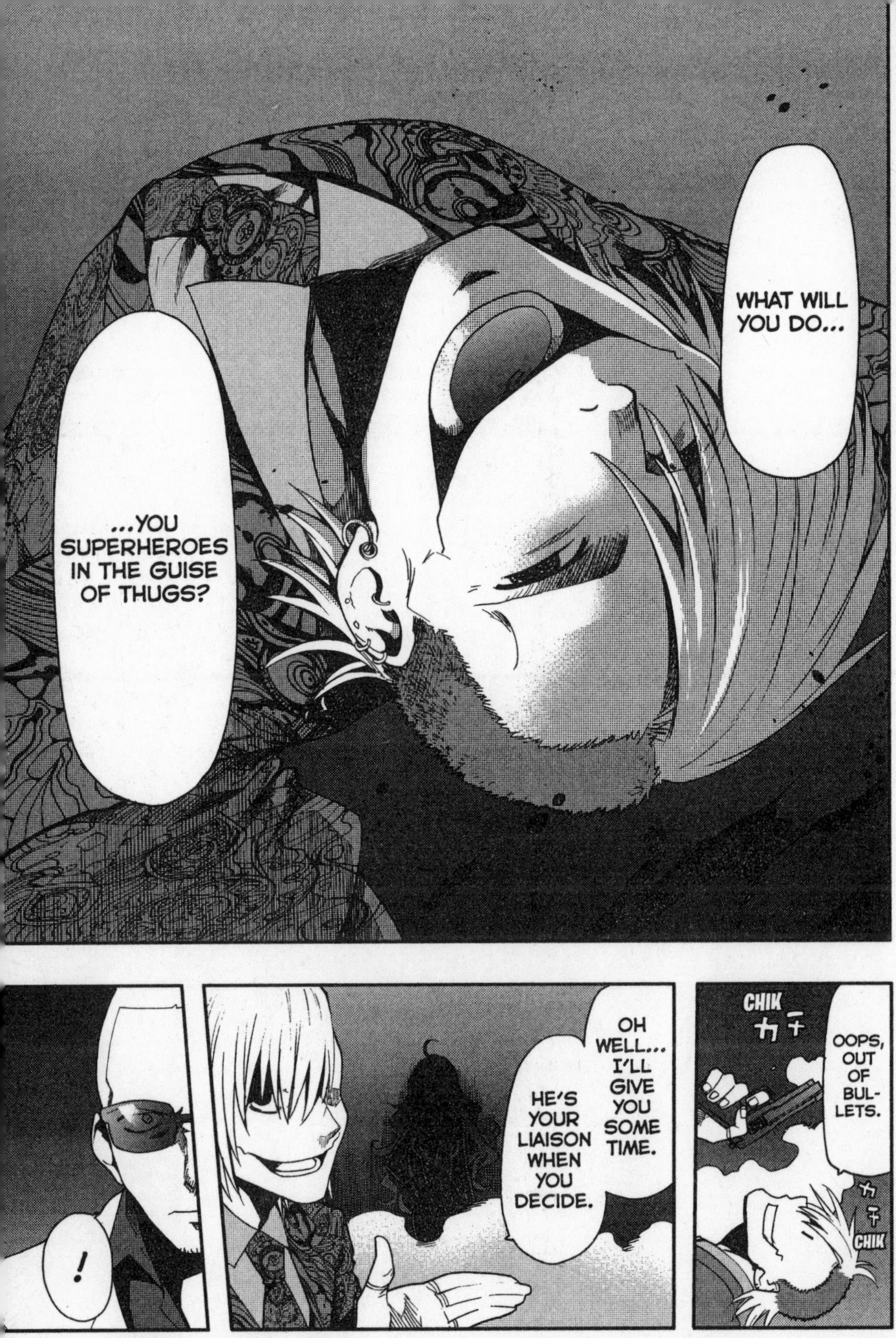
WHAT WILL YOU DO...
...YOU SUPERHEROES IN THE GUISE OF THUGS?
CHIK
OOPS, OUT OF BUL-LETS.
CHIK
OH WELL... I'LL GIVE YOU SOME TIME.
HE'S YOUR LIAISON WHEN YOU DECIDE.
!

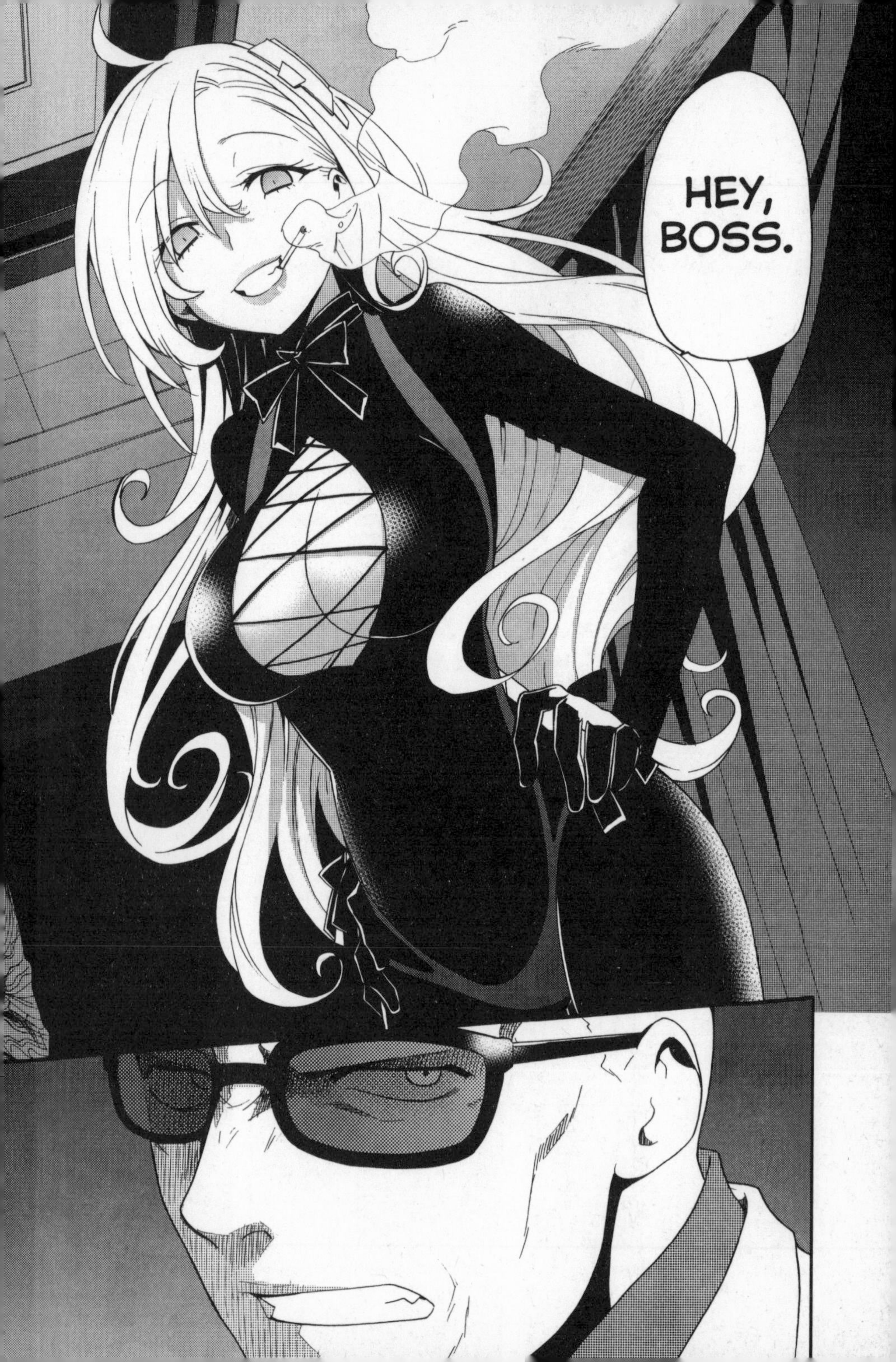
HEY, BOSS.

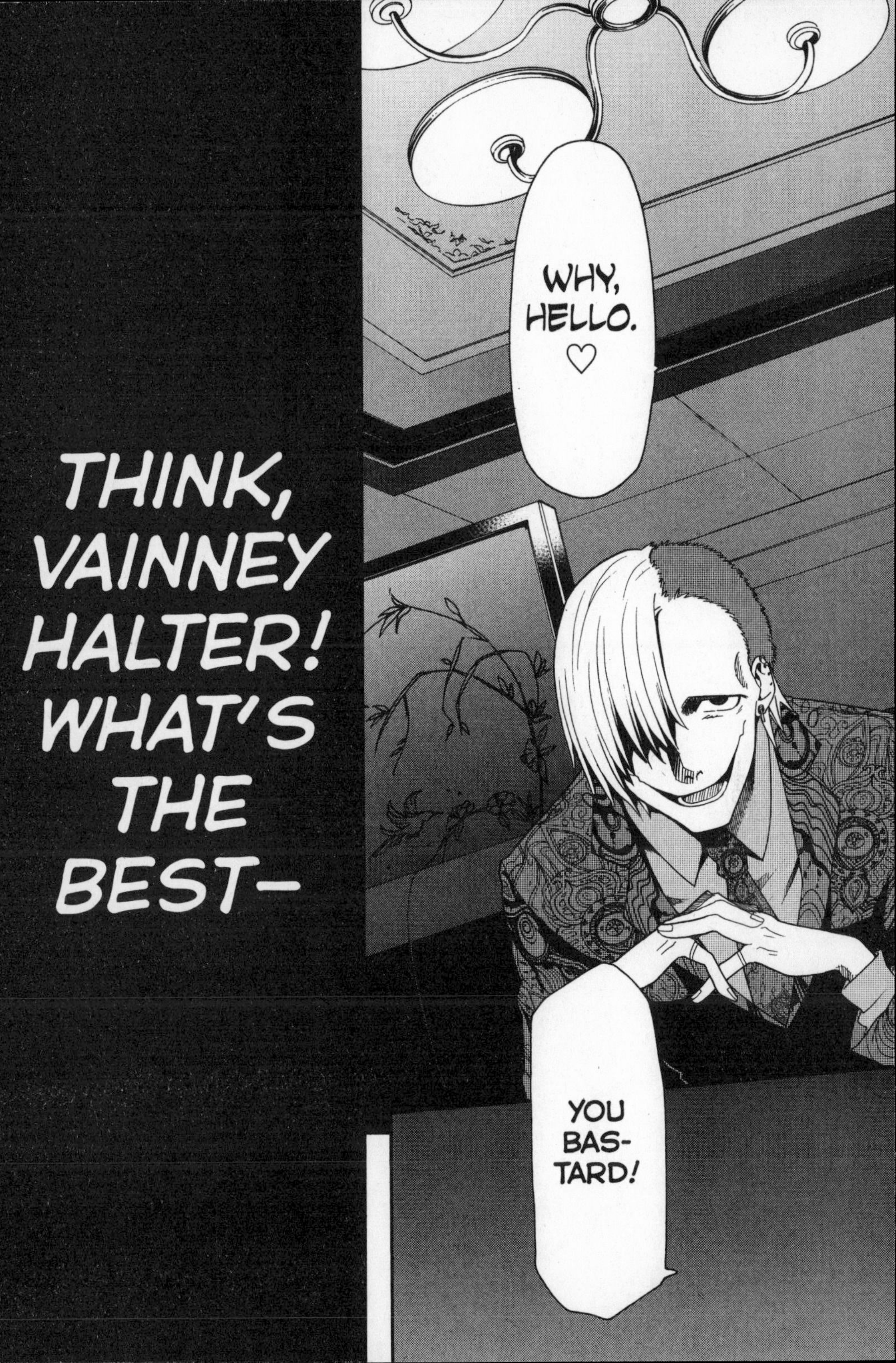
WHY, HELLO. ♡
YOU BAS-TARD!
THINK, VAINNEY HALTER! WHAT'S THE BEST—

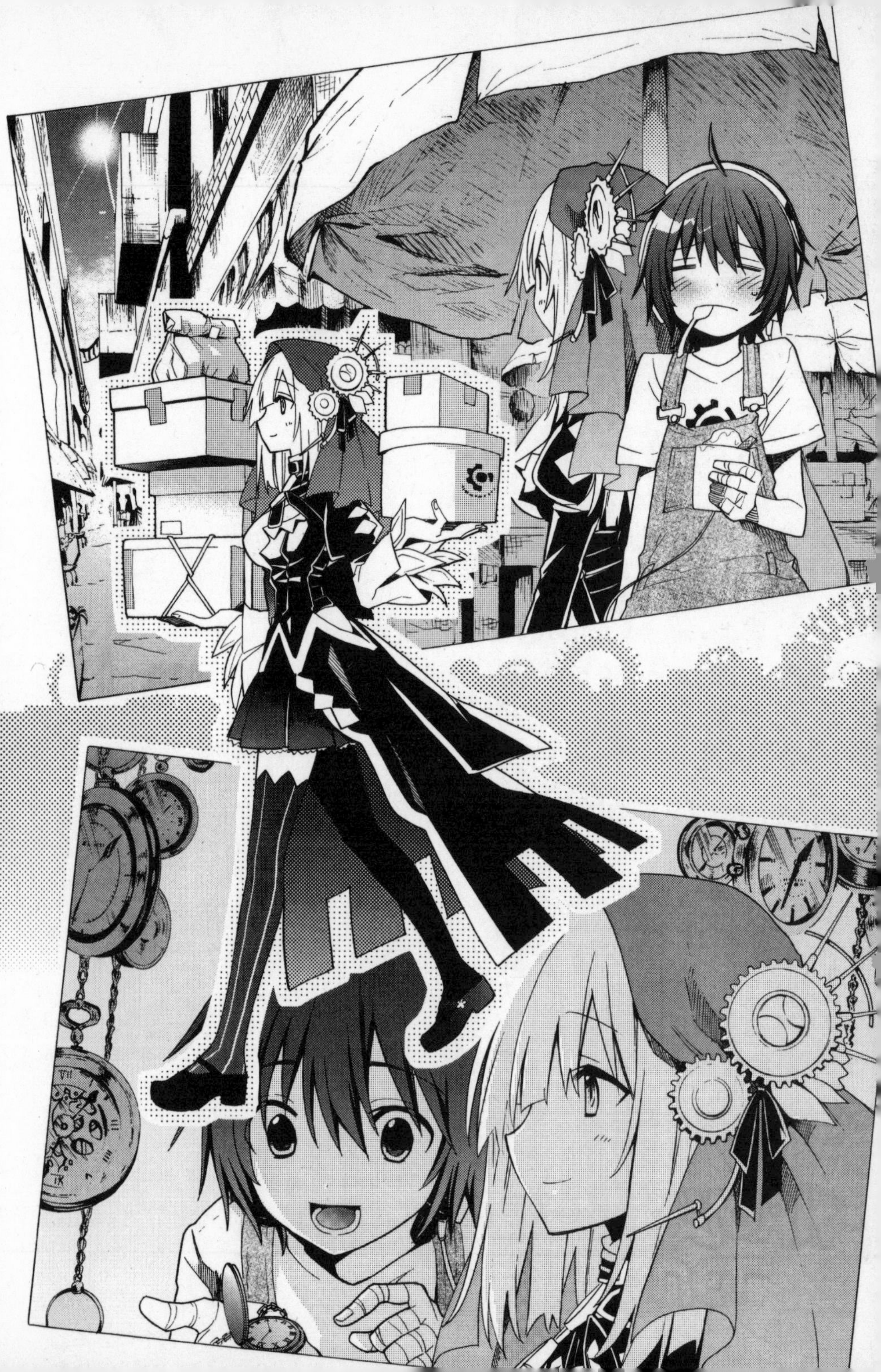

Clock 43: Kiu Tai Yu

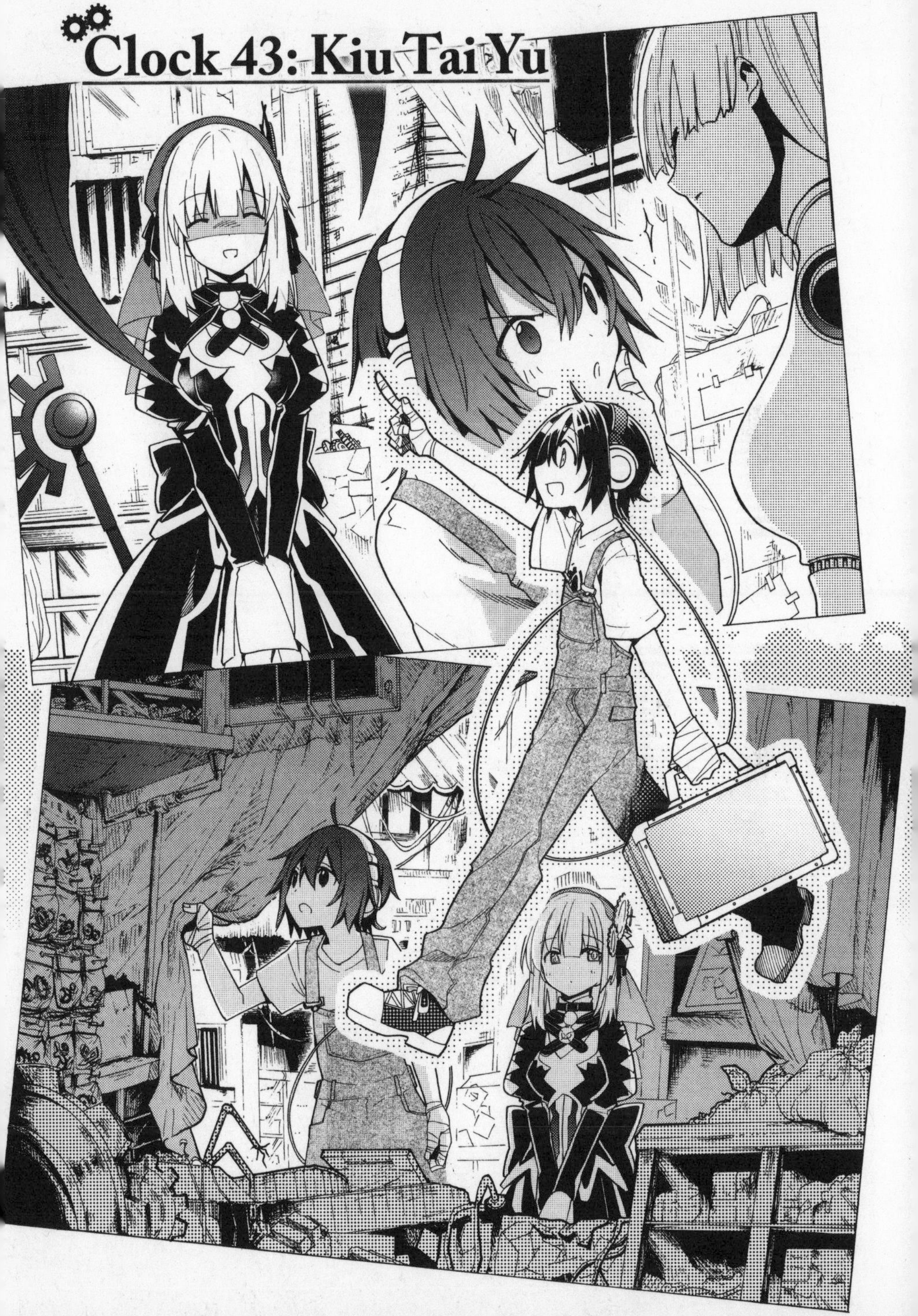

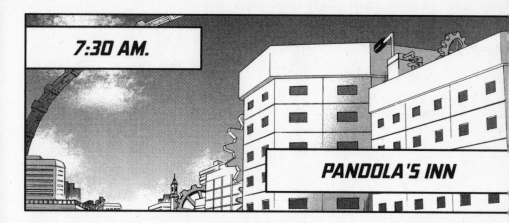

7:30 AM.

PANDOLA'S INN

CLATTER

OR THIS.

OR THIS.

THIS WON'T WORK.

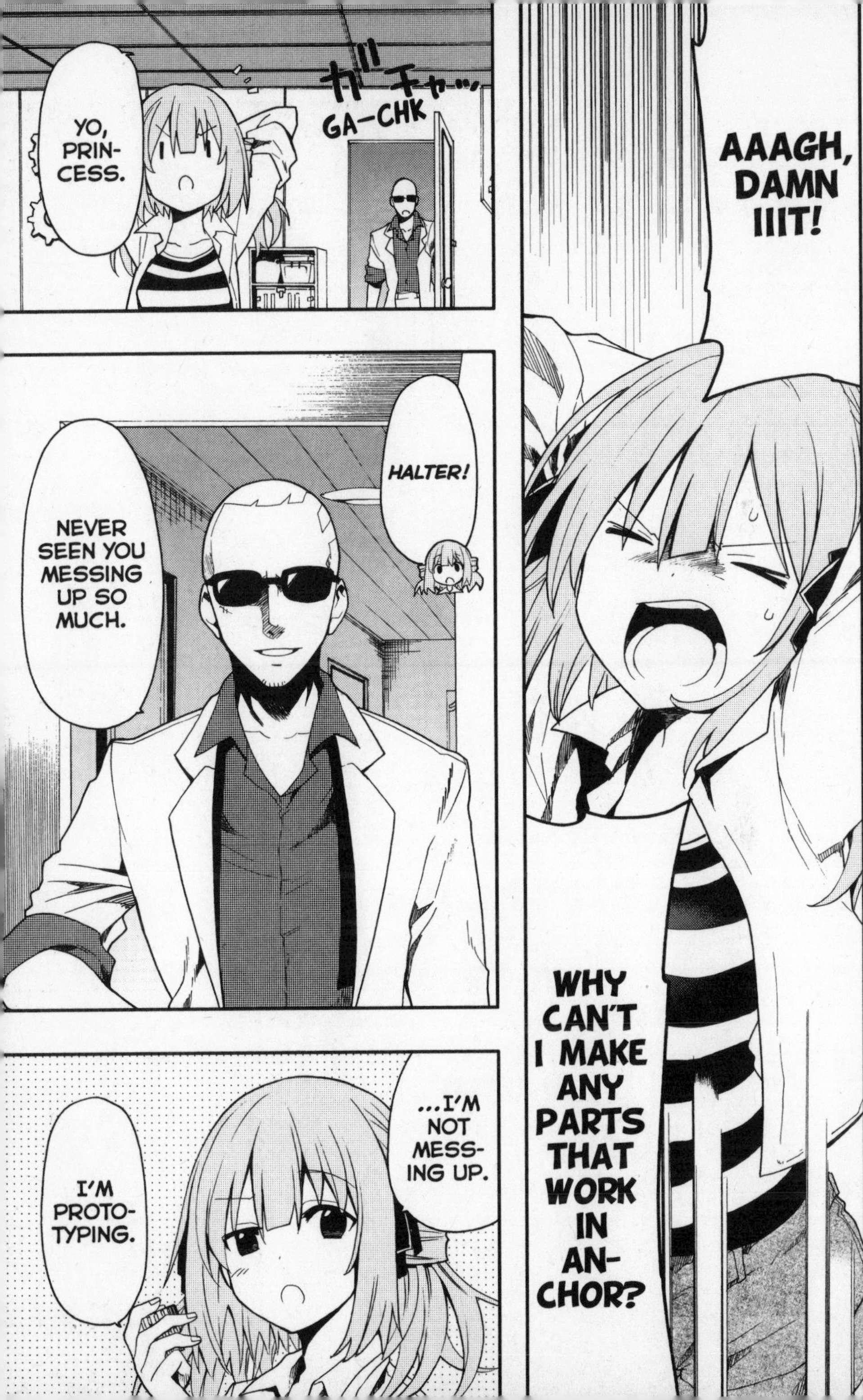
AAAGH, DAMN IIIT!
WHY CAN'T I MAKE ANY PARTS THAT WORK IN AN-CHOR?
ガチャッ
GA-CHK
YO, PRIN-CESS.
HALTER!
NEVER SEEN YOU MESSING UP SO MUCH.
...I'M NOT MESS-ING UP.
I'M PROTO-TYPING.

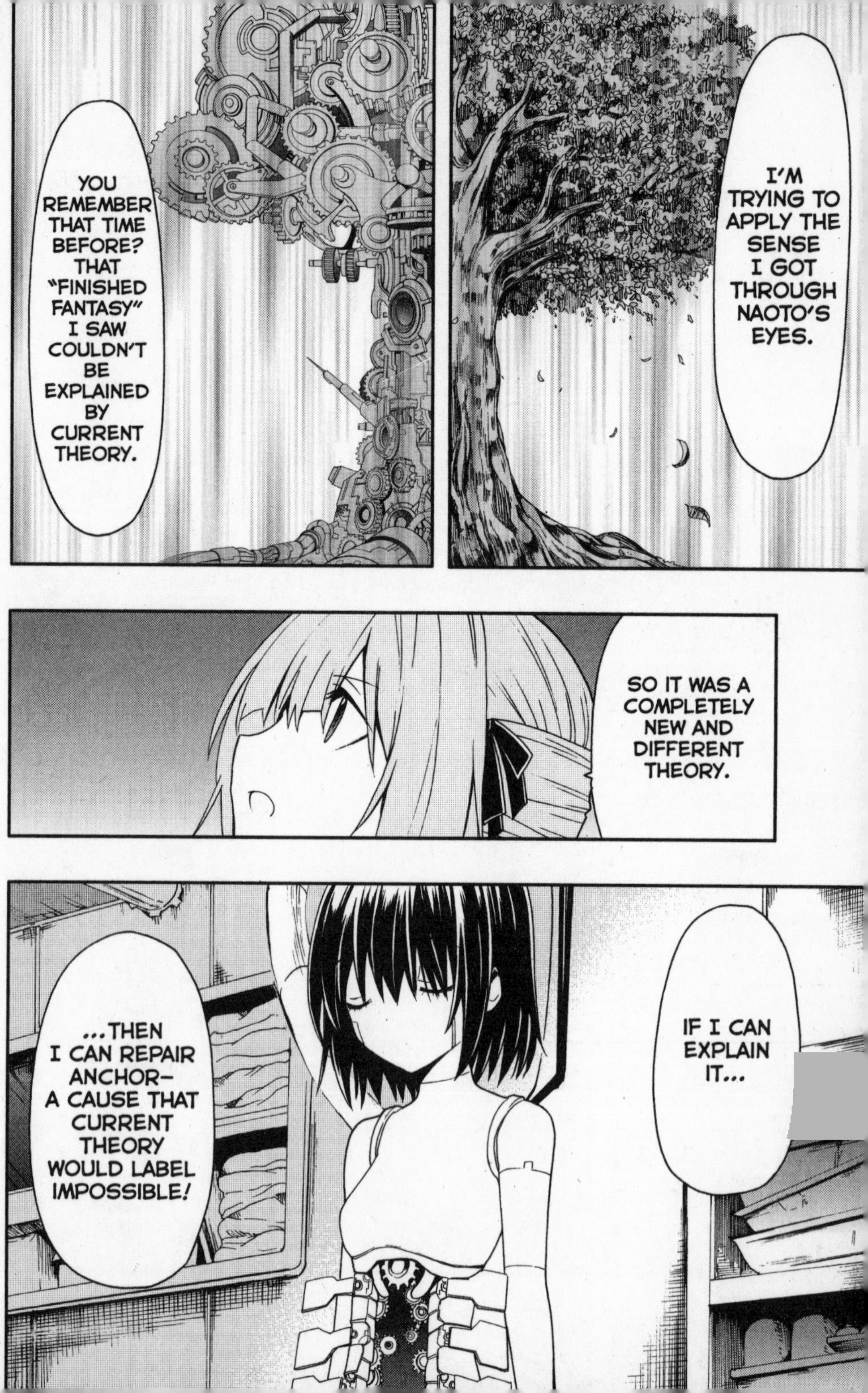
I'M TRYING TO APPLY THE SENSE I GOT THROUGH NAOTO'S EYES.
YOU REMEMBER THAT TIME BEFORE? THAT "FINISHED FANTASY" I SAW COULDN'T BE EXPLAINED BY CURRENT THEORY.
SO IT WAS A COMPLETELY NEW AND DIFFERENT THEORY.
IF I CAN EXPLAIN IT...
...THEN I CAN REPAIR ANCHOR— A CAUSE THAT CURRENT THEORY WOULD LABEL IMPOSSIBLE!

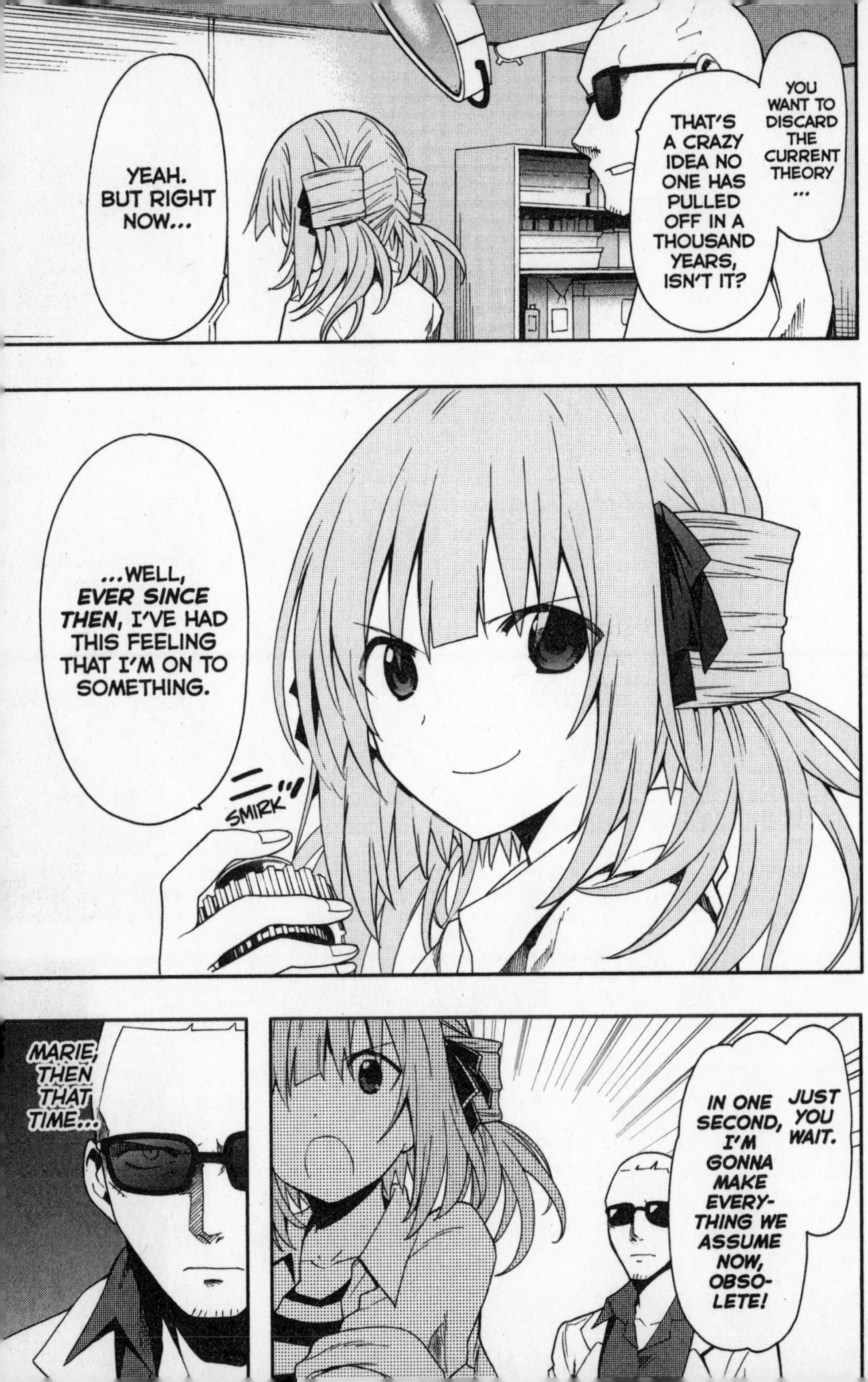
YOU WANT TO DISCARD THE CURRENT THEORY...
THAT'S A CRAZY IDEA NO ONE HAS PULLED OFF IN A THOUSAND YEARS, ISN'T IT?
YEAH. BUT RIGHT NOW...
...WELL, EVER SINCE THEN, I'VE HAD THIS FEELING THAT I'M ON TO SOMETHING.
SMIRK
JUST YOU WAIT.
IN ONE SECOND, I'M GONNA MAKE EVERYTHING WE ASSUME NOW, OBSOLETE!
MARIE, THEN THAT TIME...

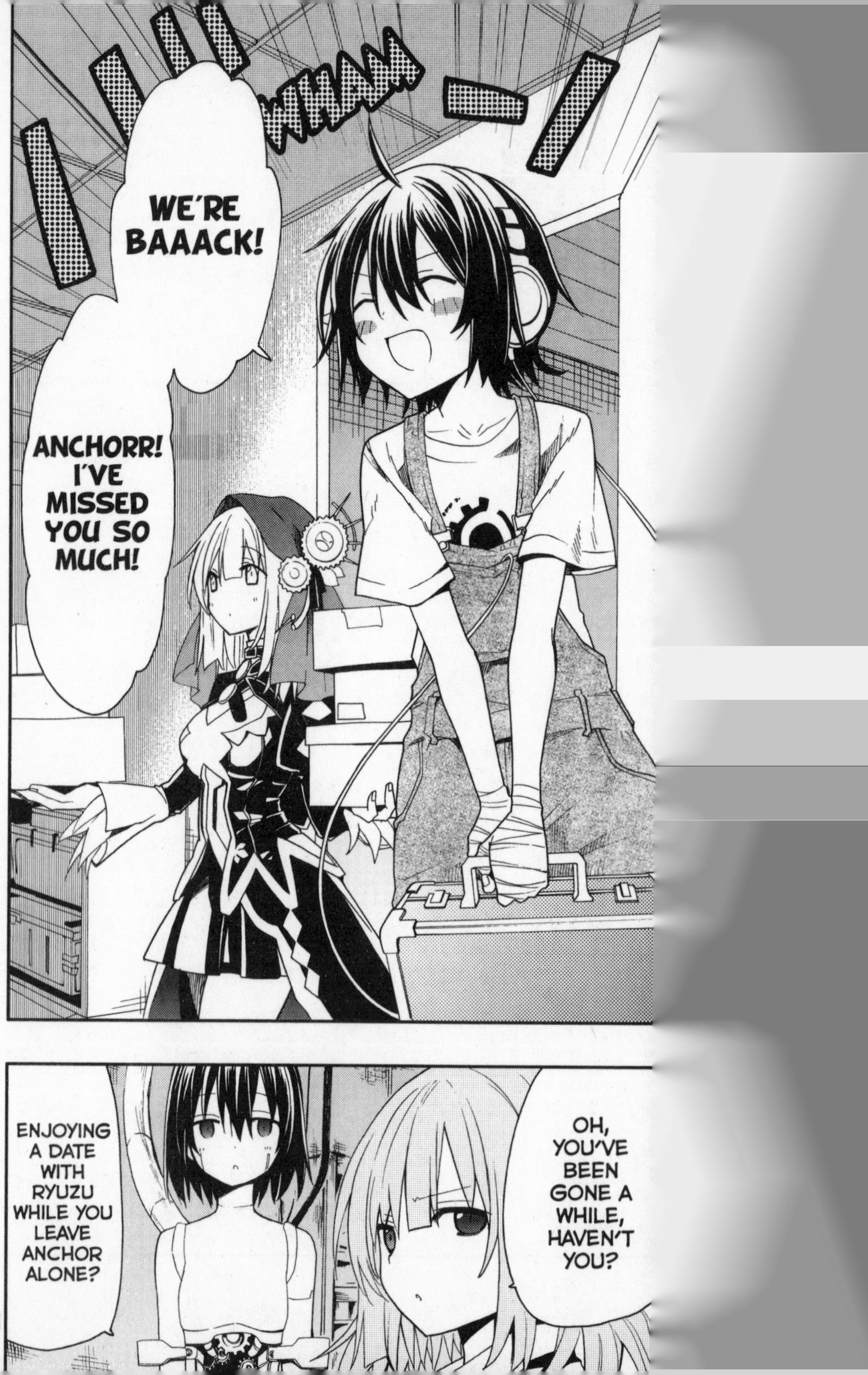
WHAM
WE'RE BAAACK!
ANCHORR! I'VE MISSED YOU SO MUCH!
OH, YOU'VE BEEN GONE A WHILE, HAVEN'T YOU?
ENJOYING A DATE WITH RYUZU WHILE YOU LEAVE ANCHOR ALONE?

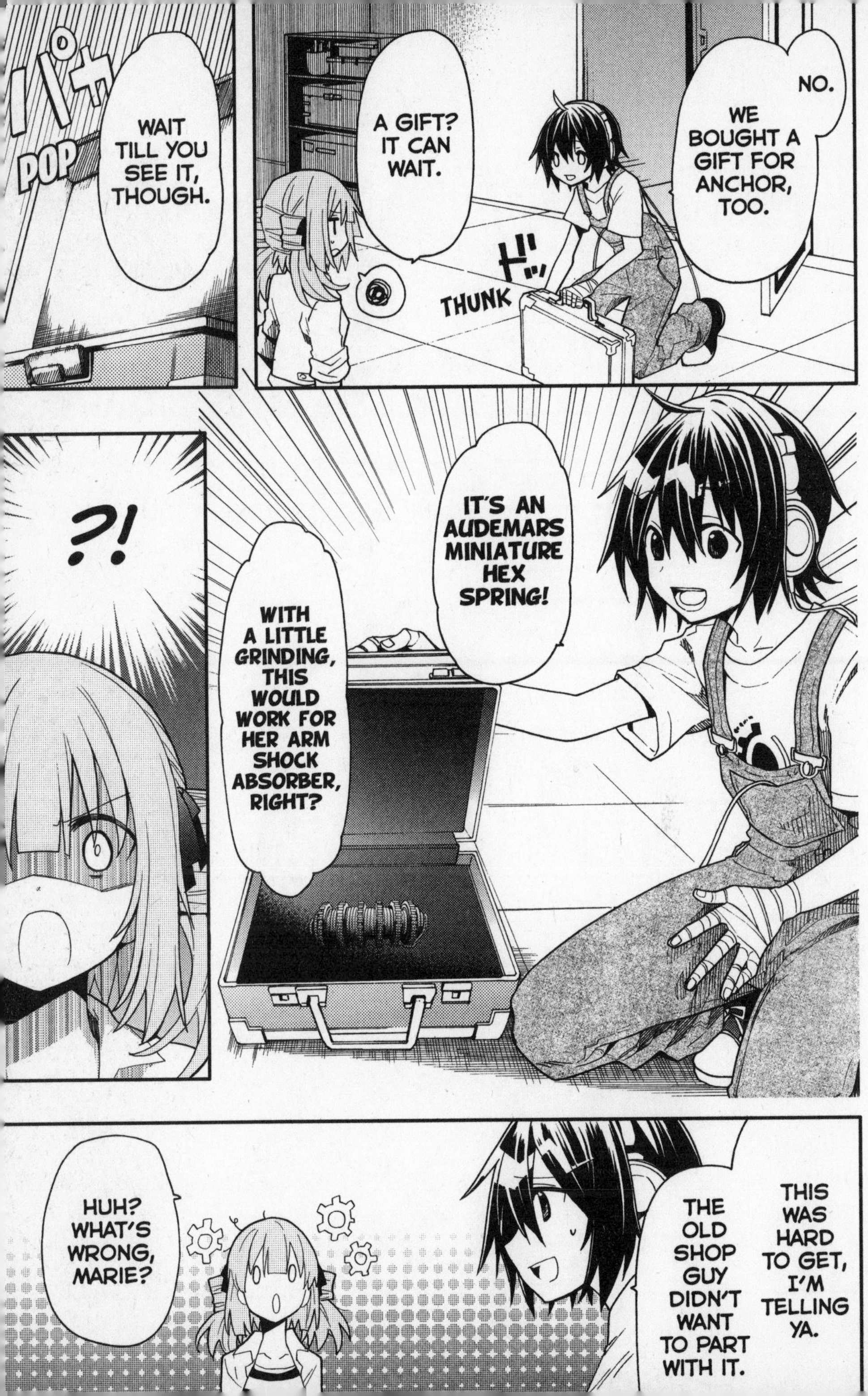
NO.
WE BOUGHT A GIFT FOR ANCHOR, TOO.
A GIFT? IT CAN WAIT.
THUNK
POP
WAIT TILL YOU SEE IT, THOUGH.
IT'S AN AUDEMARS MINIATURE HEX SPRING!
WITH A LITTLE GRINDING, THIS WOULD WORK FOR HER ARM SHOCK ABSORBER, RIGHT?
?!
THIS WAS HARD TO GET, I'M TELLING YA.
THE OLD SHOP GUY DIDN'T WANT TO PART WITH IT.
HUH? WHAT'S WRONG, MARIE?

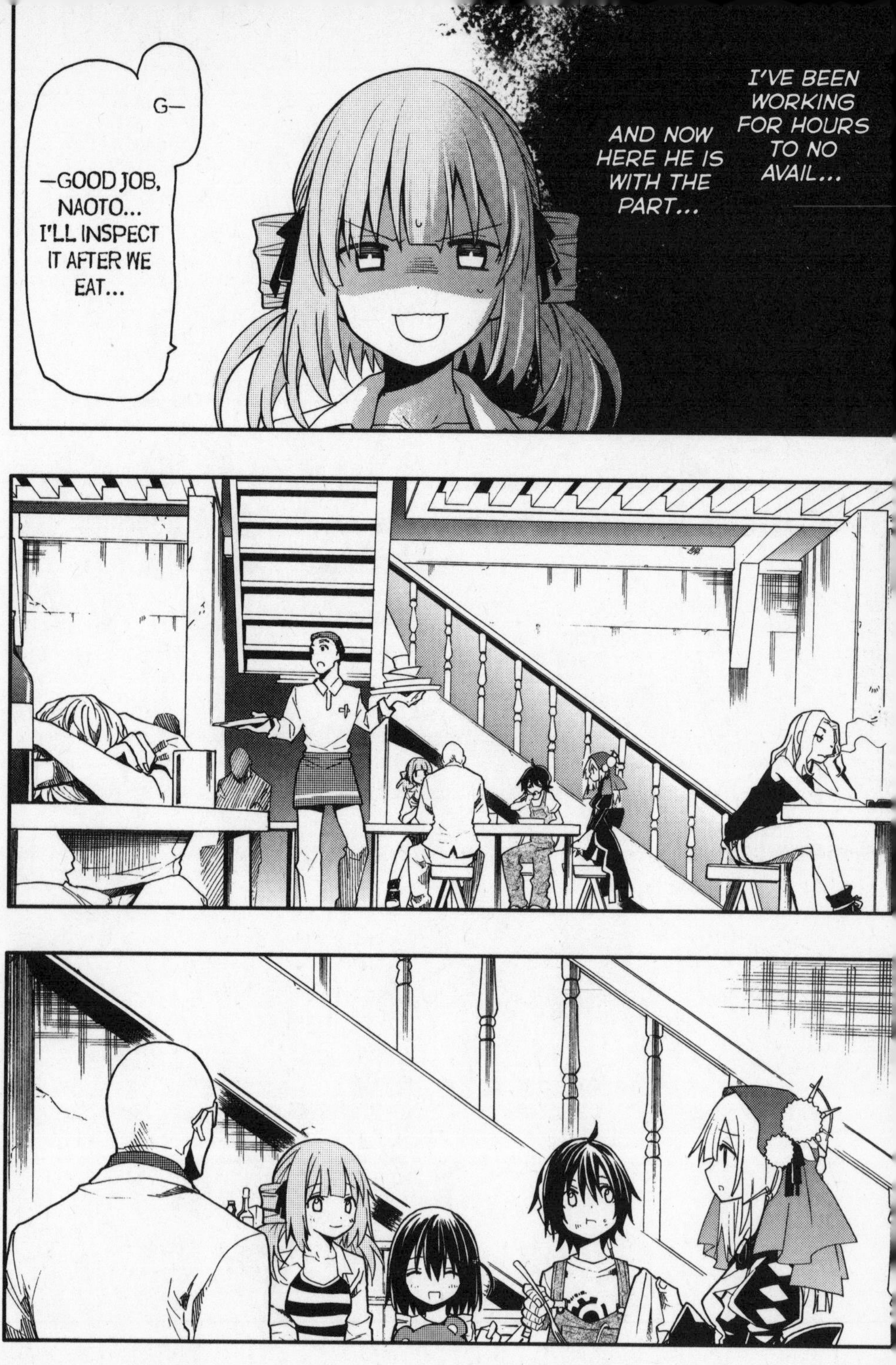
I'VE BEEN WORKING FOR HOURS TO NO AVAIL...
AND NOW HERE HE IS WITH THE PART...
G—
—GOOD JOB, NAOTO... I'LL INSPECT IT AFTER WE EAT...

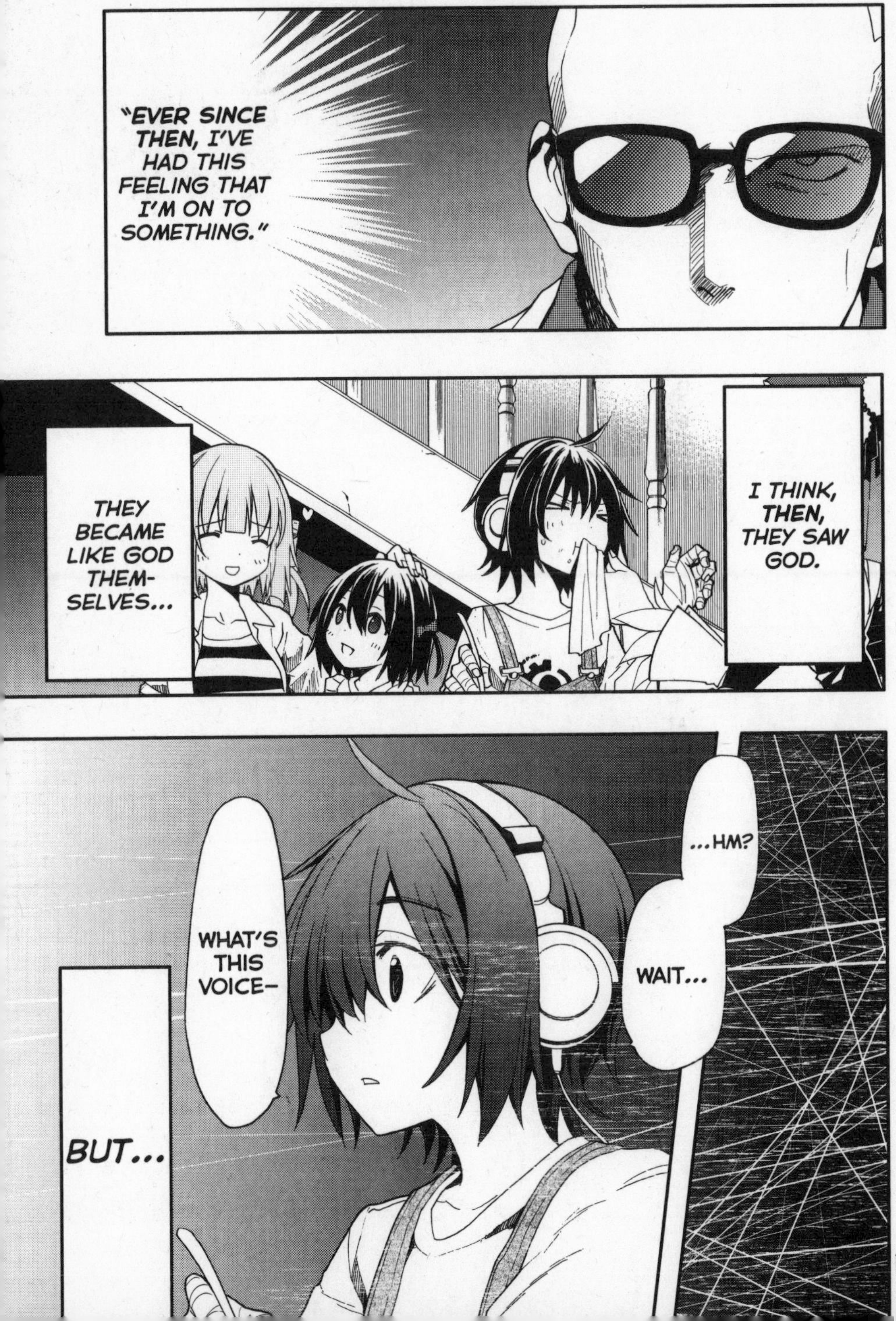
"EVER SINCE THEN, I'VE HAD THIS FEELING THAT I'M ON TO SOMETHING."
I THINK, THEN, THEY SAW GOD.
THEY BECAME LIKE GOD THEM-SELVES...
...HM?
WAIT...
WHAT'S THIS VOICE–
BUT...

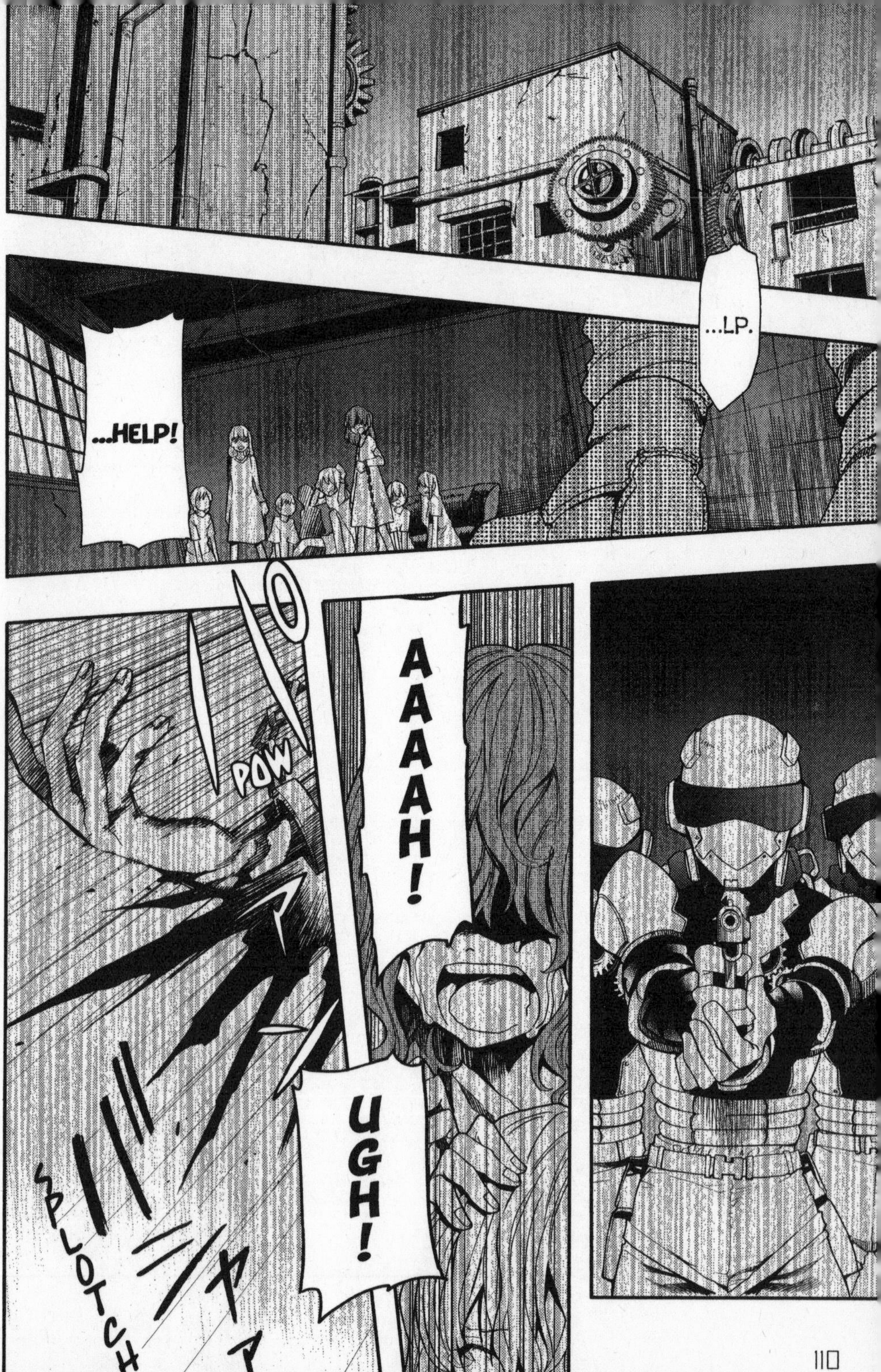
...LP.
...HELP!
AAAAAH!
UGH!
POW
SPLOTCH

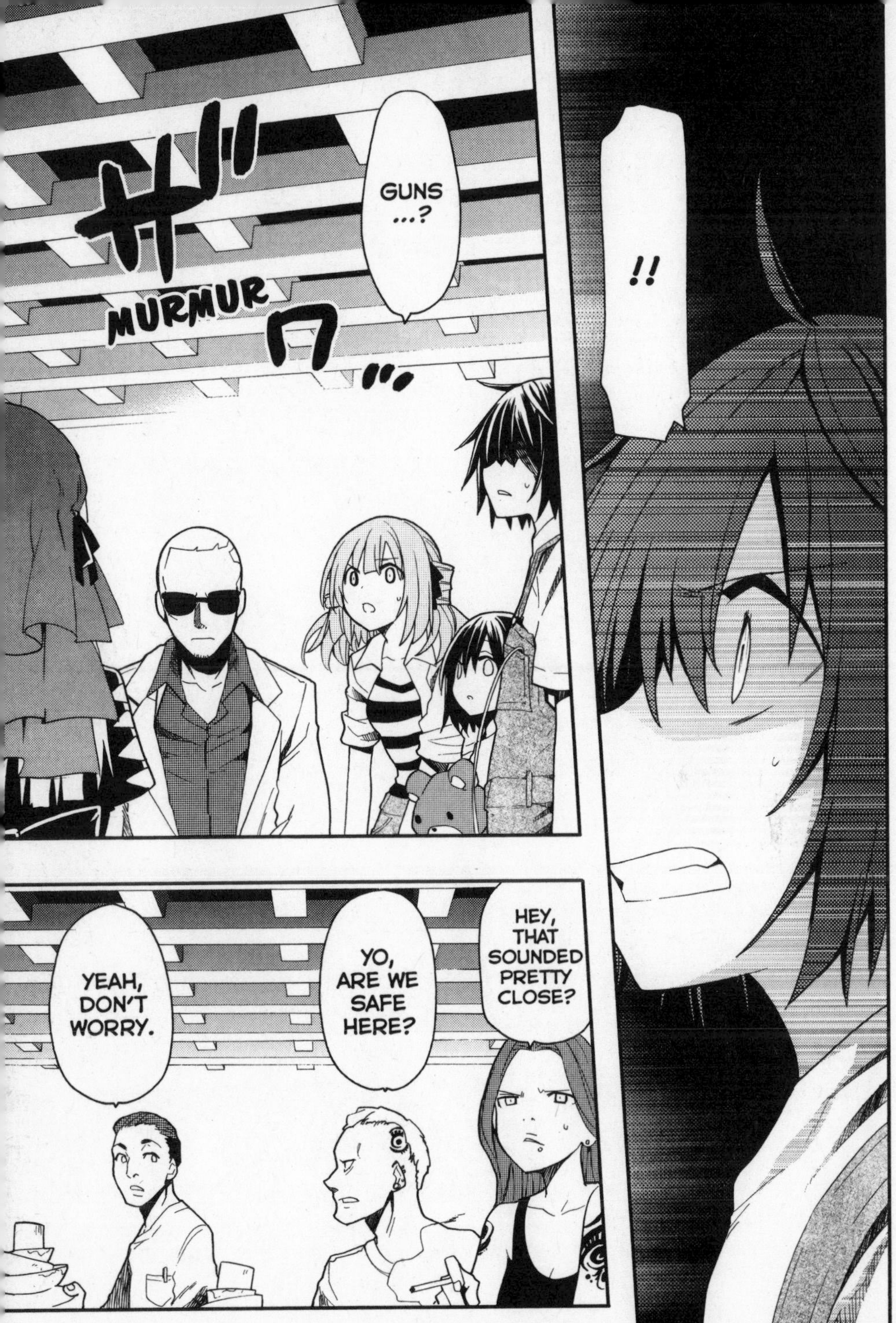
!!
GUNS ...?
ザワ
MURMUR
ワ
HEY, THAT SOUNDED PRETTY CLOSE?
YO, ARE WE SAFE HERE?
YEAH, DON'T WORRY.

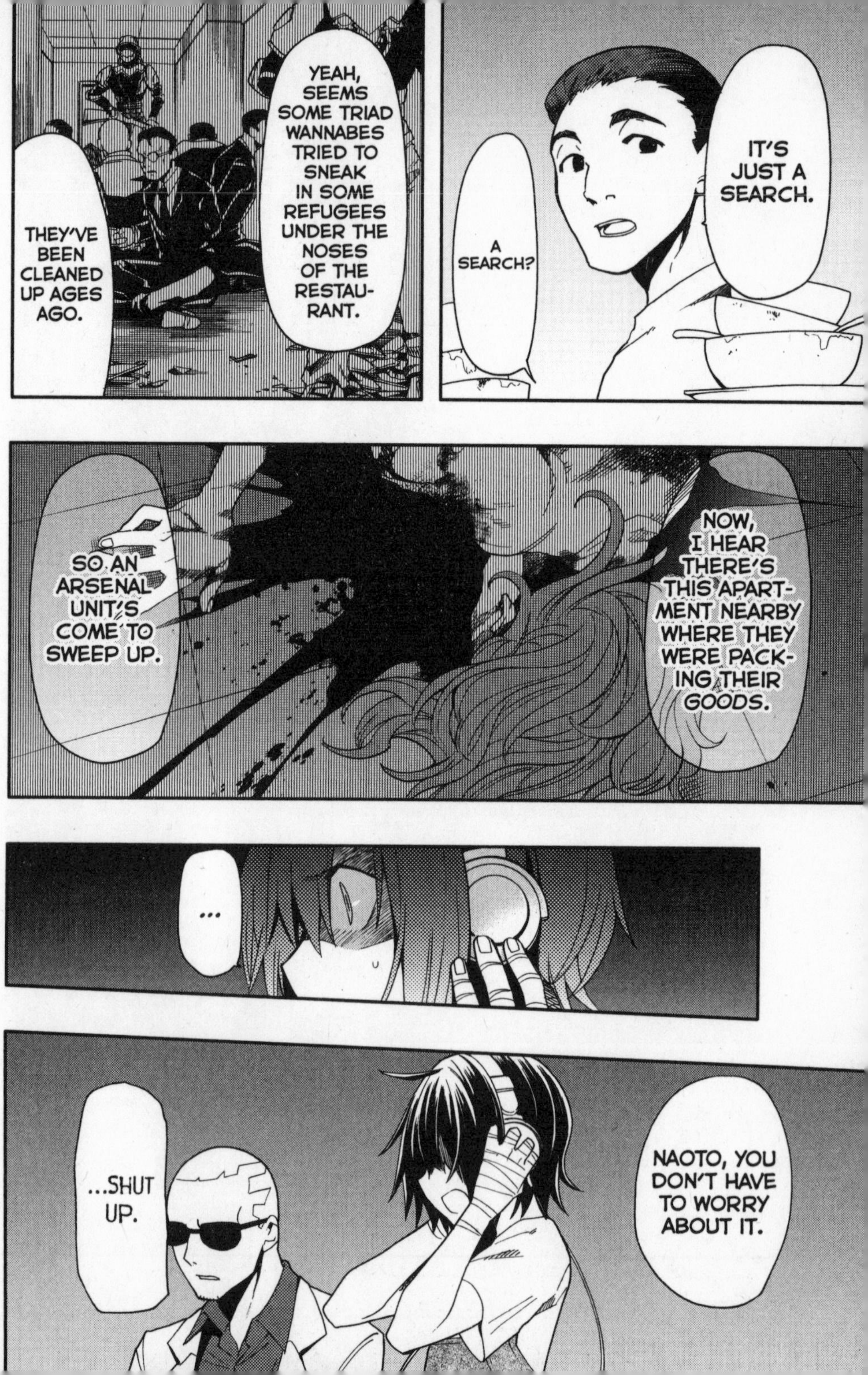
IT'S JUST A SEARCH.
A SEARCH?
YEAH, SEEMS SOME TRIAD WANNABES TRIED TO SNEAK IN SOME REFUGEES UNDER THE NOSES OF THE RESTAU-RANT.
THEY'VE BEEN CLEANED UP AGES AGO.
NOW, I HEAR THERE'S THIS APART-MENT NEARBY WHERE THEY WERE PACK-ING THEIR GOODS.
SO AN ARSENAL UNIT'S COME TO SWEEP UP.
...
NAOTO, YOU DON'T HAVE TO WORRY ABOUT IT.
...SHUT UP.

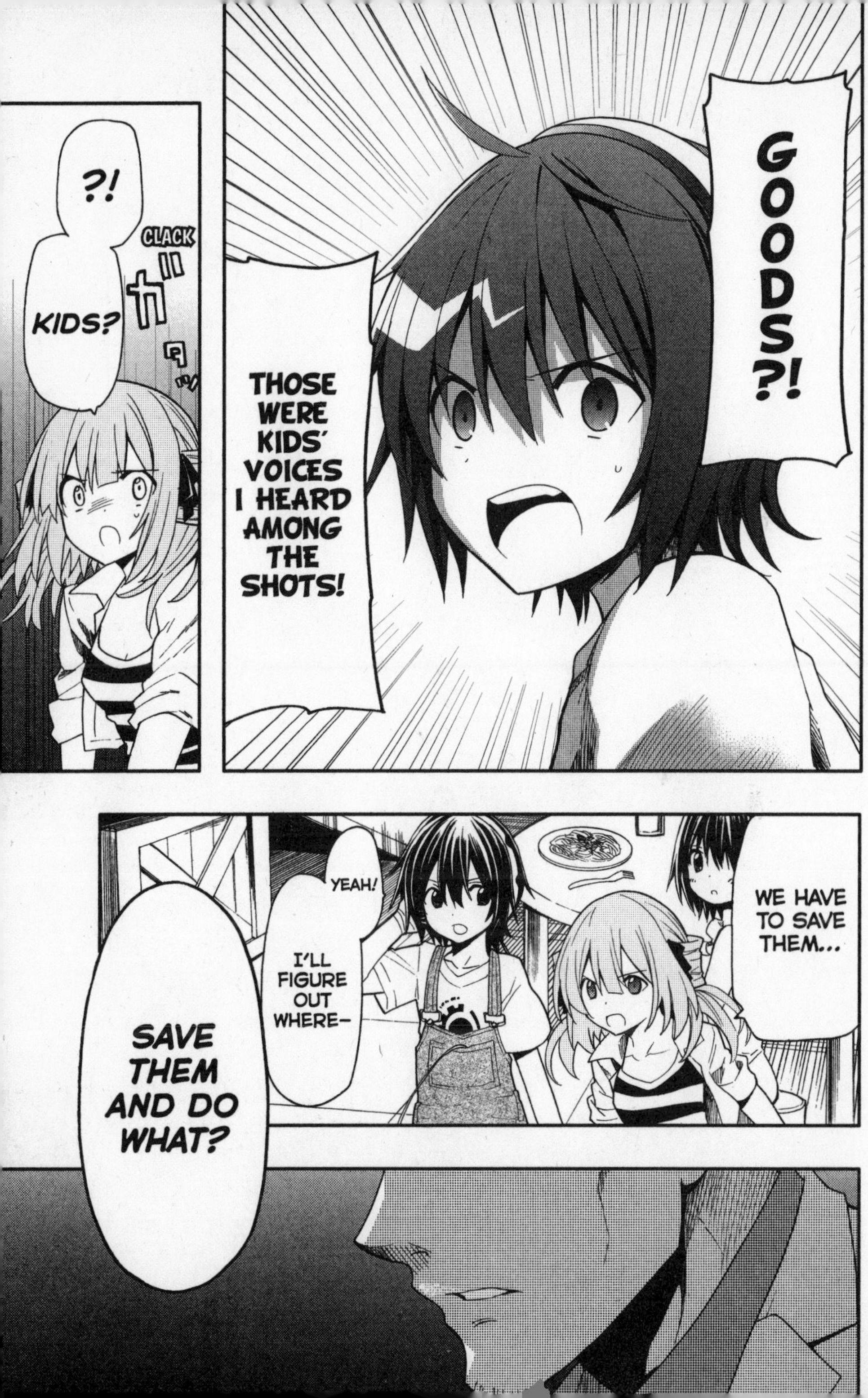
GOODS?!
THOSE WERE KIDS' VOICES I HEARD AMONG THE SHOTS!
?!
KIDS?
CLACK
WE HAVE TO SAVE THEM...
YEAH!
I'LL FIGURE OUT WHERE–
SAVE THEM AND DO WHAT?

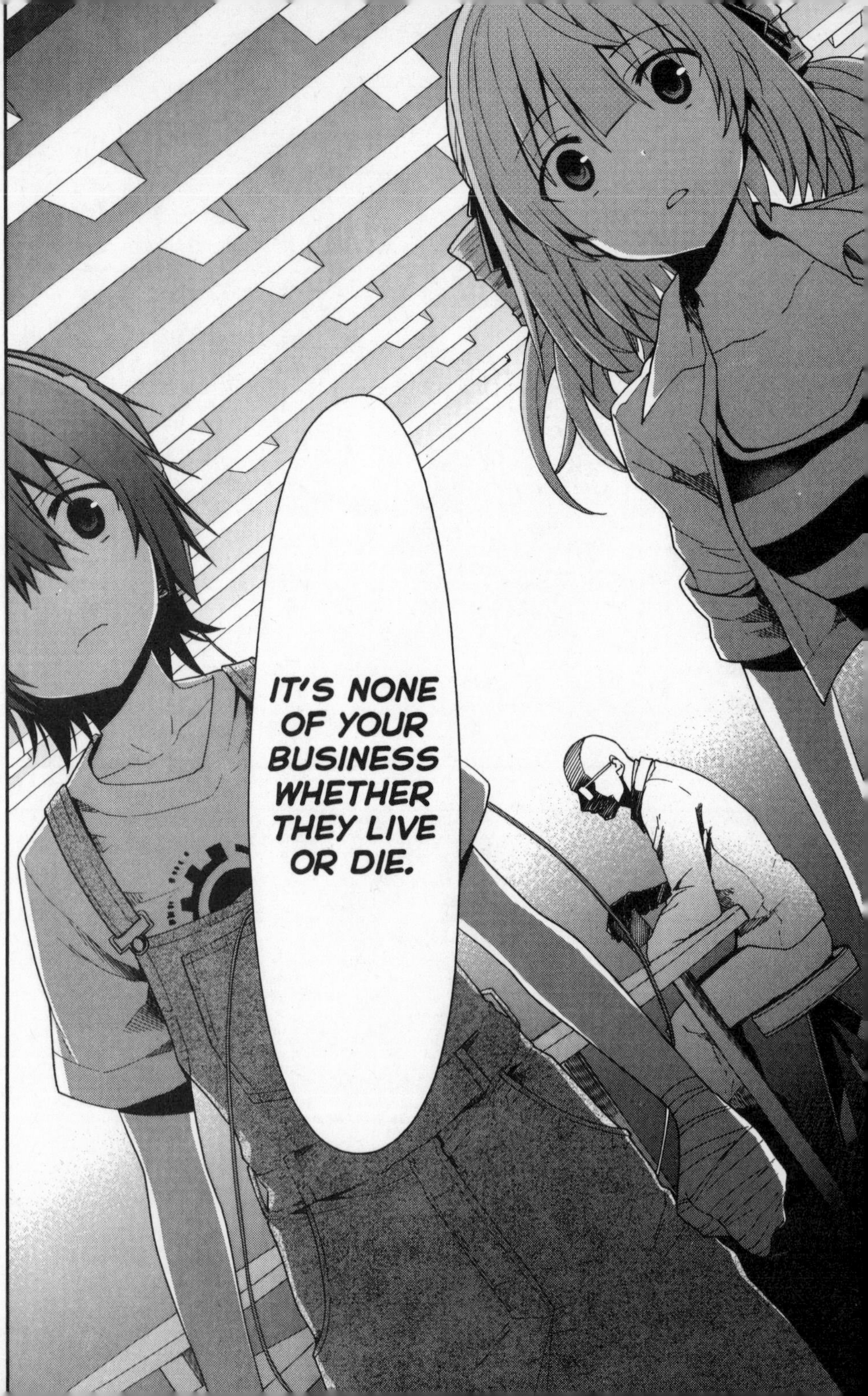
IT'S NONE OF YOUR BUSINESS WHETHER THEY LIVE OR DIE.

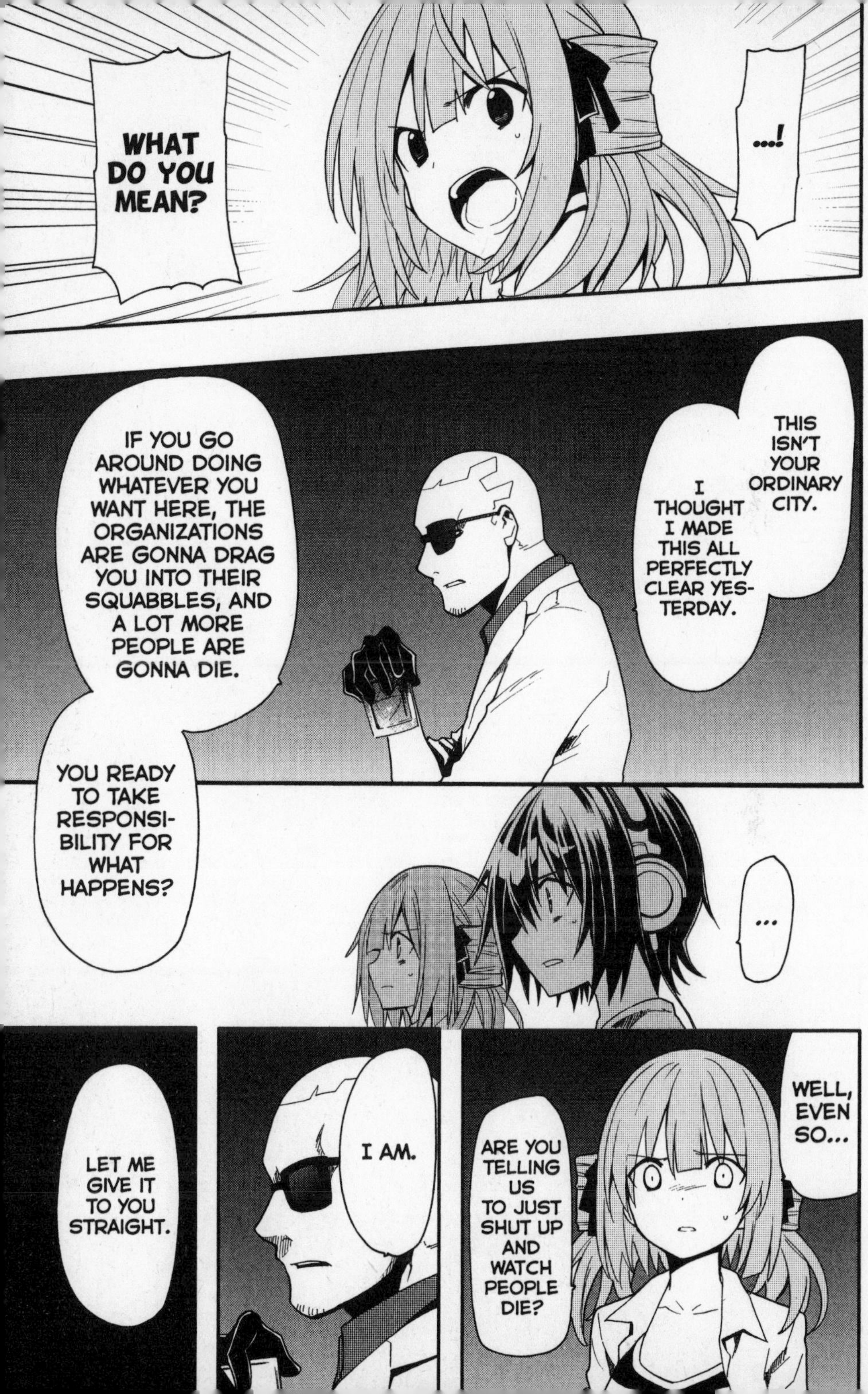
...!
WHAT DO YOU MEAN?
THIS ISN'T YOUR ORDINARY CITY.
I THOUGHT I MADE THIS ALL PERFECTLY CLEAR YES-TERDAY.
IF YOU GO AROUND DOING WHATEVER YOU WANT HERE, THE ORGANIZATIONS ARE GONNA DRAG YOU INTO THEIR SQUABBLES, AND A LOT MORE PEOPLE ARE GONNA DIE.
YOU READY TO TAKE RESPONSI-BILITY FOR WHAT HAPPENS?
...
WELL, EVEN SO...
ARE YOU TELLING US TO JUST SHUT UP AND WATCH PEOPLE DIE?
I AM.
LET ME GIVE IT TO YOU STRAIGHT.

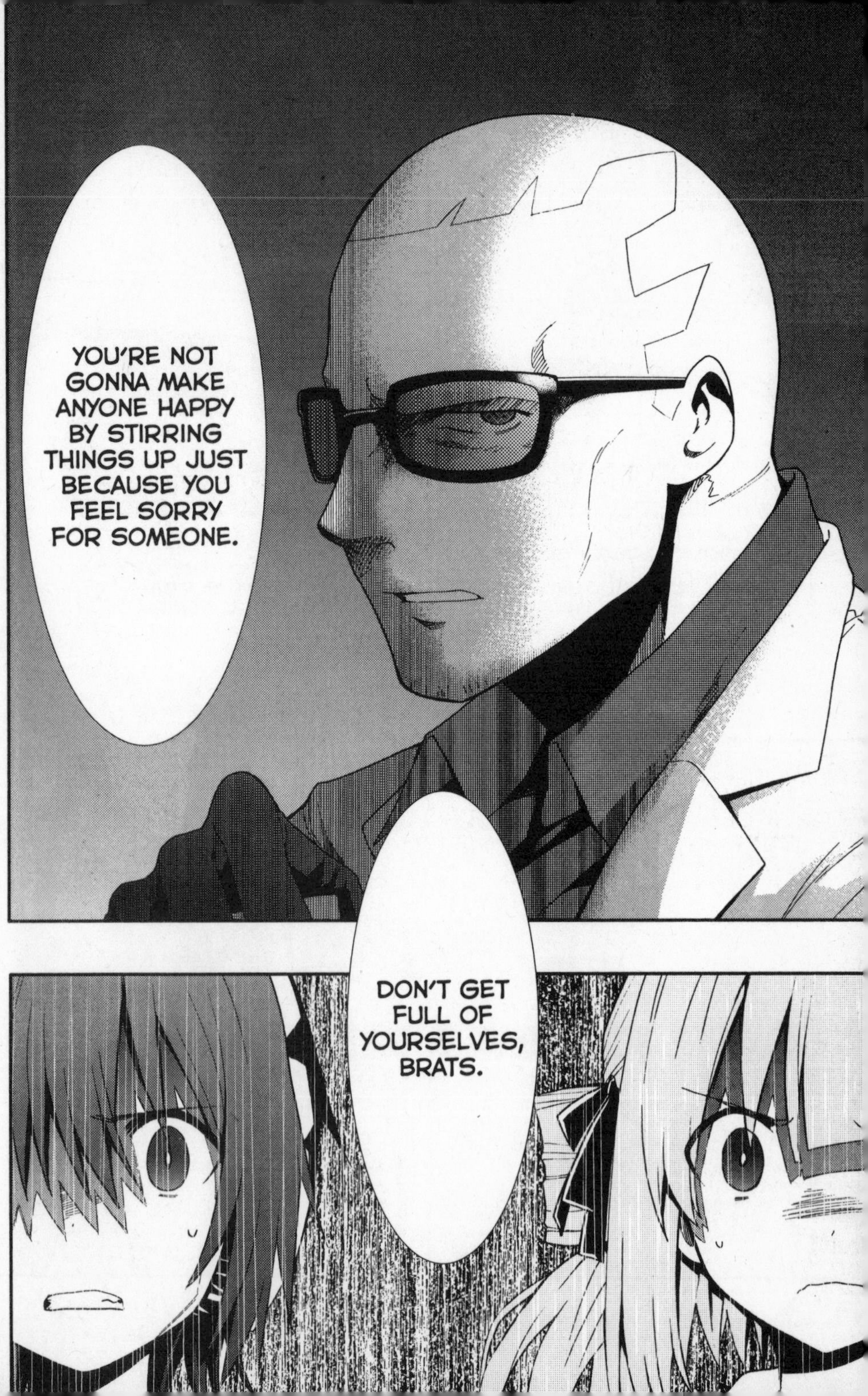
YOU'RE NOT GONNA MAKE ANYONE HAPPY BY STIRRING THINGS UP JUST BECAUSE YOU FEEL SORRY FOR SOMEONE.
DON'T GET FULL OF YOURSELVES, BRATS.

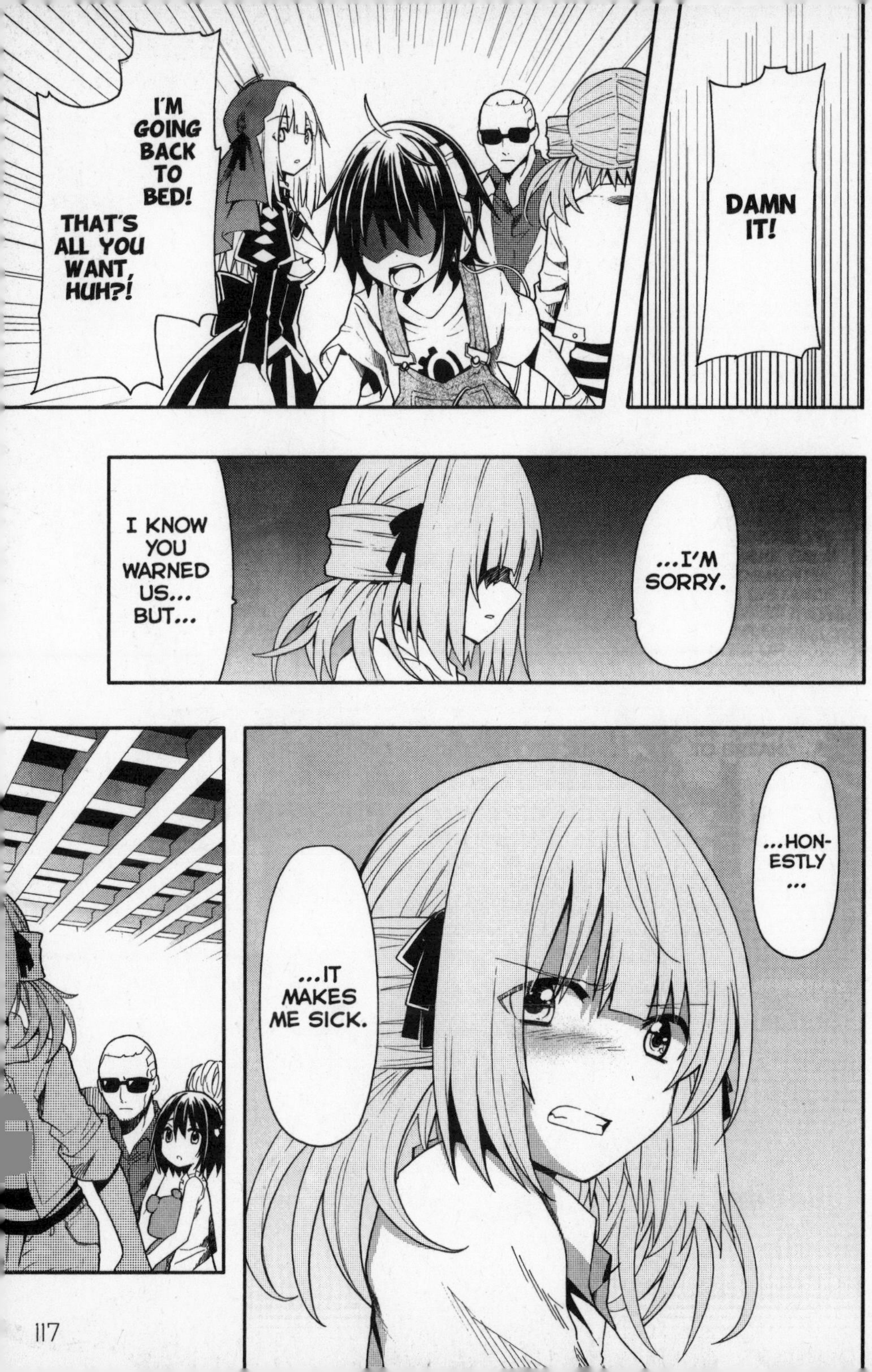
DAMN IT!
I'M GOING BACK TO BED!
THAT'S ALL YOU WANT, HUH?!
...I'M SORRY.
I KNOW YOU WARNED US... BUT...
...HON-ESTLY...
...IT MAKES ME SICK.

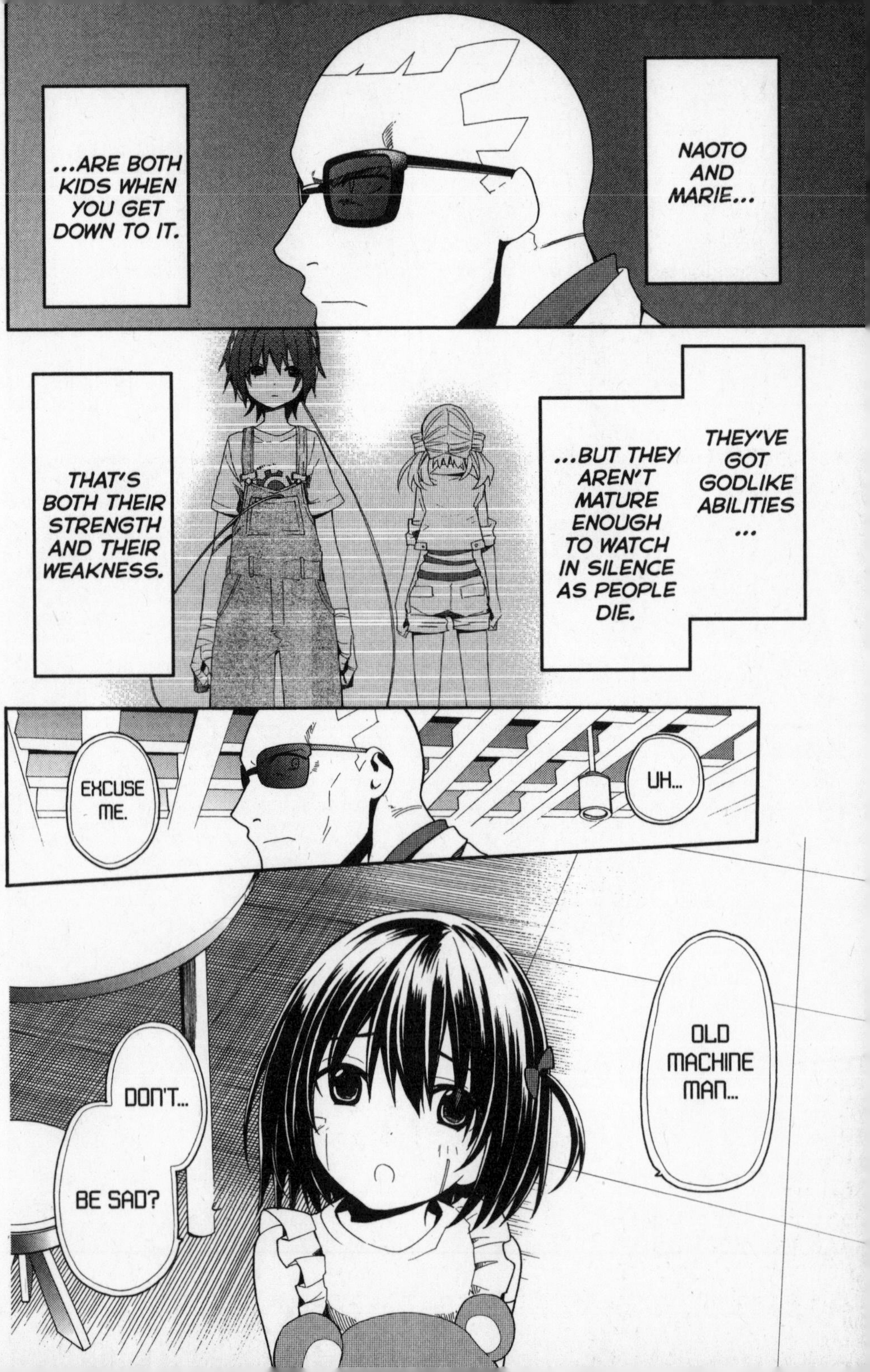
NAOTO AND MARIE...
...ARE BOTH KIDS WHEN YOU GET DOWN TO IT.
THEY'VE GOT GODLIKE ABILITIES ...
...BUT THEY AREN'T MATURE ENOUGH TO WATCH IN SILENCE AS PEOPLE DIE.
THAT'S BOTH THEIR STRENGTH AND THEIR WEAKNESS.
UH...
EXCUSE ME.
OLD MACHINE MAN...
DON'T...
BE SAD?

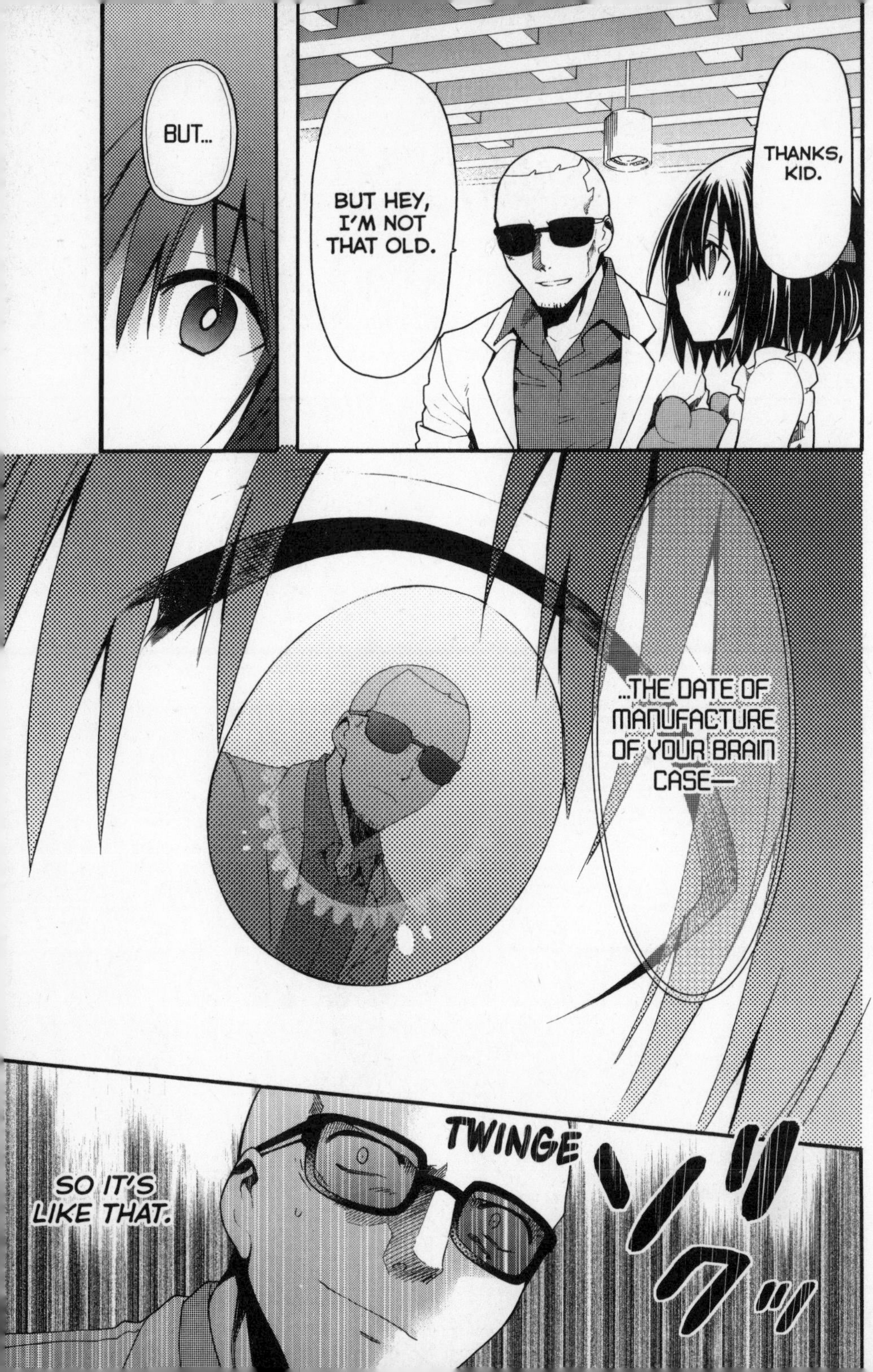
THANKS, KID.
BUT HEY, I'M NOT THAT OLD.
BUT...
...THE DATE OF MANUFACTURE OF YOUR BRAIN CASE—
TWINGE
SO IT'S LIKE THAT.

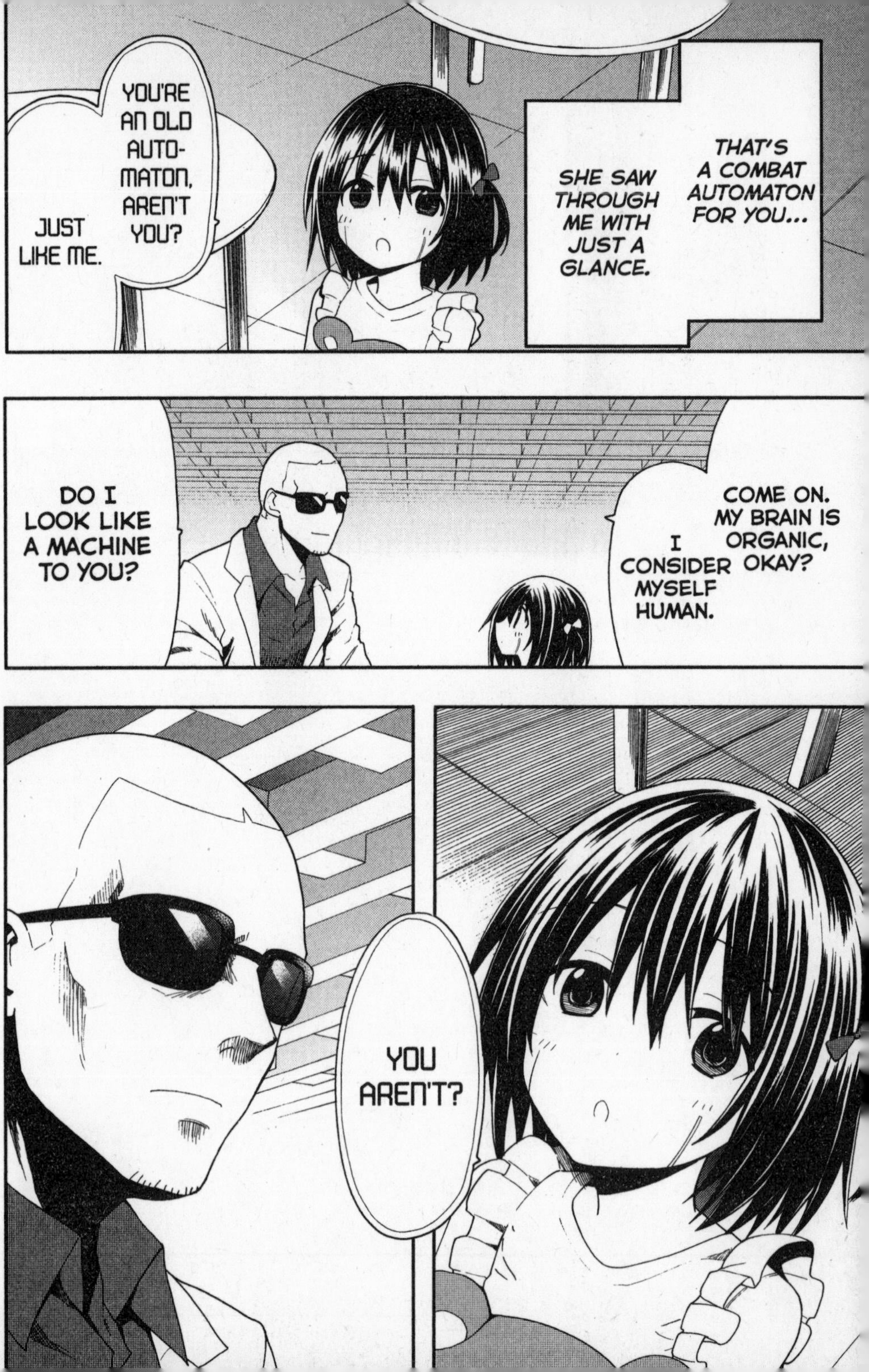
THAT'S A COMBAT AUTOMATON FOR YOU...
SHE SAW THROUGH ME WITH JUST A GLANCE.
YOU'RE AN OLD AUTO-MATON, AREN'T YOU?
JUST LIKE ME.
COME ON. MY BRAIN IS ORGANIC, OKAY?
I CONSIDER MYSELF HUMAN.
DO I LOOK LIKE A MACHINE TO YOU?
YOU AREN'T?

COME TO THINK OF IT, IT WAS LIKE THAT THEN, TOO.

THIS AUTOMATON DISTINGUISHES BETWEEN HUMANS AND MACHINES.

AND SHE DEFINES ME...

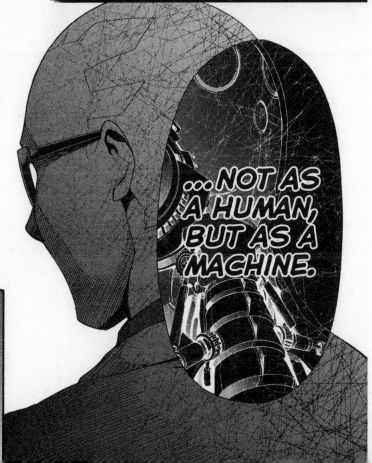

...NOT AS A HUMAN, BUT AS A MACHINE.

AN-CHOR.

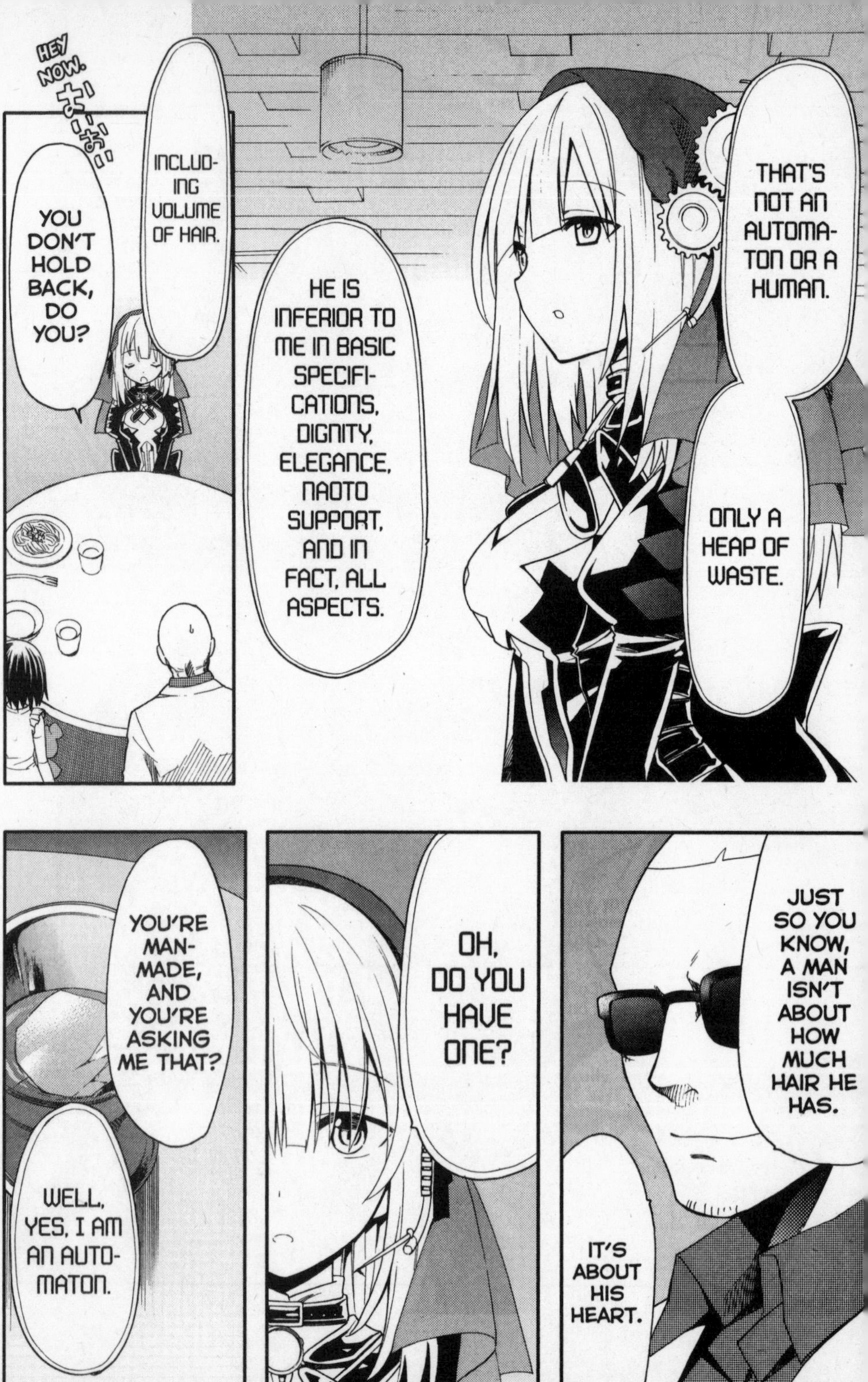
THAT'S NOT AN AUTOMATON OR A HUMAN.
ONLY A HEAP OF WASTE.
HE IS INFERIOR TO ME IN BASIC SPECIFICATIONS, DIGNITY, ELEGANCE, NAOTO SUPPORT, AND IN FACT, ALL ASPECTS.
INCLUDING VOLUME OF HAIR.
YOU DON'T HOLD BACK, DO YOU?
HEY NOW.
JUST SO YOU KNOW, A MAN ISN'T ABOUT HOW MUCH HAIR HE HAS.
IT'S ABOUT HIS HEART.
OH, DO YOU HAVE ONE?
YOU'RE MAN-MADE, AND YOU'RE ASKING ME THAT?
WELL, YES, I AM AN AUTOMATON.

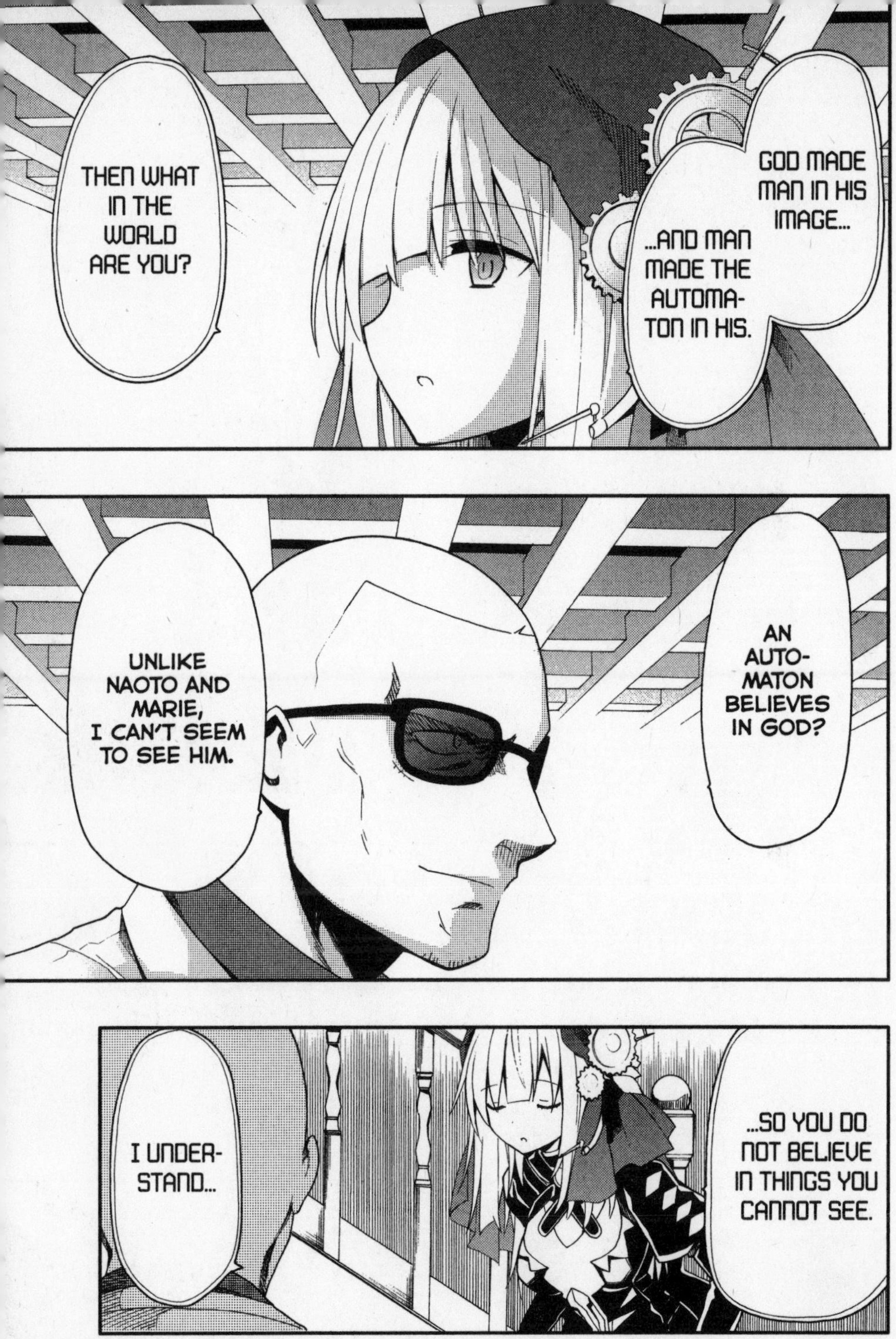
GOD MADE MAN IN HIS IMAGE...
...AND MAN MADE THE AUTOMATON IN HIS.
THEN WHAT IN THE WORLD ARE YOU?
AN AUTOMATON BELIEVES IN GOD?
UNLIKE NAOTO AND MARIE, I CAN'T SEEM TO SEE HIM.
...SO YOU DO NOT BELIEVE IN THINGS YOU CANNOT SEE.
I UNDERSTAND...

...THAT YOU ARE A FOOL...

...UNABLE TO RECOGNIZE THE EXIST-ENCE...

...OF THINGS BEYOND YOUR EYES AND EARS.

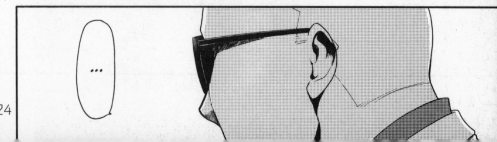

...

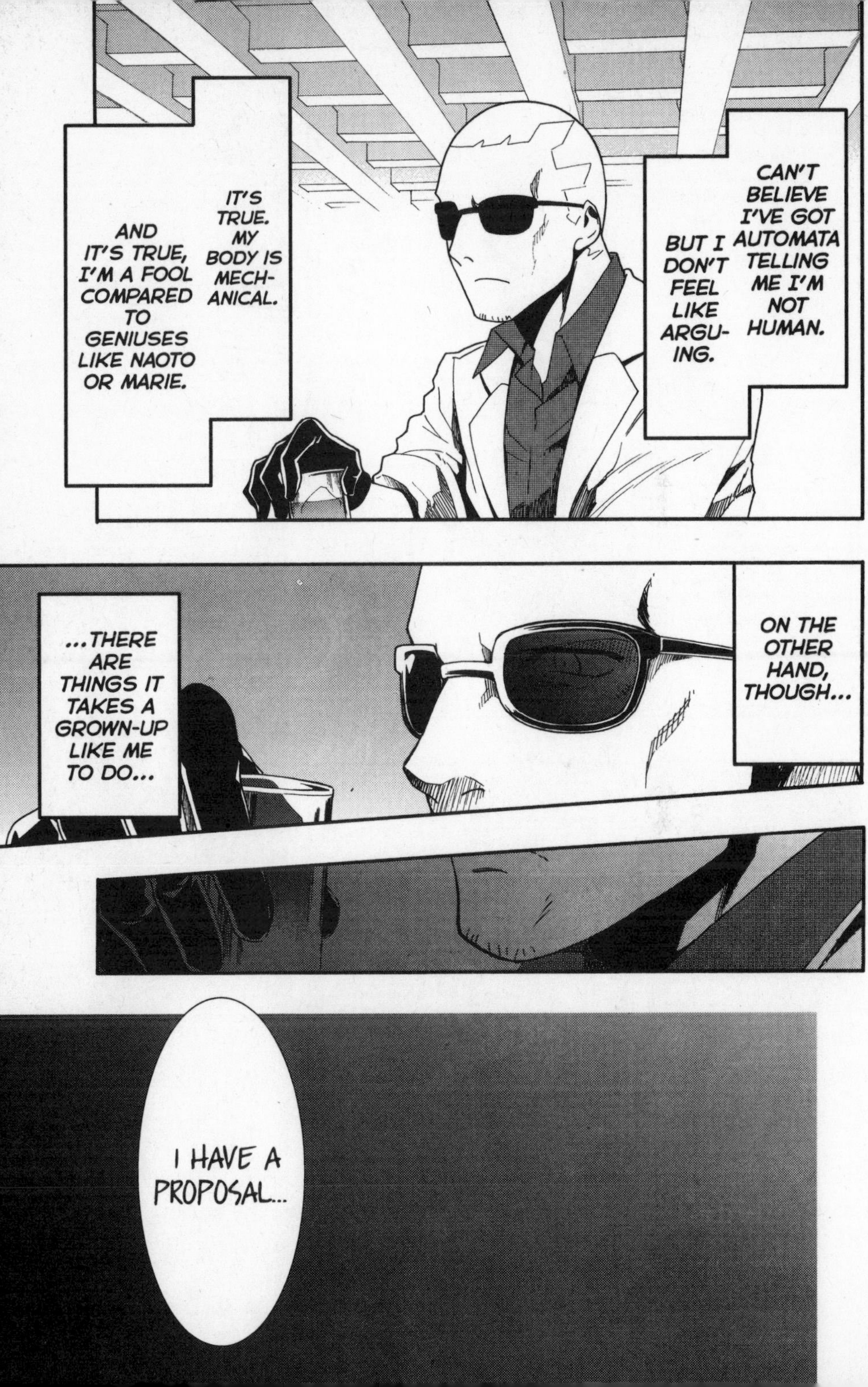
CAN'T BELIEVE I'VE GOT AUTOMATA TELLING ME I'M NOT HUMAN.
BUT I DON'T FEEL LIKE ARGU-ING.
IT'S TRUE. MY BODY IS MECH-ANICAL.
AND IT'S TRUE, I'M A FOOL COMPARED TO GENIUSES LIKE NAOTO OR MARIE.
ON THE OTHER HAND, THOUGH...
...THERE ARE THINGS IT TAKES A GROWN-UP LIKE ME TO DO...
I HAVE A PROPOSAL...

"CAN YOU DELIVER ME EITHER NAOTO OR MARIE?"

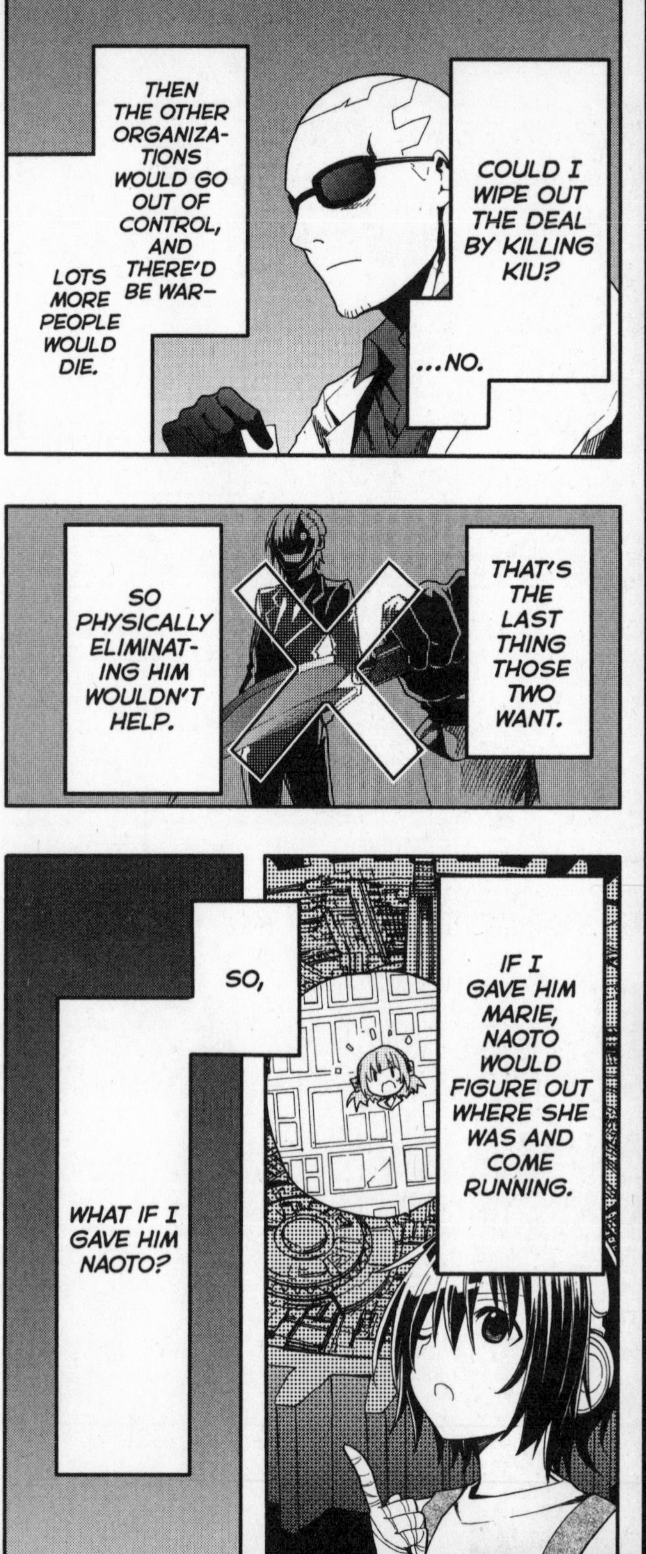

COULD I WIPE OUT THE DEAL BY KILLING KIU?
...NO.
THEN THE OTHER ORGANIZA-TIONS WOULD GO OUT OF CONTROL, AND THERE'D BE WAR—
LOTS MORE PEOPLE WOULD DIE.
THAT'S THE LAST THING THOSE TWO WANT.
SO PHYSICALLY ELIMINAT-ING HIM WOULDN'T HELP.
IF I GAVE HIM MARIE, NAOTO WOULD FIGURE OUT WHERE SHE WAS AND COME RUNNING.
SO,
WHAT IF I GAVE HIM NAOTO?

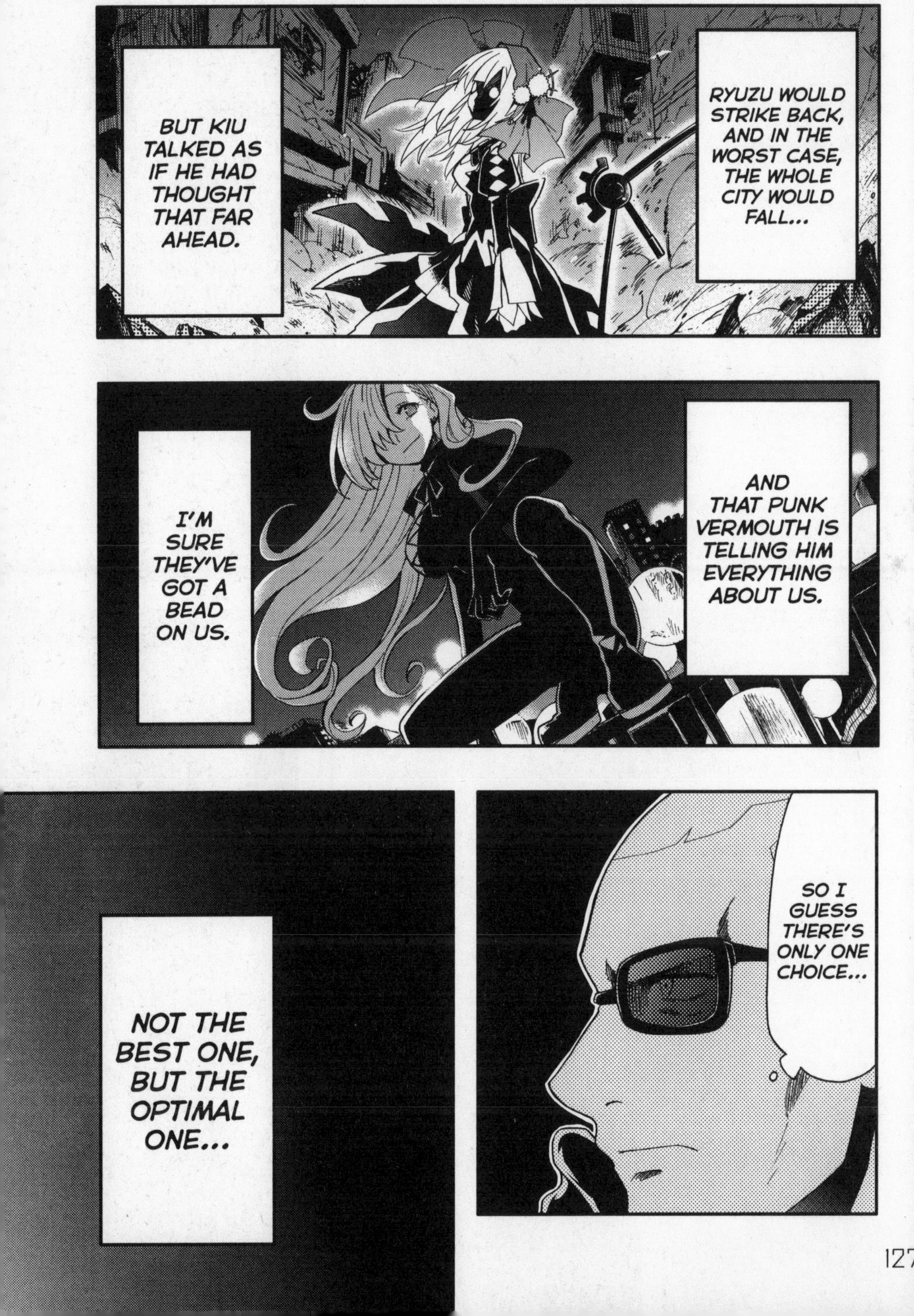
RYUZU WOULD STRIKE BACK, AND IN THE WORST CASE, THE WHOLE CITY WOULD FALL...
BUT KIU TALKED AS IF HE HAD THOUGHT THAT FAR AHEAD.
AND THAT PUNK VERMOUTH IS TELLING HIM EVERYTHING ABOUT US.
I'M SURE THEY'VE GOT A BEAD ON US.
SO I GUESS THERE'S ONLY ONE CHOICE...
NOT THE BEST ONE, BUT THE OPTIMAL ONE...

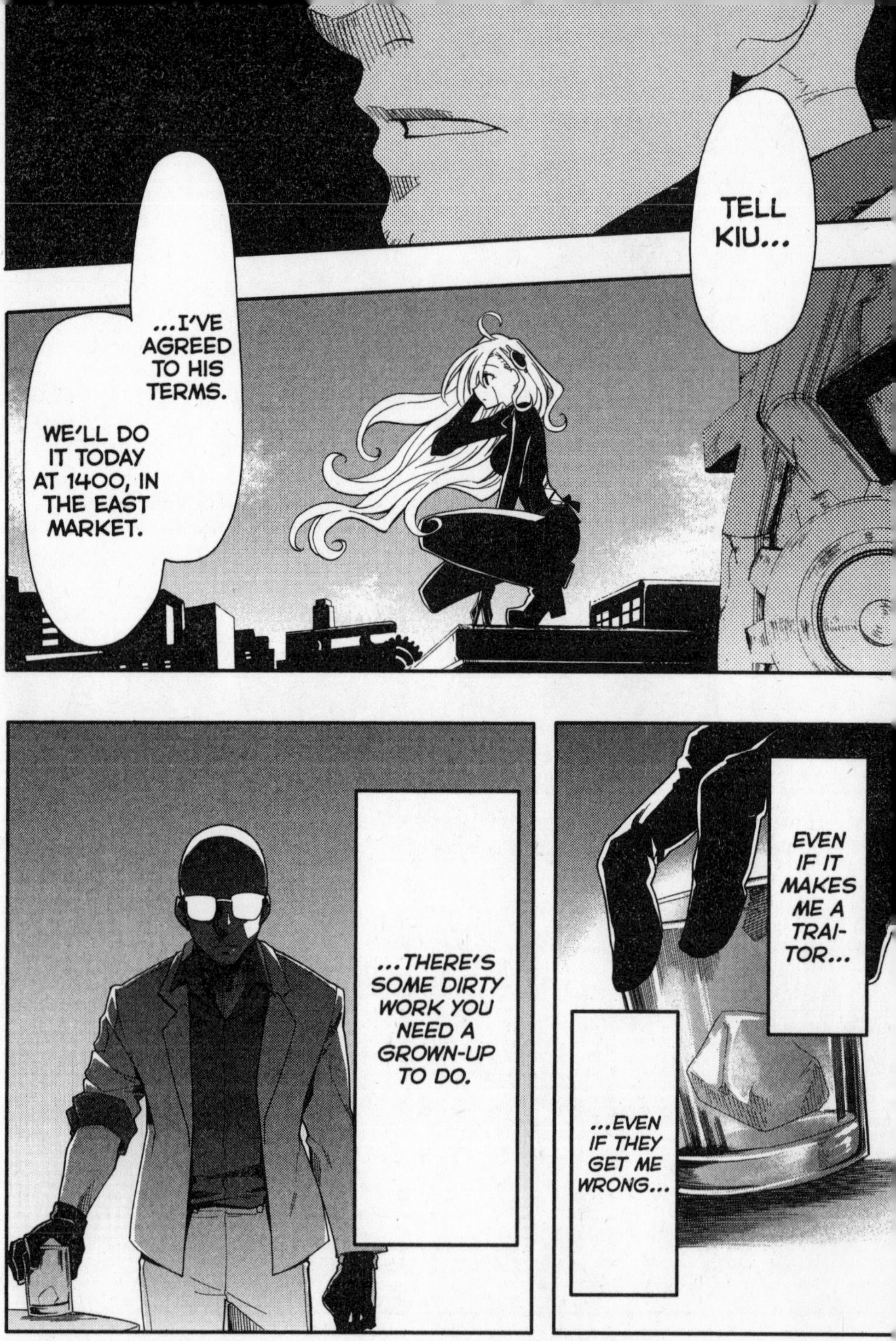
TELL KIU...
...I'VE AGREED TO HIS TERMS.
WE'LL DO IT TODAY AT 1400, IN THE EAST MARKET.
EVEN IF IT MAKES ME A TRAI-TOR...
...EVEN IF THEY GET ME WRONG...
...THERE'S SOME DIRTY WORK YOU NEED A GROWN-UP TO DO.

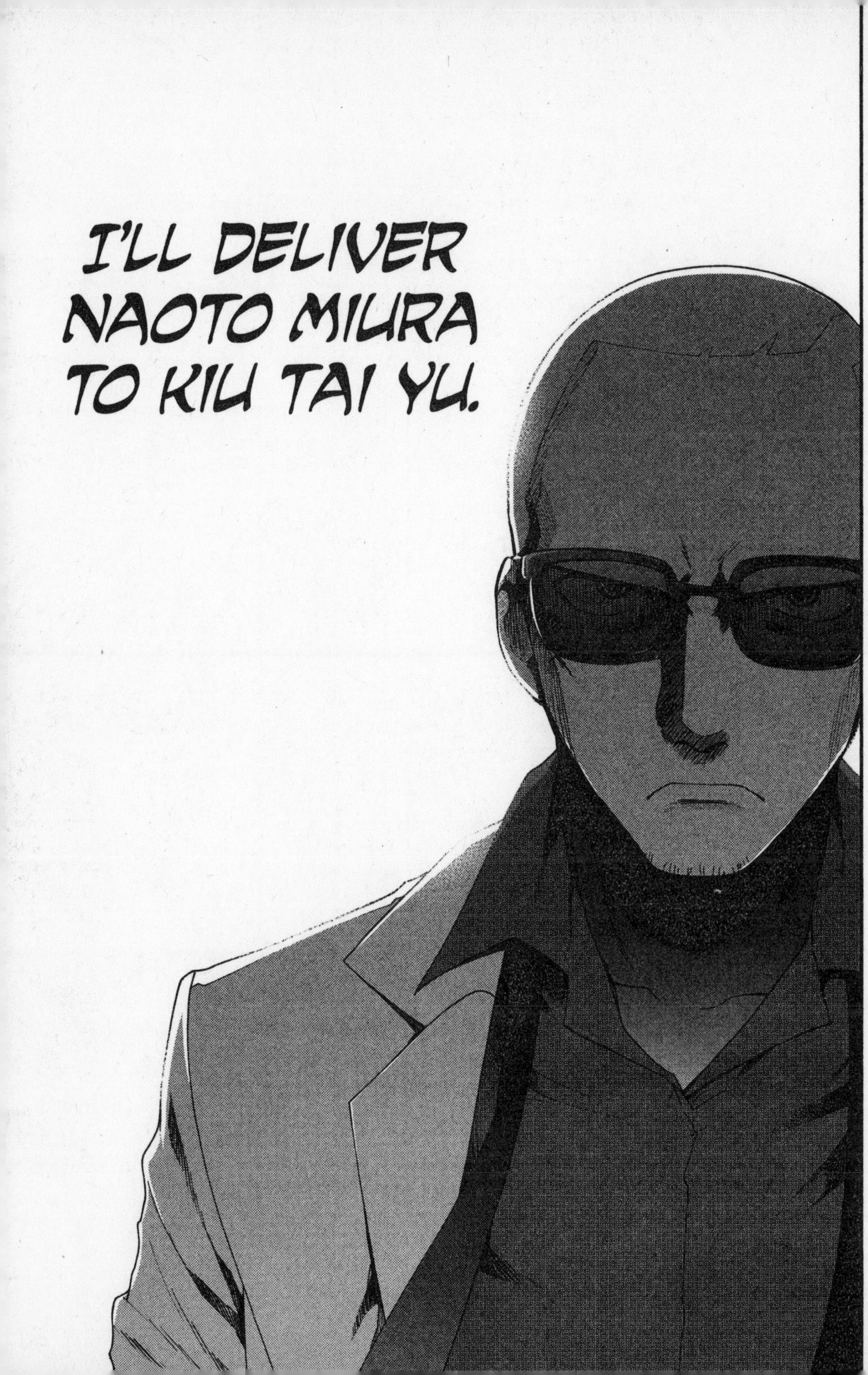
I'LL DELIVER NAOTO MIURA TO KIU TAI YU.

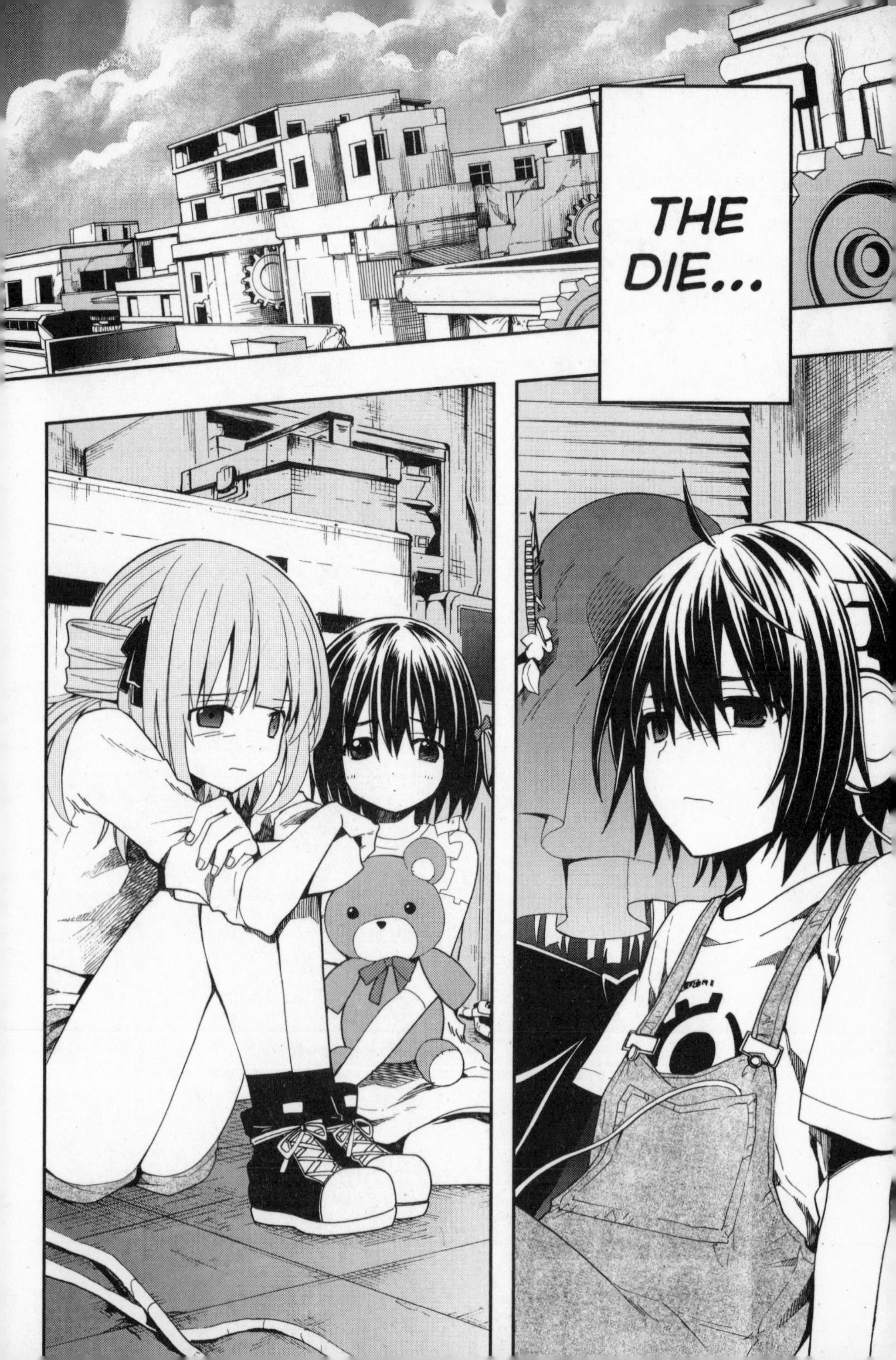
THE DIE...

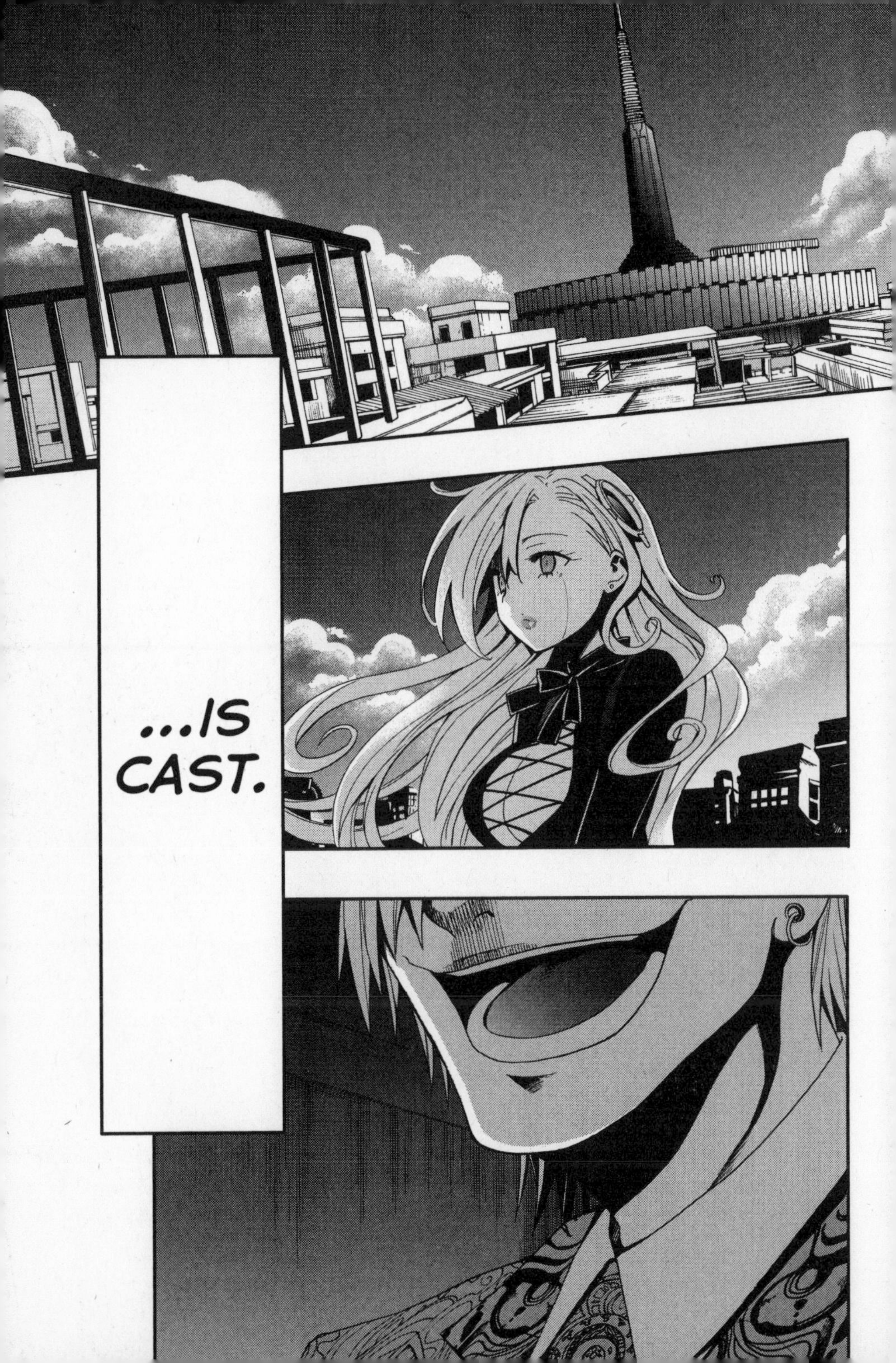
...IS
CAST.

Clockwork Planet

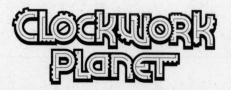

GRID SHANGRI-LA

EAST MARKET: CHAKRAN STREET

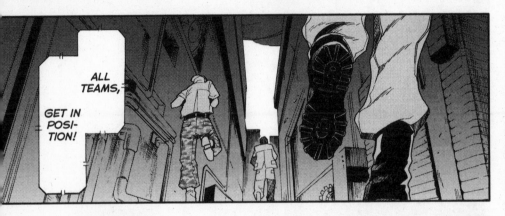

ALL TEAMS,

GET IN POSITION!

TEAM A, IN POSITION.

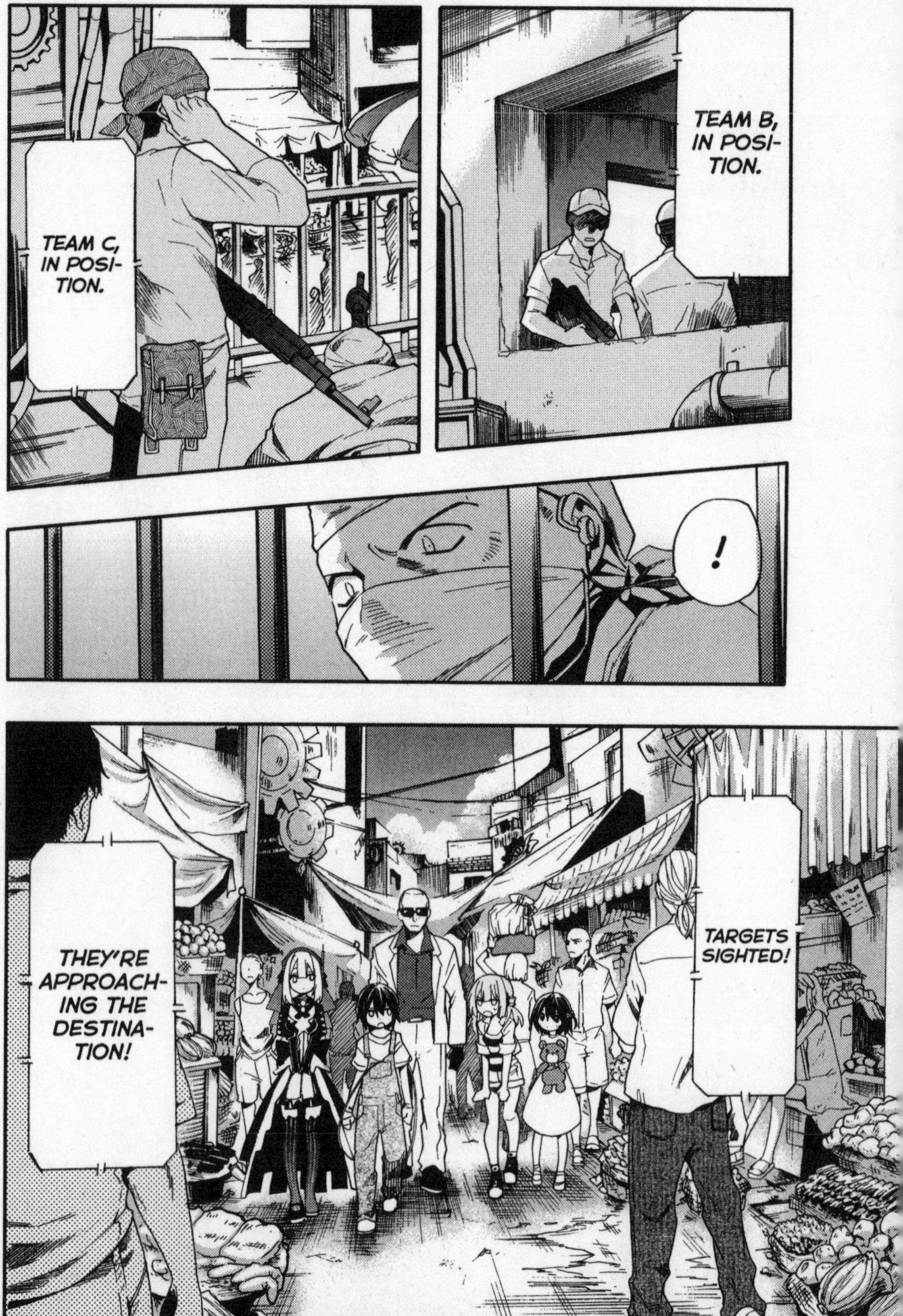
TEAM B, IN POSI-TION.
TEAM C, IN POSI-TION.
!
TARGETS SIGHTED!
THEY'RE APPROACH-ING THE DESTINA-TION!

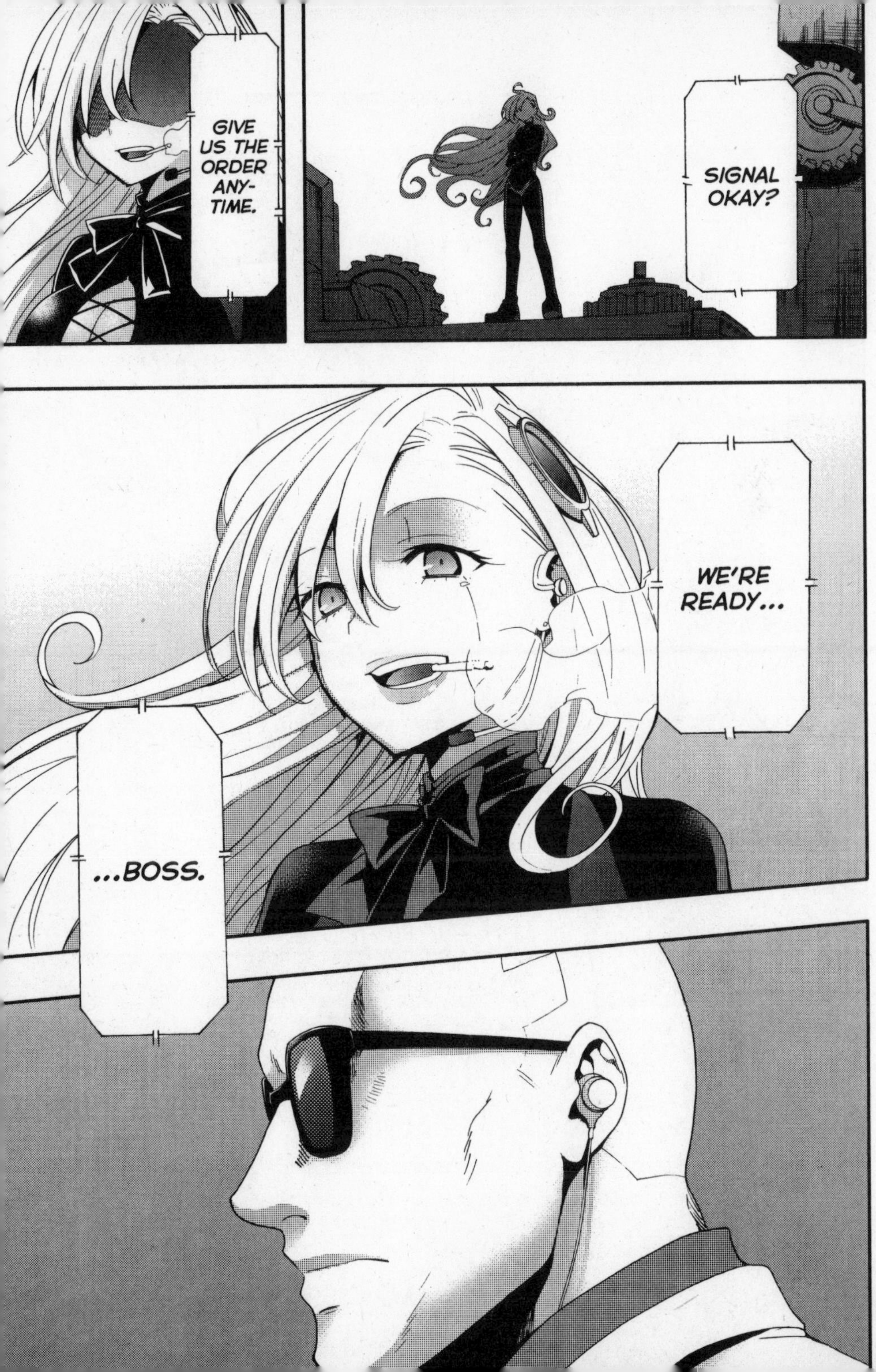
SIGNAL OKAY?
GIVE US THE ORDER ANY-TIME.
WE'RE READY...
...BOSS.

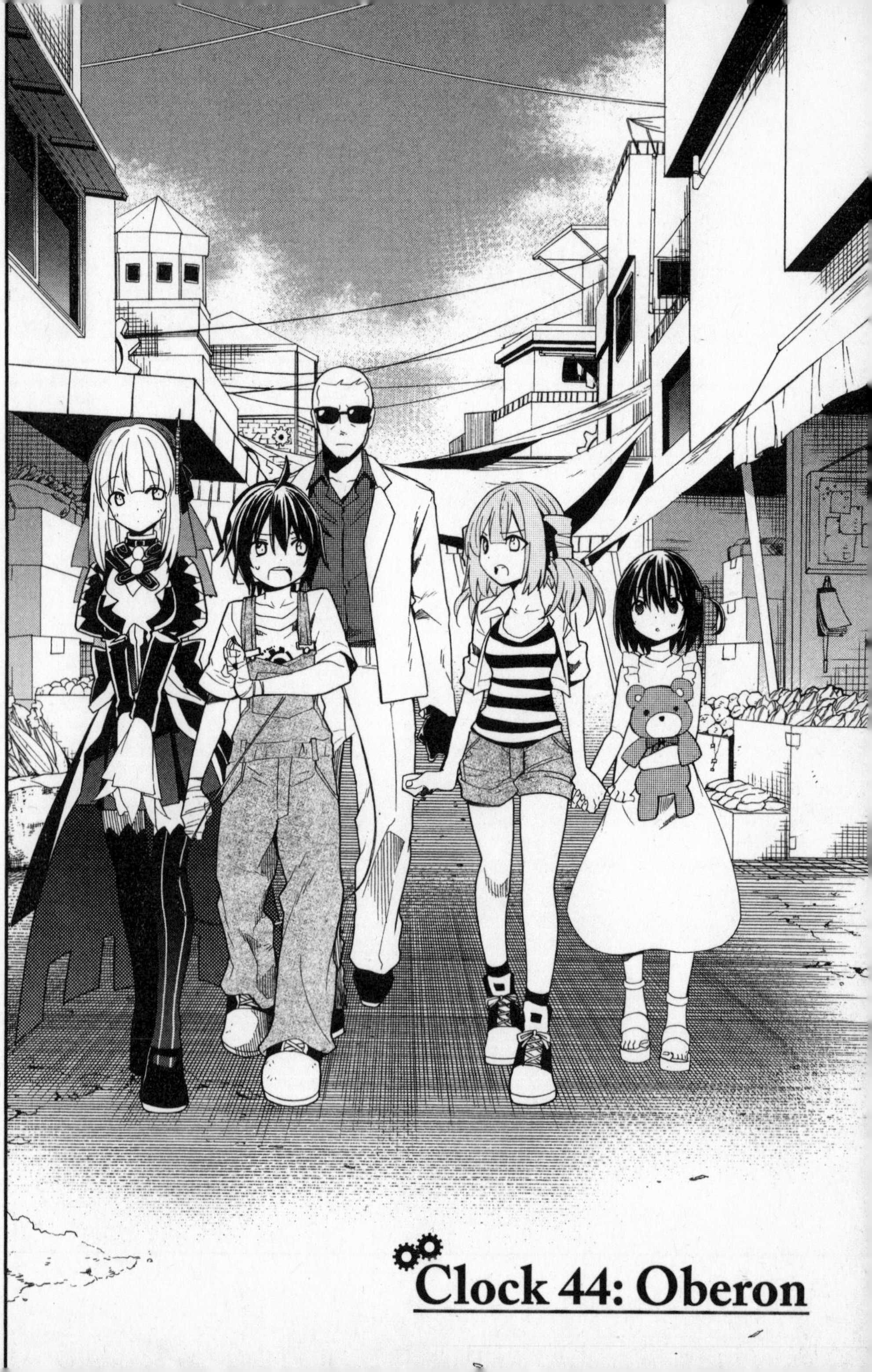

Clock 44: Oberon

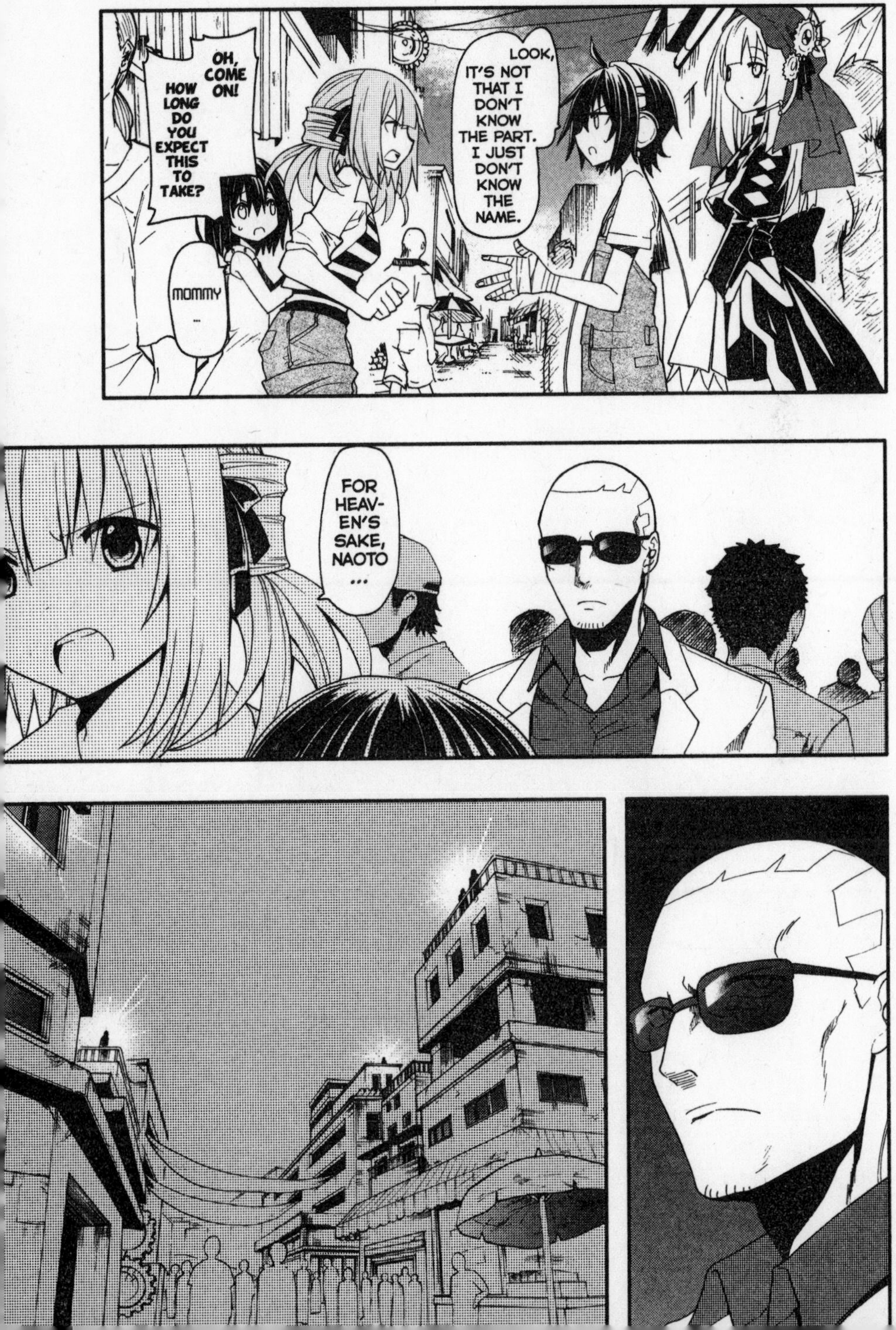
LOOK, IT'S NOT THAT I DON'T KNOW THE PART. I JUST DON'T KNOW THE NAME.
OH, COME ON! HOW LONG DO YOU EXPECT THIS TO TAKE?
MOMMY ...
FOR HEAVEN'S SAKE, NAOTO ...

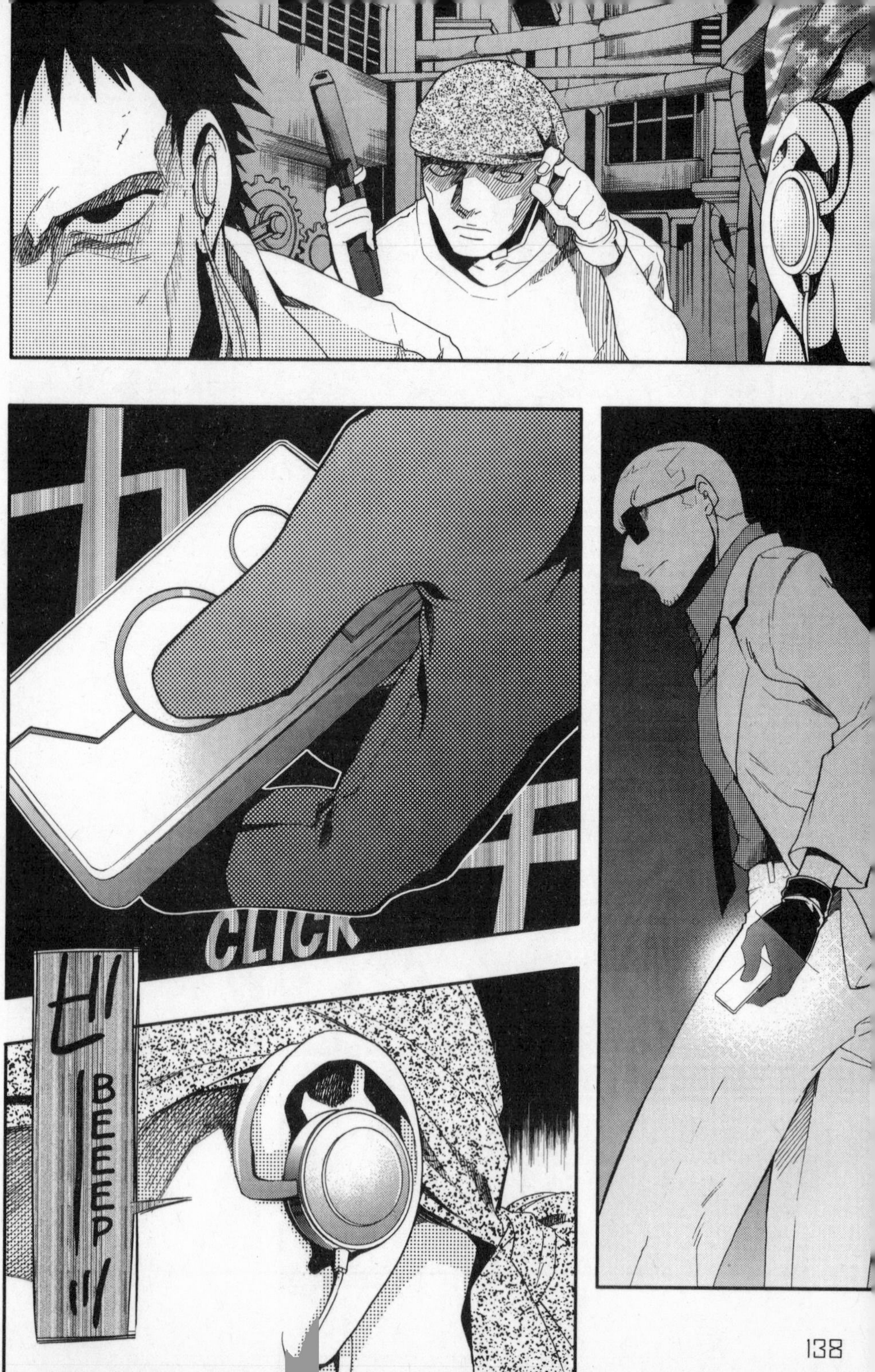
CLICK
ピーーッ
BEEEEP

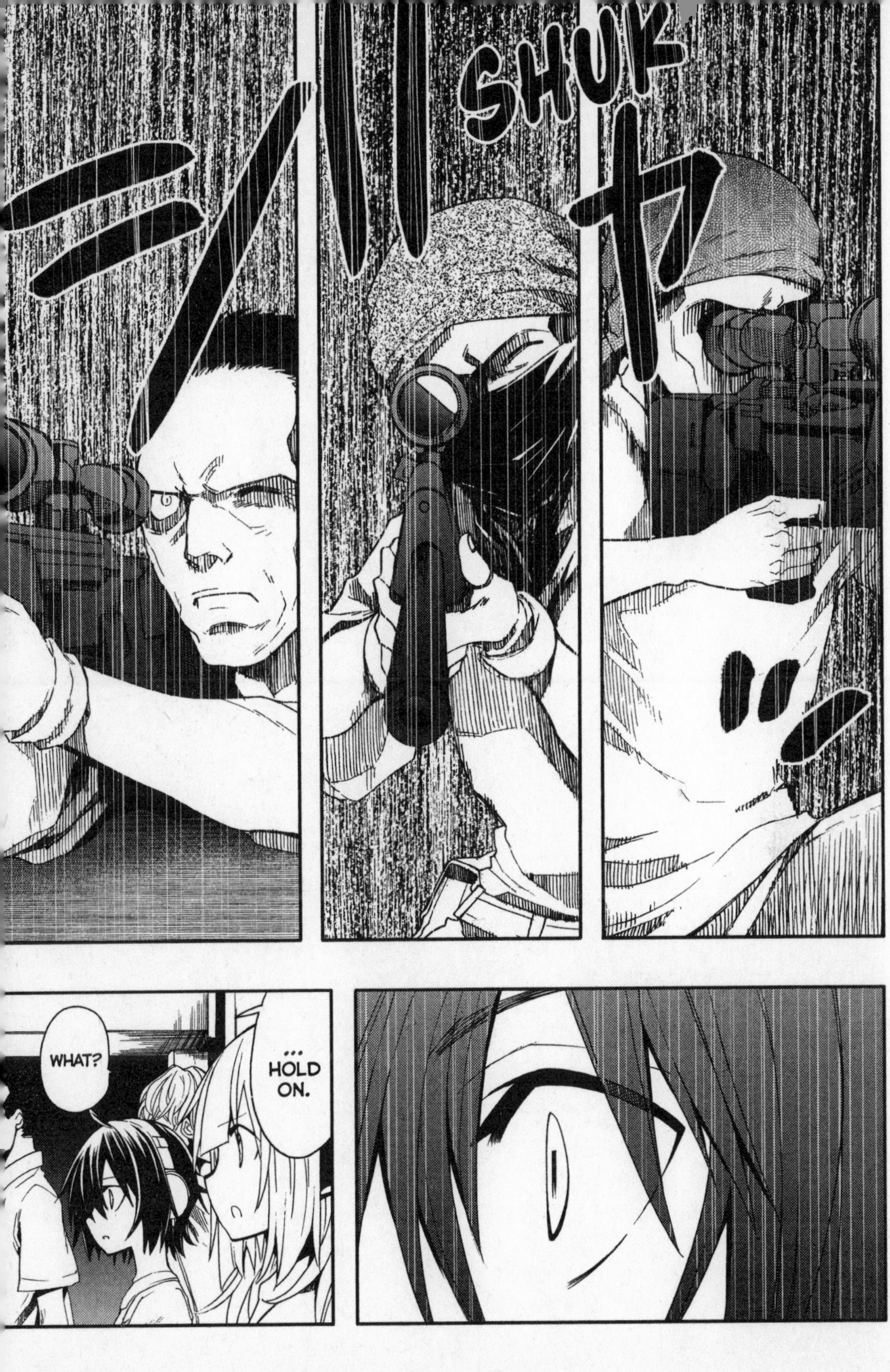
SHUK
...HOLD ON.
WHAT?

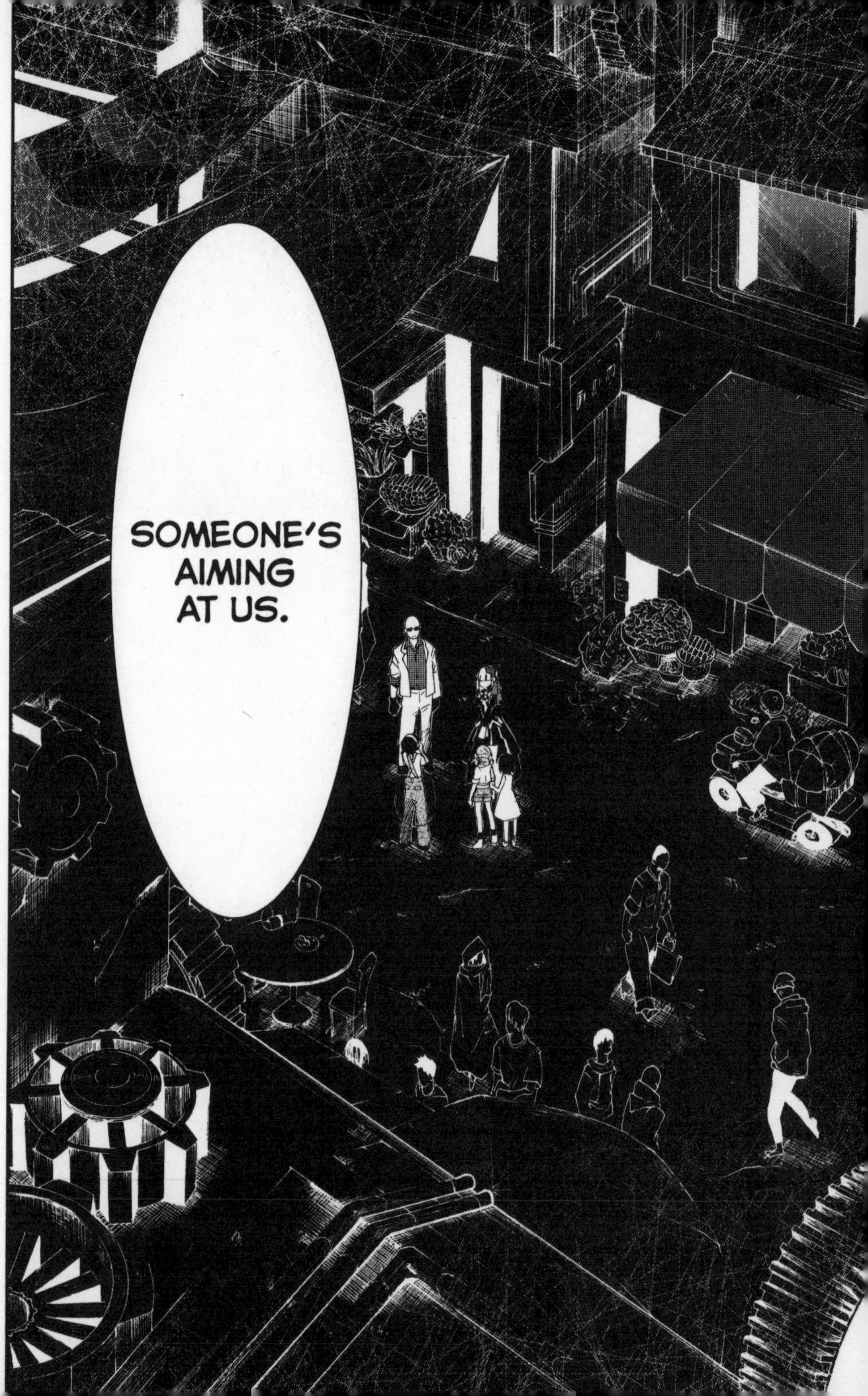
SOMEONE'S AIMING AT US.

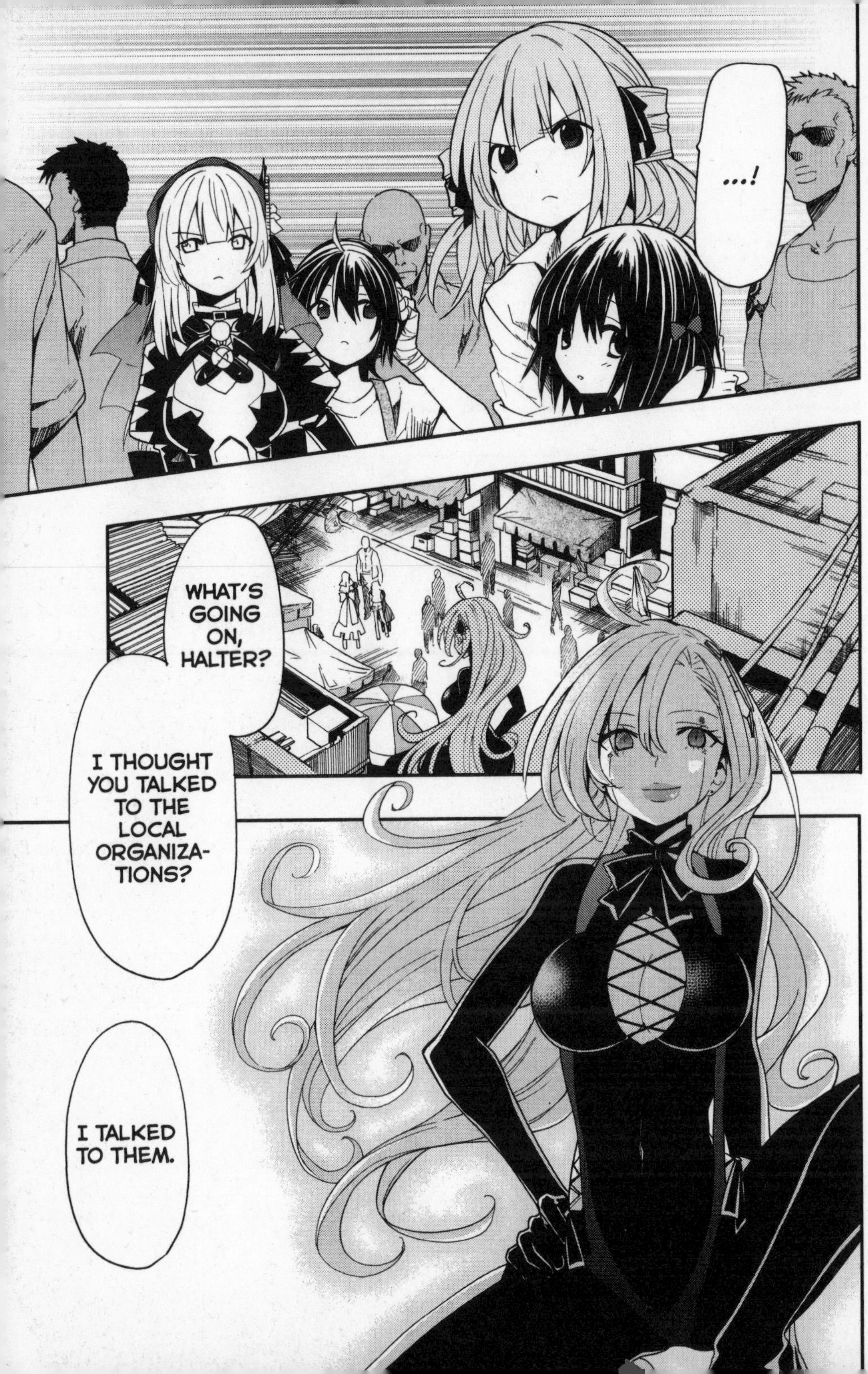
...!
WHAT'S GOING ON, HALTER?
I THOUGHT YOU TALKED TO THE LOCAL ORGANIZATIONS?
I TALKED TO THEM.

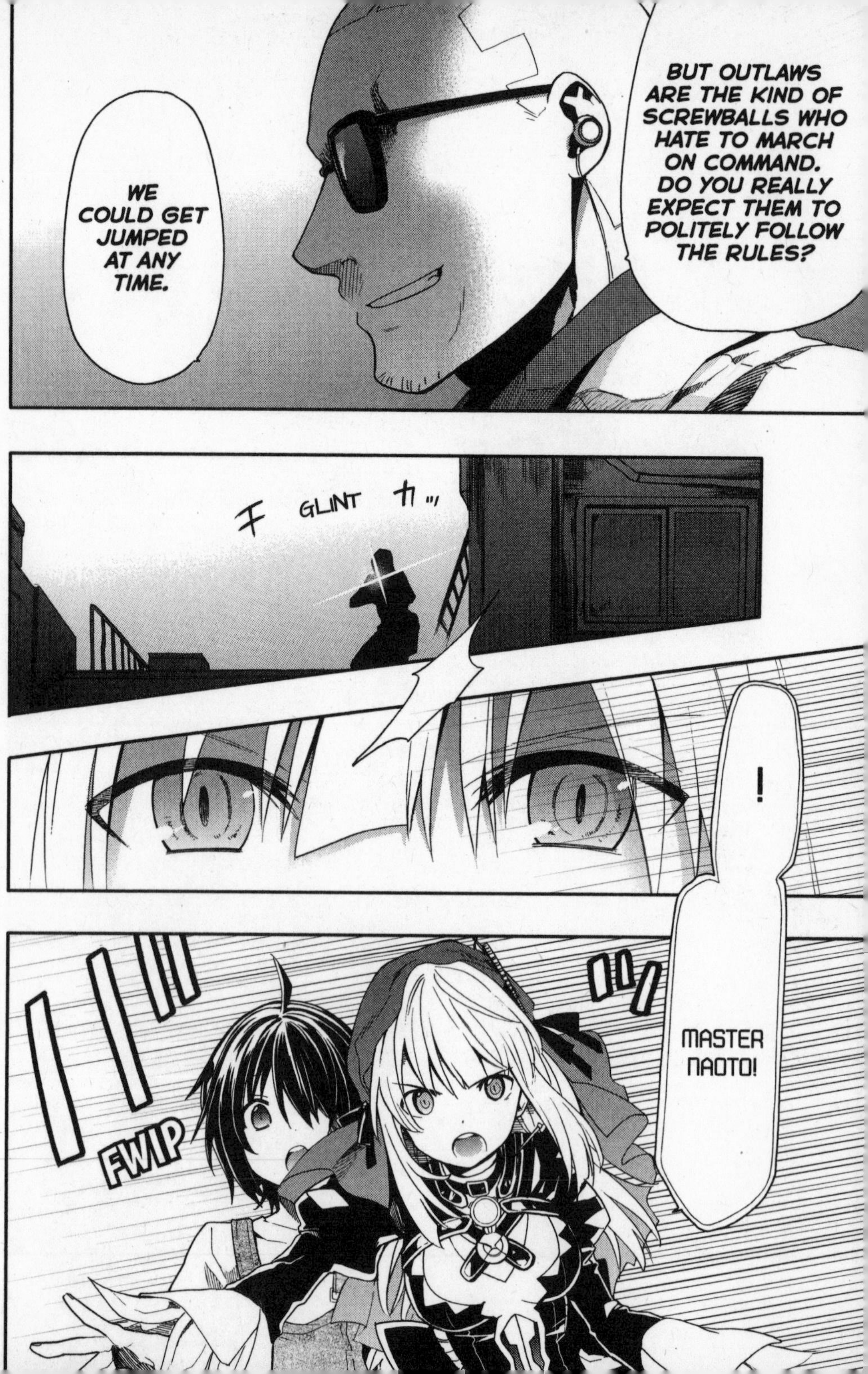
BUT OUTLAWS ARE THE KIND OF SCREWBALLS WHO HATE TO MARCH ON COMMAND. DO YOU REALLY EXPECT THEM TO POLITELY FOLLOW THE RULES?
WE COULD GET JUMPED AT ANY TIME.
GLINT
!
MASTER NAOTO!
FWIP

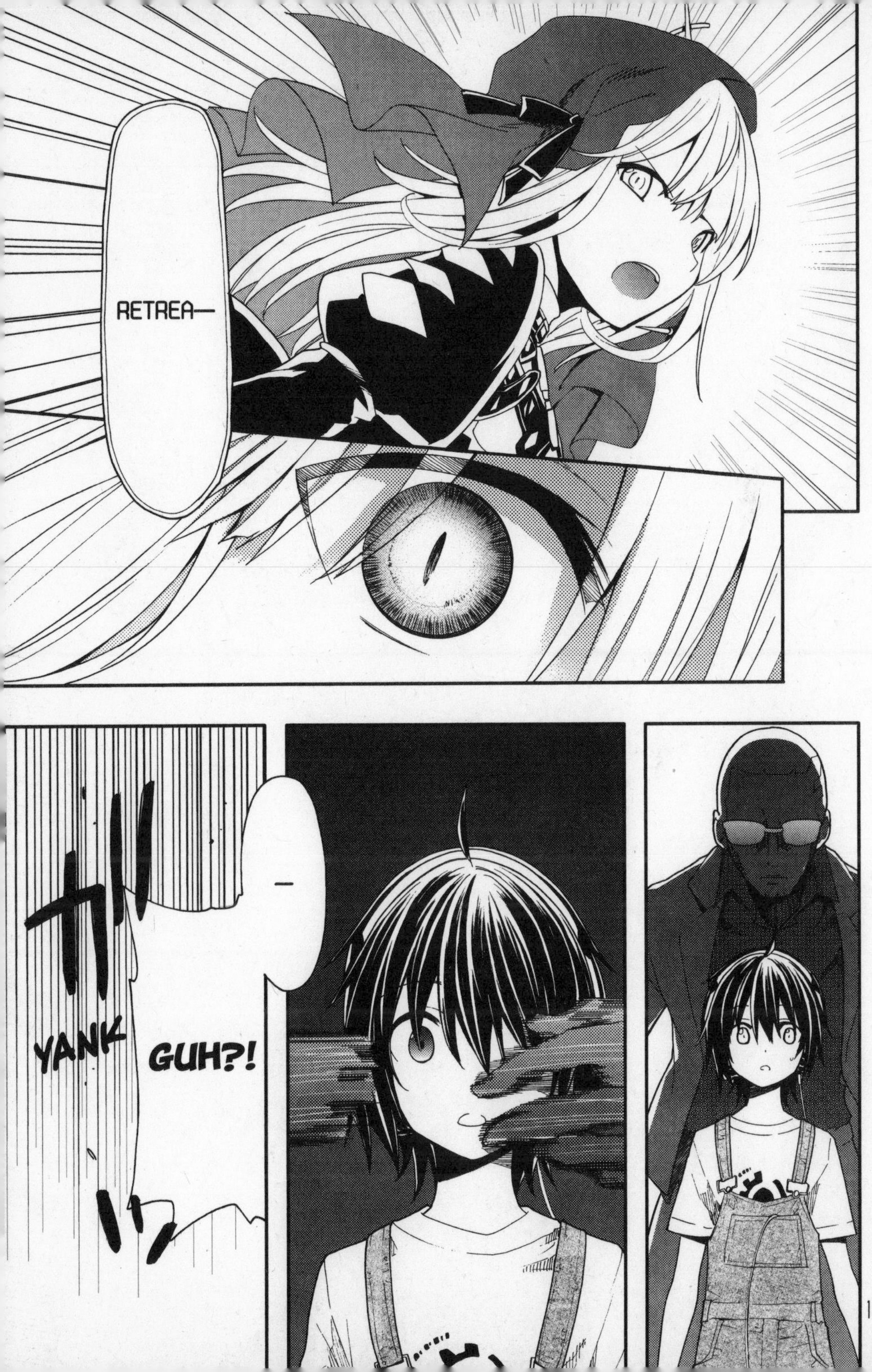
RETREA—
—
GUH?!
ガッ
YANK

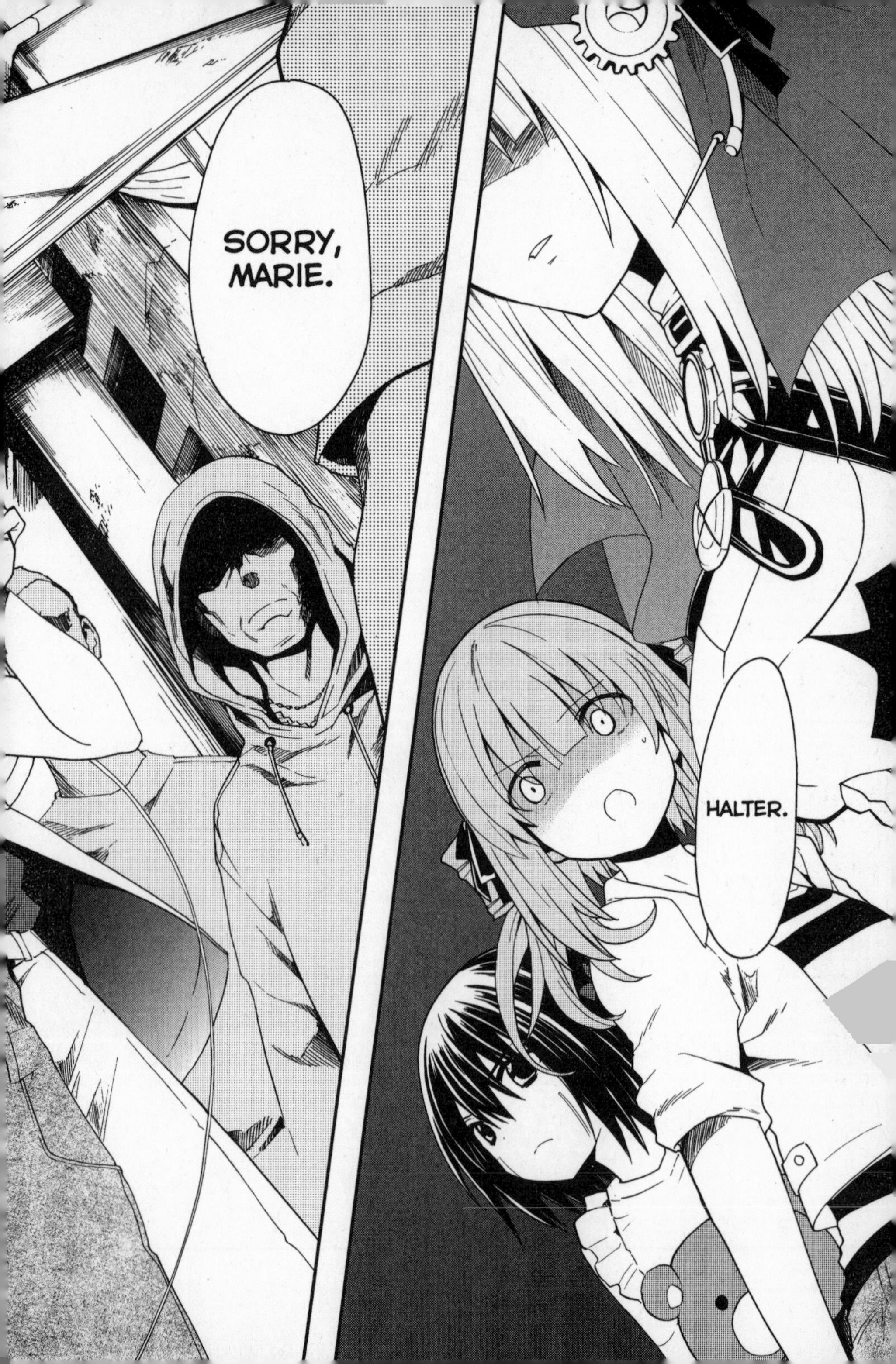
HALTER.
SORRY, MARIE.

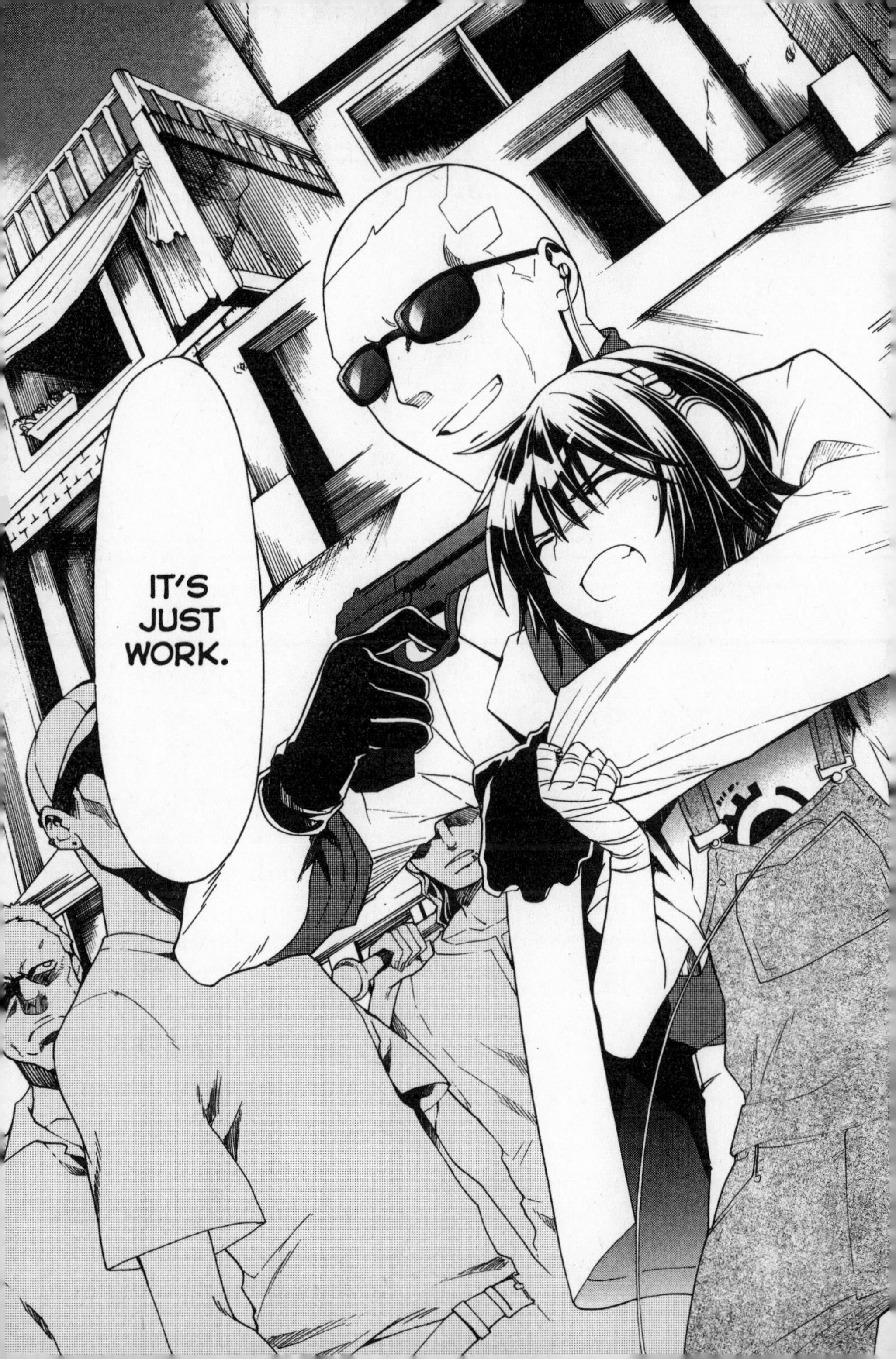
IT'S JUST WORK.

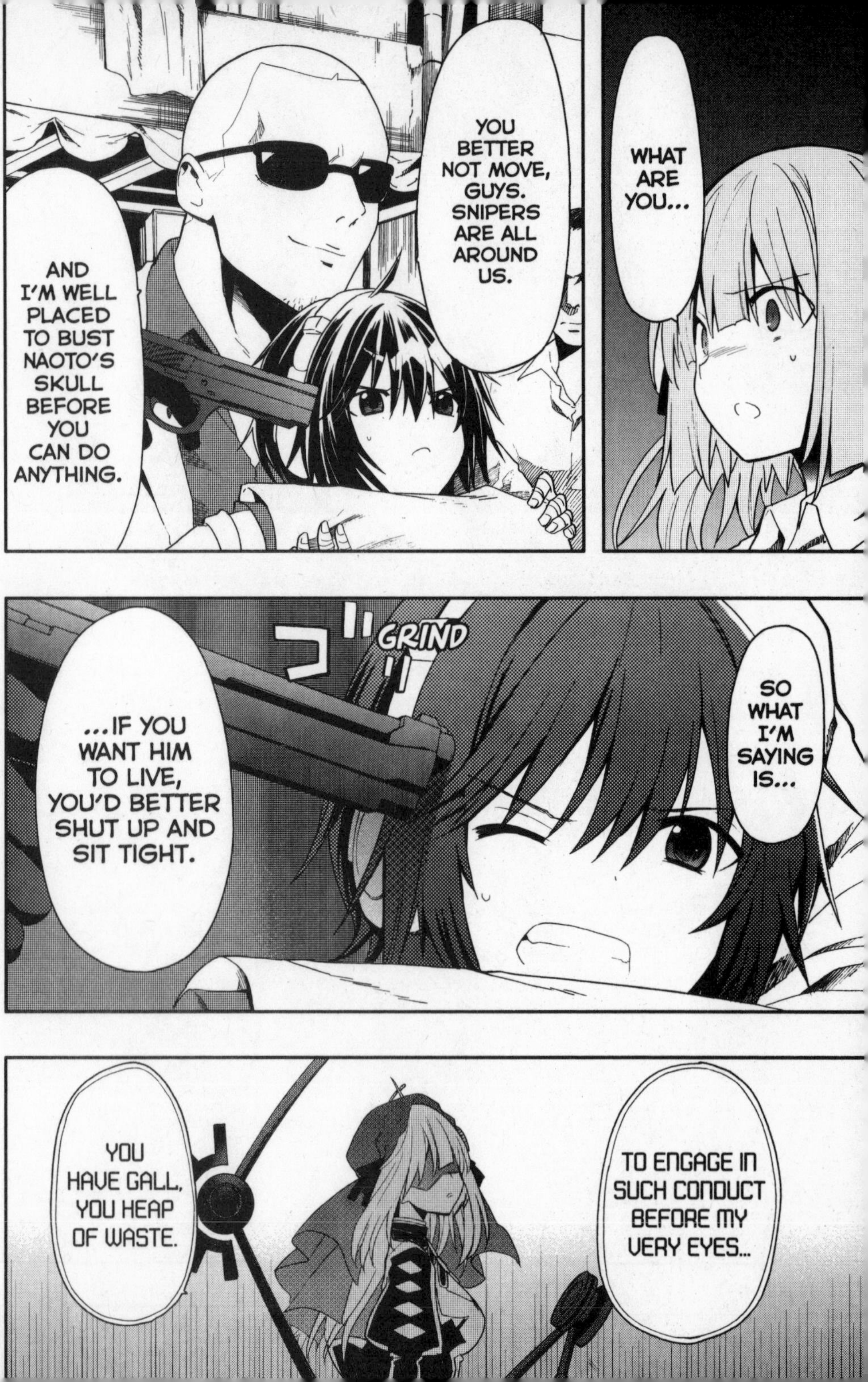
WHAT ARE YOU...
YOU BETTER NOT MOVE, GUYS. SNIPERS ARE ALL AROUND US.
AND I'M WELL PLACED TO BUST NAOTO'S SKULL BEFORE YOU CAN DO ANYTHING.
SO WHAT I'M SAYING IS...
GRIND
...IF YOU WANT HIM TO LIVE, YOU'D BETTER SHUT UP AND SIT TIGHT.
TO ENGAGE IN SUCH CONDUCT BEFORE MY VERY EYES...
YOU HAVE GALL, YOU HEAP OF WASTE.

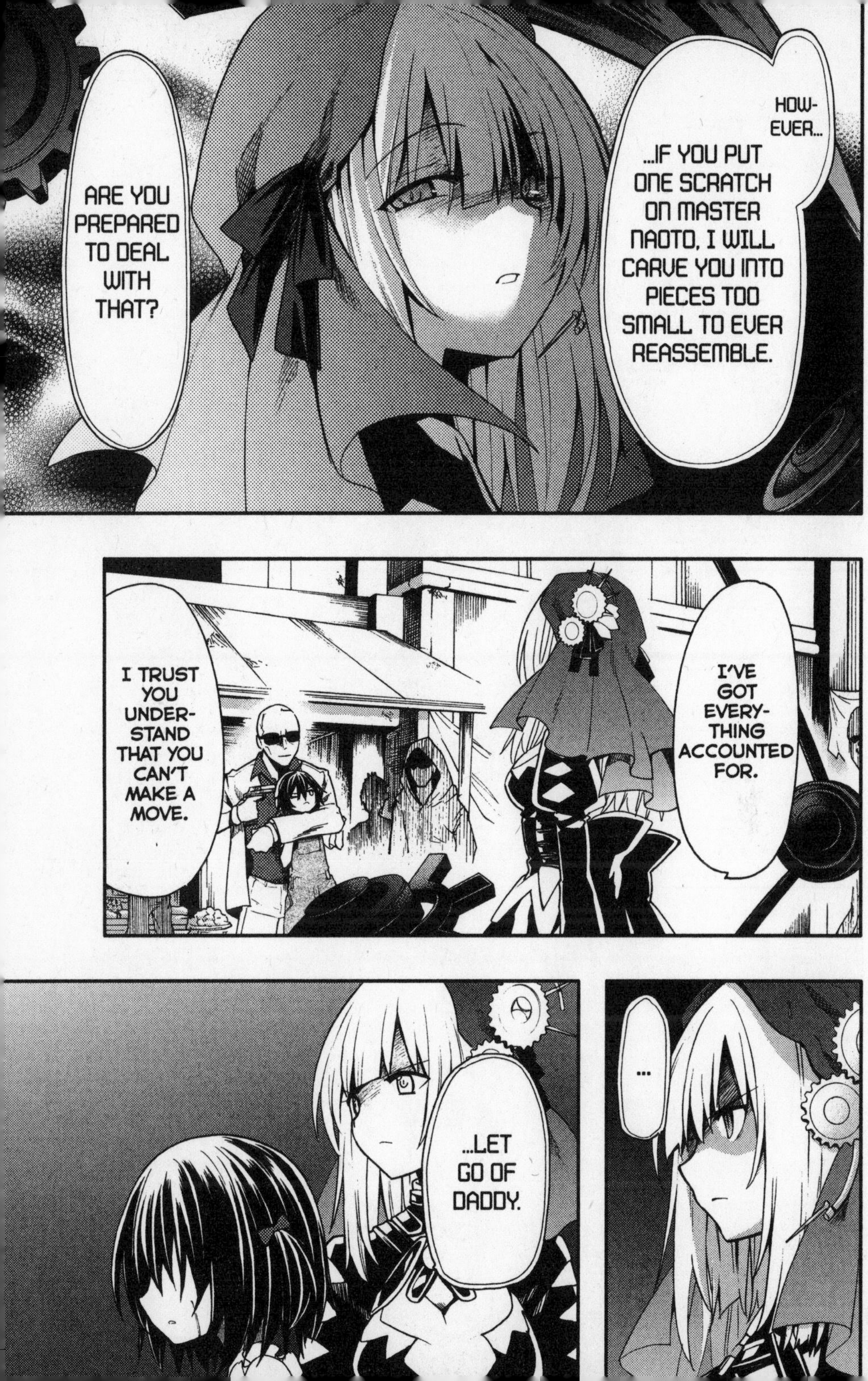
HOW-EVER...
...IF YOU PUT ONE SCRATCH ON MASTER NAOTO, I WILL CARVE YOU INTO PIECES TOO SMALL TO EVER REASSEMBLE.
ARE YOU PREPARED TO DEAL WITH THAT?
I'VE GOT EVERY-THING ACCOUNTED FOR.
I TRUST YOU UNDER-STAND THAT YOU CAN'T MAKE A MOVE.
...
...LET GO OF DADDY.

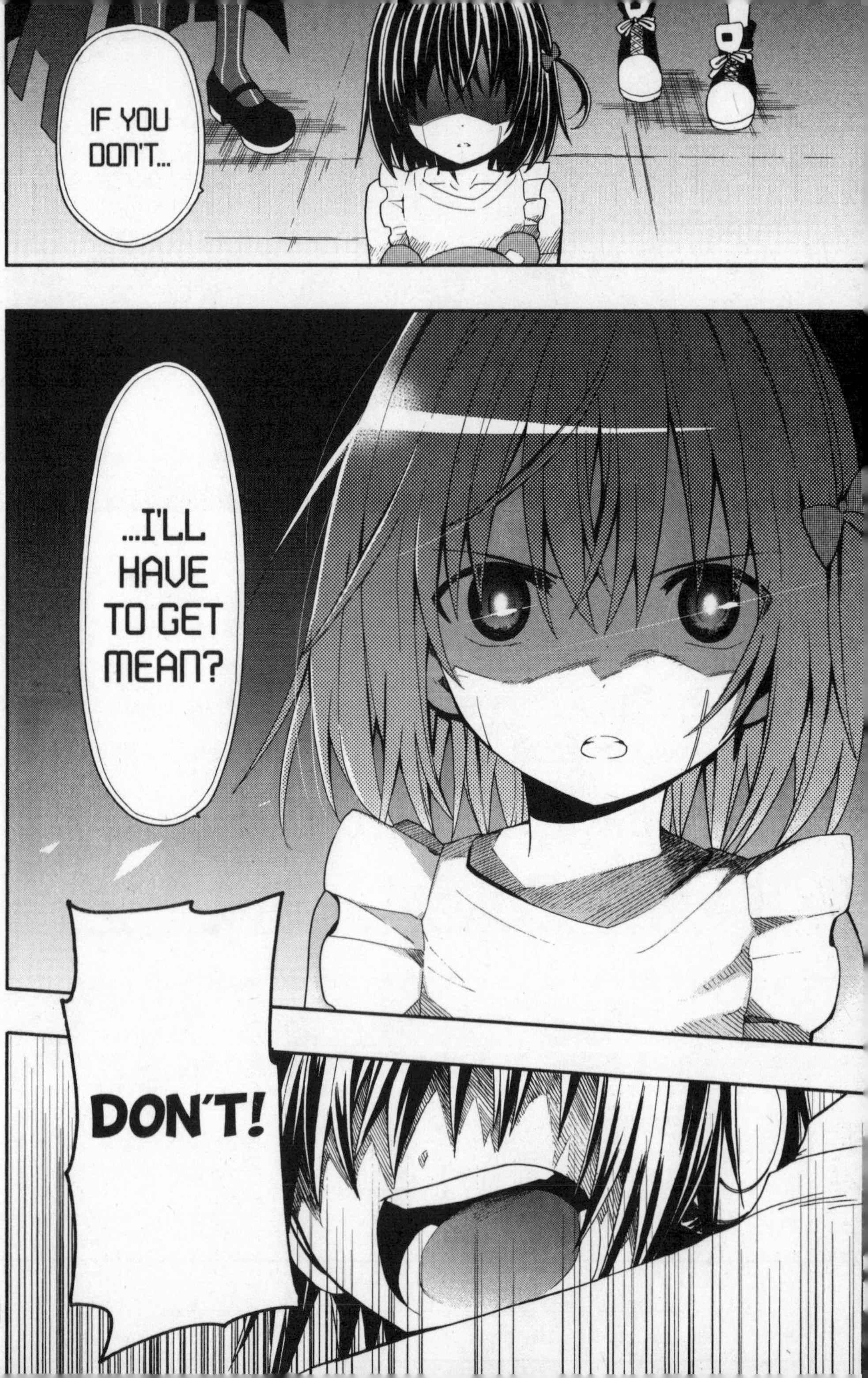
IF YOU DON'T...
...I'LL HAVE TO GET MEAN?
DON'T!

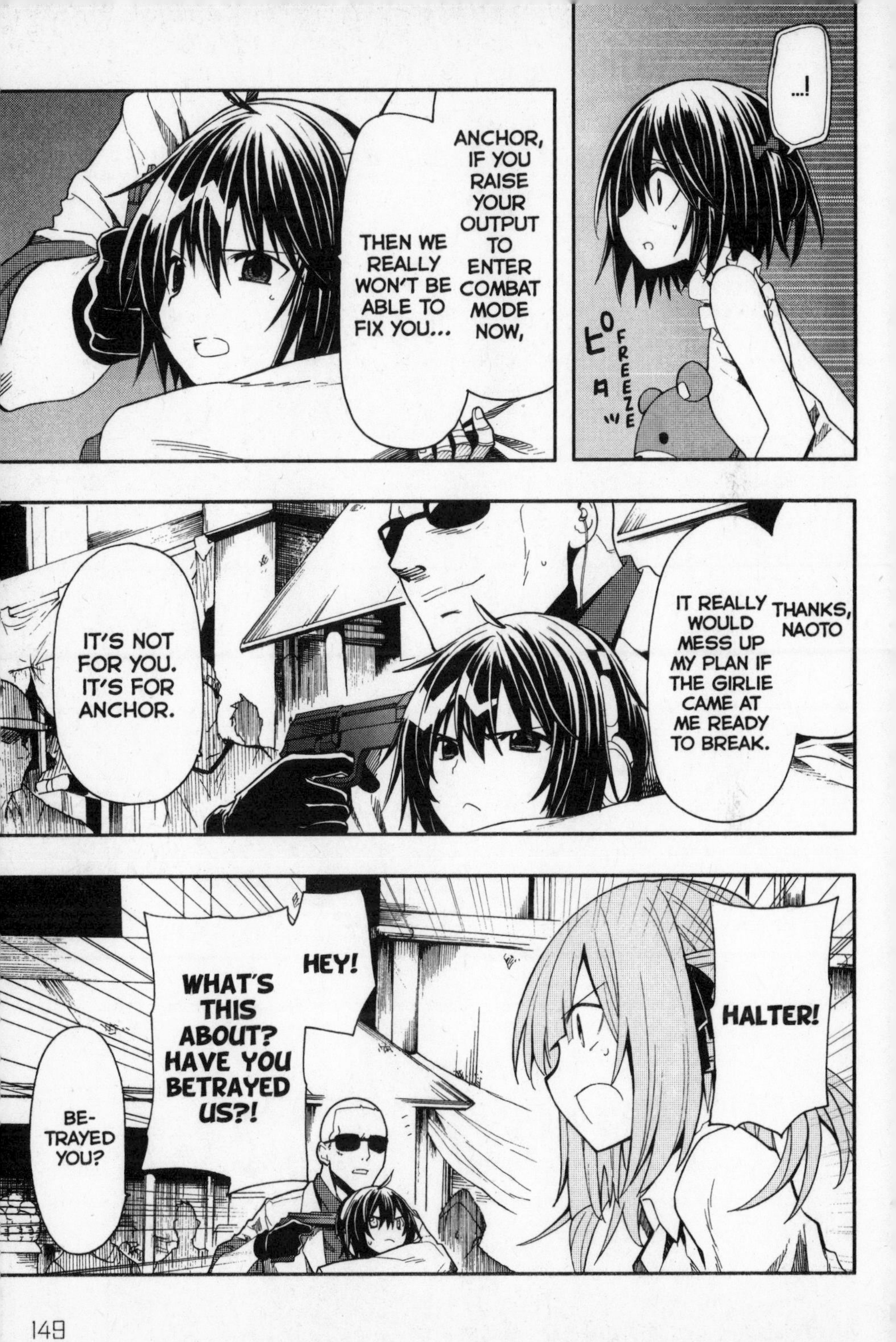
...!
FREEZE
ANCHOR, IF YOU RAISE YOUR OUTPUT TO ENTER COMBAT MODE NOW,
THEN WE REALLY WON'T BE ABLE TO FIX YOU...
THANKS, NAOTO
IT REALLY WOULD MESS UP MY PLAN IF THE GIRLIE CAME AT ME READY TO BREAK.
IT'S NOT FOR YOU. IT'S FOR ANCHOR.
HALTER!
HEY!
WHAT'S THIS ABOUT? HAVE YOU BETRAYED US?!
BE-TRAYED YOU?

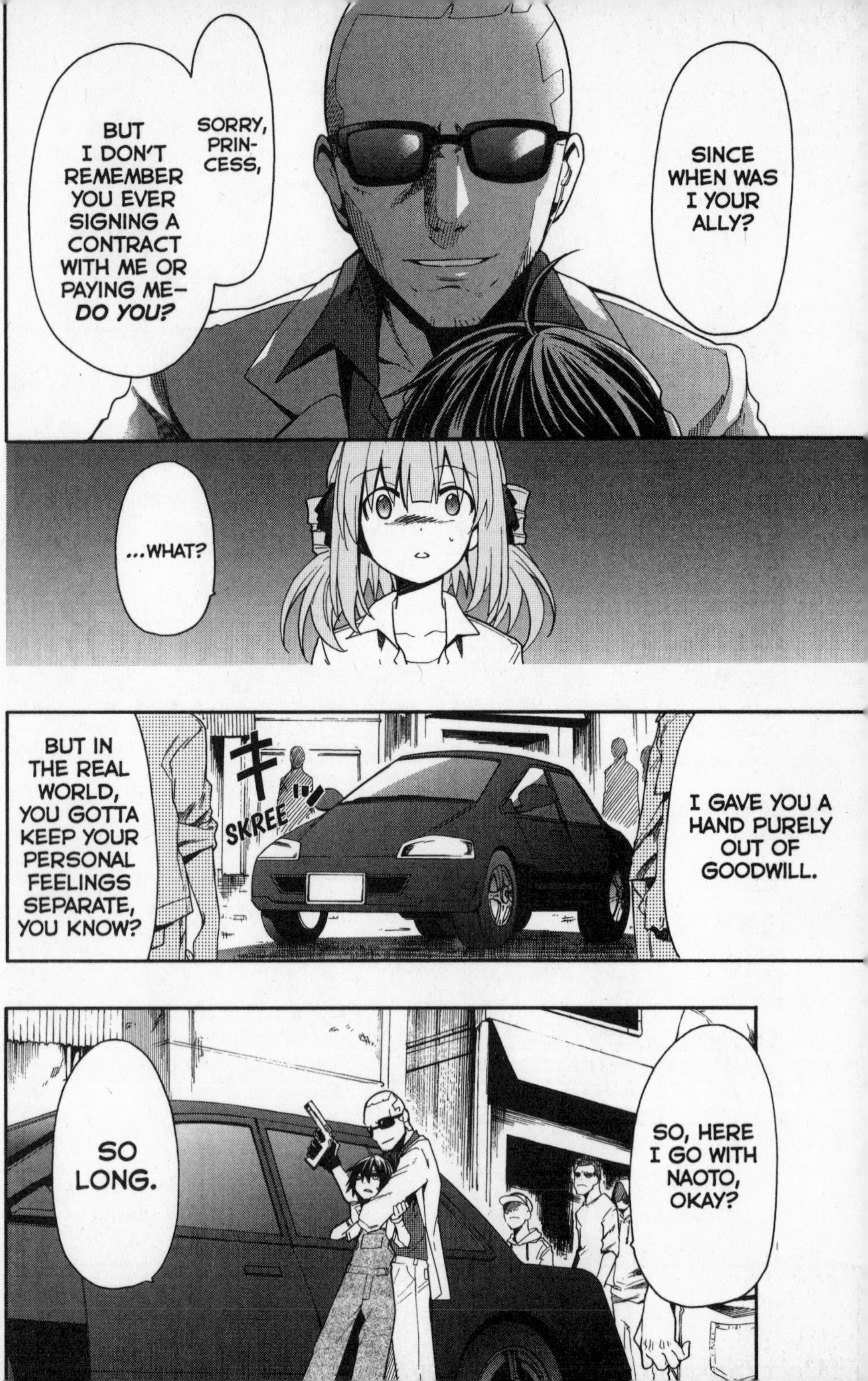
SINCE WHEN WAS I YOUR ALLY?
SORRY, PRIN-CESS,
BUT I DON'T REMEMBER YOU EVER SIGNING A CONTRACT WITH ME OR PAYING ME— *DO YOU?*
...WHAT?
I GAVE YOU A HAND PURELY OUT OF GOODWILL.
SKREE
BUT IN THE REAL WORLD, YOU GOTTA KEEP YOUR PERSONAL FEELINGS SEPARATE, YOU KNOW?
SO, HERE I GO WITH NAOTO, OKAY?
SO LONG.

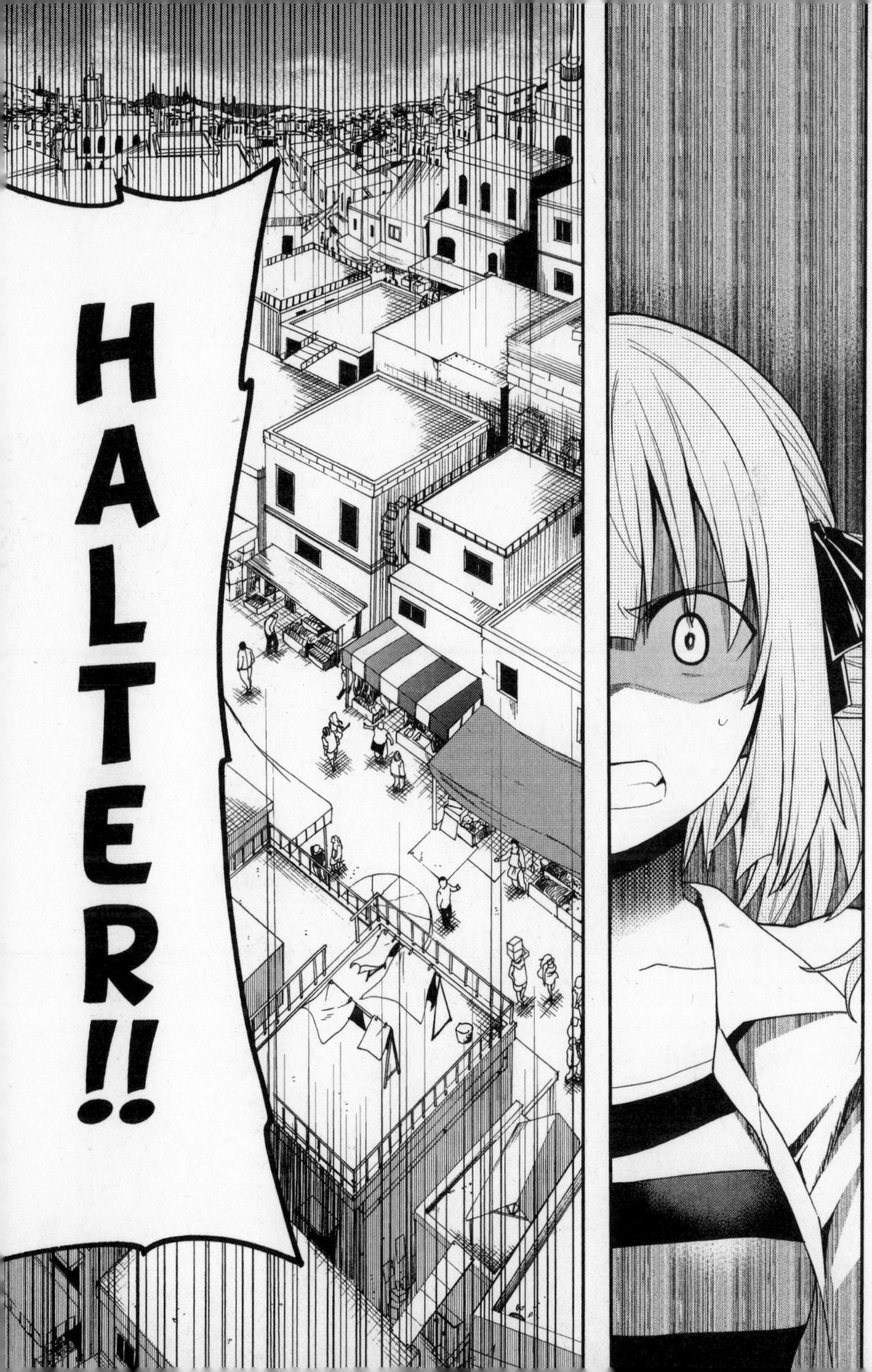
HALTER!!

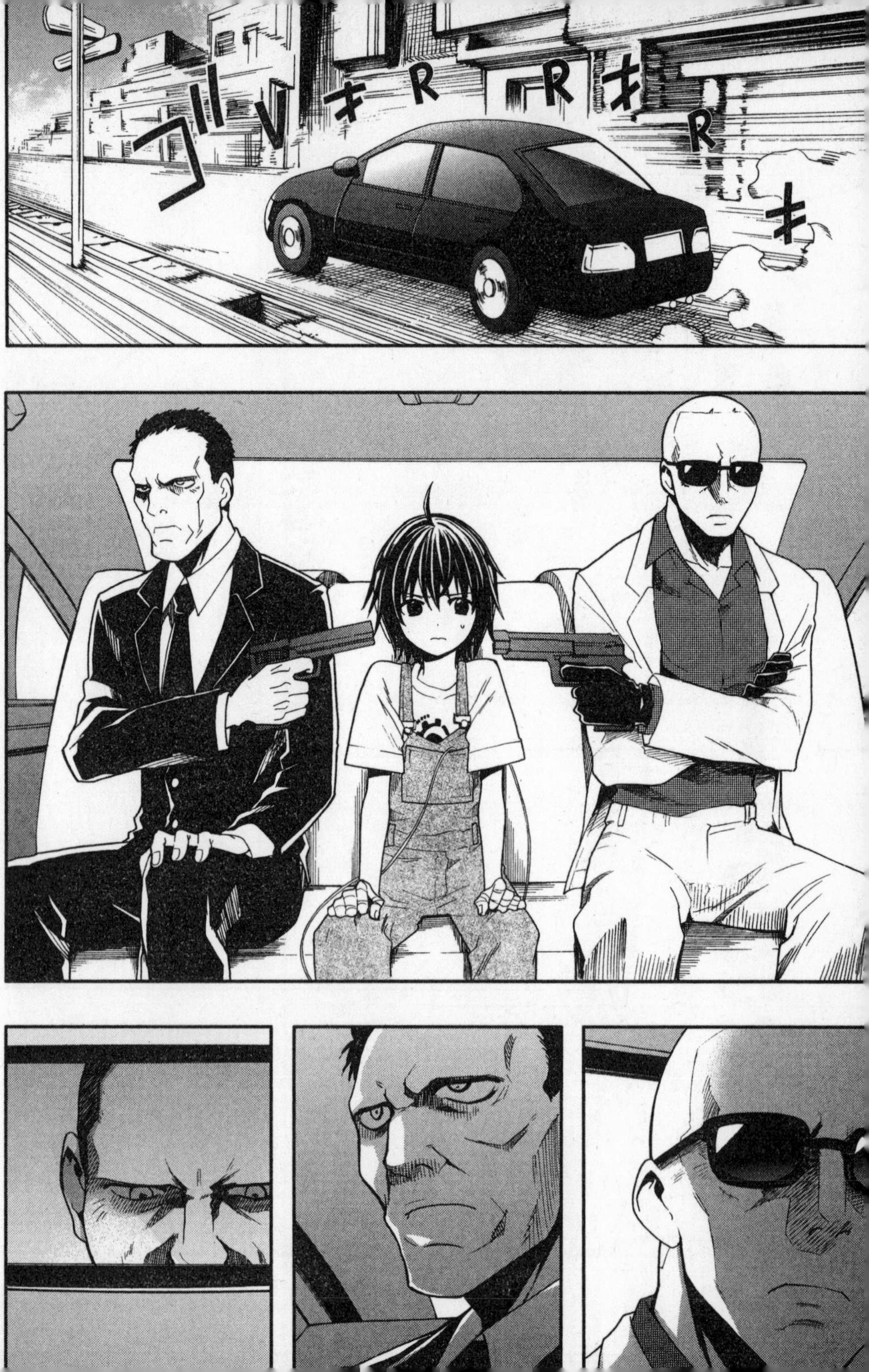
フルVォRRォRォ

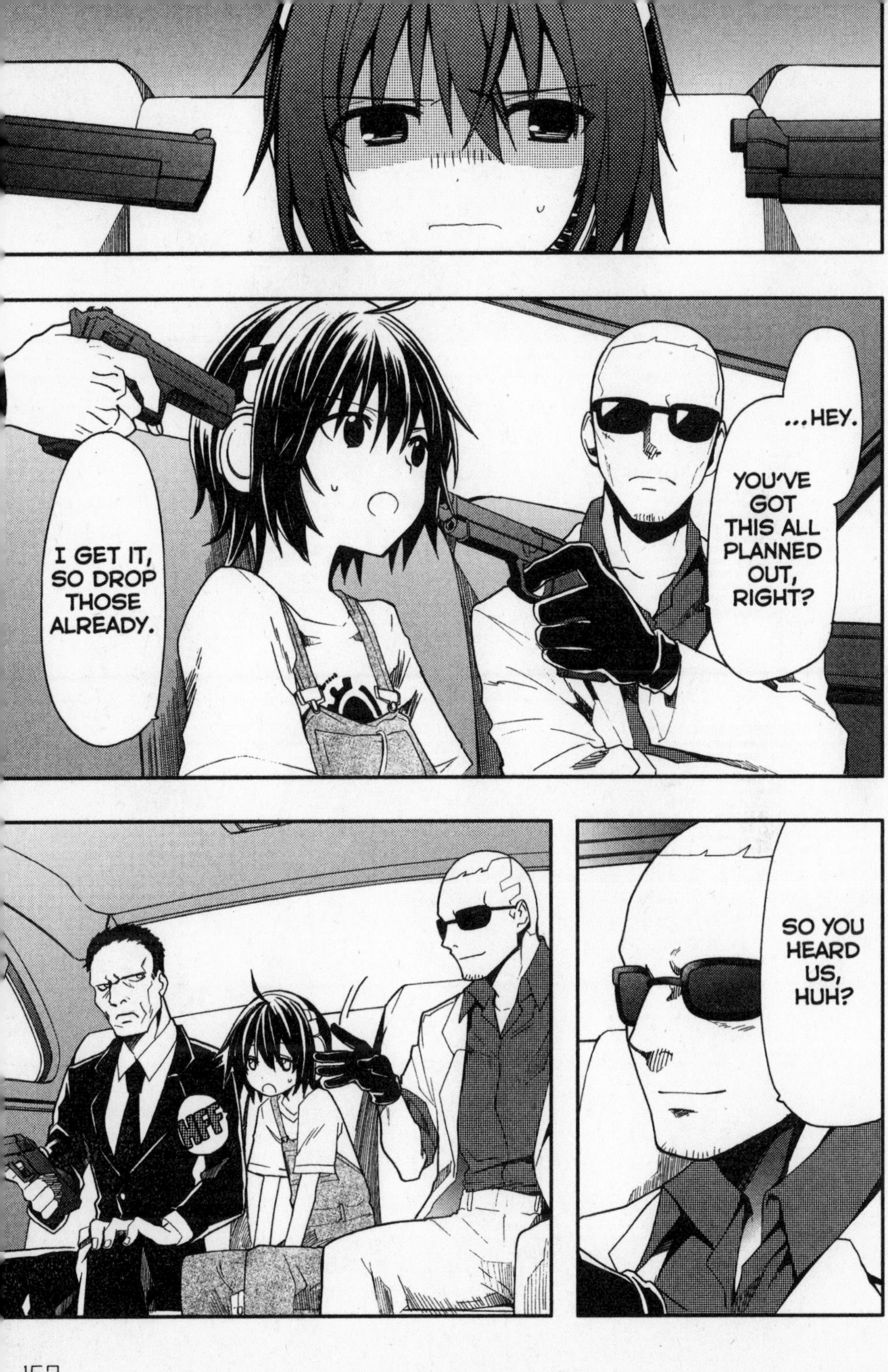
...HEY.
YOU'VE GOT THIS ALL PLANNED OUT, RIGHT?
I GET IT, SO DROP THOSE ALREADY.
SO YOU HEARD US, HUH?

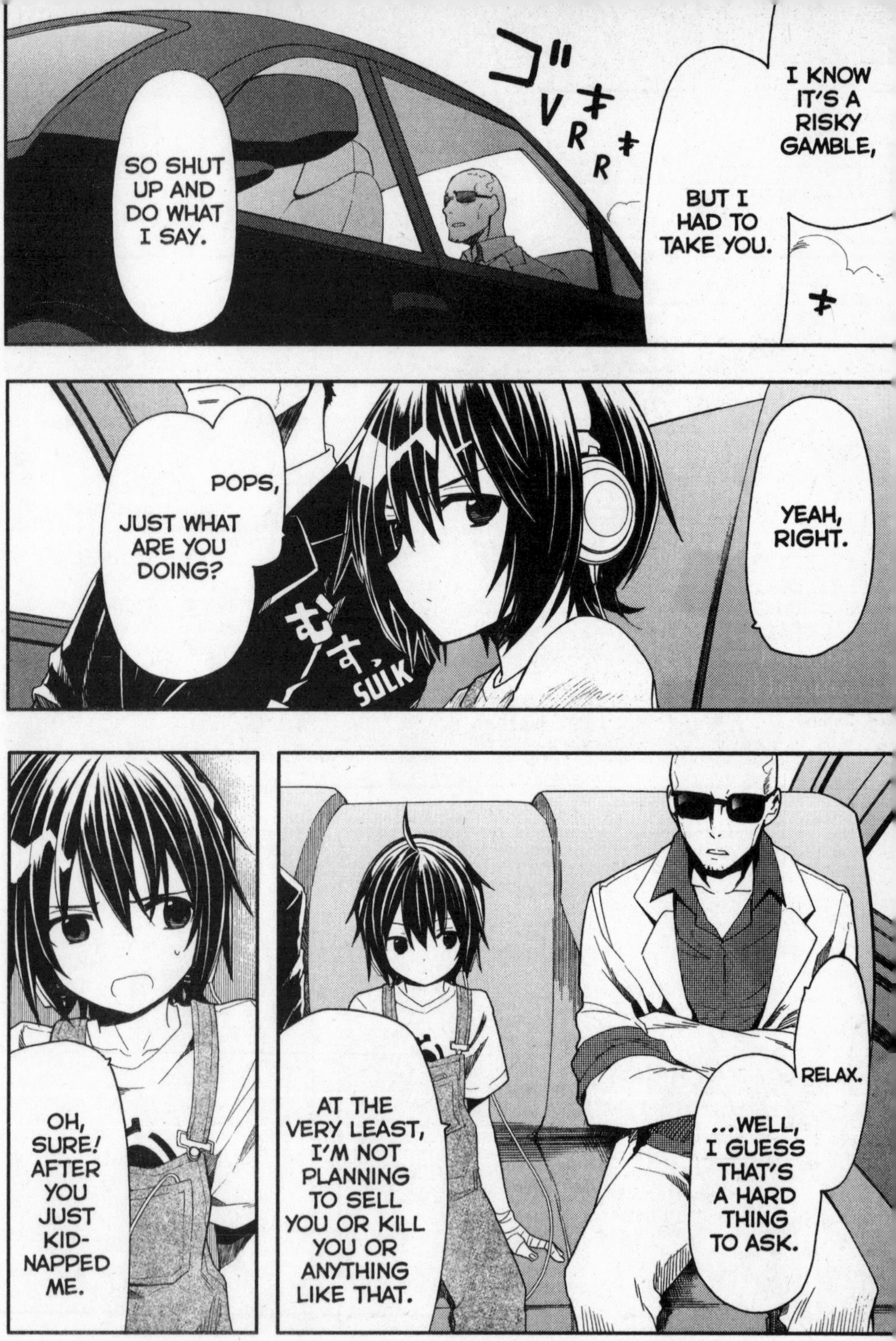
I KNOW IT'S A RISKY GAMBLE,
BUT I HAD TO TAKE YOU.
ゴキ
VRRR
キ
SO SHUT UP AND DO WHAT I SAY.
YEAH, RIGHT.
POPS,
JUST WHAT ARE YOU DOING?
むすっ
SULK
RELAX.
...WELL, I GUESS THAT'S A HARD THING TO ASK.
AT THE VERY LEAST, I'M NOT PLANNING TO SELL YOU OR KILL YOU OR ANYTHING LIKE THAT.
OH, SURE! AFTER YOU JUST KID-NAPPED ME.

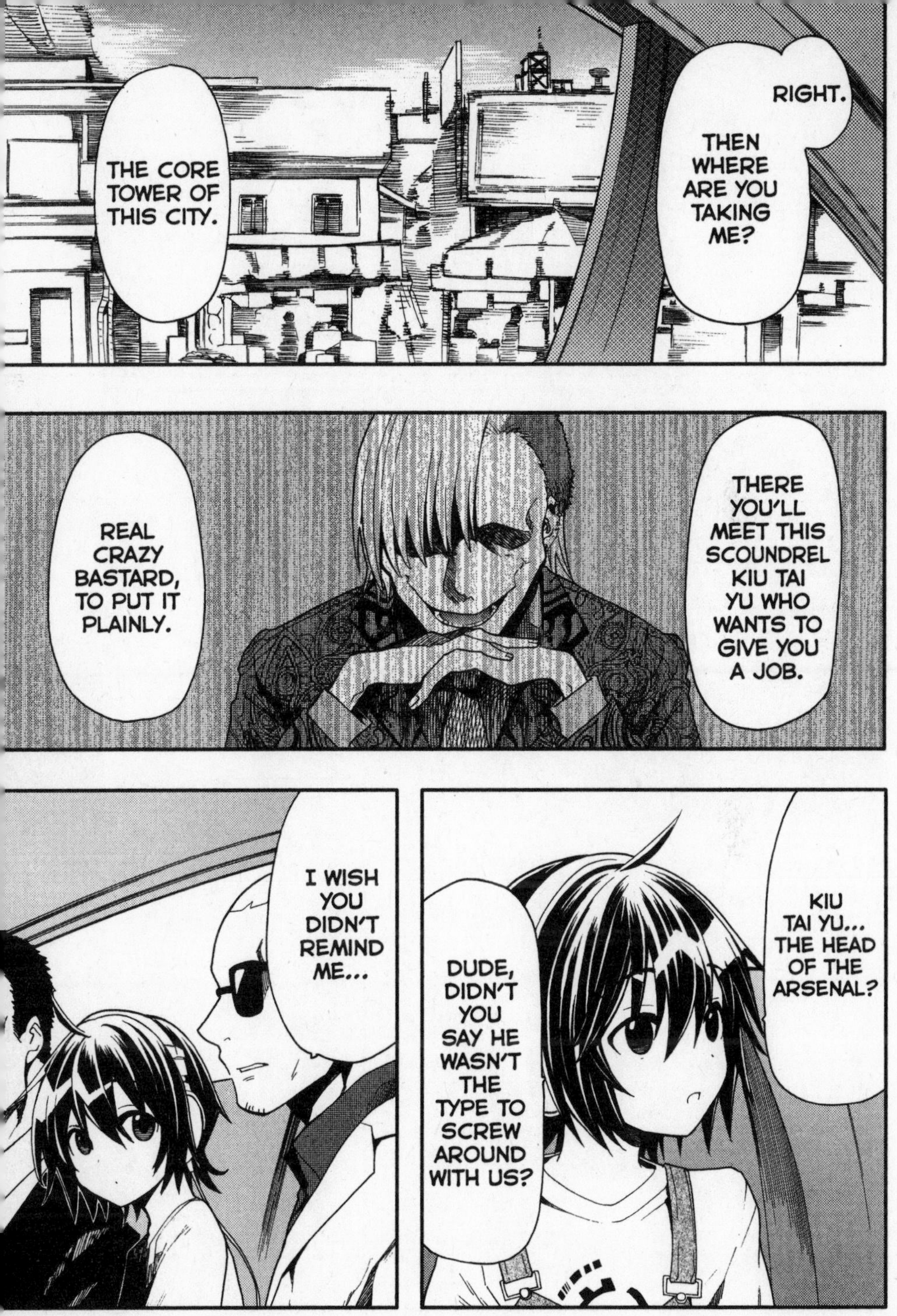
RIGHT.
THEN WHERE ARE YOU TAKING ME?
THE CORE TOWER OF THIS CITY.
THERE YOU'LL MEET THIS SCOUNDREL KIU TAI YU WHO WANTS TO GIVE YOU A JOB.
REAL CRAZY BASTARD, TO PUT IT PLAINLY.
KIU TAI YU... THE HEAD OF THE ARSENAL?
DUDE, DIDN'T YOU SAY HE WASN'T THE TYPE TO SCREW AROUND WITH US?
I WISH YOU DIDN'T REMIND ME...

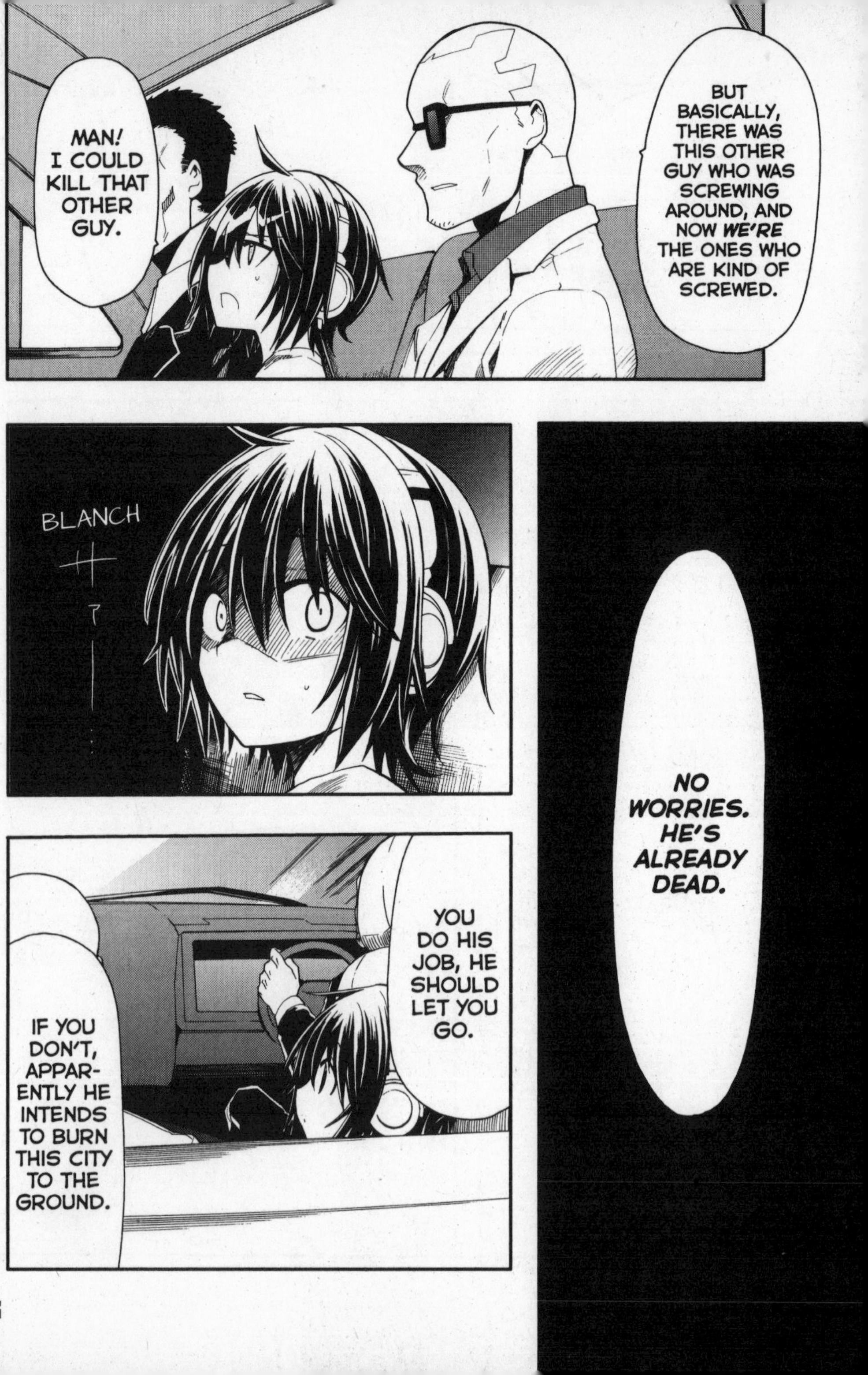
BUT BASICALLY, THERE WAS THIS OTHER GUY WHO WAS SCREWING AROUND, AND NOW *WE'RE* THE ONES WHO ARE KIND OF SCREWED.
MAN! I COULD KILL THAT OTHER GUY.
NO WORRIES. HE'S ALREADY DEAD.
BLANCH
YOU DO HIS JOB, HE SHOULD LET YOU GO.
IF YOU DON'T, APPARENTLY HE INTENDS TO BURN THIS CITY TO THE GROUND.

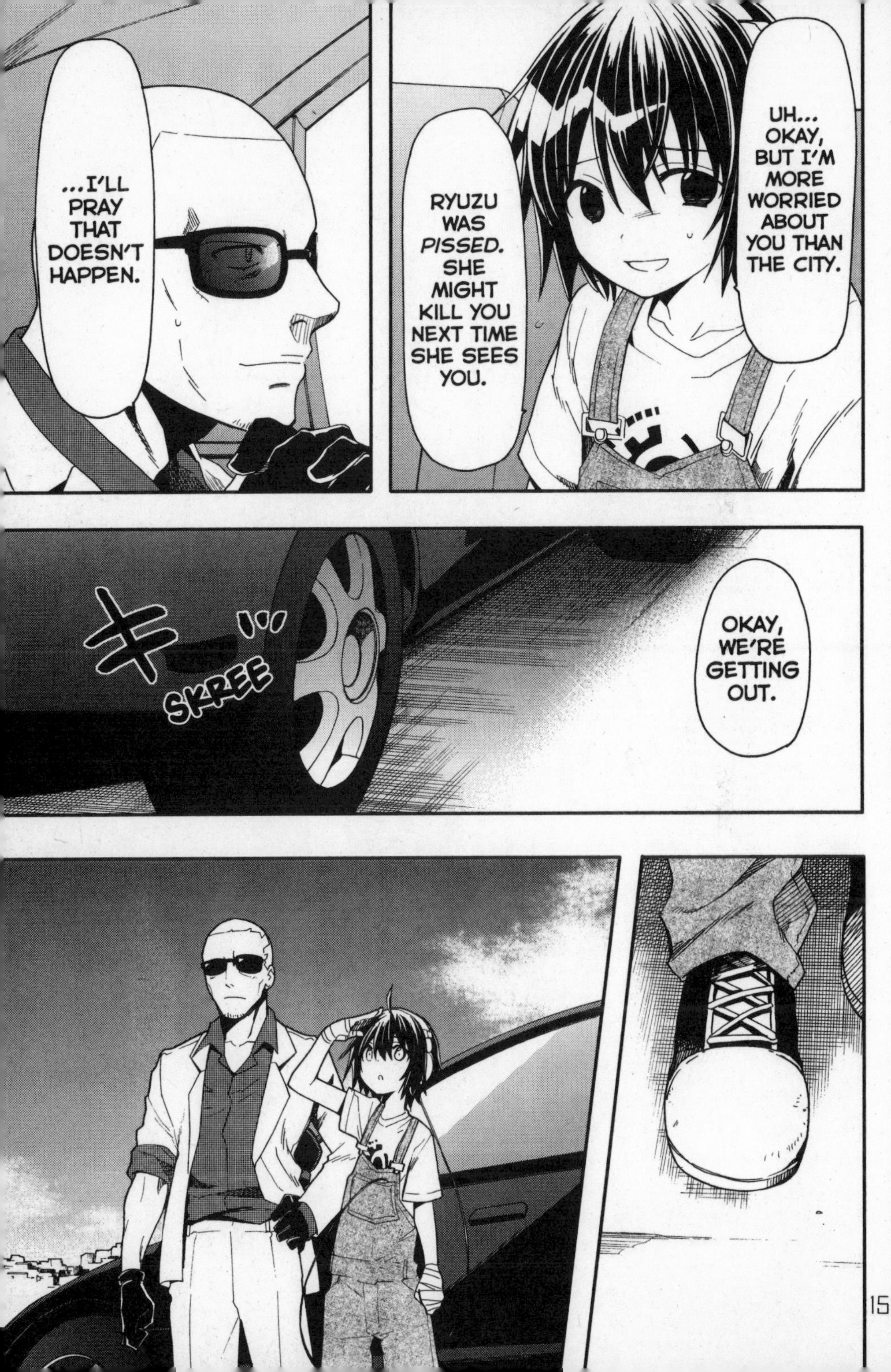
UH... OKAY, BUT I'M MORE WORRIED ABOUT YOU THAN THE CITY.
RYUZU WAS *PISSED.* SHE MIGHT KILL YOU NEXT TIME SHE SEES YOU.
...I'LL PRAY THAT DOESN'T HAPPEN.
OKAY, WE'RE GETTING OUT.
SKREE

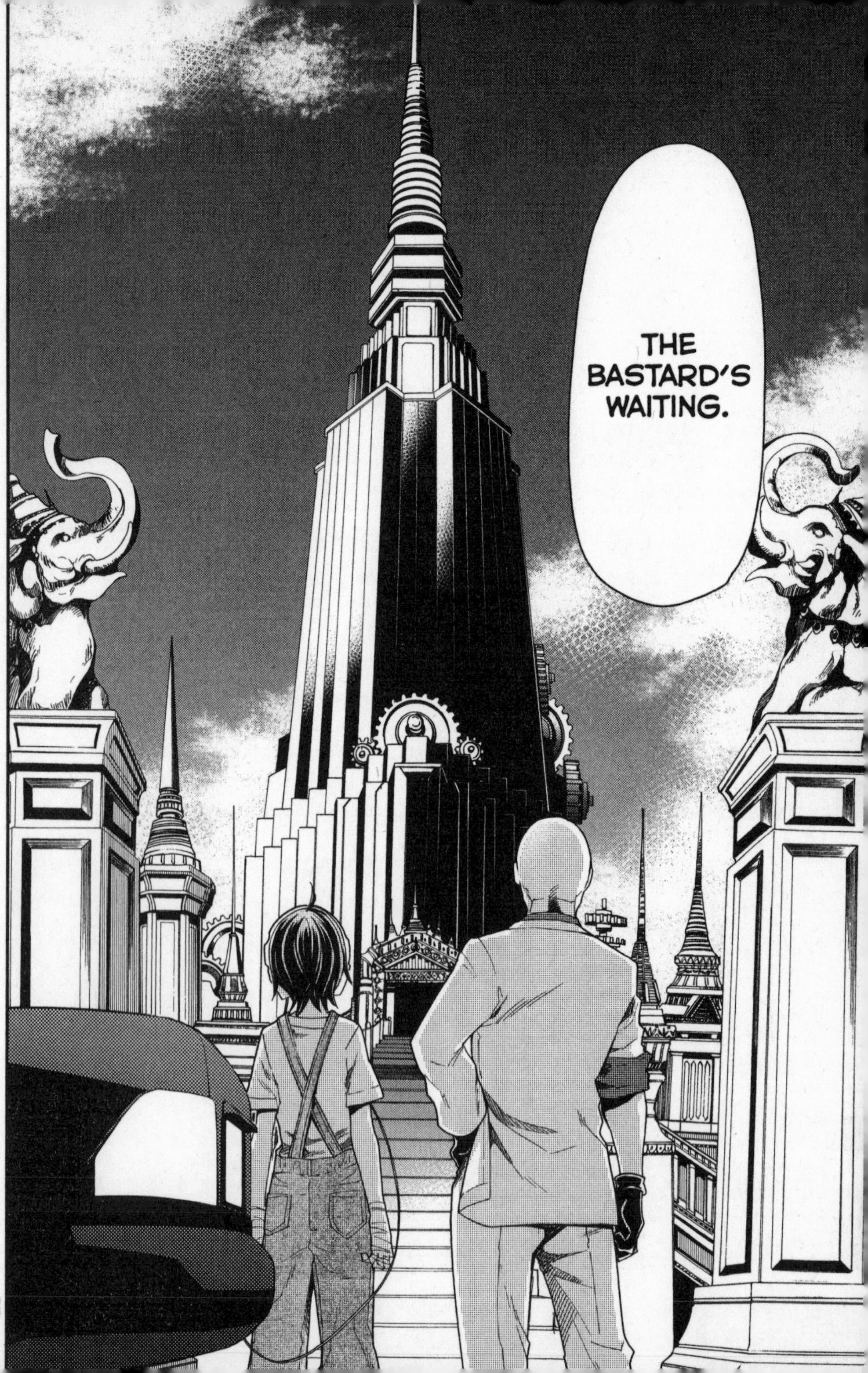
THE BASTARD'S WAITING.

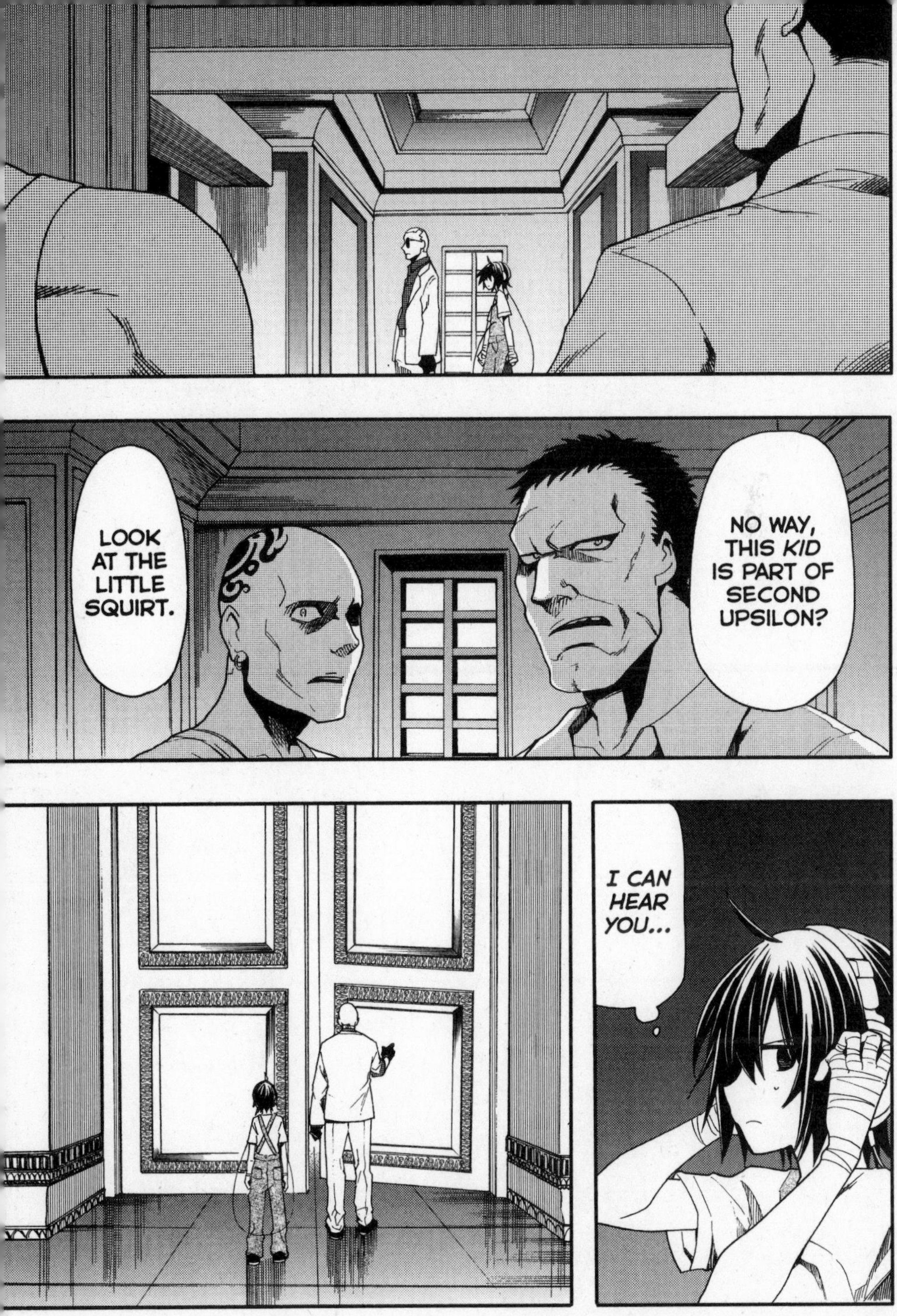
NO WAY, THIS *KID* IS PART OF SECOND UPSILON?
LOOK AT THE LITTLE SQUIRT.
I CAN HEAR YOU...

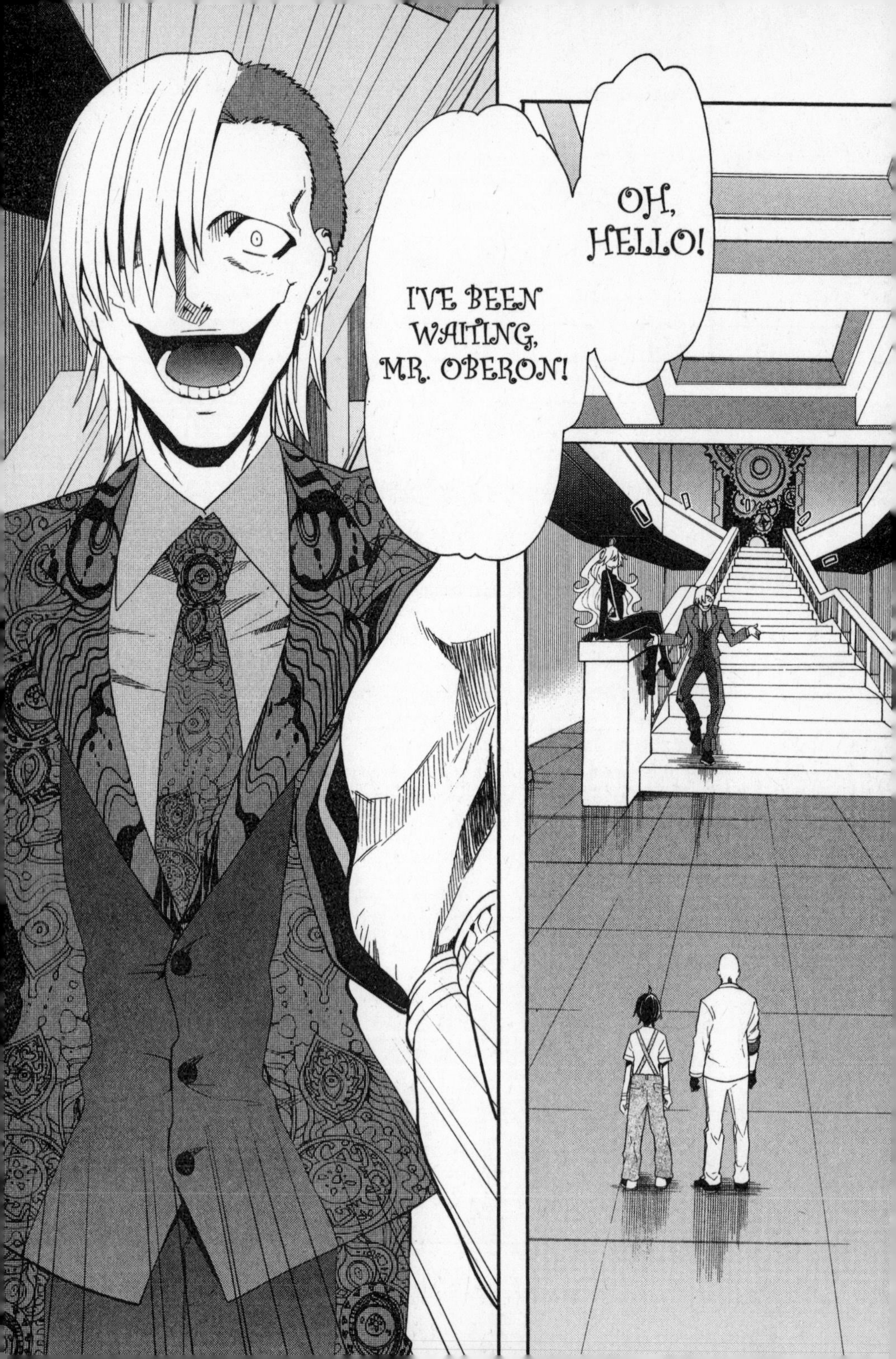
OH, HELLO!
I'VE BEEN WAITING, MR. OBERON!

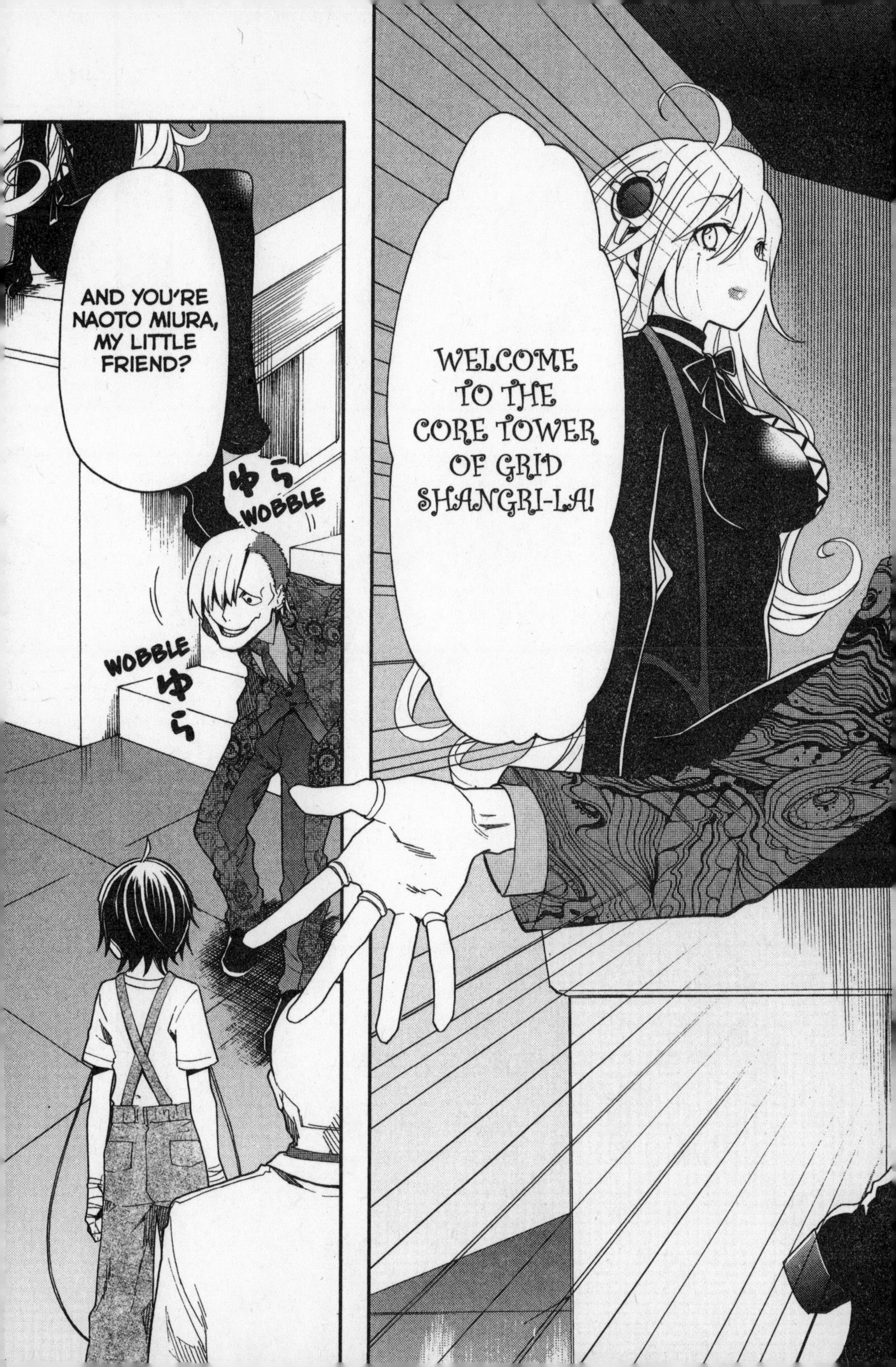
WELCOME TO THE CORE TOWER OF GRID SHANGRI-LA!
AND YOU'RE NAOTO MIURA, MY LITTLE FRIEND?
ゆら
WOBBLE
WOBBLE
ゆら

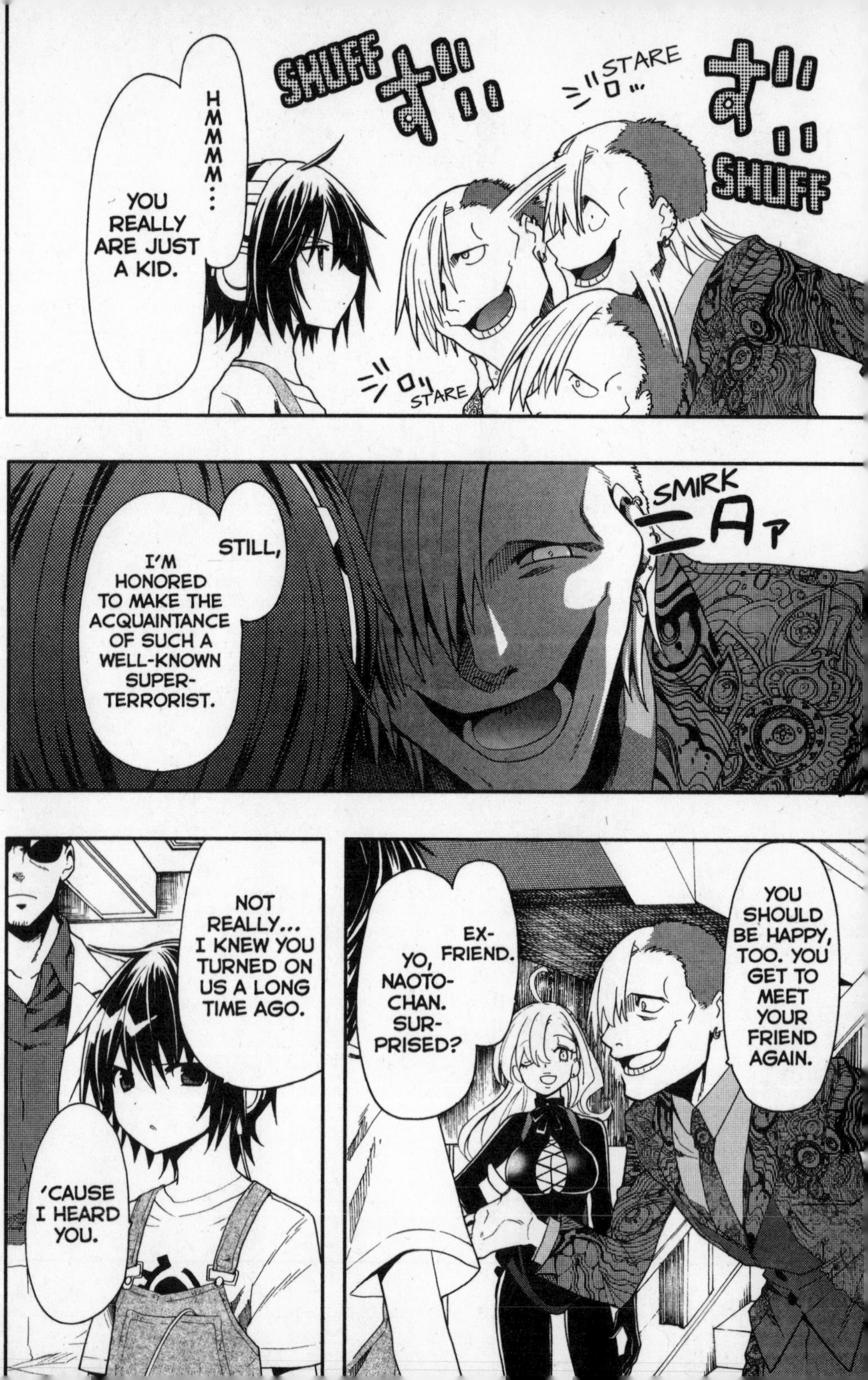
SHUFF
STARE
HMMMM... YOU REALLY ARE JUST A KID.
SHUFF
STARE
SMIRK
STILL, I'M HONORED TO MAKE THE ACQUAINTANCE OF SUCH A WELL-KNOWN SUPER-TERRORIST.
YOU SHOULD BE HAPPY, TOO. YOU GET TO MEET YOUR FRIEND AGAIN.
EX-FRIEND.
YO, NAOTO-CHAN. SURPRISED?
NOT REALLY... I KNEW YOU TURNED ON US A LONG TIME AGO.
'CAUSE I HEARD YOU.

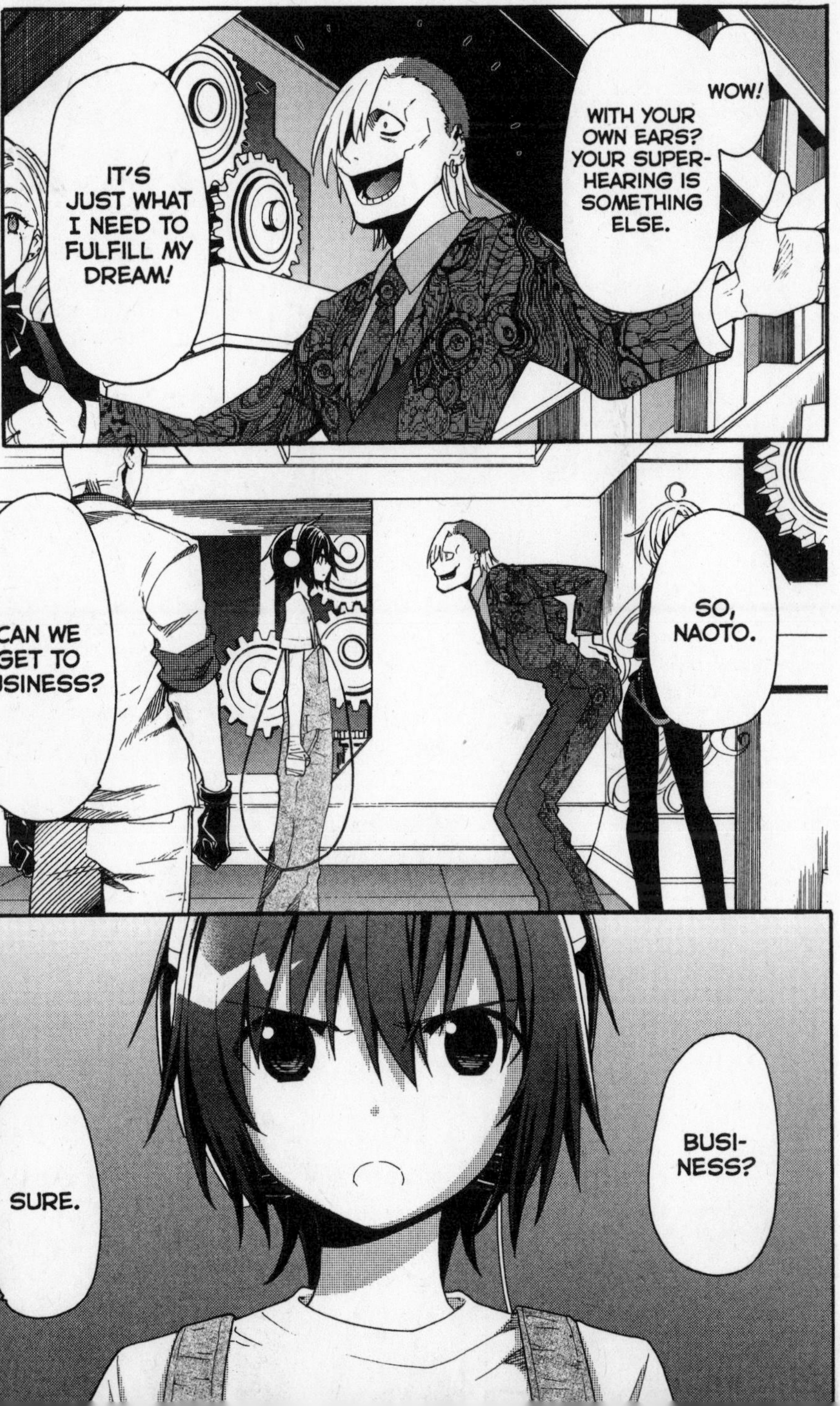
WOW!
WITH YOUR OWN EARS? YOUR SUPER-HEARING IS SOMETHING ELSE.
IT'S JUST WHAT I NEED TO FULFILL MY DREAM!
SO, NAOTO.
CAN WE GET TO BUSINESS?
BUSI-NESS?
SURE.

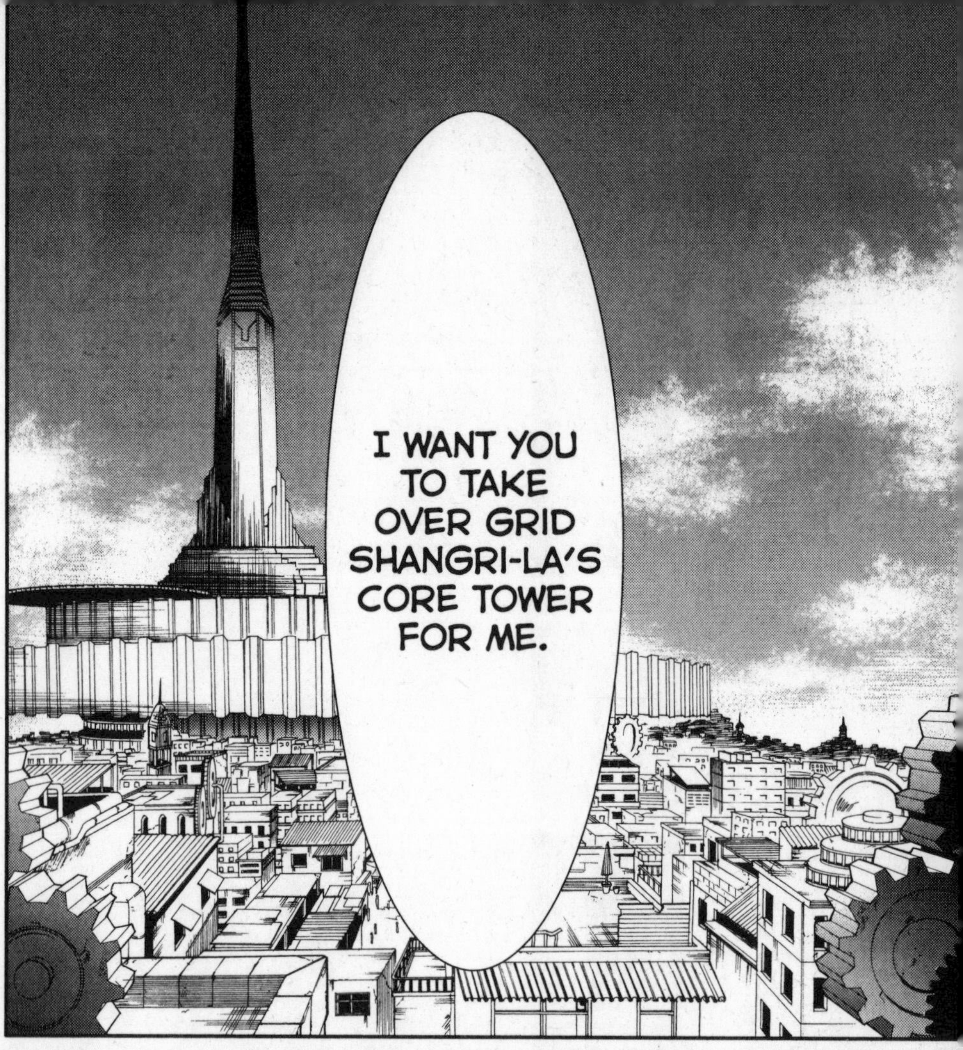
I WANT YOU TO TAKE OVER GRID SHANGRI-LA'S CORE TOWER FOR ME.

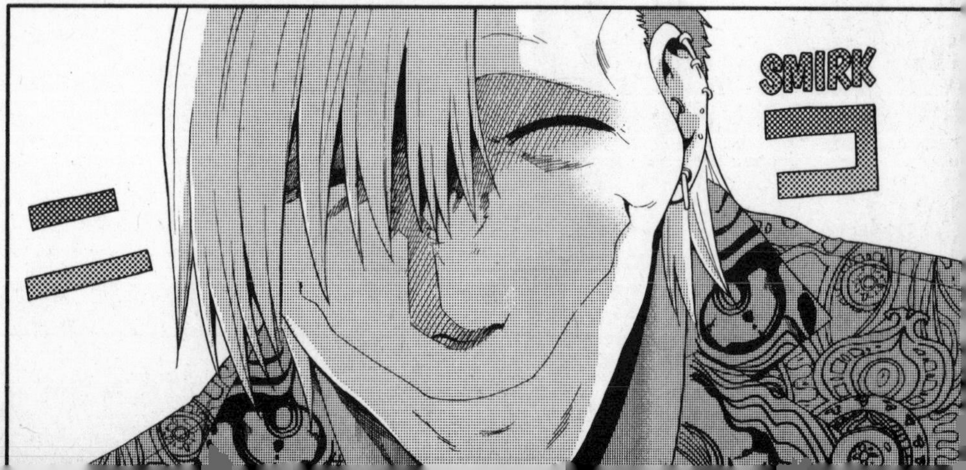
SMIRK

CLOCKWORK PLANET

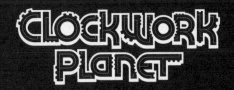

CLOCKWORK PLANET

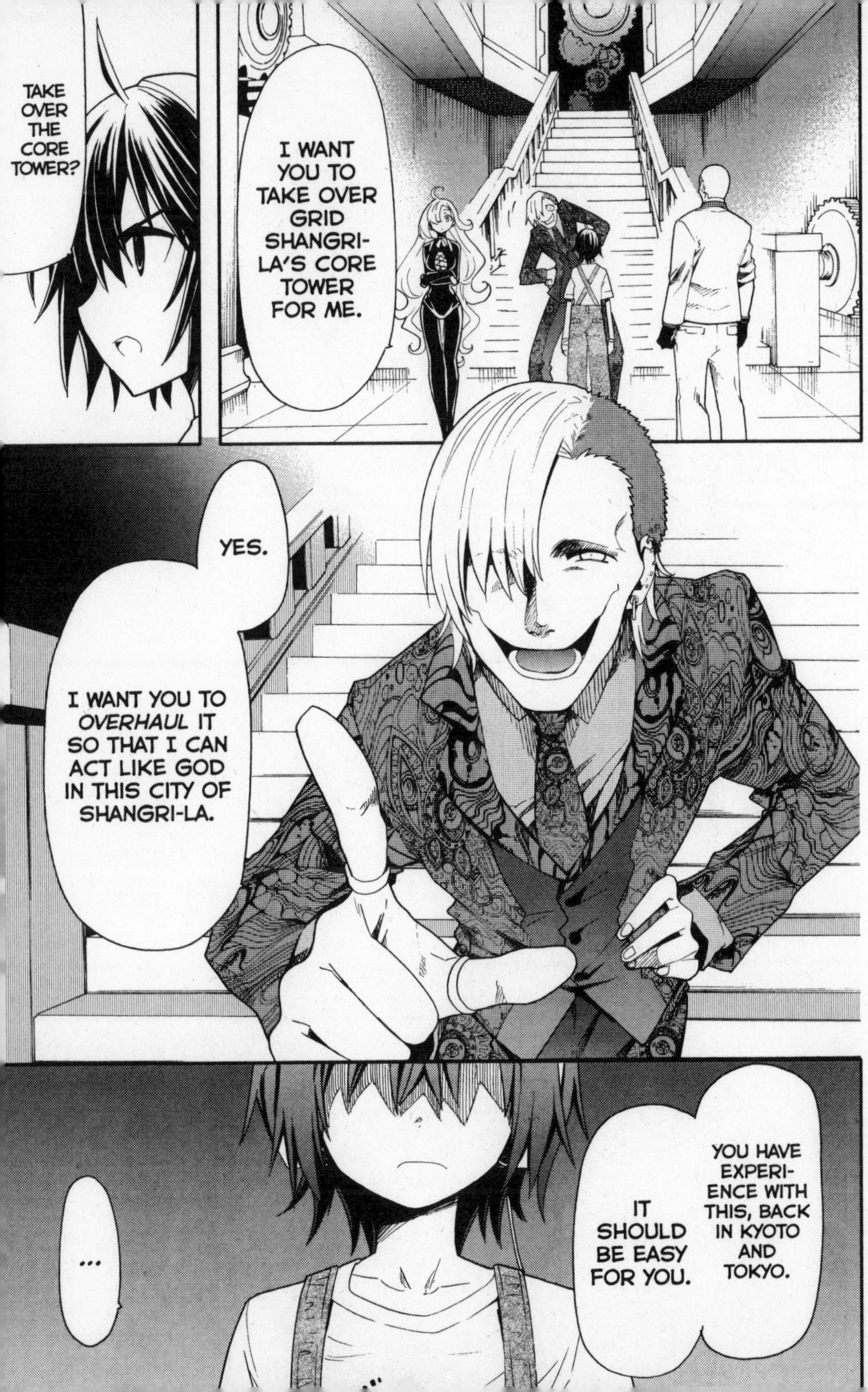
I WANT YOU TO TAKE OVER GRID SHANGRI-LA'S CORE TOWER FOR ME.
TAKE OVER THE CORE TOWER?
YES.
I WANT YOU TO *OVERHAUL* IT SO THAT I CAN ACT LIKE GOD IN THIS CITY OF SHANGRI-LA.
YOU HAVE EXPERIENCE WITH THIS, BACK IN KYOTO AND TOKYO.
IT SHOULD BE EASY FOR YOU.
...

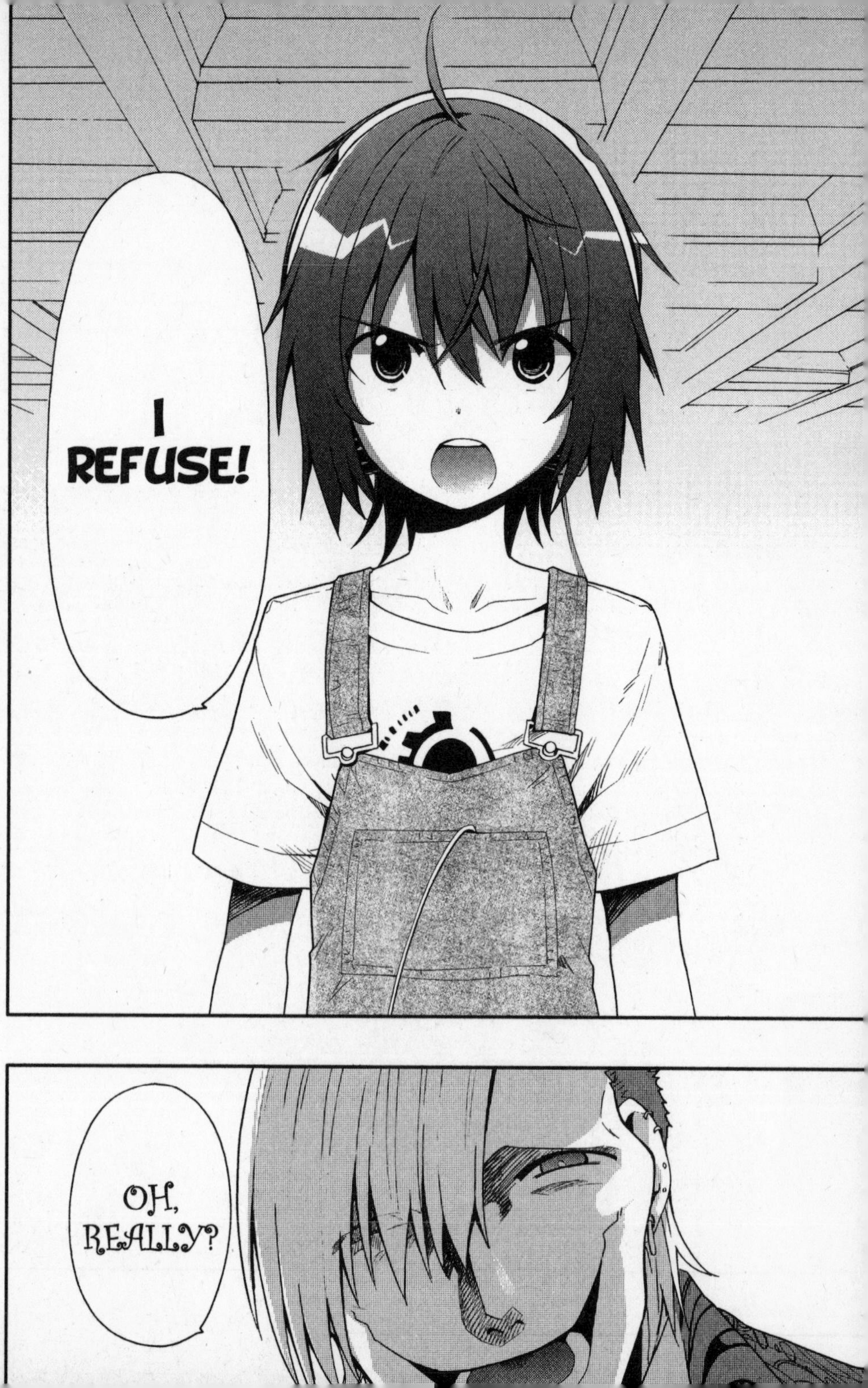
I REFUSE!
OH, REALLY?

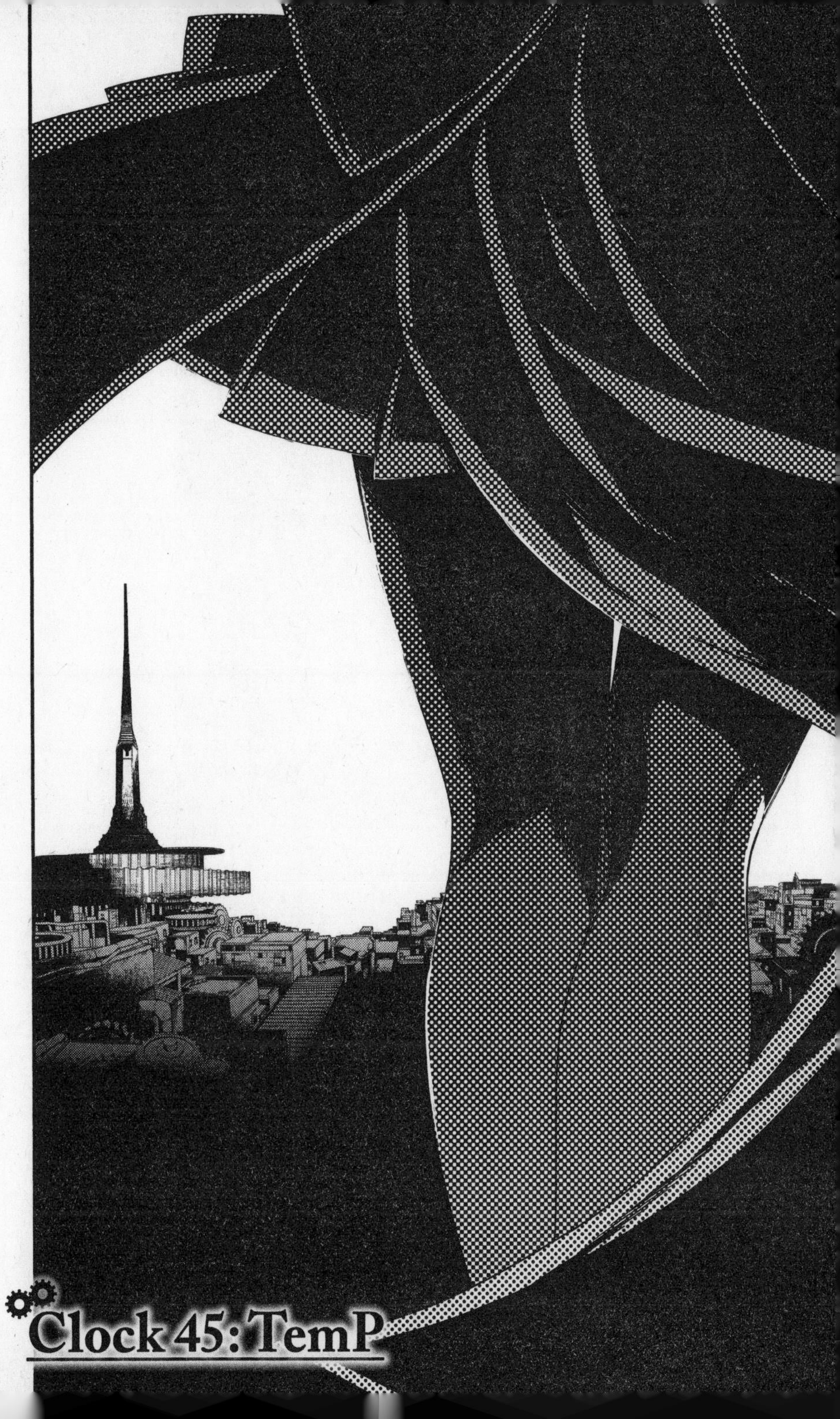
Clock 45: TemP

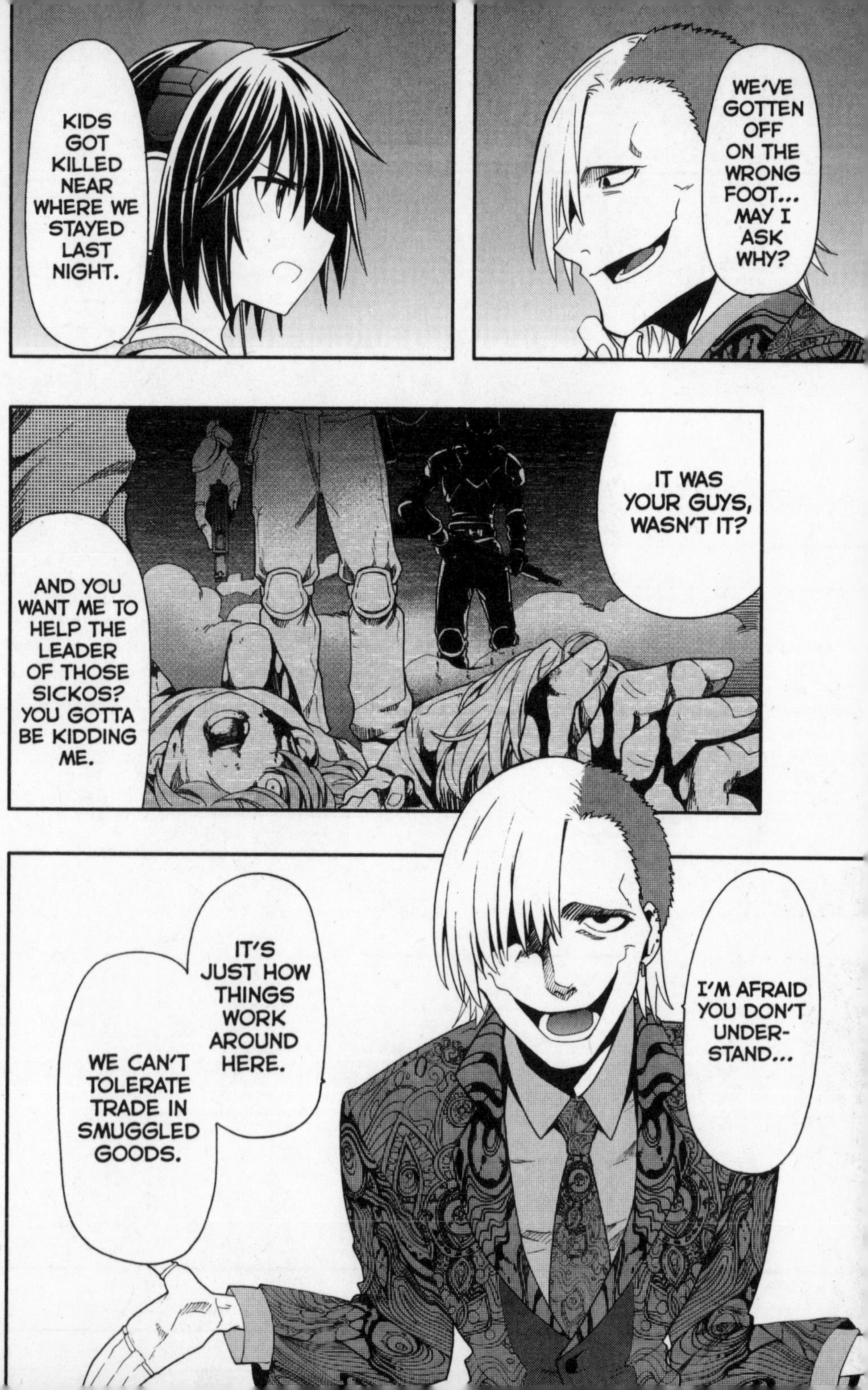
WE'VE GOTTEN OFF ON THE WRONG FOOT... MAY I ASK WHY?
KIDS GOT KILLED NEAR WHERE WE STAYED LAST NIGHT.
IT WAS YOUR GUYS, WASN'T IT?
AND YOU WANT ME TO HELP THE LEADER OF THOSE SICKOS? YOU GOTTA BE KIDDING ME.
I'M AFRAID YOU DON'T UNDER-STAND...
IT'S JUST HOW THINGS WORK AROUND HERE.
WE CAN'T TOLERATE TRADE IN SMUGGLED GOODS.

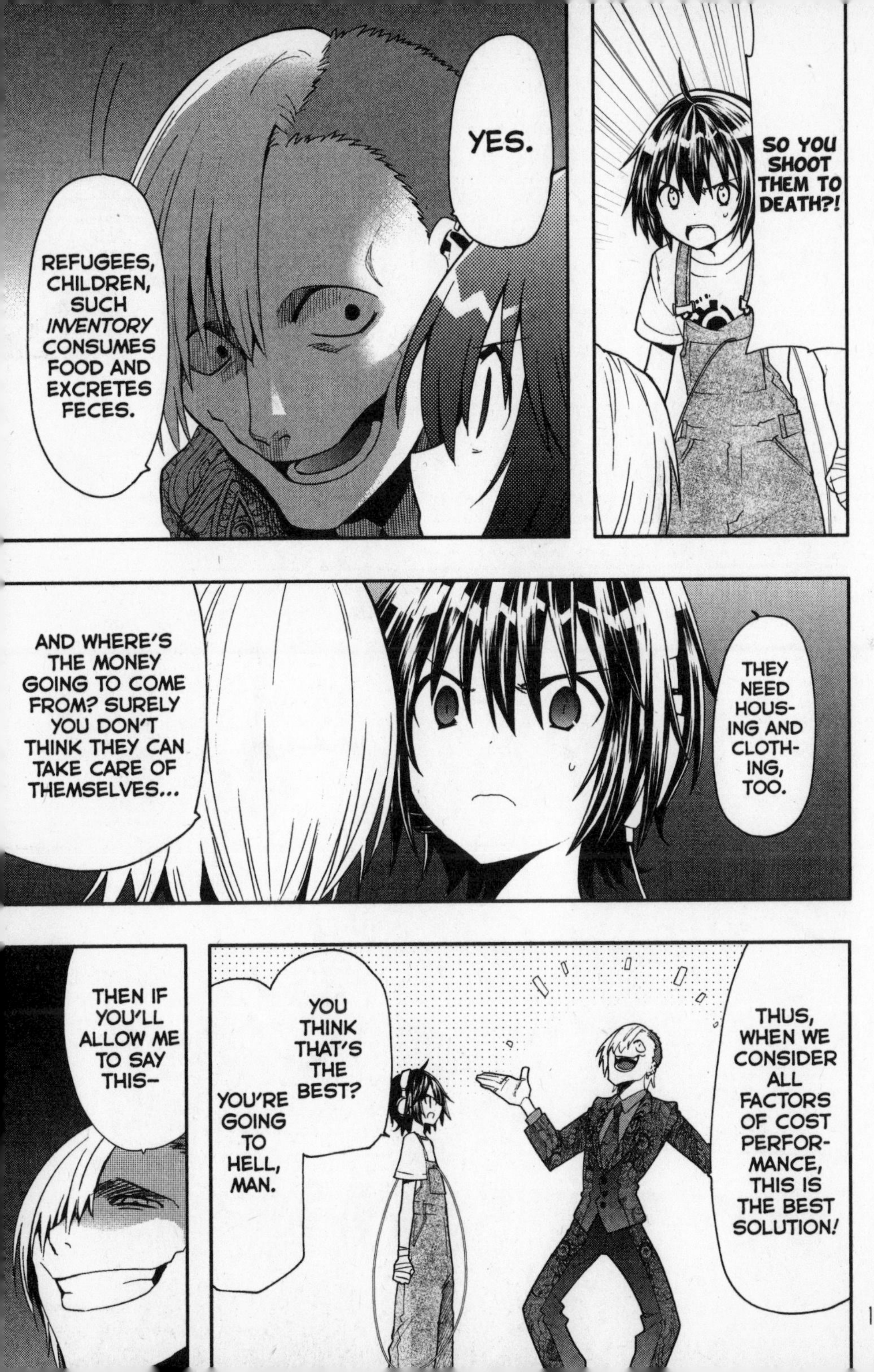
SO YOU SHOOT THEM TO DEATH?!
YES.
REFUGEES, CHILDREN, SUCH *INVENTORY* CONSUMES FOOD AND EXCRETES FECES.
THEY NEED HOUSING AND CLOTHING, TOO.
AND WHERE'S THE MONEY GOING TO COME FROM? SURELY YOU DON'T THINK THEY CAN TAKE CARE OF THEMSELVES...
THUS, WHEN WE CONSIDER ALL FACTORS OF COST PERFORMANCE, THIS IS THE BEST SOLUTION!
YOU THINK THAT'S THE BEST?
YOU'RE GOING TO HELL, MAN.
THEN IF YOU'LL ALLOW ME TO SAY THIS–

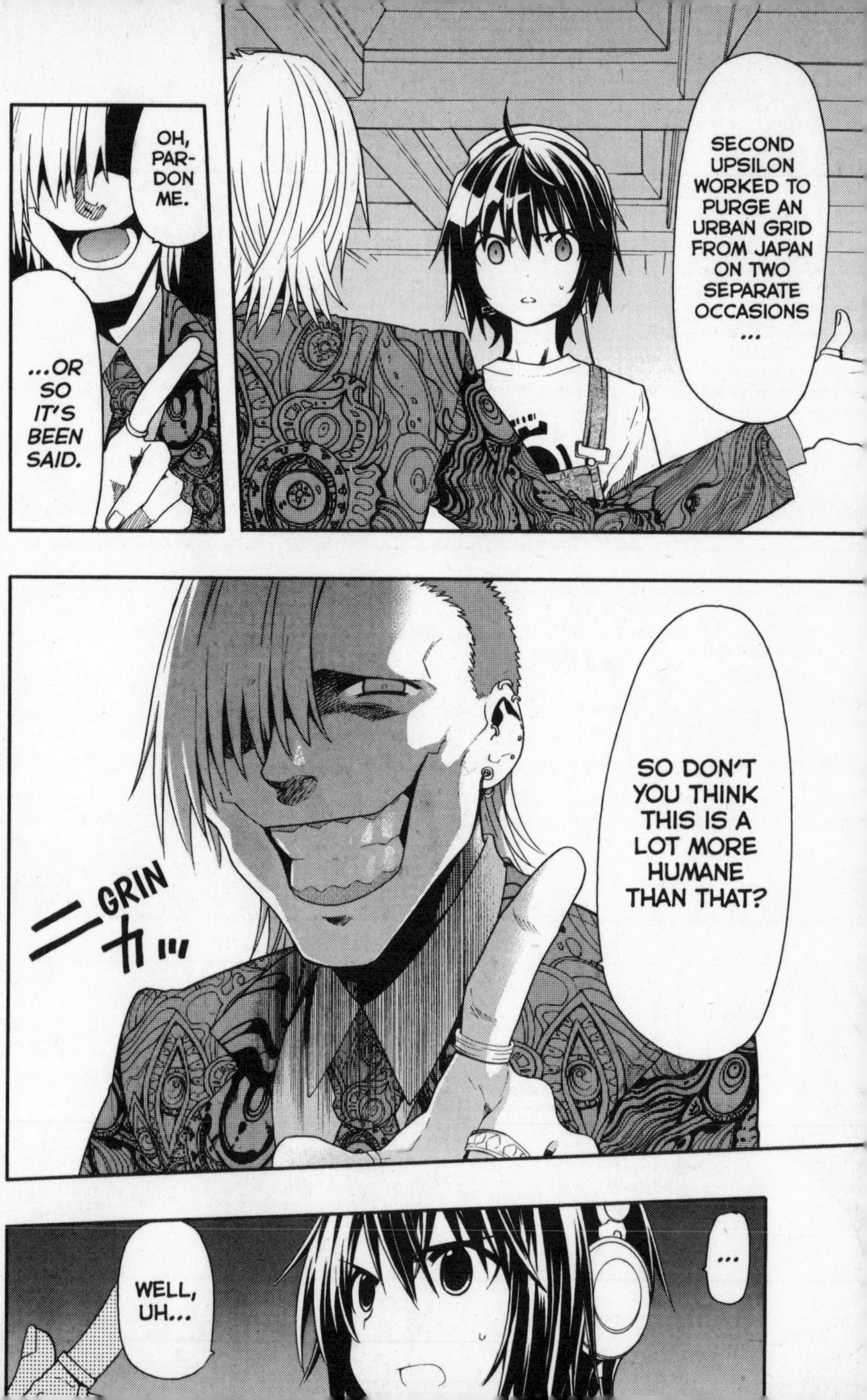
SECOND UPSILON WORKED TO PURGE AN URBAN GRID FROM JAPAN ON TWO SEPARATE OCCASIONS ...
OH, PAR-DON ME.
...OR SO IT'S BEEN SAID.
SO DON'T YOU THINK THIS IS A LOT MORE HUMANE THAN THAT?
GRIN
...
WELL, UH...

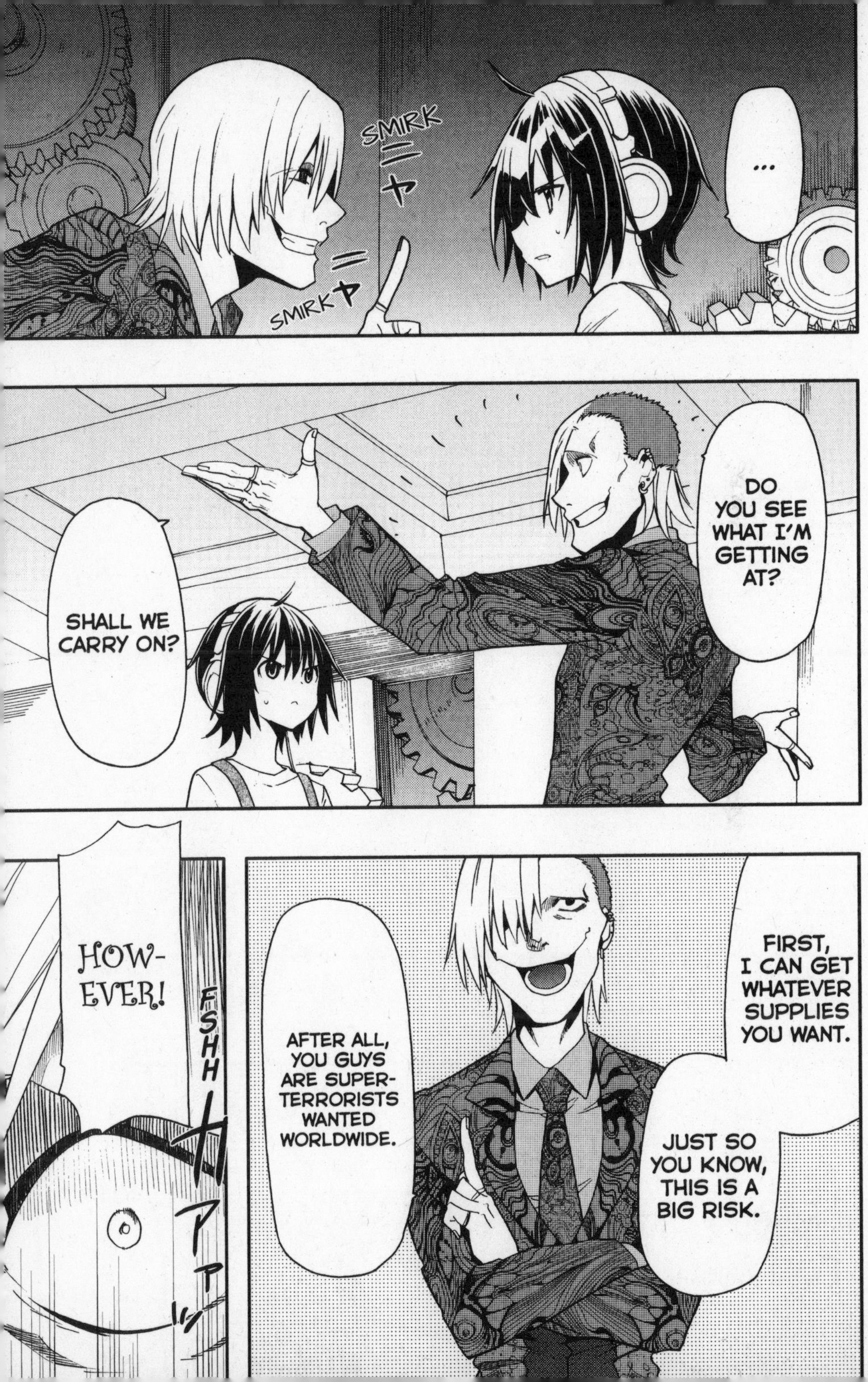

...
SMIRK
SMIRK
DO YOU SEE WHAT I'M GETTING AT?
SHALL WE CARRY ON?
FIRST, I CAN GET WHATEVER SUPPLIES YOU WANT.
JUST SO YOU KNOW, THIS IS A BIG RISK.
AFTER ALL, YOU GUYS ARE SUPER-TERRORISTS WANTED WORLDWIDE.
HOW-EVER!
FSHH

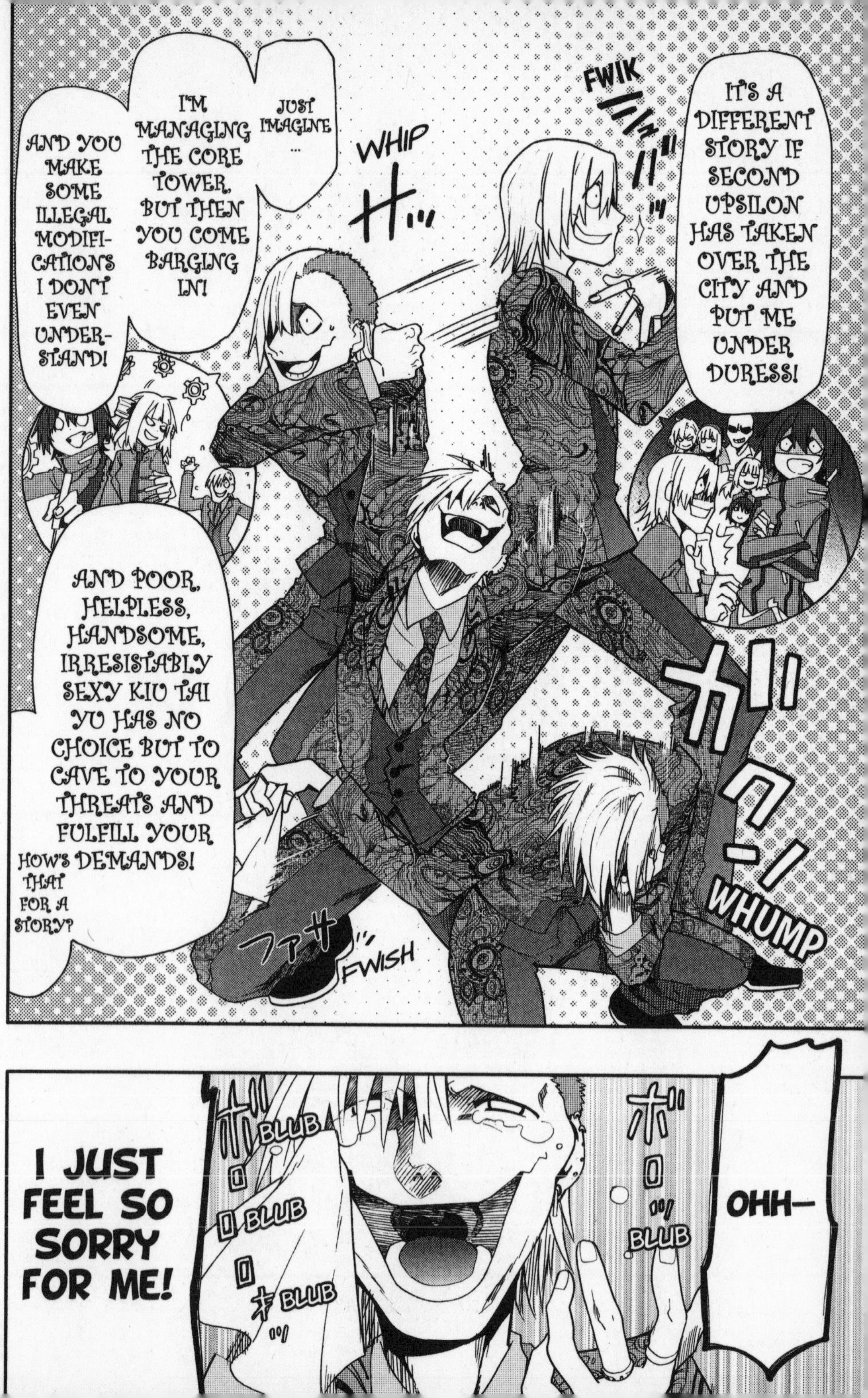
IT'S A DIFFERENT STORY IF SECOND UPSILON HAS TAKEN OVER THE CITY AND PUT ME UNDER DURESS!
FWIK
WHIP
JUST IMAGINE...
I'M MANAGING THE CORE TOWER, BUT THEN YOU COME BARGING IN!
AND YOU MAKE SOME ILLEGAL MODIFI-CATIONS I DON'T EVEN UNDER-STAND!
WHUMP
AND POOR, HELPLESS, HANDSOME, IRRESISTABLY SEXY KIU TAI YU HAS NO CHOICE BUT TO CAVE TO YOUR THREATS AND FULFILL YOUR DEMANDS!
HOW'S THAT FOR A STORY?
FWISH
OHH—
BLUB
BLUB
BLUB
BLUB
I JUST FEEL SO SORRY FOR ME!

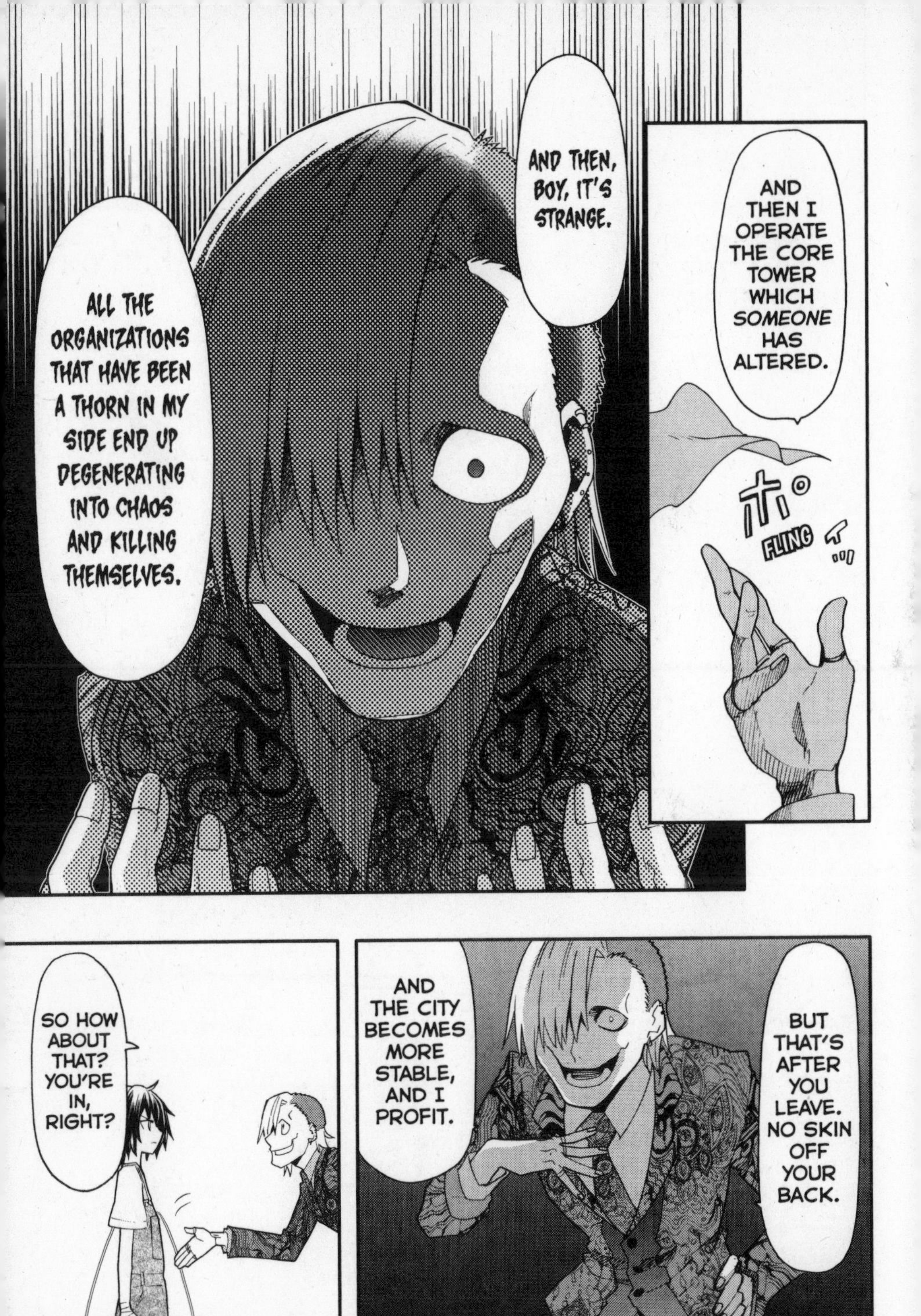
AND THEN I OPERATE THE CORE TOWER WHICH *SOMEONE* HAS ALTERED.
FLING
AND THEN, BOY, IT'S STRANGE.
ALL THE ORGANIZATIONS THAT HAVE BEEN A THORN IN MY SIDE END UP DEGENERATING INTO CHAOS AND KILLING THEMSELVES.
BUT THAT'S AFTER YOU LEAVE. NO SKIN OFF YOUR BACK.
AND THE CITY BECOMES MORE STABLE, AND I PROFIT.
SO HOW ABOUT THAT? YOU'RE IN, RIGHT?

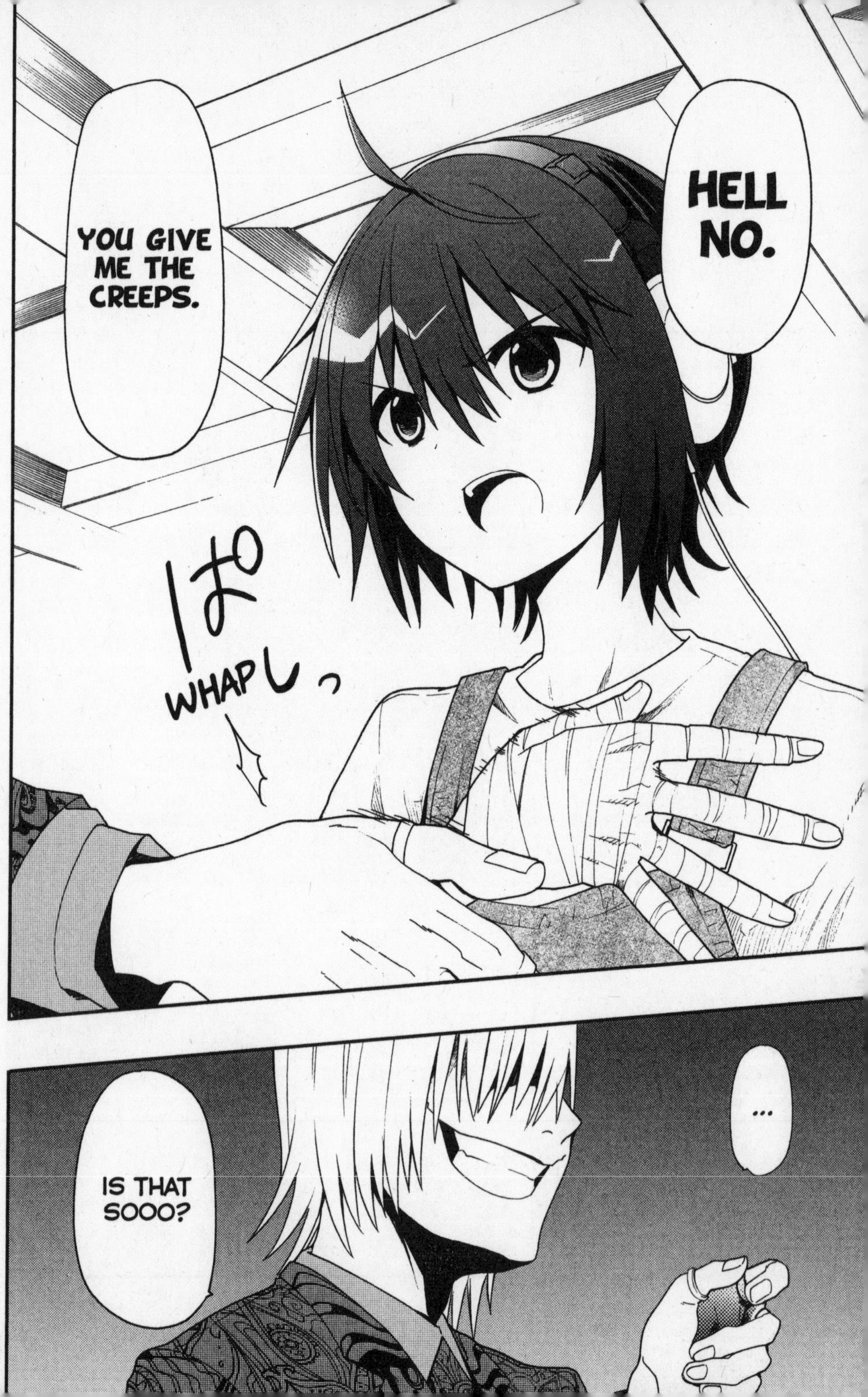
HELL NO.
YOU GIVE ME THE CREEPS.
ぱしっ
WHAP
...
IS THAT SOOO?

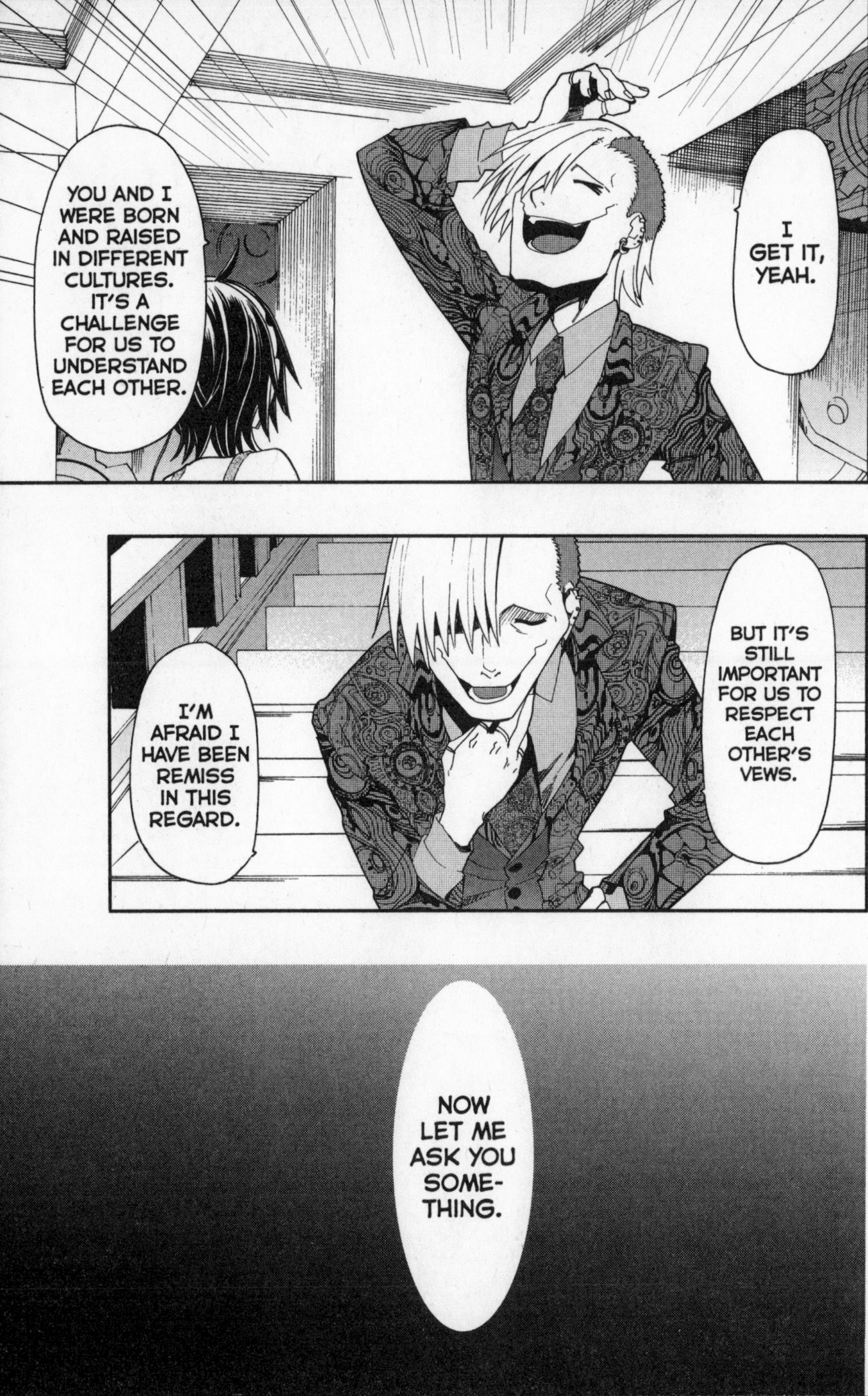
I GET IT, YEAH.
YOU AND I WERE BORN AND RAISED IN DIFFERENT CULTURES. IT'S A CHALLENGE FOR US TO UNDERSTAND EACH OTHER.
BUT IT'S STILL IMPORTANT FOR US TO RESPECT EACH OTHER'S VEWS.
I'M AFRAID I HAVE BEEN REMISS IN THIS REGARD.
NOW LET ME ASK YOU SOME-THING.

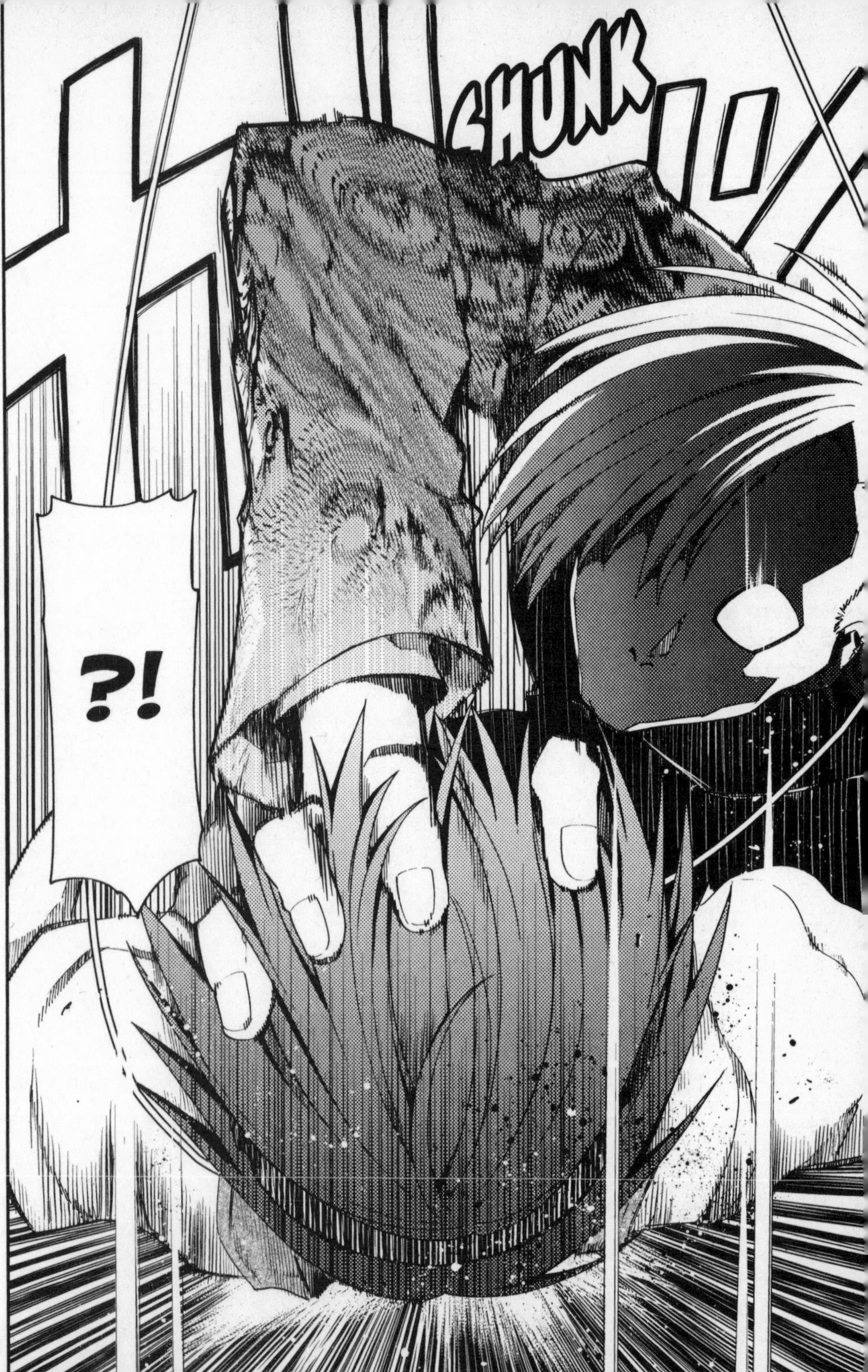
SHUNK
?!

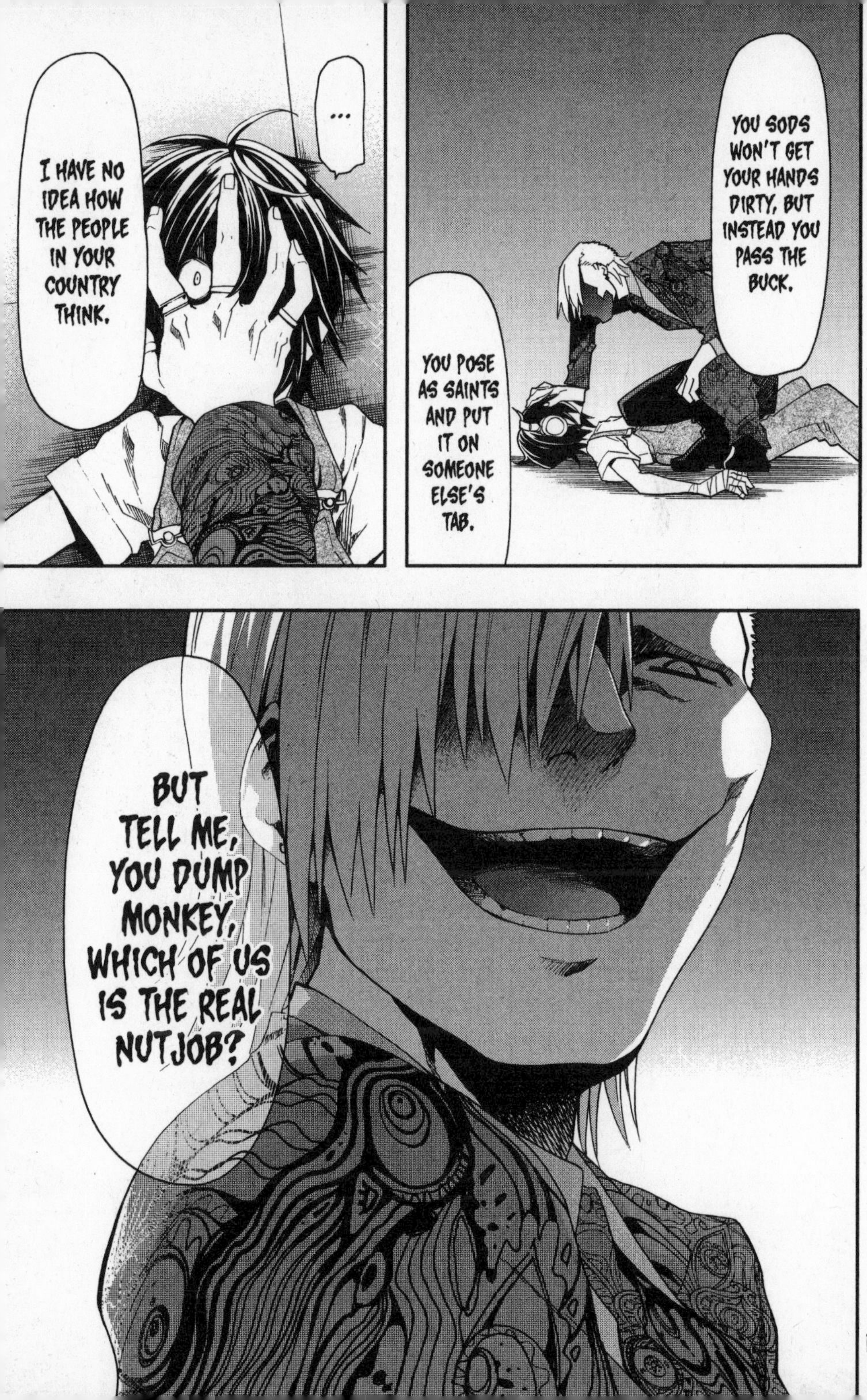
YOU SODS WON'T GET YOUR HANDS DIRTY, BUT INSTEAD YOU PASS THE BUCK.
YOU POSE AS SAINTS AND PUT IT ON SOMEONE ELSE'S TAB.
...
I HAVE NO IDEA HOW THE PEOPLE IN YOUR COUNTRY THINK.
BUT TELL ME, YOU DUMP MONKEY, WHICH OF US IS THE REAL NUTJOB?

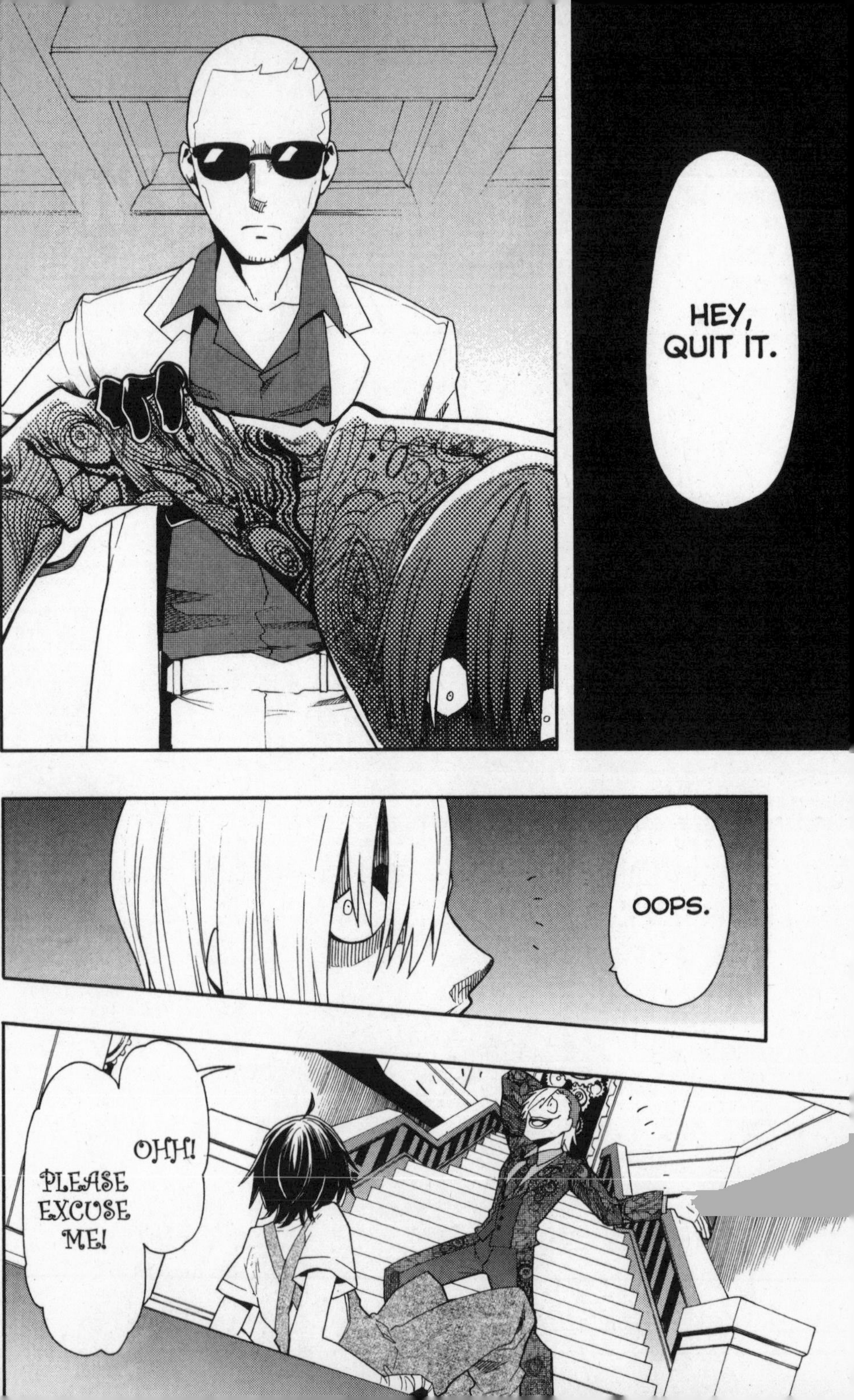
HEY, QUIT IT.
OOPS.
OHH! PLEASE EXCUSE ME!

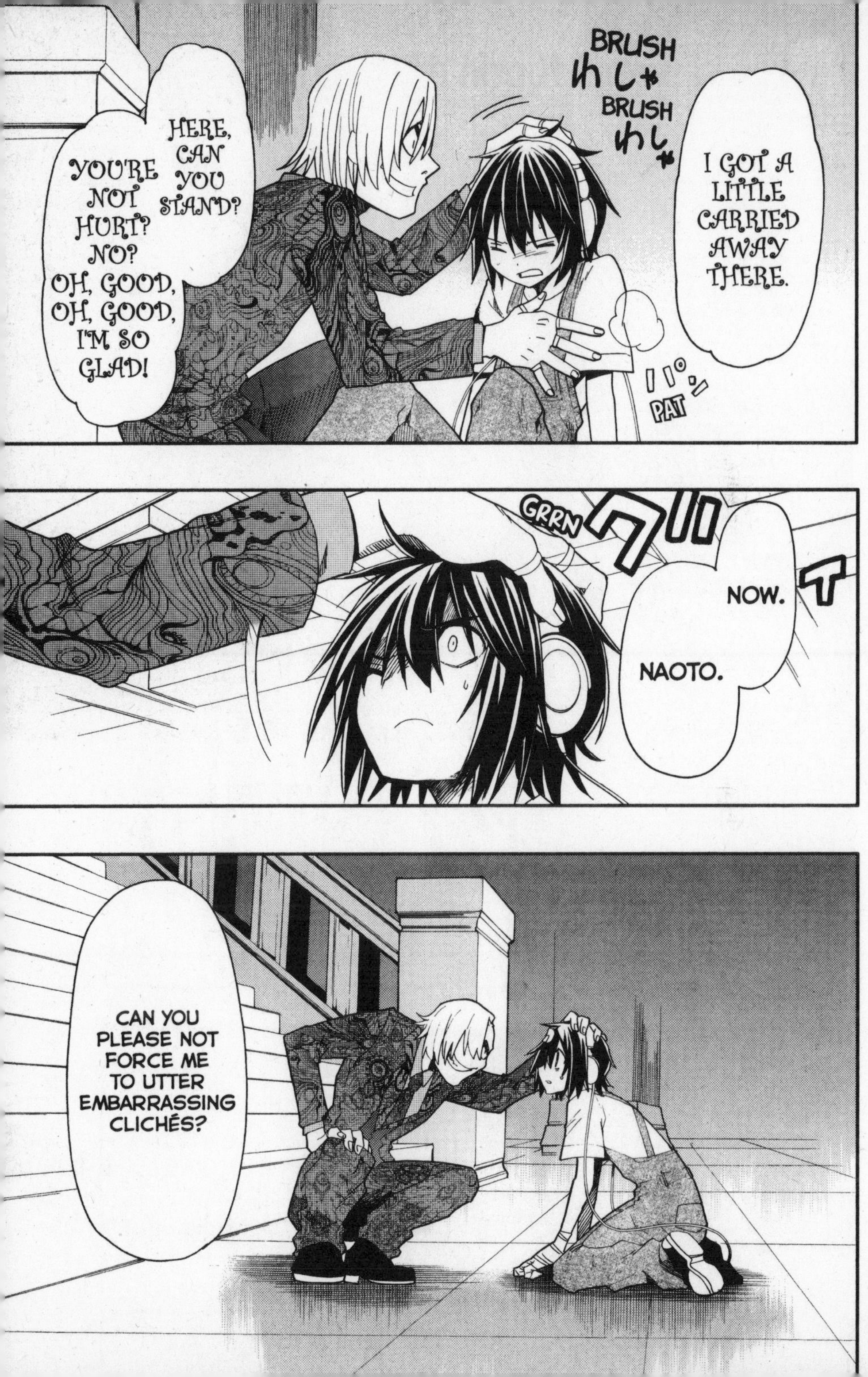

BRUSH
わしゃ
BRUSH
わしゃ
I GOT A LITTLE CARRIED AWAY THERE.
HERE, CAN YOU STAND?
YOU'RE NOT HURT? NO? OH, GOOD, OH, GOOD, I'M SO GLAD!
PAT
GRRN
NOW.
NAOTO.
CAN YOU PLEASE NOT FORCE ME TO UTTER EMBARRASSING CLICHÉS?

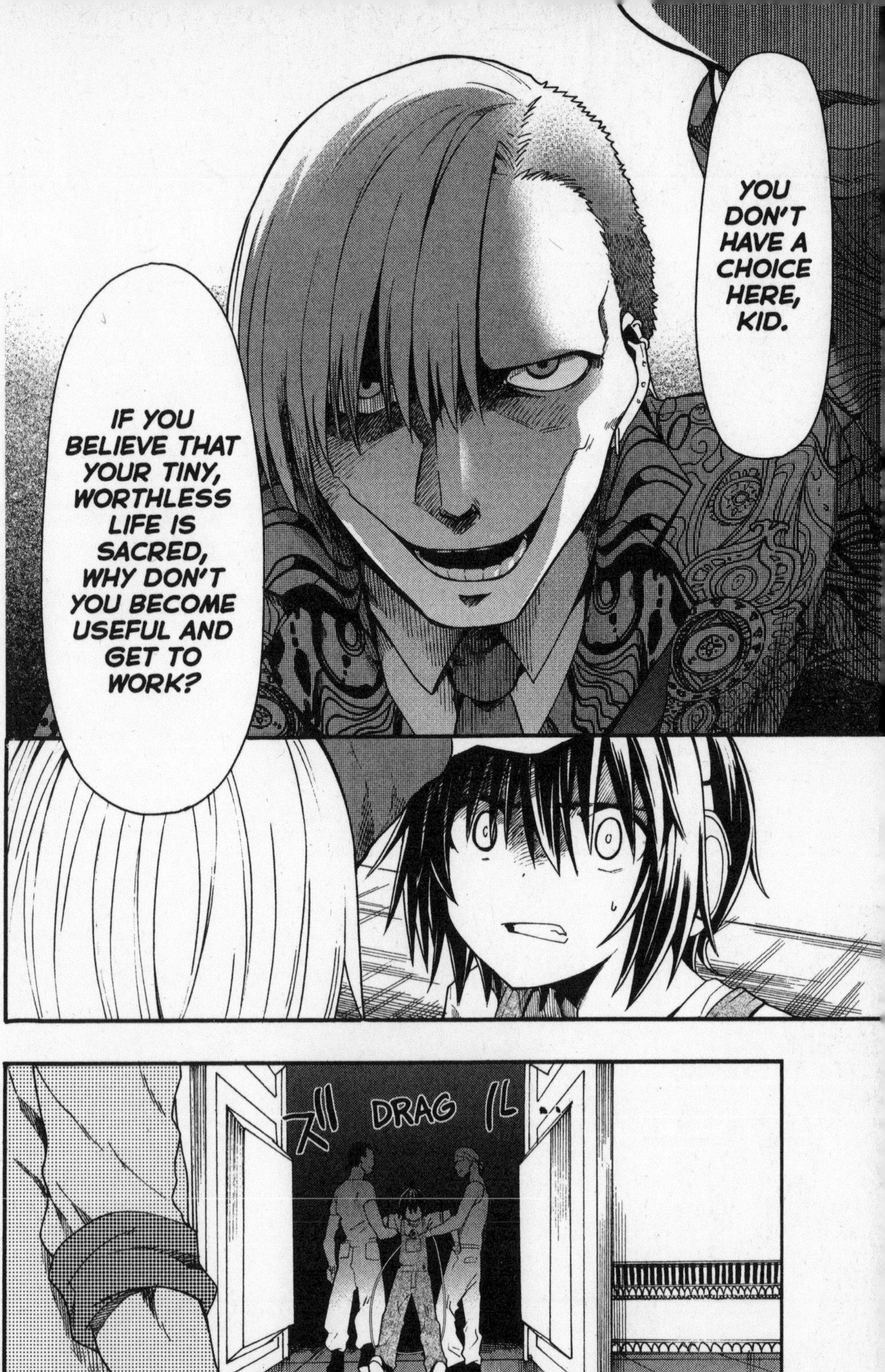
YOU DON'T HAVE A CHOICE HERE, KID.
IF YOU BELIEVE THAT YOUR TINY, WORTHLESS LIFE IS SACRED, WHY DON'T YOU BECOME USEFUL AND GET TO WORK?
DRAG

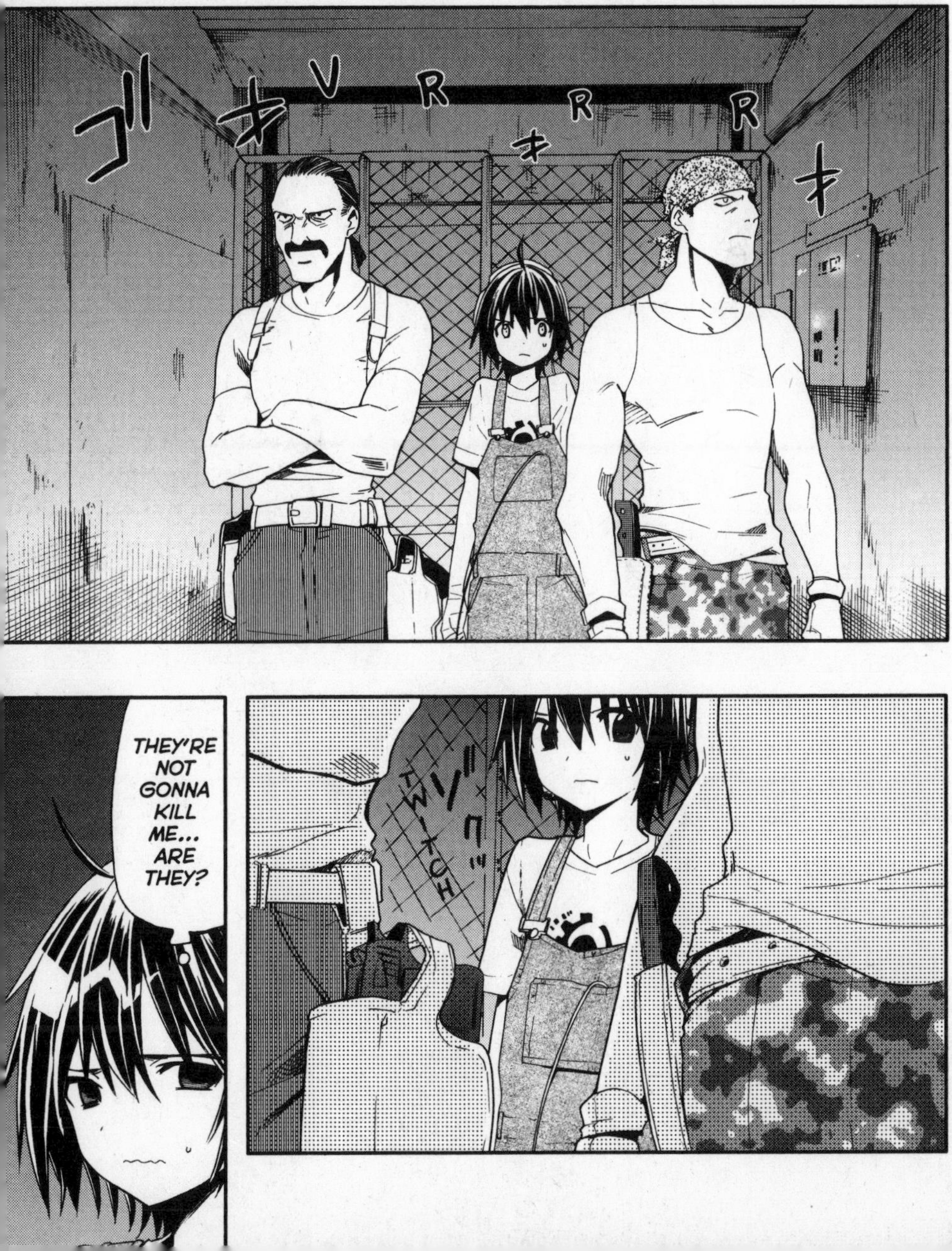
VRRR
TWITCH
THEY'RE NOT GONNA KILL ME... ARE THEY?

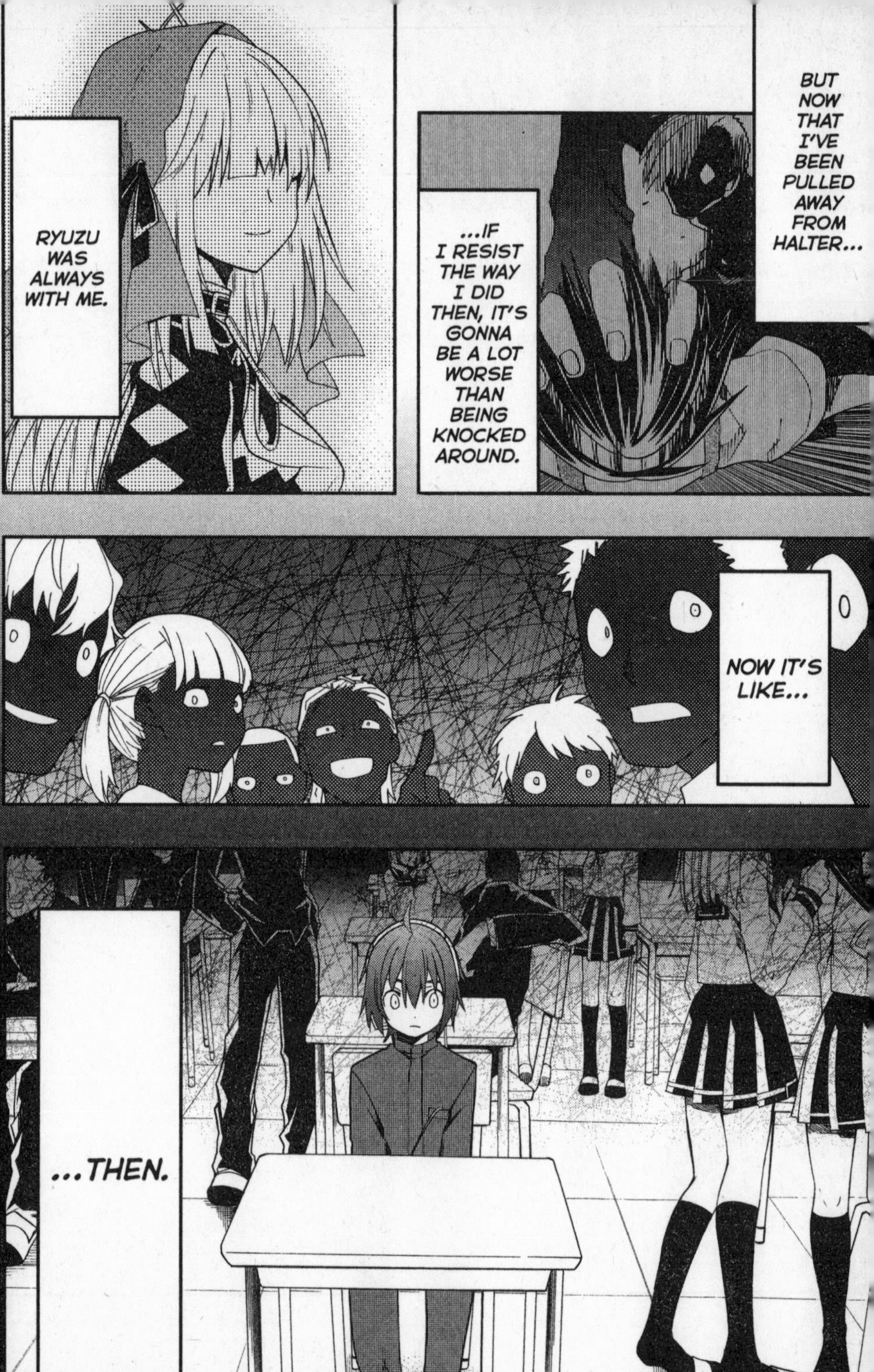
BUT NOW THAT I'VE BEEN PULLED AWAY FROM HALTER...
...IF I RESIST THE WAY I DID THEN, IT'S GONNA BE A LOT WORSE THAN BEING KNOCKED AROUND.
RYUZU WAS ALWAYS WITH ME.
NOW IT'S LIKE...
...THEN.

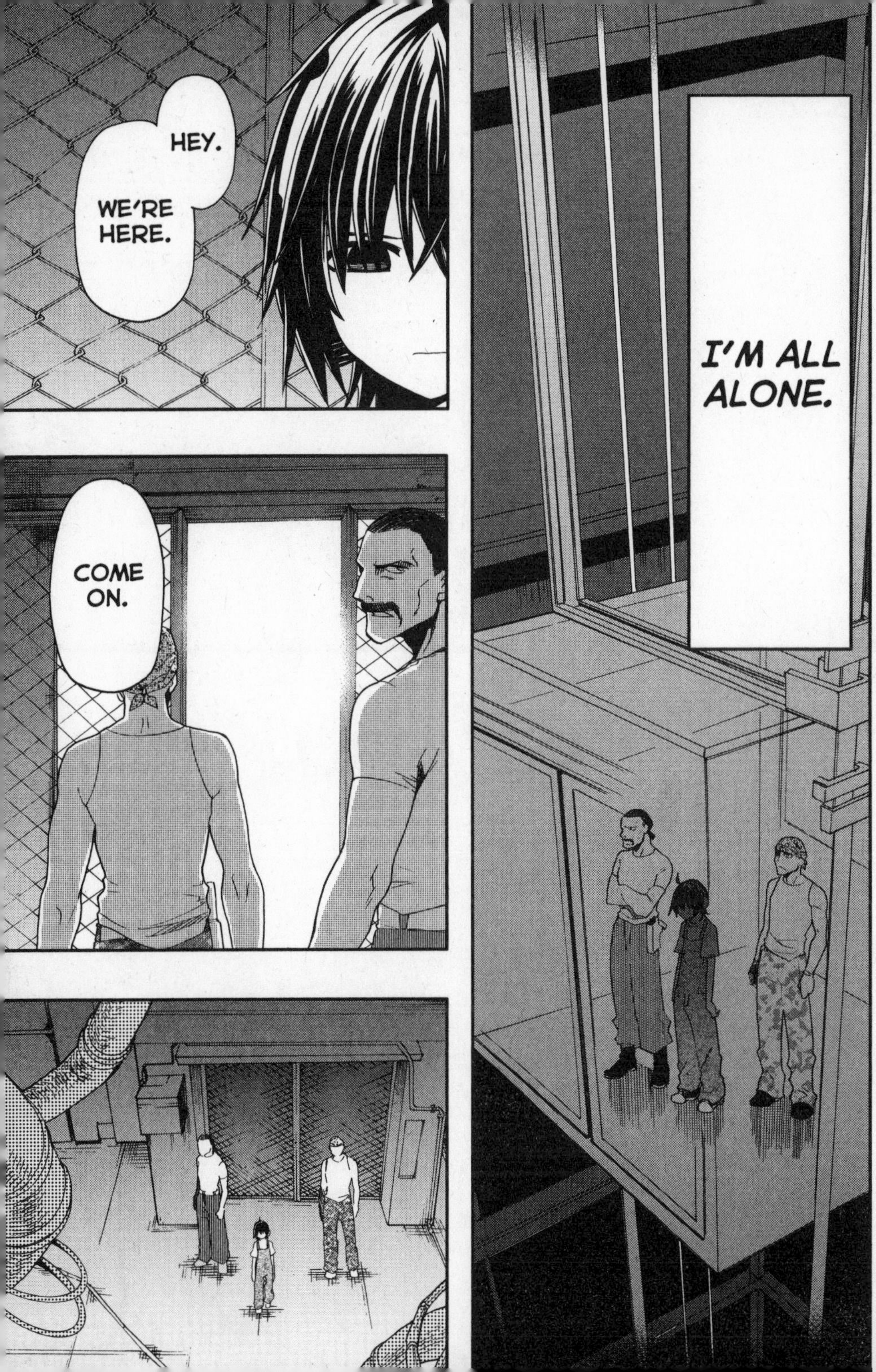
I'M ALL ALONE.
HEY.
WE'RE HERE.
COME ON.

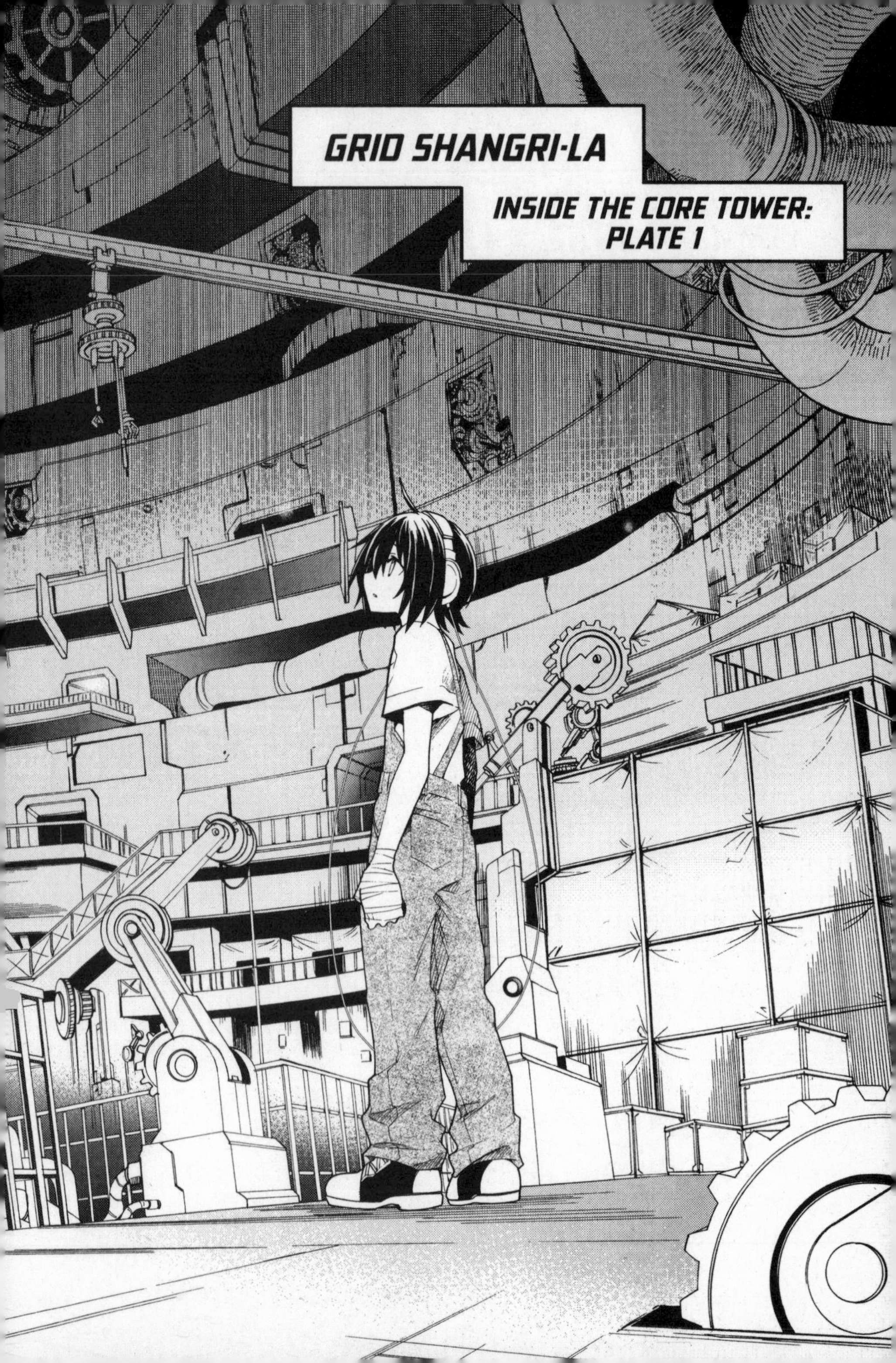
GRID SHANGRI-LA
INSIDE THE CORE TOWER:
PLATE 1

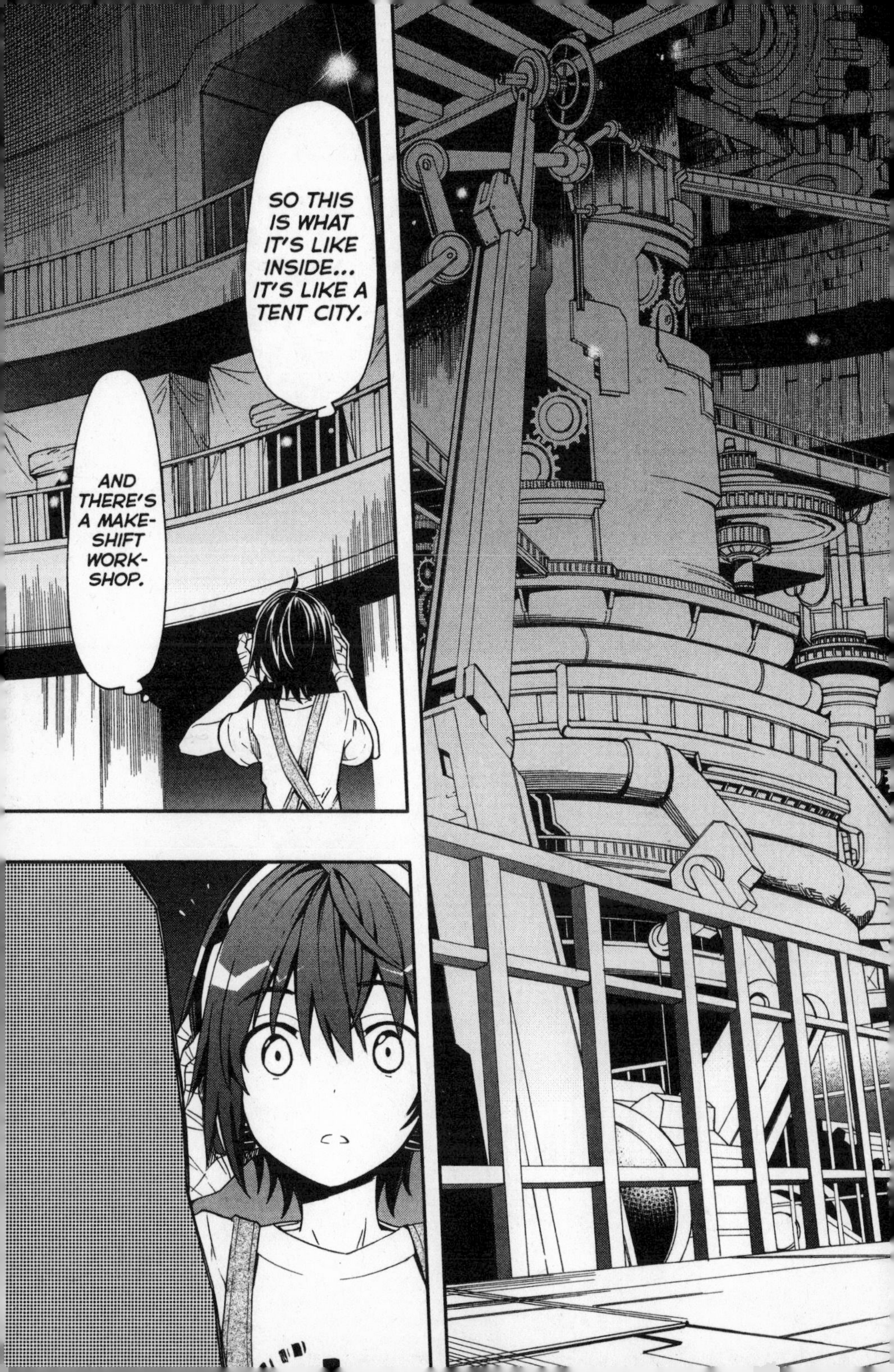
SO THIS IS WHAT IT'S LIKE INSIDE... IT'S LIKE A TENT CITY.
AND THERE'S A MAKE-SHIFT WORK-SHOP.

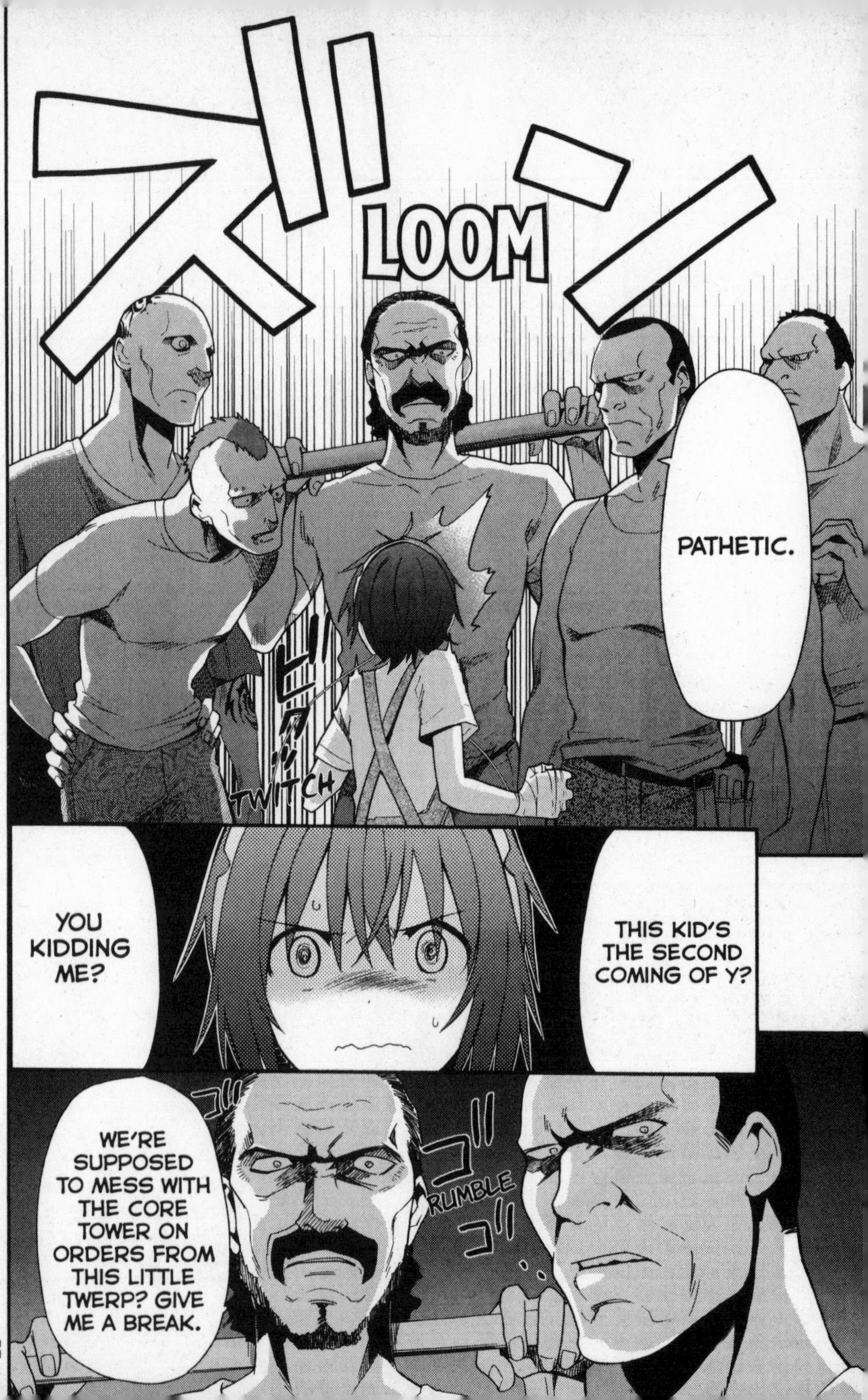
LOOM
PATHETIC.
TWITCH
THIS KID'S THE SECOND COMING OF Y?
YOU KIDDING ME?
RUMBLE
WE'RE SUPPOSED TO MESS WITH THE CORE TOWER ON ORDERS FROM THIS LITTLE TWERP? GIVE ME A BREAK.

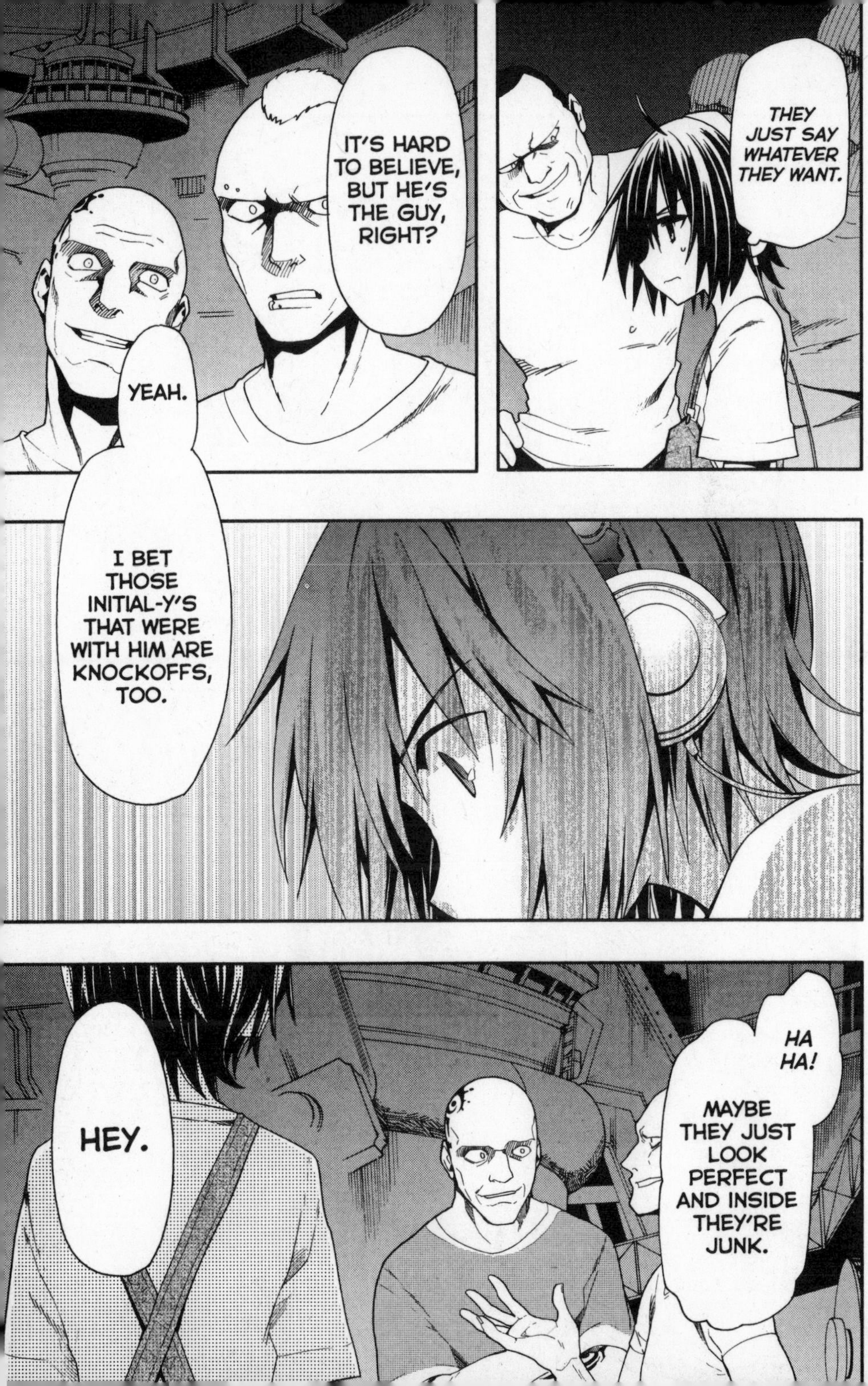
THEY JUST SAY WHATEVER THEY WANT.
IT'S HARD TO BELIEVE, BUT HE'S THE GUY, RIGHT?
YEAH.
I BET THOSE INITIAL-Y'S THAT WERE WITH HIM ARE KNOCKOFFS, TOO.
HA HA!
MAYBE THEY JUST LOOK PERFECT AND INSIDE THEY'RE JUNK.
HEY.

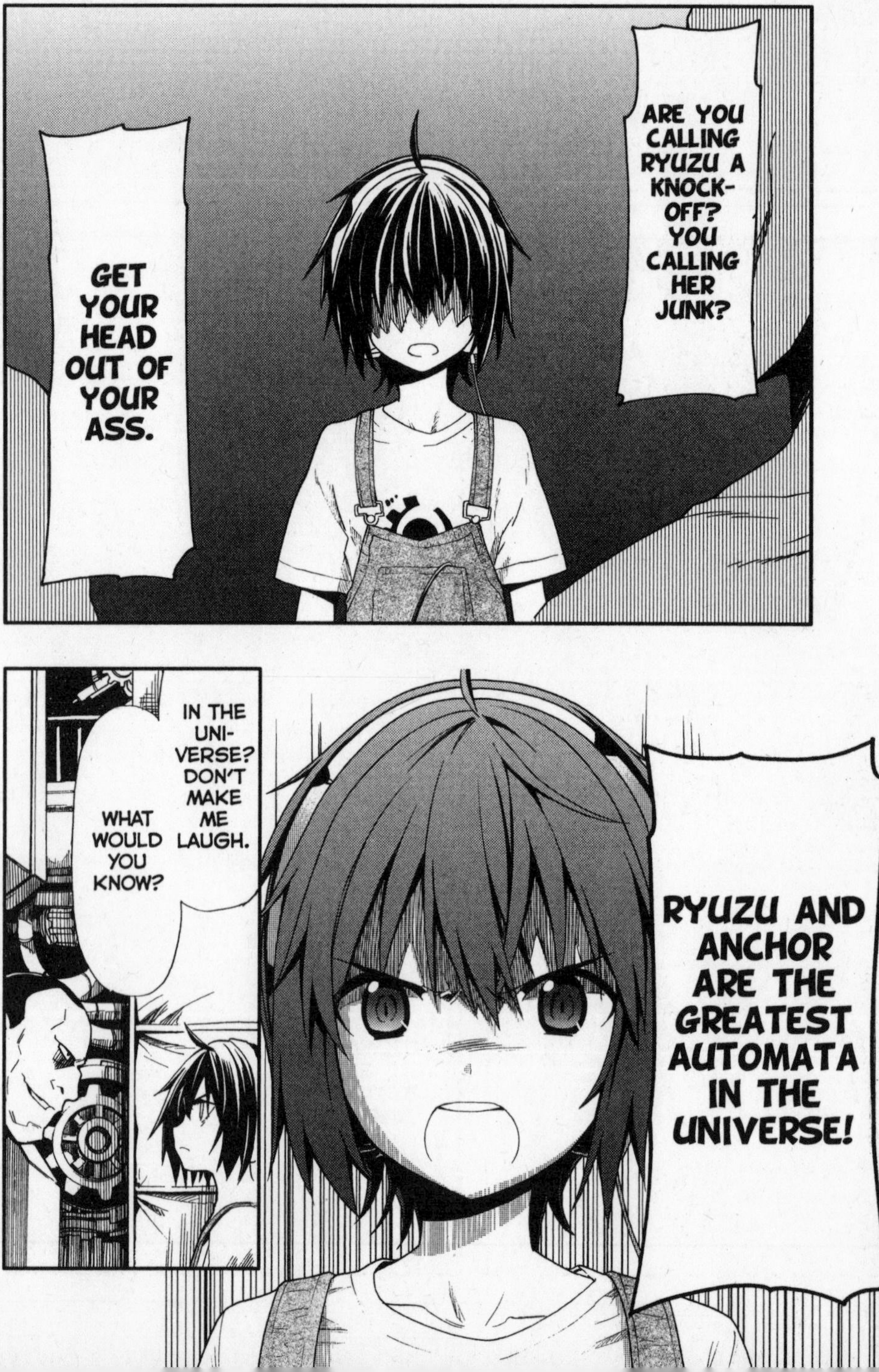
ARE YOU CALLING RYUZU A KNOCK-OFF? YOU CALLING HER JUNK?
GET YOUR HEAD OUT OF YOUR ASS.
RYUZU AND ANCHOR ARE THE GREATEST AUTOMATA IN THE UNIVERSE!
IN THE UNI-VERSE? DON'T MAKE ME LAUGH.
WHAT WOULD YOU KNOW?

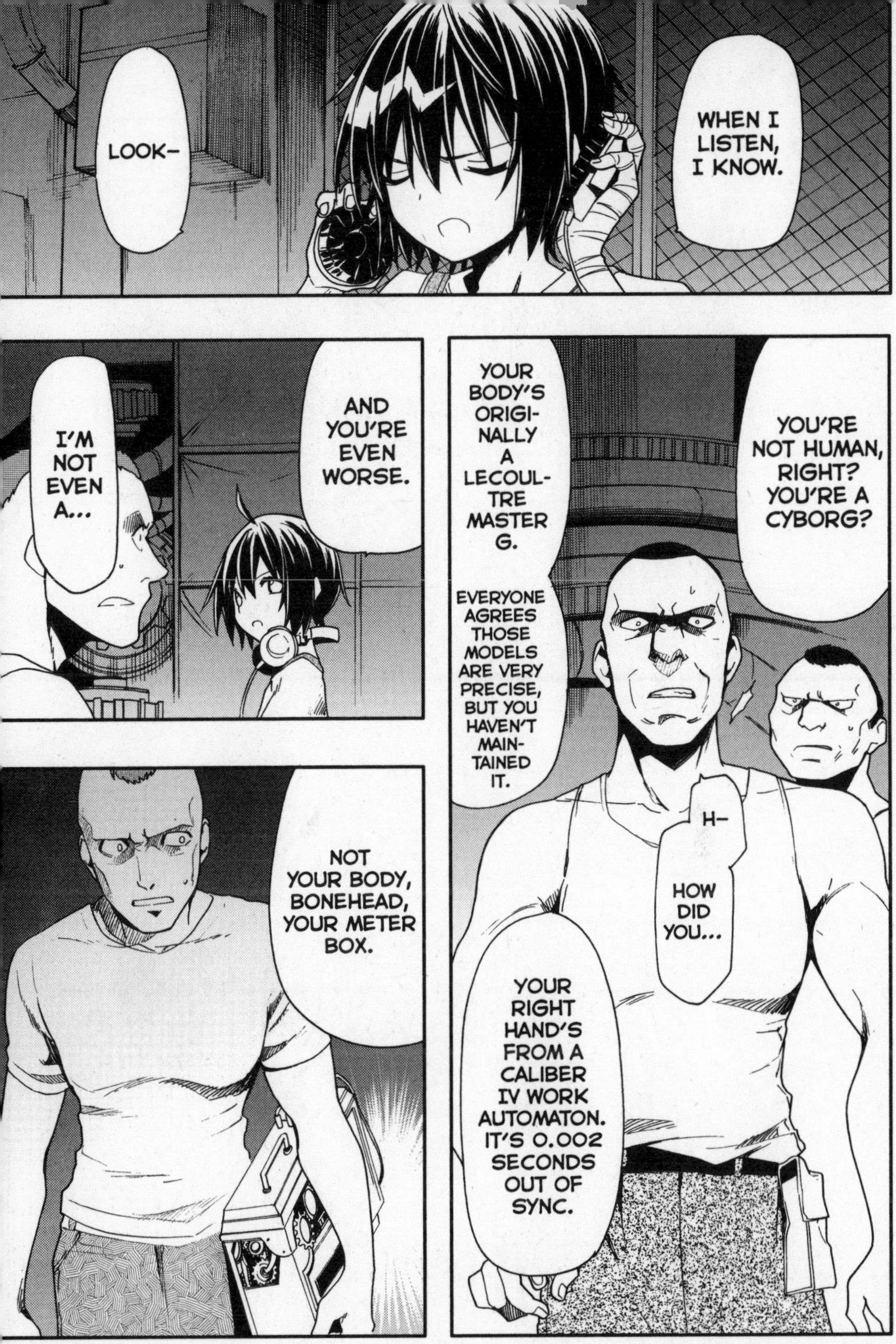
WHEN I LISTEN, I KNOW.
LOOK—
YOU'RE NOT HUMAN, RIGHT? YOU'RE A CYBORG?
YOUR BODY'S ORIGI-NALLY A LECOUL-TRE MASTER G.
EVERYONE AGREES THOSE MODELS ARE VERY PRECISE, BUT YOU HAVEN'T MAIN-TAINED IT.
H—
HOW DID YOU...
YOUR RIGHT HAND'S FROM A CALIBER IV WORK AUTOMATON. IT'S 0.002 SECONDS OUT OF SYNC.
AND YOU'RE EVEN WORSE.
I'M NOT EVEN A...
NOT YOUR BODY, BONEHEAD, YOUR METER BOX.

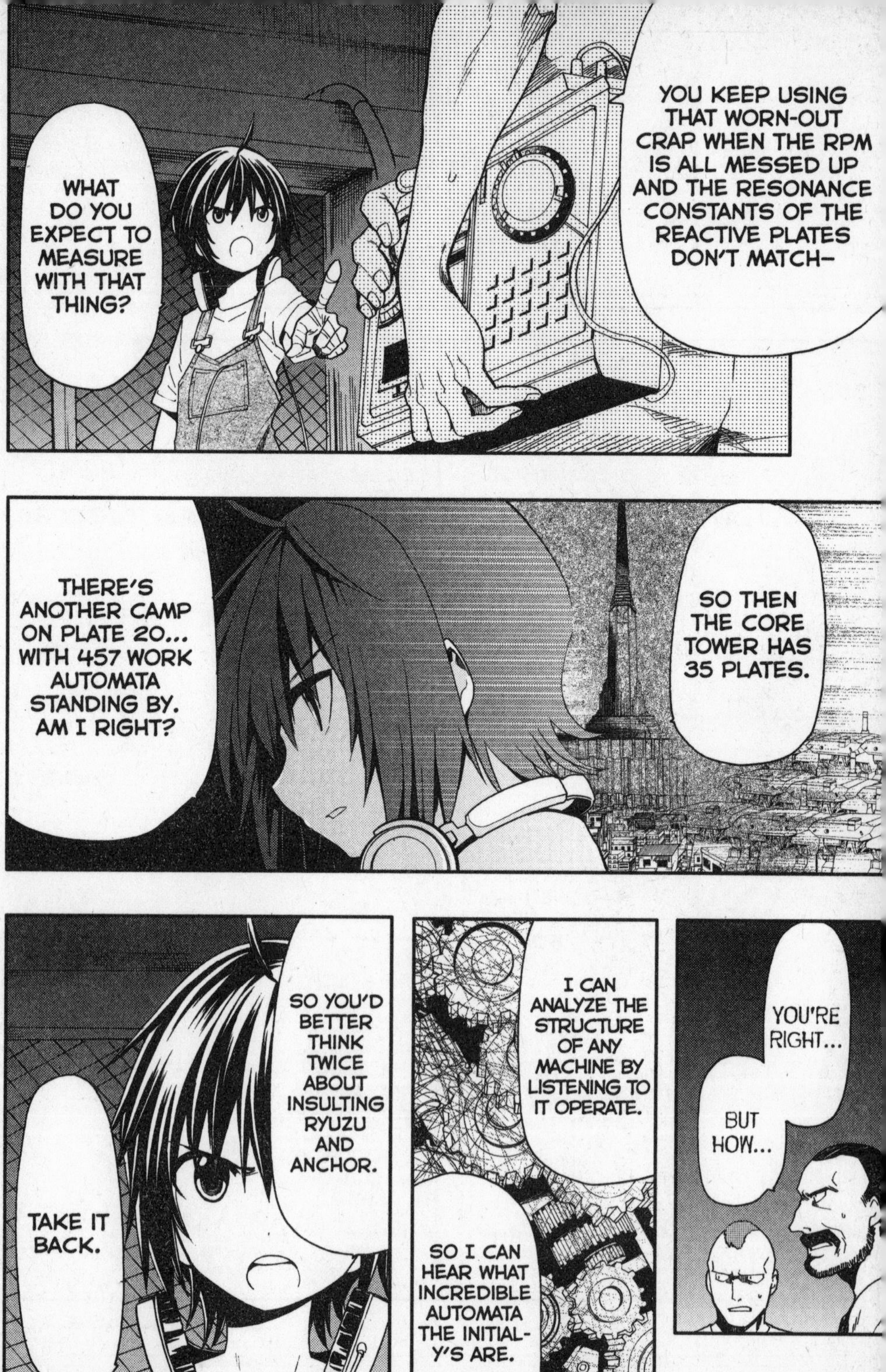
YOU KEEP USING THAT WORN-OUT CRAP WHEN THE RPM IS ALL MESSED UP AND THE RESONANCE CONSTANTS OF THE REACTIVE PLATES DON'T MATCH–
WHAT DO YOU EXPECT TO MEASURE WITH THAT THING?
SO THEN THE CORE TOWER HAS 35 PLATES.
THERE'S ANOTHER CAMP ON PLATE 20... WITH 457 WORK AUTOMATA STANDING BY. AM I RIGHT?
YOU'RE RIGHT...
BUT HOW...
I CAN ANALYZE THE STRUCTURE OF ANY MACHINE BY LISTENING TO IT OPERATE.
SO I CAN HEAR WHAT INCREDIBLE AUTOMATA THE INITIAL-Y'S ARE.
SO YOU'D BETTER THINK TWICE ABOUT INSULTING RYUZU AND ANCHOR.
TAKE IT BACK.

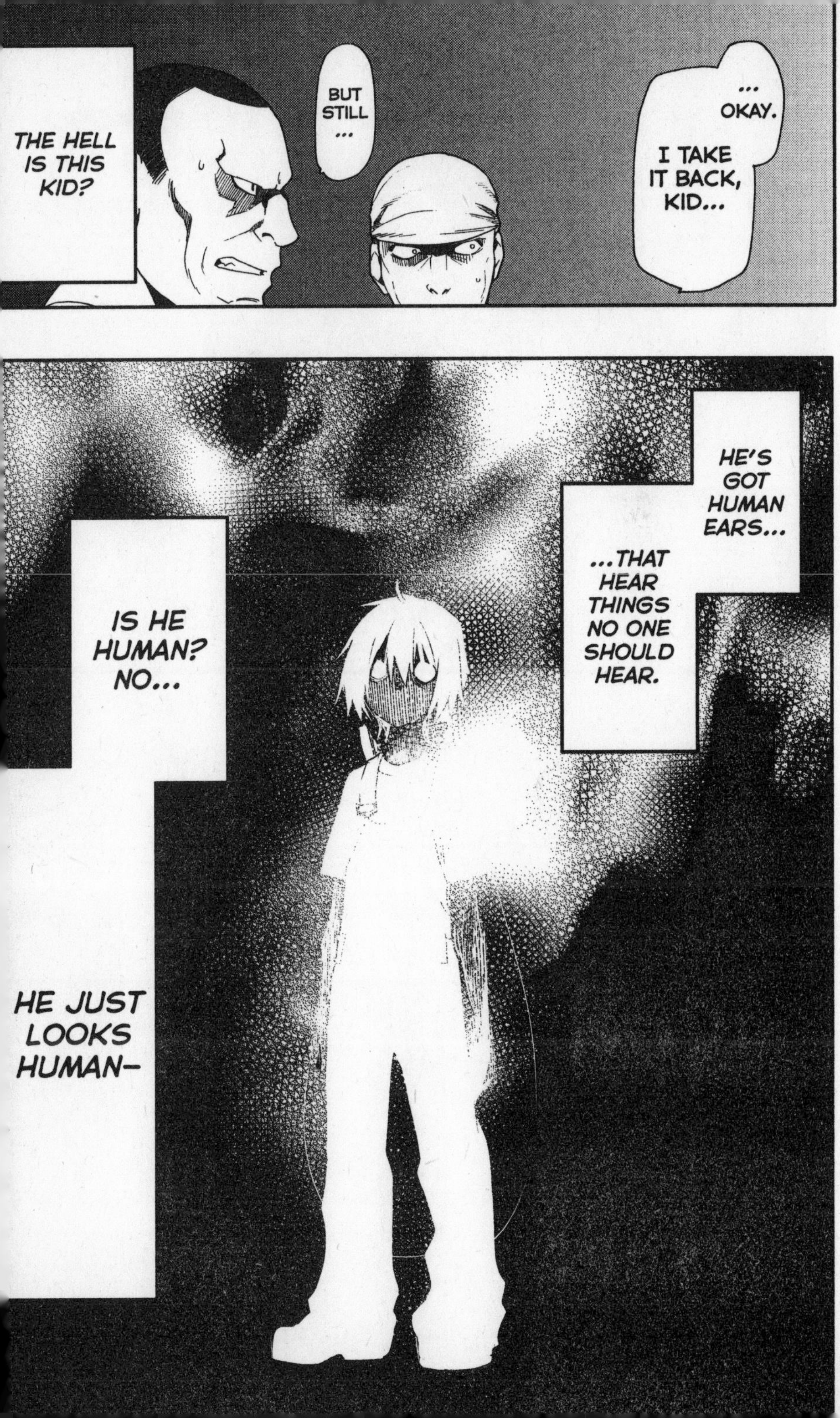
... OKAY.
I TAKE IT BACK, KID...
BUT STILL ...
THE HELL IS THIS KID?
HE'S GOT HUMAN EARS...
...THAT HEAR THINGS NO ONE SHOULD HEAR.
IS HE HUMAN? NO...
HE JUST LOOKS HUMAN-

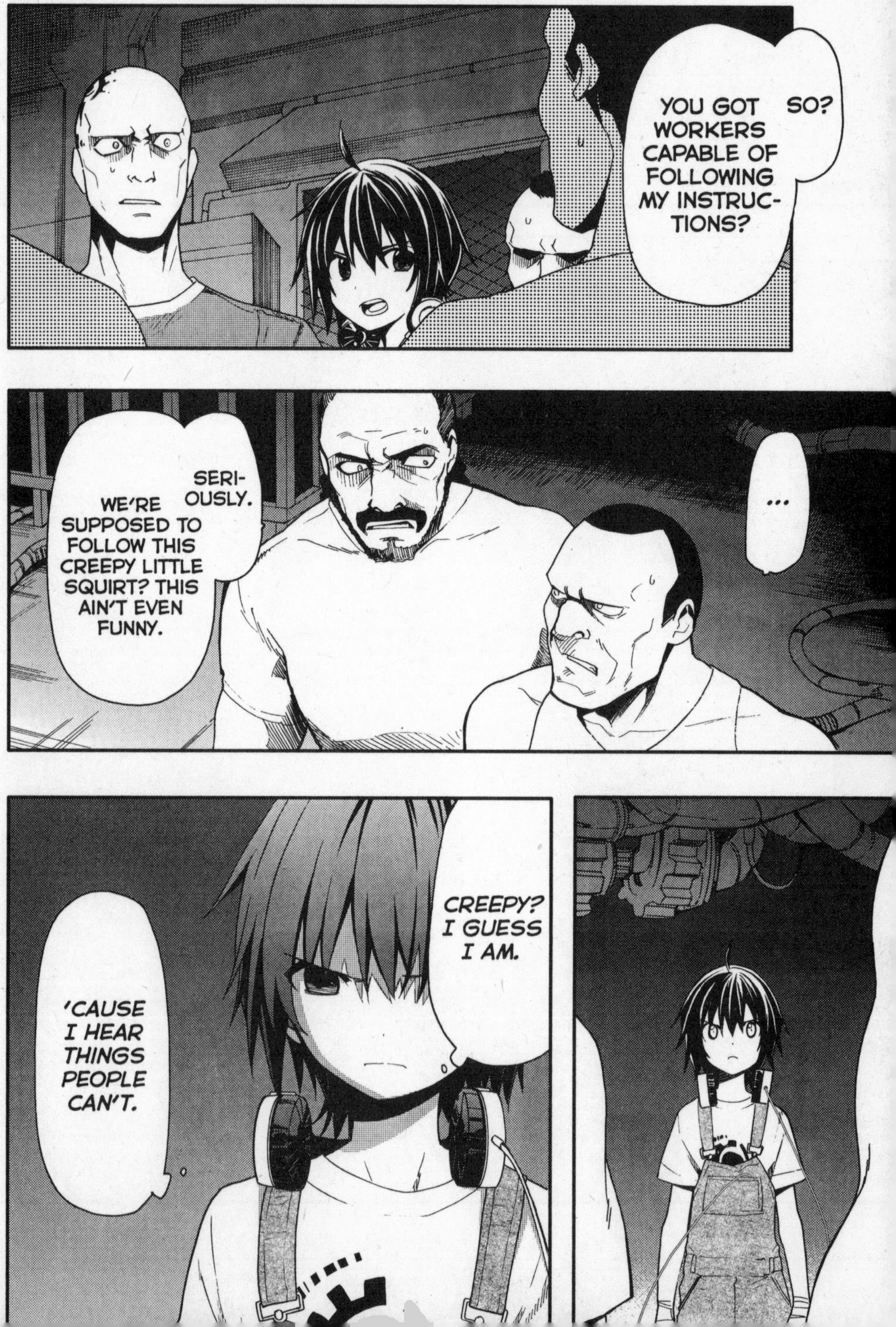
SO?
YOU GOT WORKERS CAPABLE OF FOLLOWING MY INSTRUCTIONS?
...
SERIOUSLY. WE'RE SUPPOSED TO FOLLOW THIS CREEPY LITTLE SQUIRT? THIS AIN'T EVEN FUNNY.
CREEPY? I GUESS I AM.
'CAUSE I HEAR THINGS PEOPLE CAN'T.

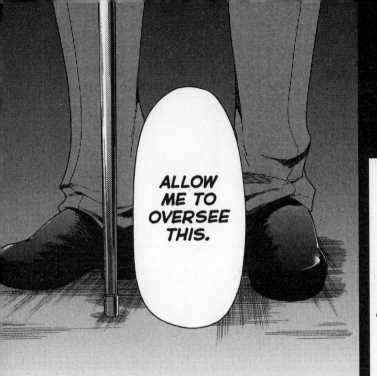

ALLOW ME TO OVERSEE THIS.

WHO'S GONNA...

FOLLOW ME...

!

UH—

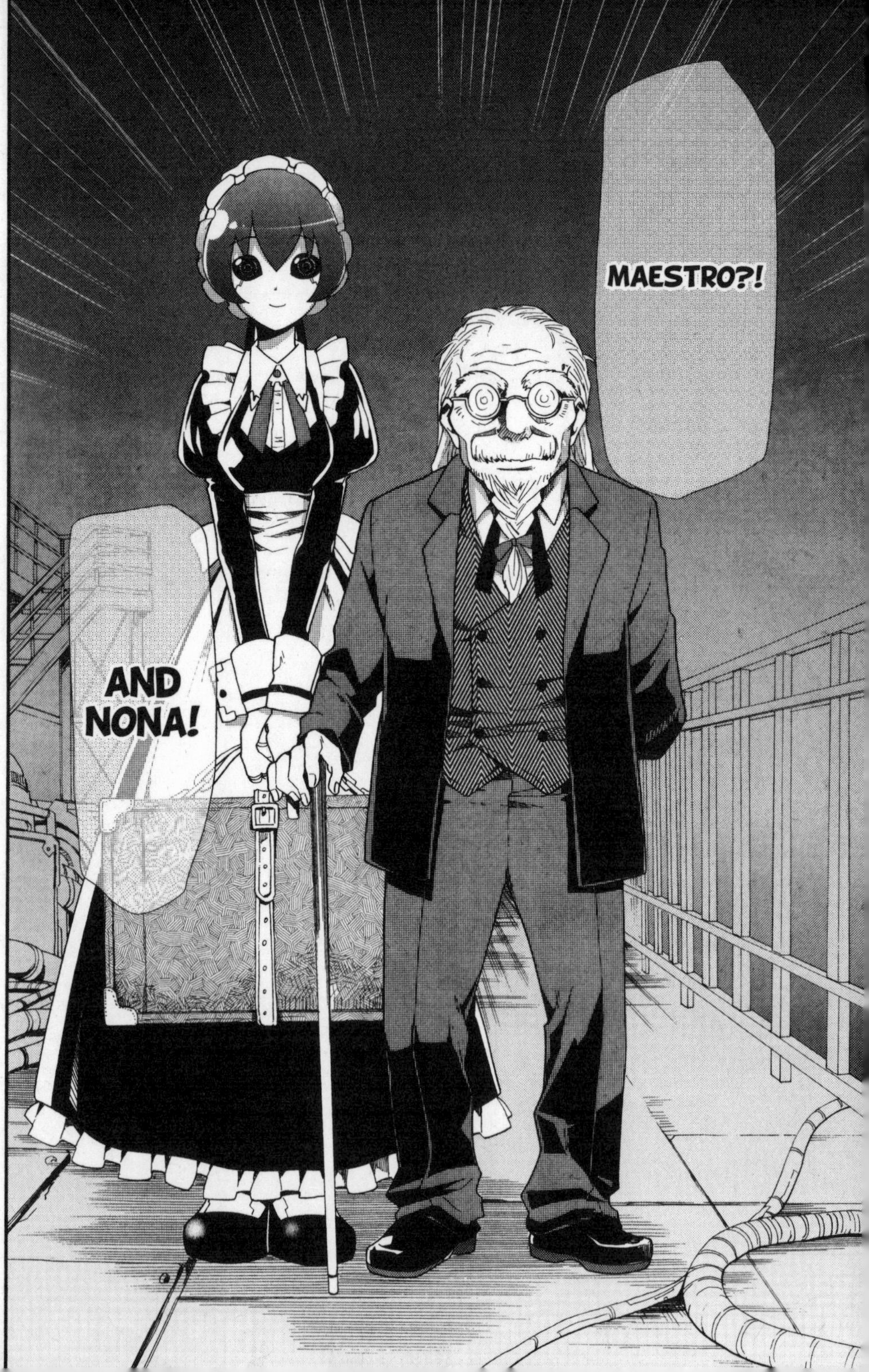
MAESTRO?!
AND NONA!

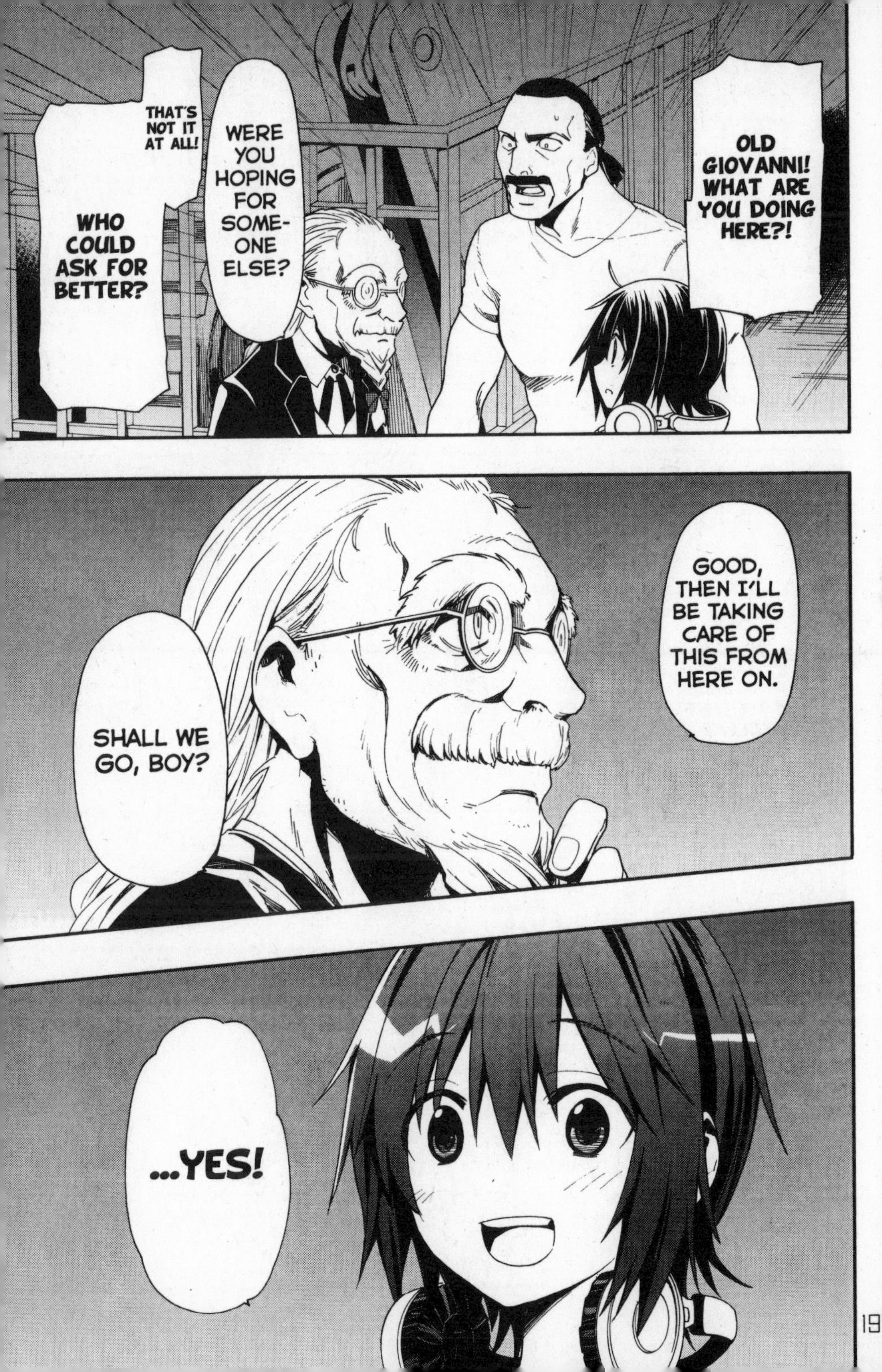
OLD GIOVANNI! WHAT ARE YOU DOING HERE?!
WERE YOU HOPING FOR SOME-ONE ELSE?
THAT'S NOT IT AT ALL!
WHO COULD ASK FOR BETTER?
GOOD, THEN I'LL BE TAKING CARE OF THIS FROM HERE ON.
SHALL WE GO, BOY?
...YES!

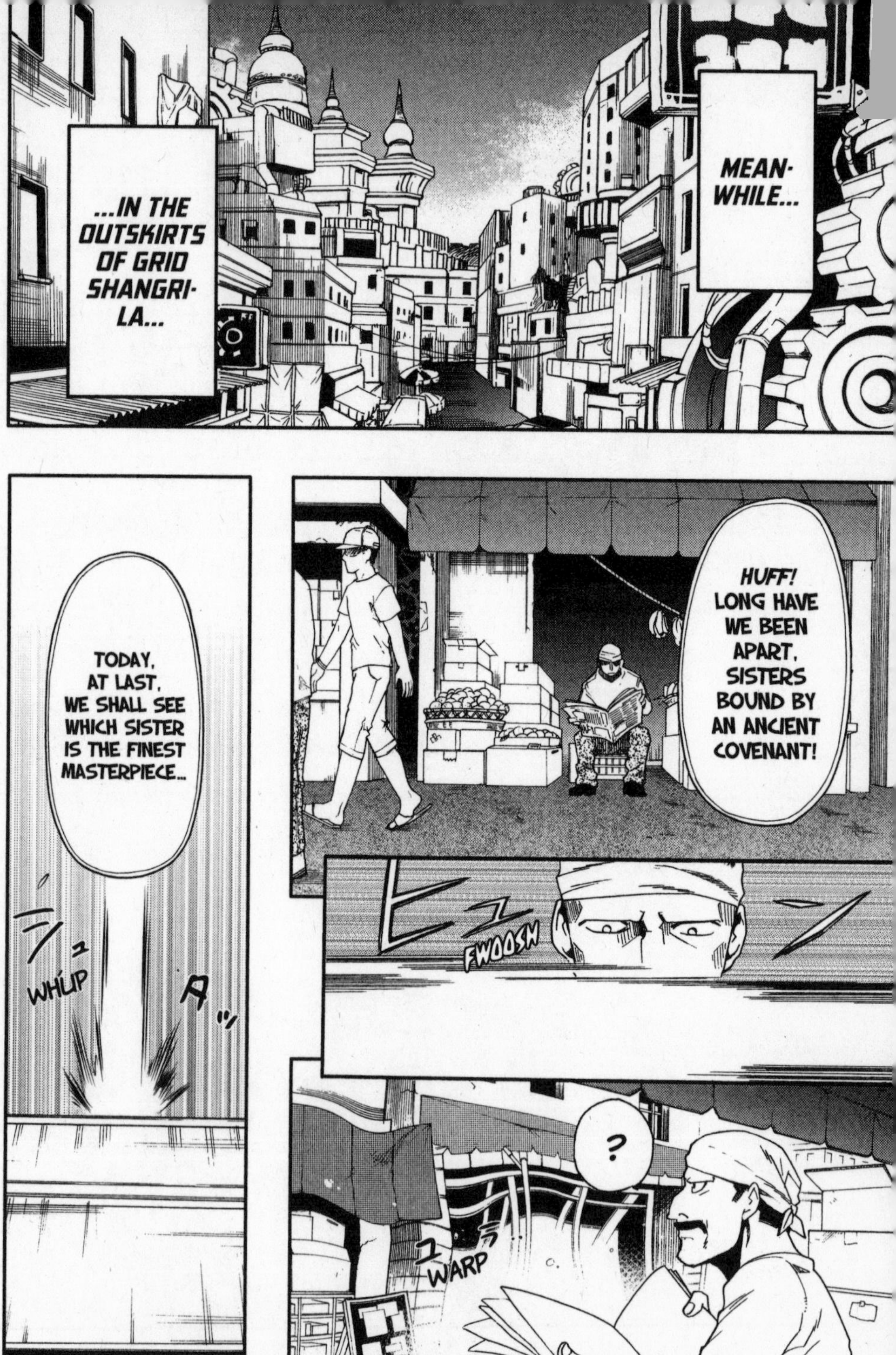
MEAN-WHILE...
...IN THE OUTSKIRTS OF GRID SHANGRI-LA...
HUFF! LONG HAVE WE BEEN APART, SISTERS BOUND BY AN ANCIENT COVENANT!
FWOOSH
?
WARP
TODAY, AT LAST, WE SHALL SEE WHICH SISTER IS THE FINEST MASTERPIECE...
WHUP

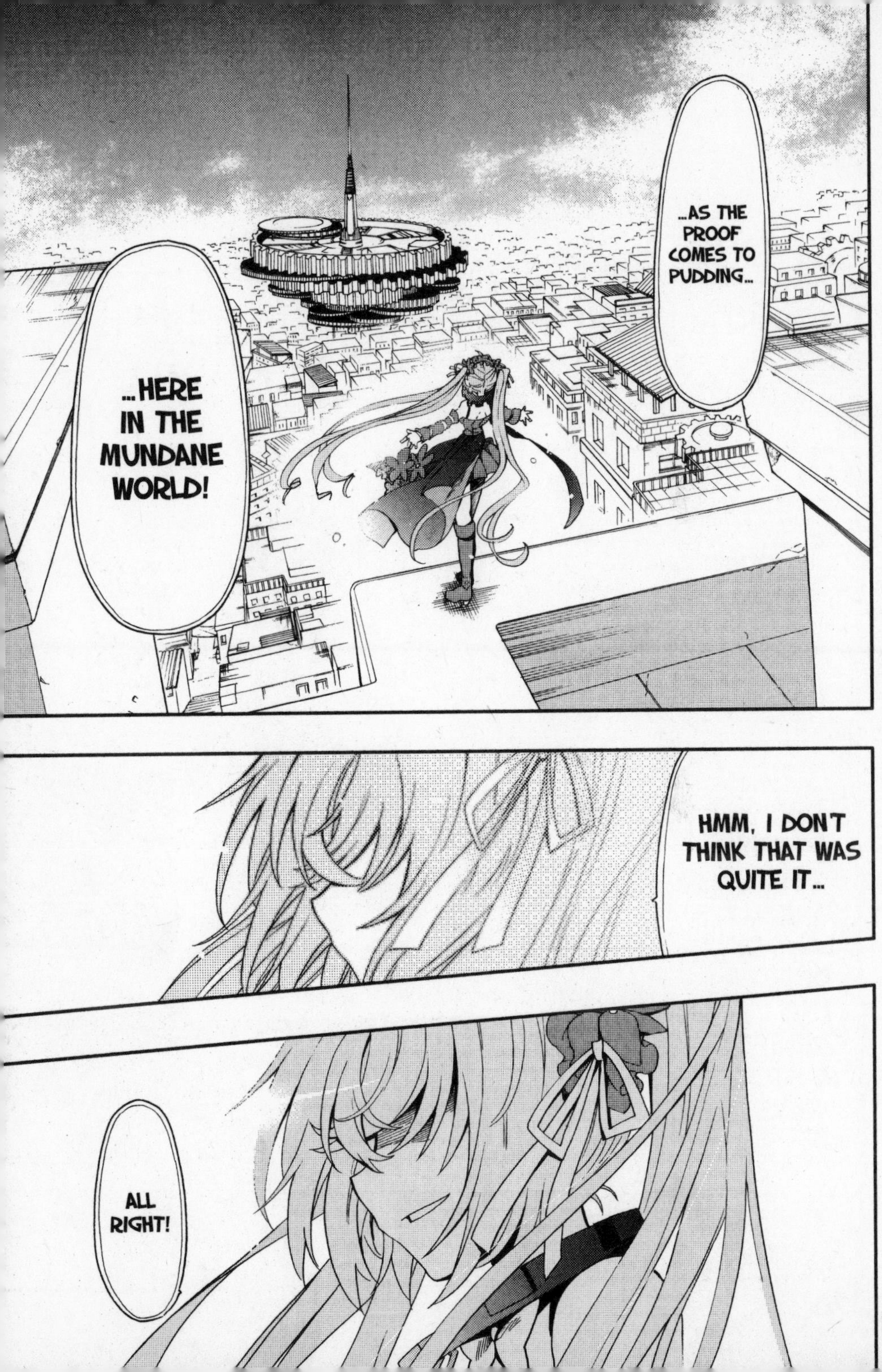
...AS THE PROOF COMES TO PUDDING...
...HERE IN THE MUNDANE WORLD!
HMM, I DON'T THINK THAT WAS QUITE IT...
ALL RIGHT!

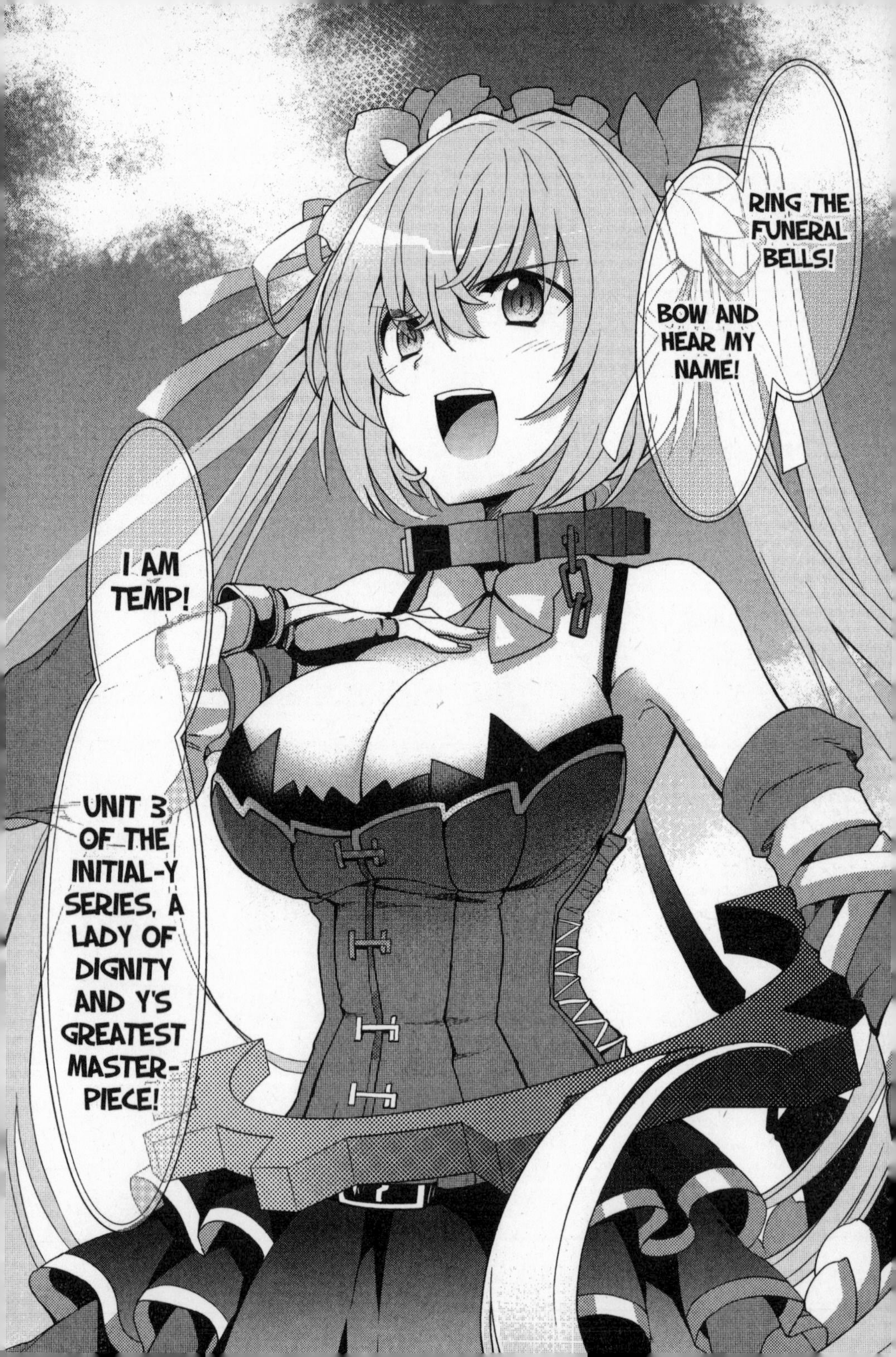
RING THE FUNERAL BELLS!
BOW AND HEAR MY NAME!
I AM TEMP!
UNIT 3 OF THE INITIAL-Y SERIES, A LADY OF DIGNITY AND Y'S GREATEST MASTER-PIECE!

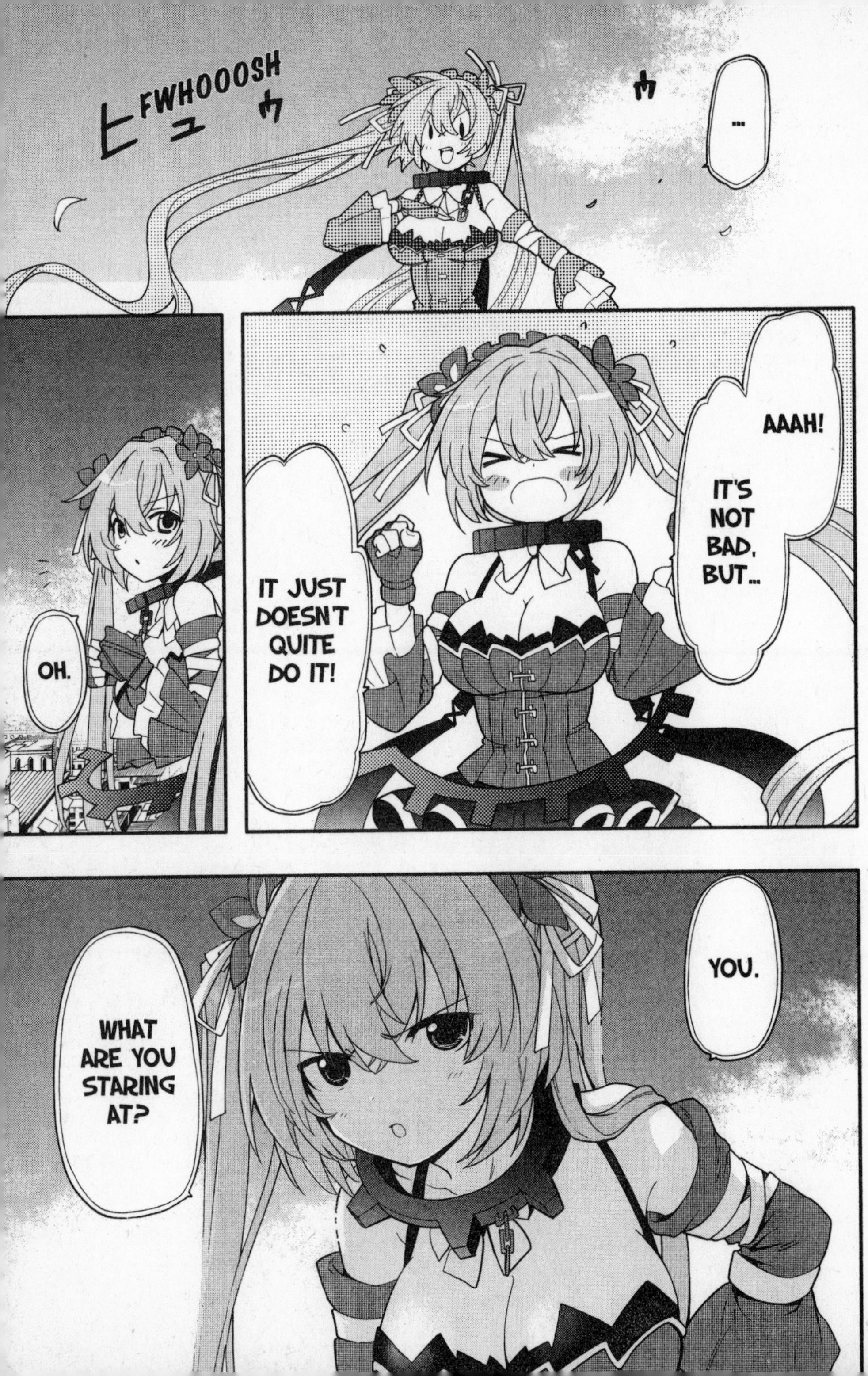

FWHOOOSH
...
AAAH!
IT'S NOT BAD, BUT...
IT JUST DOESN'T QUITE DO IT!
OH.
YOU.
WHAT ARE YOU STARING AT?

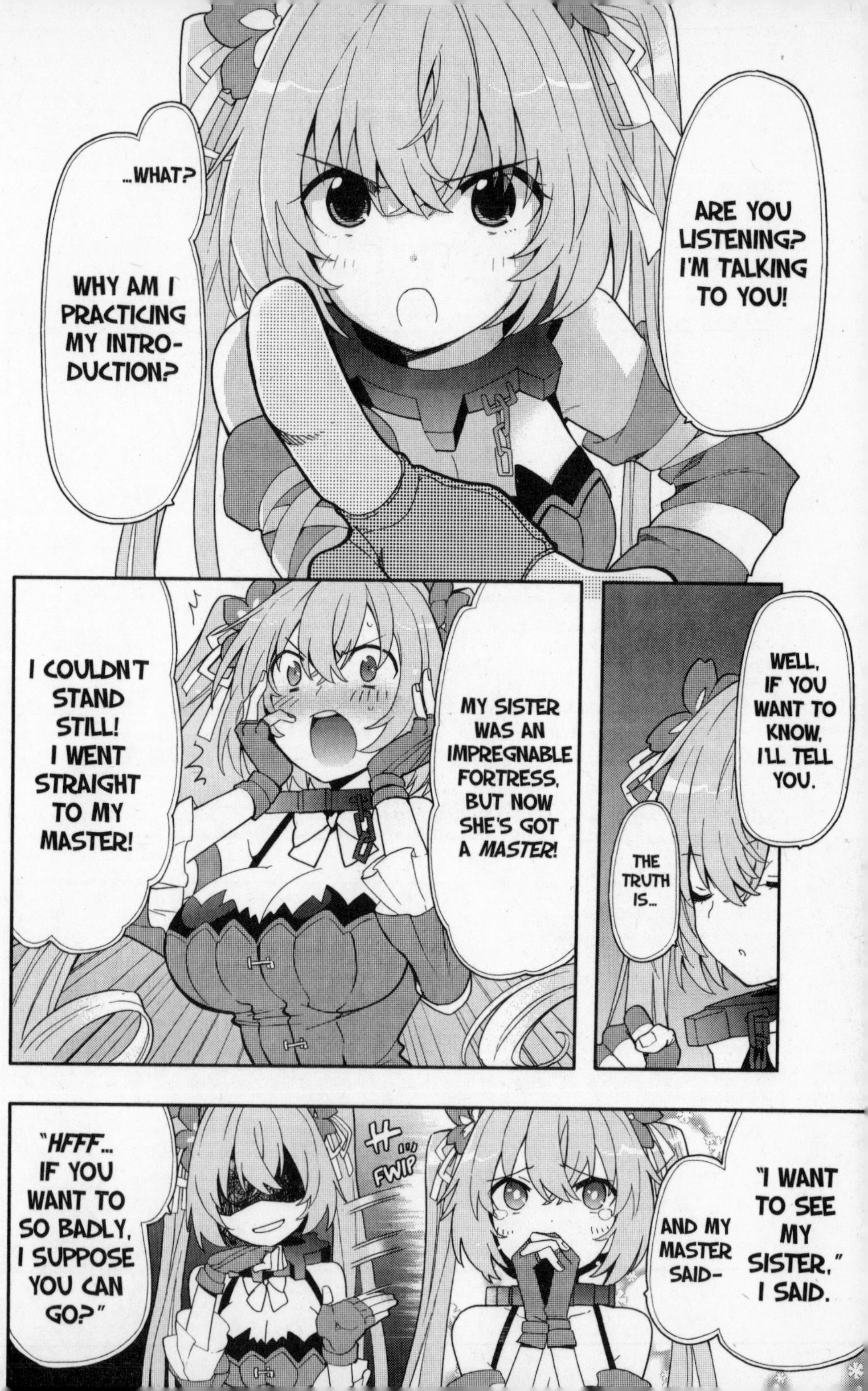
ARE YOU LISTENING? I'M TALKING TO YOU!
...WHAT?
WHY AM I PRACTICING MY INTRODUCTION?
WELL, IF YOU WANT TO KNOW, I'LL TELL YOU.
THE TRUTH IS...
MY SISTER WAS AN IMPREGNABLE FORTRESS, BUT NOW SHE'S GOT A *MASTER*!
I COULDN'T STAND STILL! I WENT STRAIGHT TO MY MASTER!
"I WANT TO SEE MY SISTER," I SAID.
AND MY MASTER SAID-
FWIP
"*HFFF*... IF YOU WANT TO SO BADLY, I SUPPOSE YOU CAN GO?"

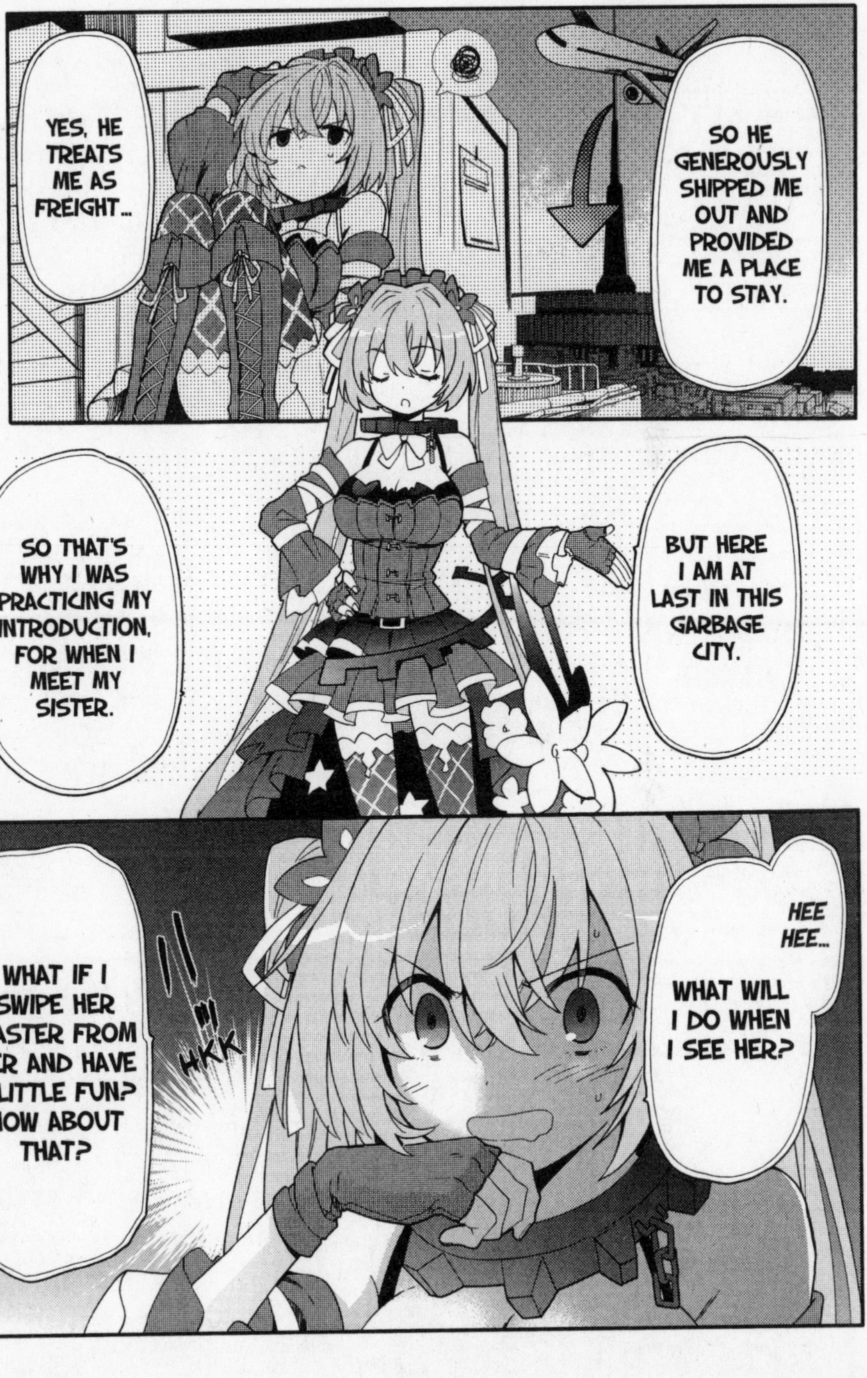
SO HE GENEROUSLY SHIPPED ME OUT AND PROVIDED ME A PLACE TO STAY.
YES, HE TREATS ME AS FREIGHT...
BUT HERE I AM AT LAST IN THIS GARBAGE CITY.
SO THAT'S WHY I WAS PRACTICING MY INTRODUCTION, FOR WHEN I MEET MY SISTER.
HEE HEE...
WHAT WILL I DO WHEN I SEE HER?
HKK
WHAT IF I SWIPE HER MASTER FROM HER AND HAVE A LITTLE FUN? HOW ABOUT THAT?

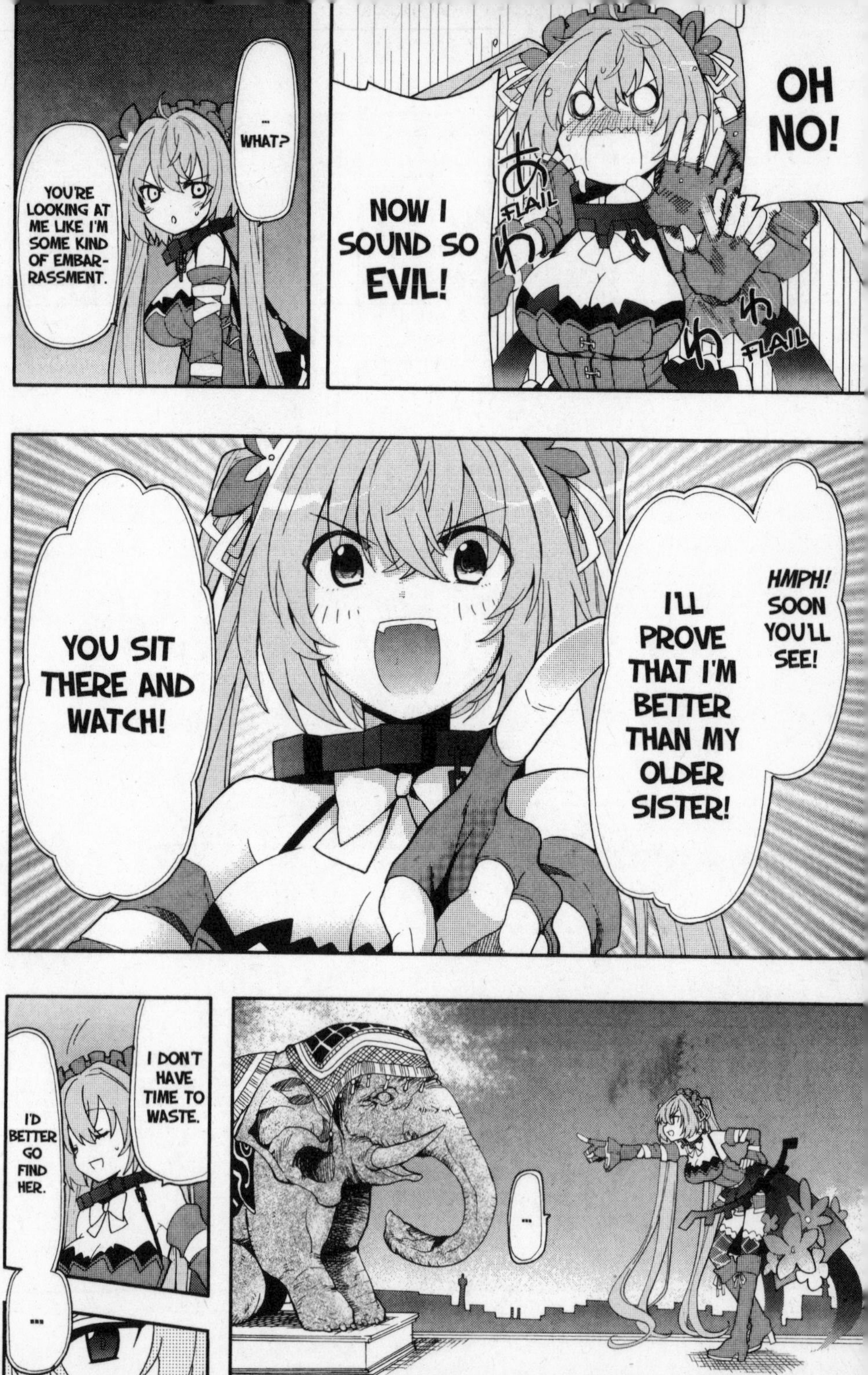

OH NO!
わわ FLAIL
あわ FLAIL
NOW I SOUND SO EVIL!
... WHAT?
YOU'RE LOOKING AT ME LIKE I'M SOME KIND OF EMBAR-RASSMENT.
HMPH! SOON YOU'LL SEE!
I'LL PROVE THAT I'M BETTER THAN MY OLDER SISTER!
YOU SIT THERE AND WATCH!
...
I DON'T HAVE TIME TO WASTE.
I'D BETTER GO FIND HER.
...

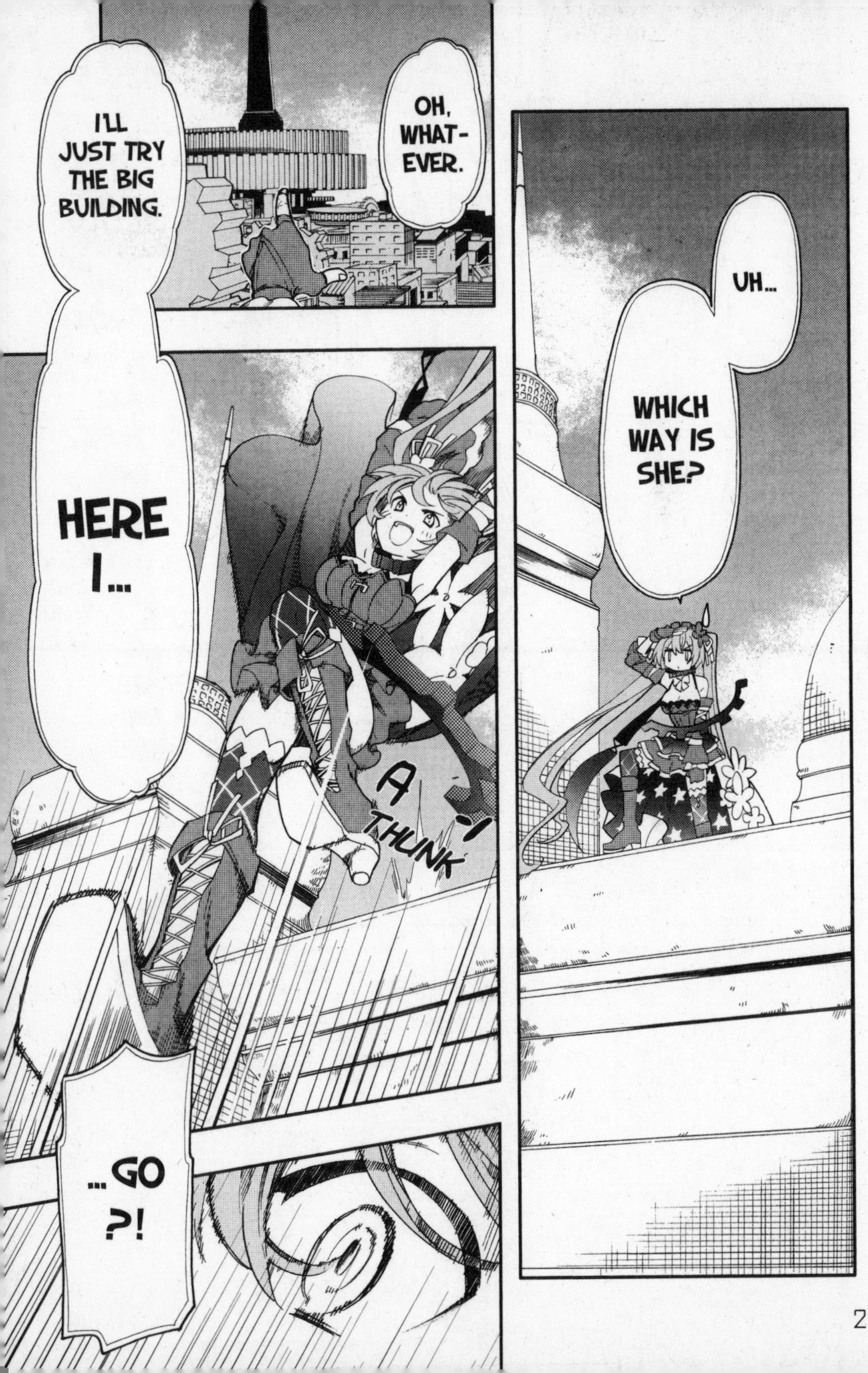
UH...
WHICH WAY IS SHE?
OH, WHAT-EVER.
I'LL JUST TRY THE BIG BUILDING.
HERE I...
A THUNK
...GO ?!

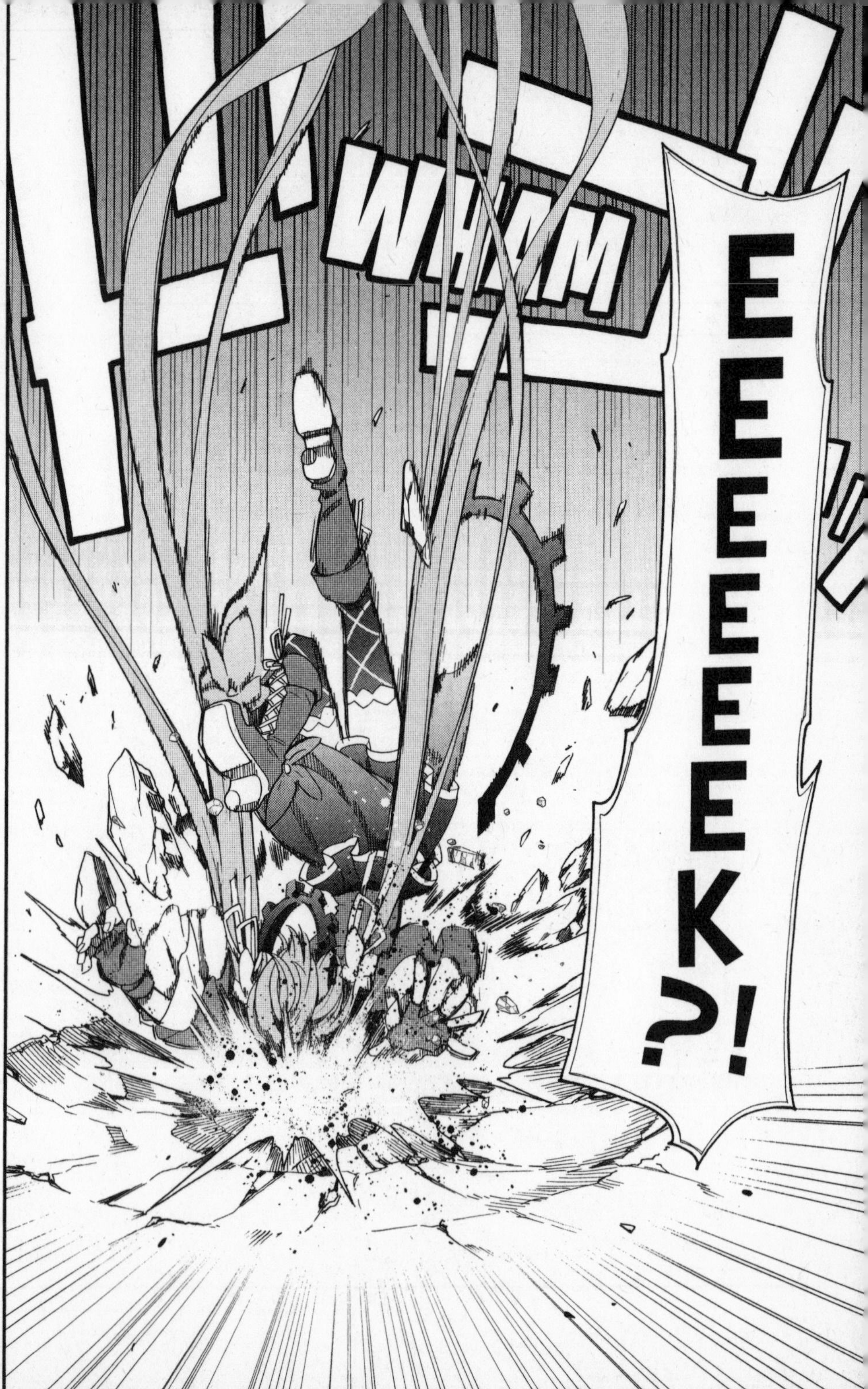
WHAM
EEEEEEEK?!

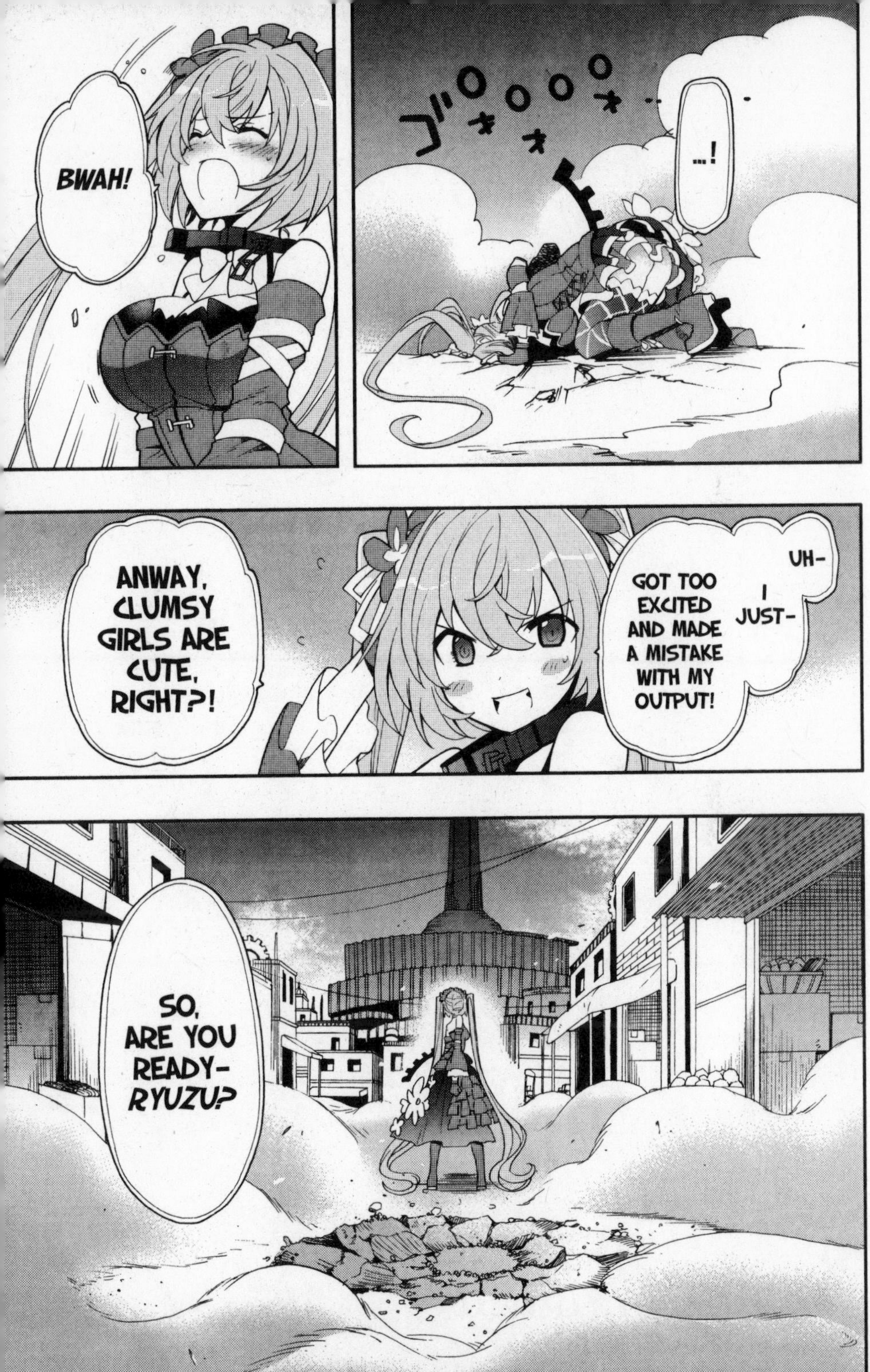
...!
BWAH!
UH- I JUST-
GOT TOO EXCITED AND MADE A MISTAKE WITH MY OUTPUT!
ANWAY, CLUMSY GIRLS ARE CUTE, RIGHT?!
SO, ARE YOU READY- RYUZU?

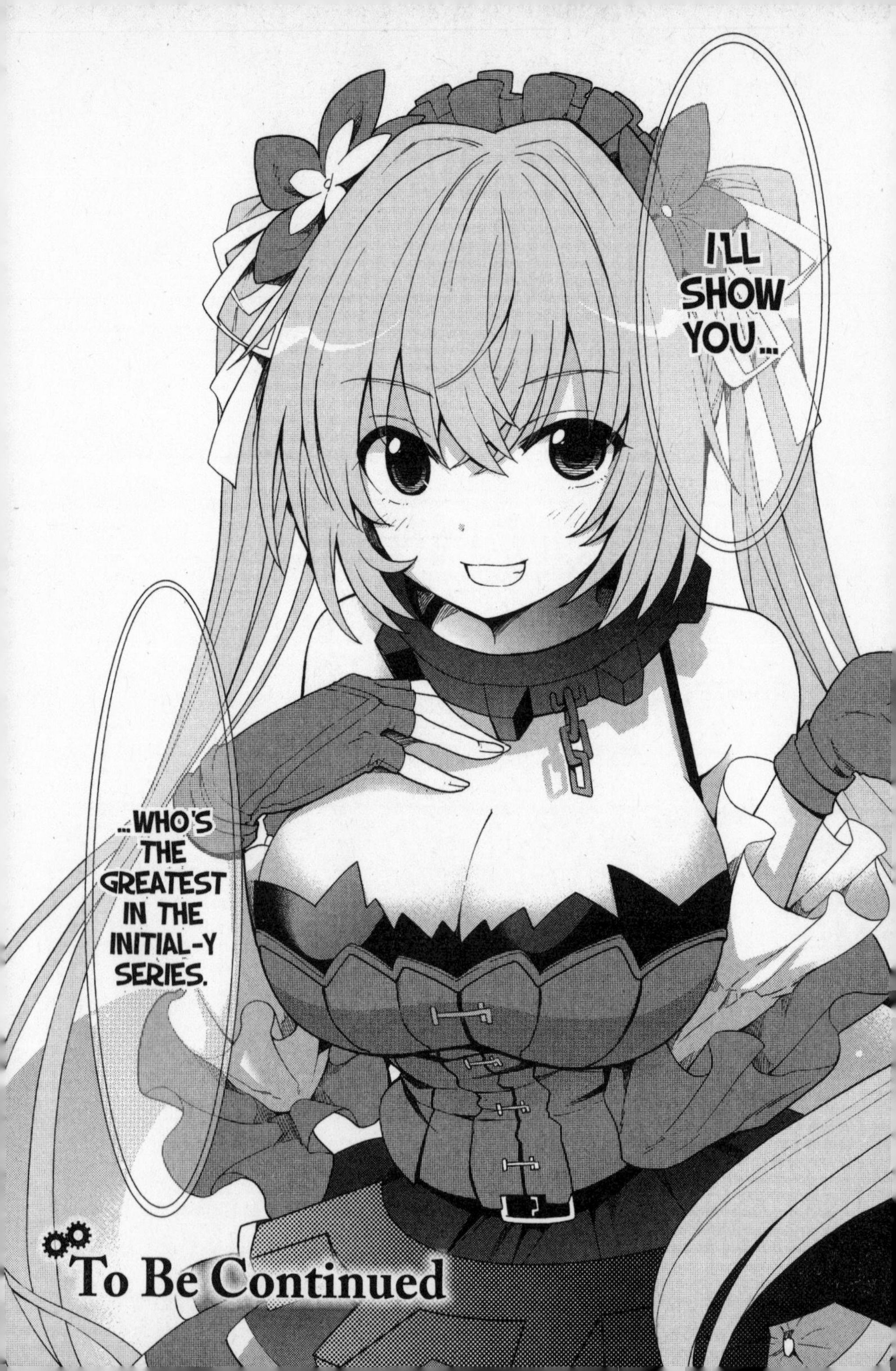
I'LL SHOW YOU...
...WHO'S THE GREATEST IN THE INITIAL-Y SERIES.
To Be Continued

CLOCKWORK FOUR-PANEL THEATER

Kodansha Japanese light novels, including *Clockwork Planet*,
include flyers full of information about adpatations and other works,
as well as four-panel comics. For the eight months from April to November 2017,
the four-panel comics were based on *Clockwork Planet*. Now, for the first time,
these special comic strips are being collected in a book. Please enjoy!

RyuZU PR

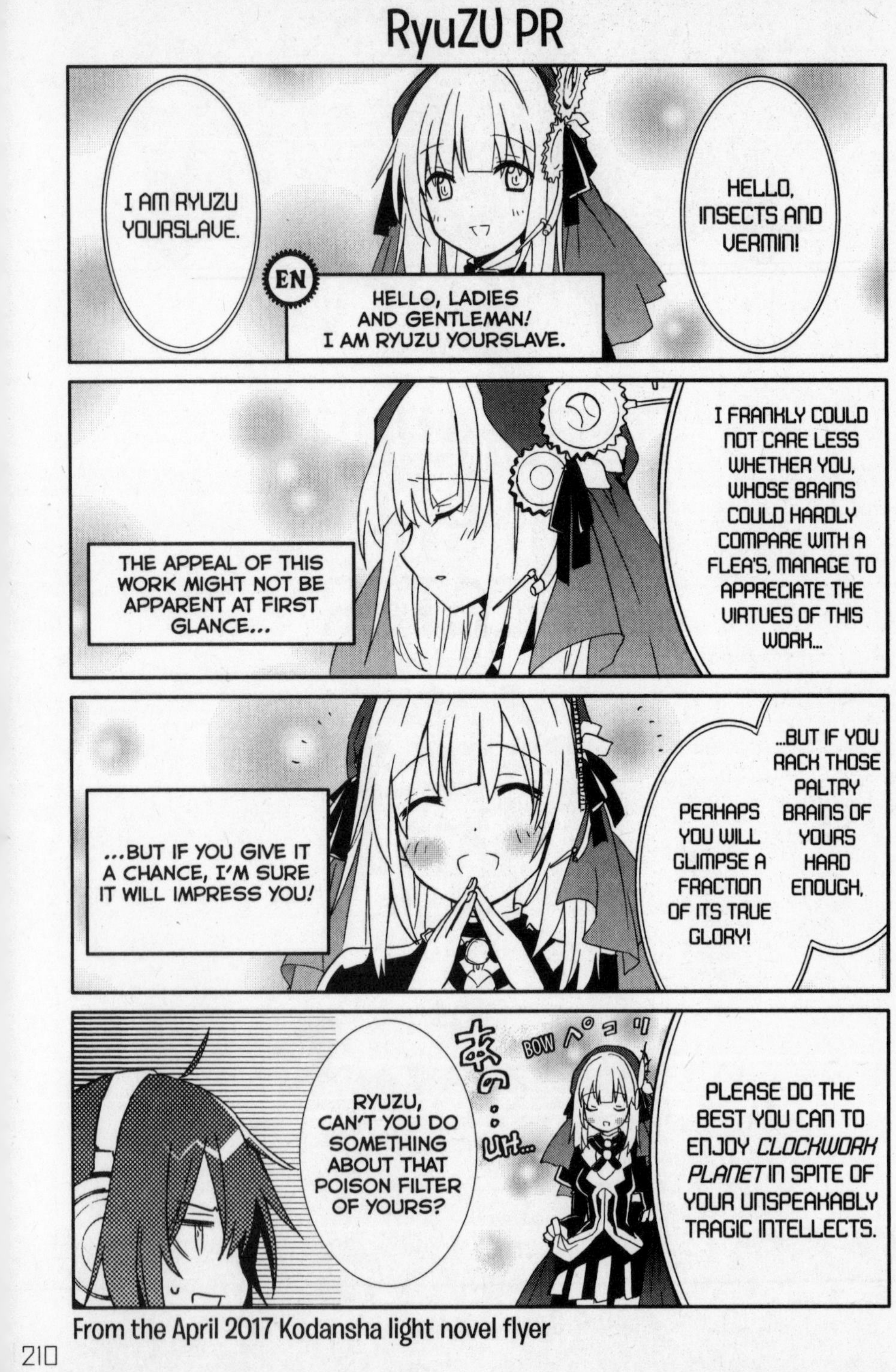

HELLO, INSECTS AND VERMIN!
I AM RYUZU YOURSLAVE.
EN
HELLO, LADIES AND GENTLEMAN! I AM RYUZU YOURSLAVE.
I FRANKLY COULD NOT CARE LESS WHETHER YOU, WHOSE BRAINS COULD HARDLY COMPARE WITH A FLEA'S, MANAGE TO APPRECIATE THE VIRTUES OF THIS WORK...
THE APPEAL OF THIS WORK MIGHT NOT BE APPARENT AT FIRST GLANCE...
...BUT IF YOU RACK THOSE PALTRY BRAINS OF YOURS HARD ENOUGH, PERHAPS YOU WILL GLIMPSE A FRACTION OF ITS TRUE GLORY!
...BUT IF YOU GIVE IT A CHANCE, I'M SURE IT WILL IMPRESS YOU!
PLEASE DO THE BEST YOU CAN TO ENJOY *CLOCKWORK PLANET* IN SPITE OF YOUR UNSPEAKABLY TRAGIC INTELLECTS.
ペコリ BOW
あの…… UH...
RYUZU, CAN'T YOU DO SOMETHING ABOUT THAT POISON FILTER OF YOURS?

From the April 2017 Kodansha light novel flyer

How to use a Naoto

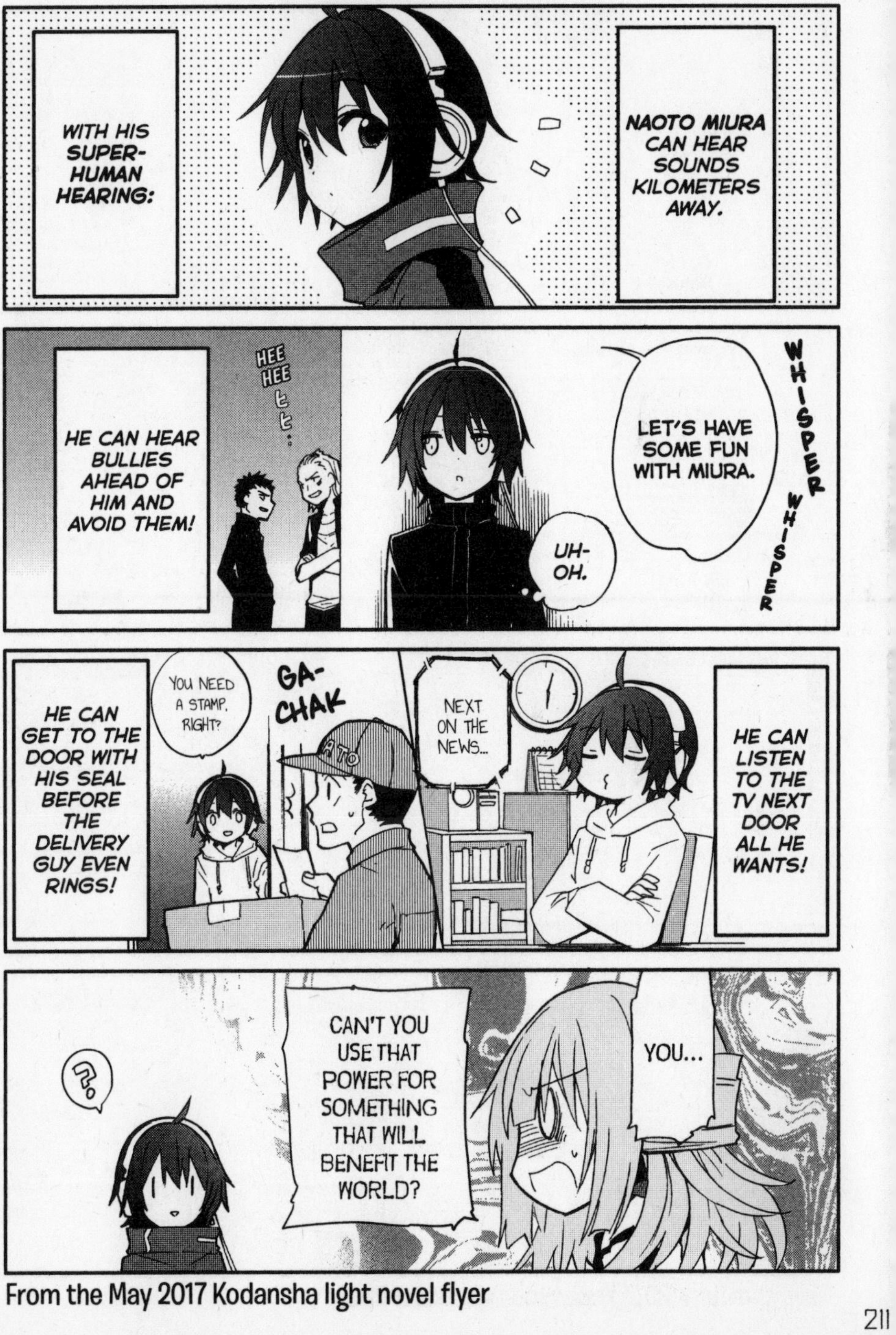
NAOTO MIURA CAN HEAR SOUNDS KILOMETERS AWAY.
WITH HIS SUPER-HUMAN HEARING:
WHISPER
WHISPER
LET'S HAVE SOME FUN WITH MIURA.
UH-OH.
HEE HEE ヒヒ..
HE CAN HEAR BULLIES AHEAD OF HIM AND AVOID THEM!
HE CAN LISTEN TO THE TV NEXT DOOR ALL HE WANTS!
NEXT ON THE NEWS...
GA-CHAK
YOU NEED A STAMP, RIGHT?
HE CAN GET TO THE DOOR WITH HIS SEAL BEFORE THE DELIVERY GUY EVEN RINGS!
YOU...
CAN'T YOU USE THAT POWER FOR SOMETHING THAT WILL BENEFIT THE WORLD?
?

From the May 2017 Kodansha light novel flyer

Marie's Image

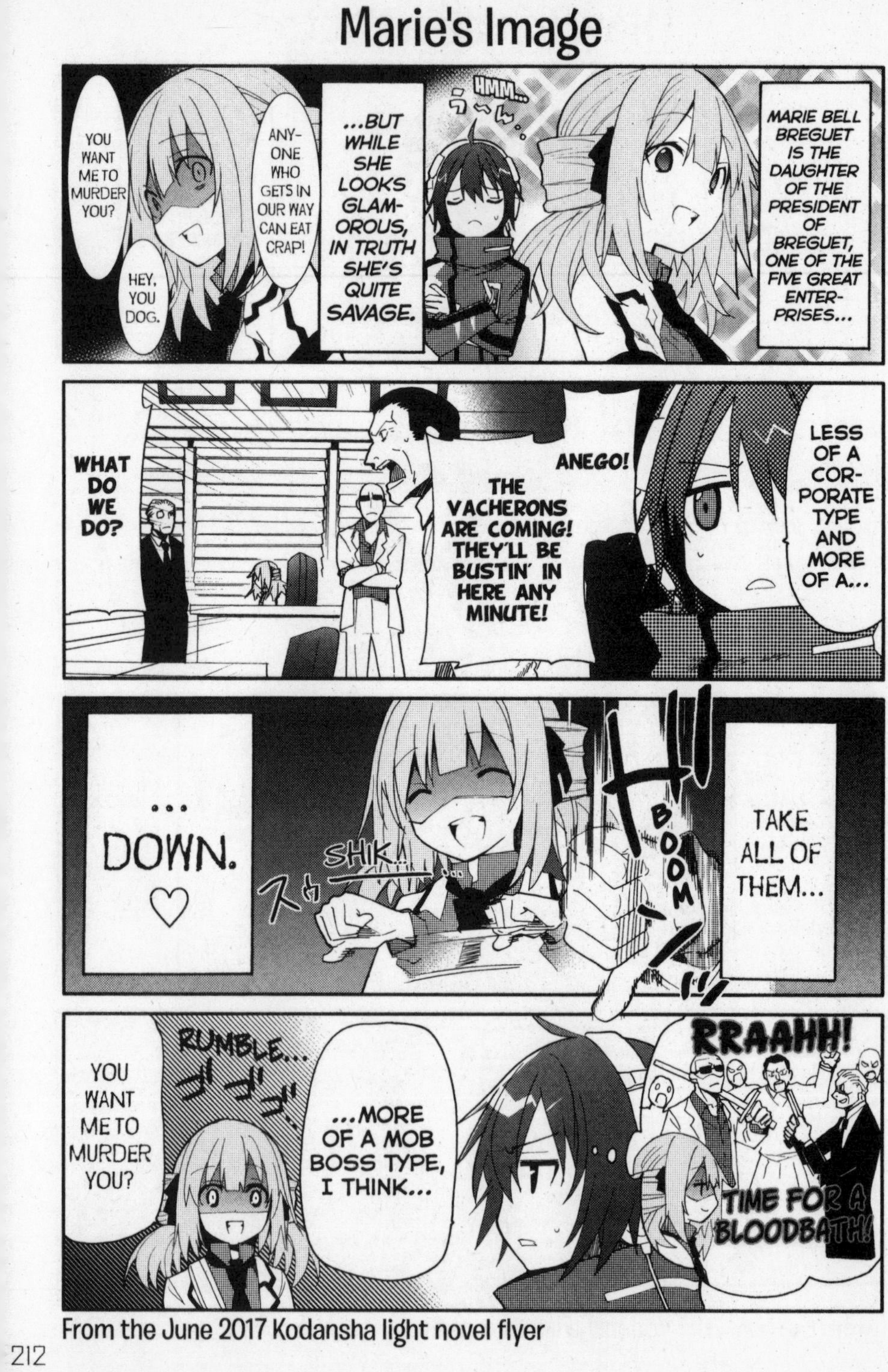

MARIE BELL BREGUET IS THE DAUGHTER OF THE PRESIDENT OF BREGUET, ONE OF THE FIVE GREAT ENTERPRISES...
HMM... うーん。。
...BUT WHILE SHE LOOKS GLAMOROUS, IN TRUTH SHE'S QUITE SAVAGE.
ANYONE WHO GETS IN OUR WAY CAN EAT CRAP!
YOU WANT ME TO MURDER YOU?
HEY, YOU DOG.
LESS OF A CORPORATE TYPE AND MORE OF A...
ANEGO!
THE VACHERONS ARE COMING! THEY'LL BE BUSTIN' IN HERE ANY MINUTE!
WHAT DO WE DO?
TAKE ALL OF THEM...
BOOM
SHIK... スゥー
...DOWN. ♡
RRAAHH!
TIME FOR A BLOODBATH!
...MORE OF A MOB BOSS TYPE, I THINK...
RUMBLE... ゴゴゴ
YOU WANT ME TO MURDER YOU?

From the June 2017 Kodansha light novel flyer

The Truth about Halter

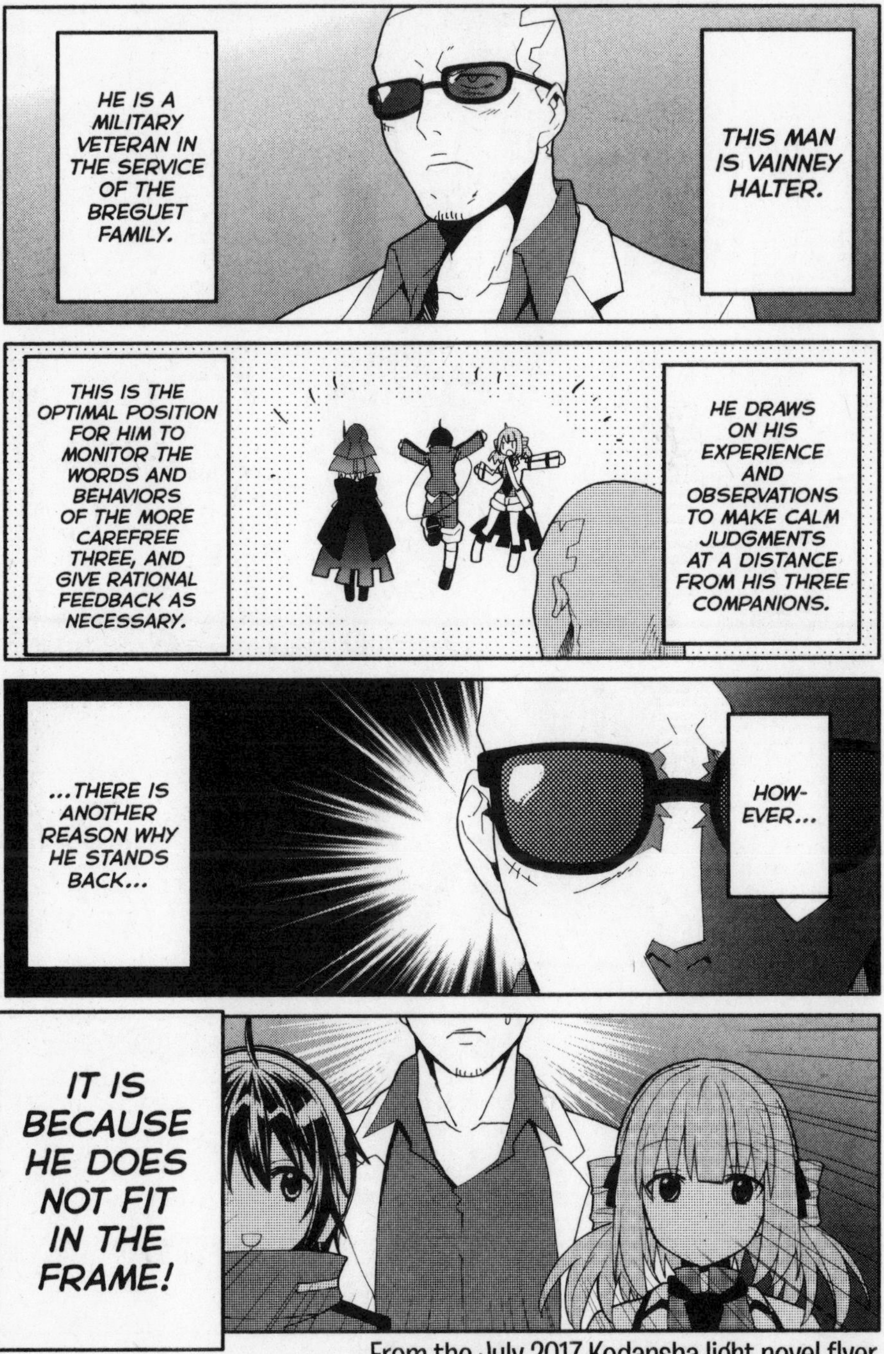
THIS MAN IS VAINNEY HALTER.
HE IS A MILITARY VETERAN IN THE SERVICE OF THE BREGUET FAMILY.
HE DRAWS ON HIS EXPERIENCE AND OBSERVATIONS TO MAKE CALM JUDGMENTS AT A DISTANCE FROM HIS THREE COMPANIONS.
THIS IS THE OPTIMAL POSITION FOR HIM TO MONITOR THE WORDS AND BEHAVIORS OF THE MORE CAREFREE THREE, AND GIVE RATIONAL FEEDBACK AS NECESSARY.
HOW-EVER...
...THERE IS ANOTHER REASON WHY HE STANDS BACK...
IT IS BECAUSE HE DOES NOT FIT IN THE FRAME!

From the July 2017 Kodansha light novel flyer

Anchor's Thoughts

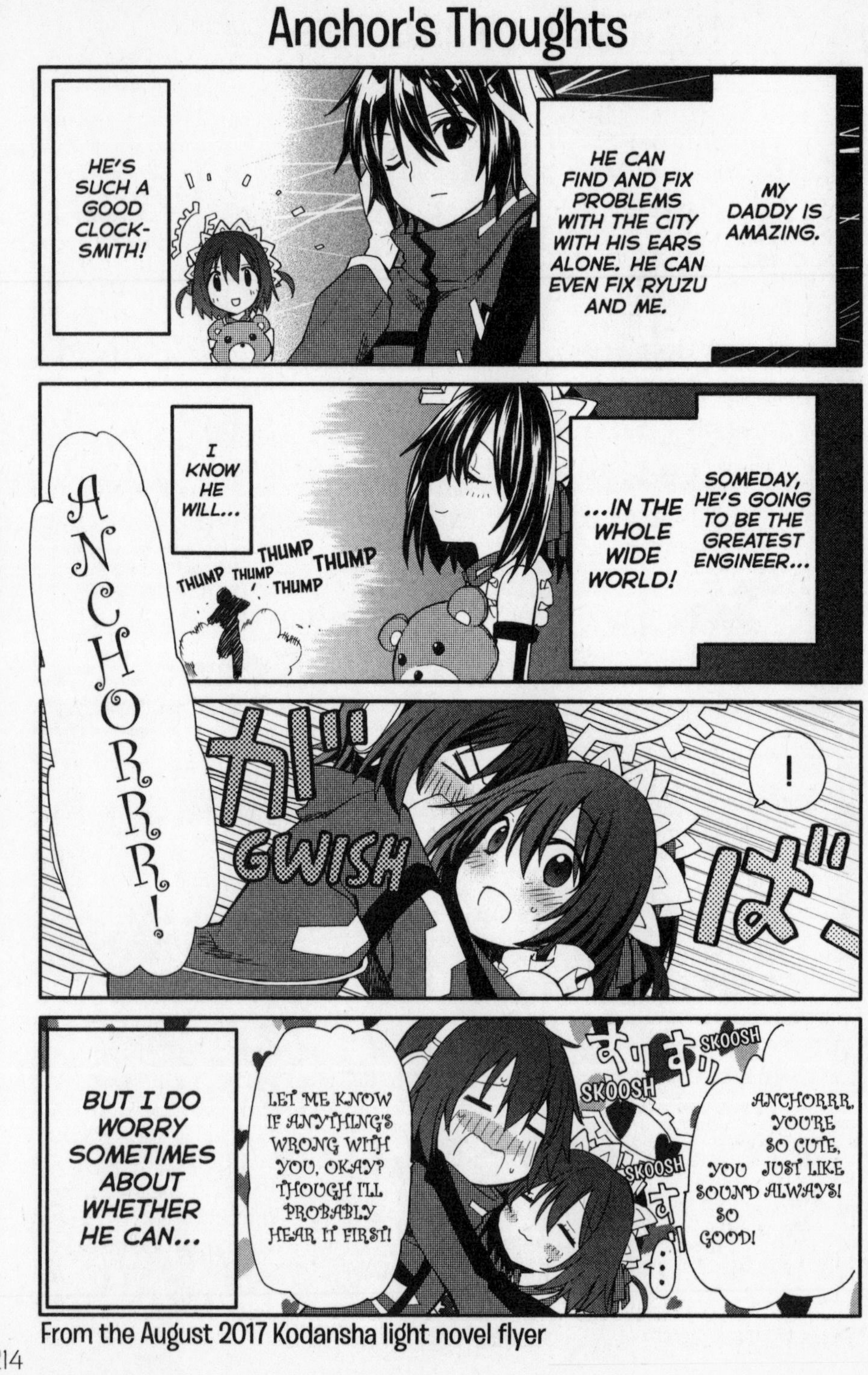

MY DADDY IS AMAZING.
HE CAN FIND AND FIX PROBLEMS WITH THE CITY WITH HIS EARS ALONE. HE CAN EVEN FIX RYUZU AND ME.
HE'S SUCH A GOOD CLOCK-SMITH!
SOMEDAY, HE'S GOING TO BE THE GREATEST ENGINEER...
...IN THE WHOLE WIDE WORLD!
I KNOW HE WILL...
THUMP THUMP THUMP THUMP THUMP
ANCHORRR!
!
ばー
GWISH
ガバ
ANCHORRR, YOU'RE SO CUTE, JUST LIKE ALWAYS!
YOU SOUND SO GOOD!
SKOOSH
すりすり
SKOOSH
SKOOSH
す
...
LET ME KNOW IF ANYTHING'S WRONG WITH YOU, OKAY? THOUGH I'LL PROBABLY HEAR IT FIRST!
BUT I DO WORRY SOMETIMES ABOUT WHETHER HE CAN...

From the August 2017 Kodansha light novel flyer

No, Thank You, Lump of Meat

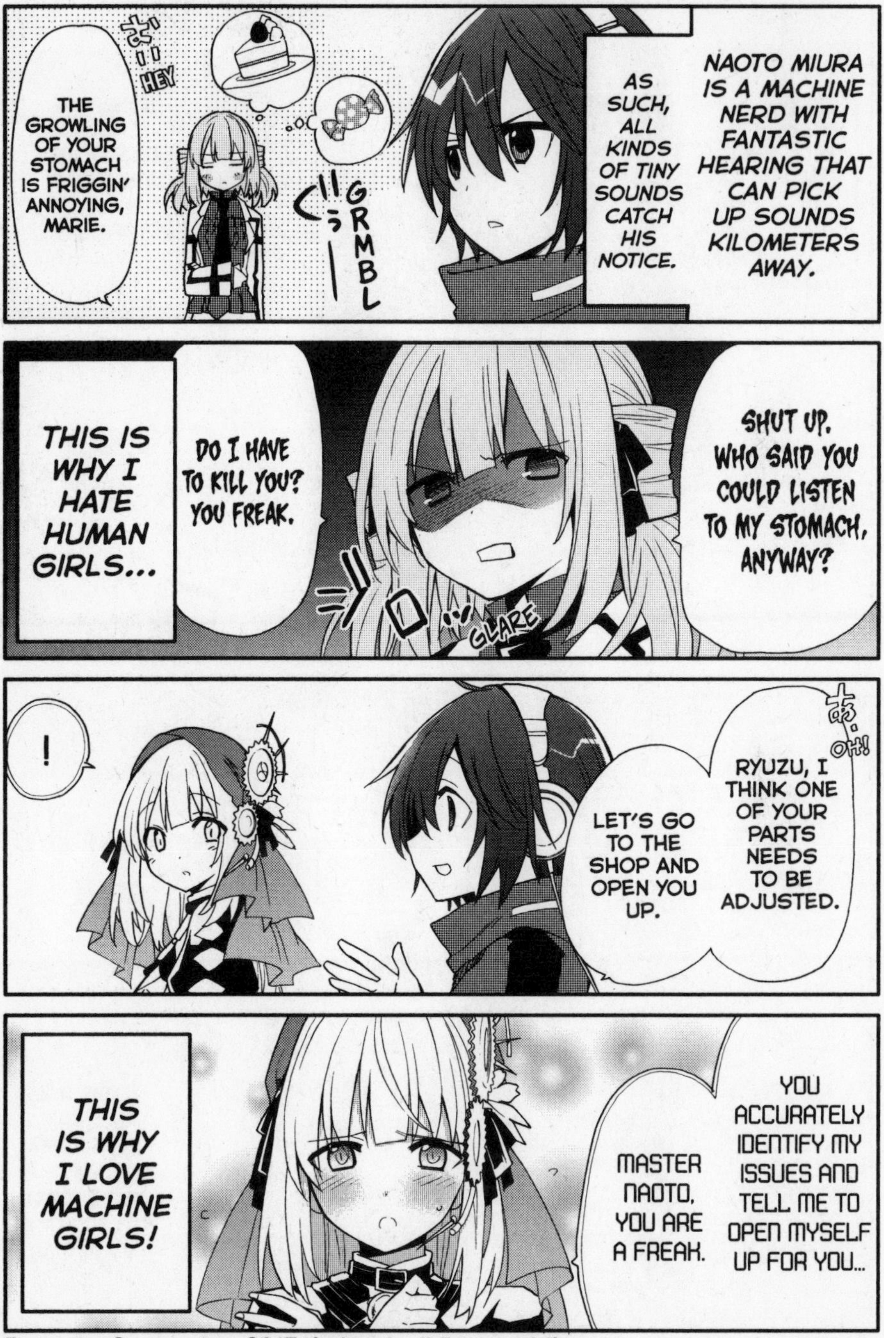
NAOTO MIURA IS A MACHINE NERD WITH FANTASTIC HEARING THAT CAN PICK UP SOUNDS KILOMETERS AWAY.
AS SUCH, ALL KINDS OF TINY SOUNDS CATCH HIS NOTICE.
GRMBL
HEY
THE GROWLING OF YOUR STOMACH IS FRIGGIN' ANNOYING, MARIE.
SHUT UP. WHO SAID YOU COULD LISTEN TO MY STOMACH, ANYWAY?
GLARE
DO I HAVE TO KILL YOU? YOU FREAK.
THIS IS WHY I HATE HUMAN GIRLS...
OH!
RYUZU, I THINK ONE OF YOUR PARTS NEEDS TO BE ADJUSTED.
LET'S GO TO THE SHOP AND OPEN YOU UP.
!
YOU ACCURATELY IDENTIFY MY ISSUES AND TELL ME TO OPEN MYSELF UP FOR YOU...
MASTER NAOTO, YOU ARE A FREAK.
THIS IS WHY I LOVE MACHINE GIRLS!

From the September 2017 Kodansha light novel flyer

Welcome, Machine Girl

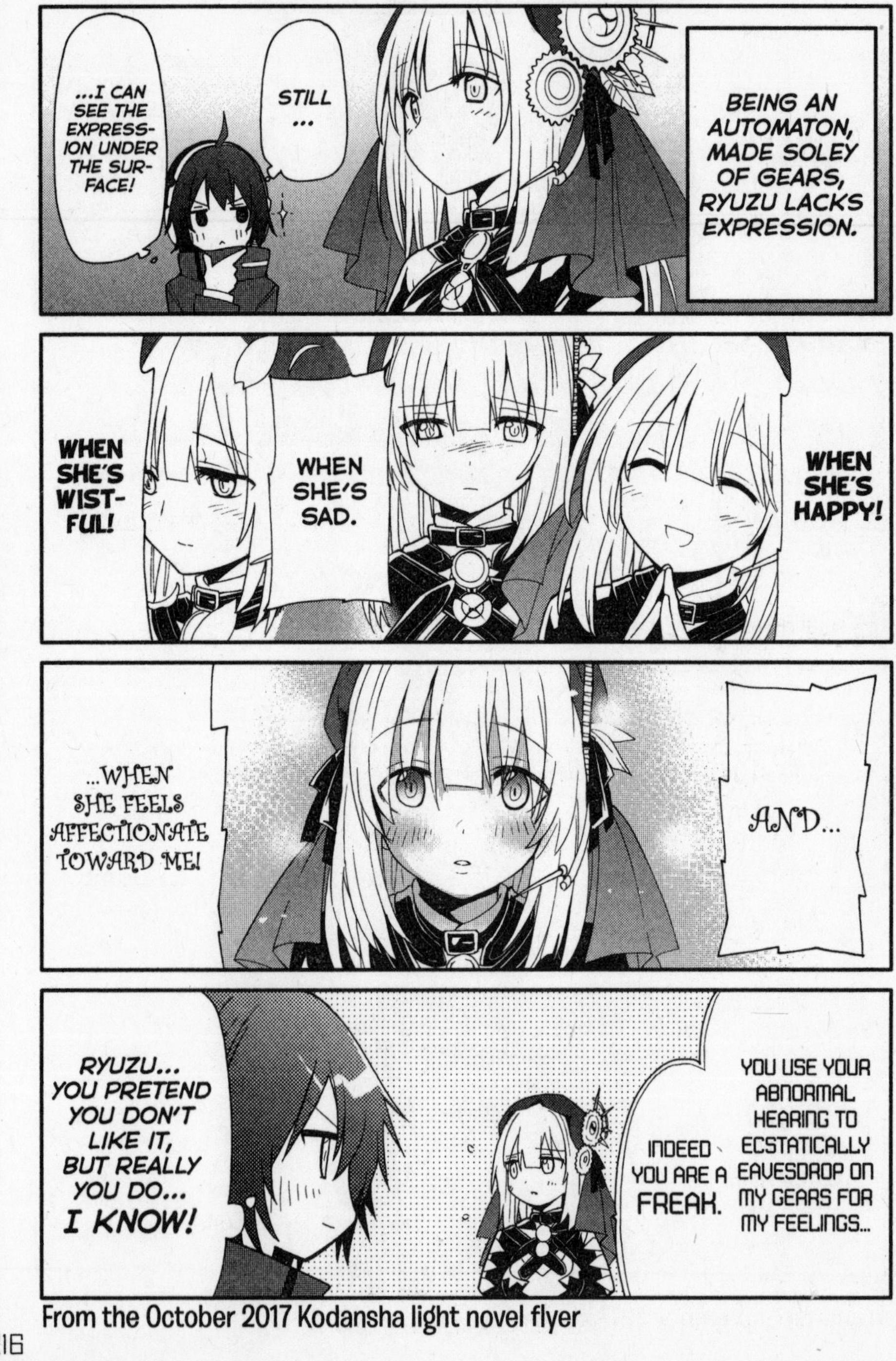
BEING AN AUTOMATON, MADE SOLEY OF GEARS, RYUZU LACKS EXPRESSION.
STILL...
...I CAN SEE THE EXPRESSION UNDER THE SURFACE!
WHEN SHE'S HAPPY!
WHEN SHE'S SAD.
WHEN SHE'S WISTFUL!
AND...
...WHEN SHE FEELS AFFECTIONATE TOWARD ME!
YOU USE YOUR ABNORMAL HEARING TO ECSTATICALLY EAVESDROP ON MY GEARS FOR MY FEELINGS...
INDEED YOU ARE A FREAK.
RYUZU... YOU PRETEND YOU DON'T LIKE IT, BUT REALLY YOU DO... I KNOW!

From the October 2017 Kodansha light novel flyer

Houko's Anguish

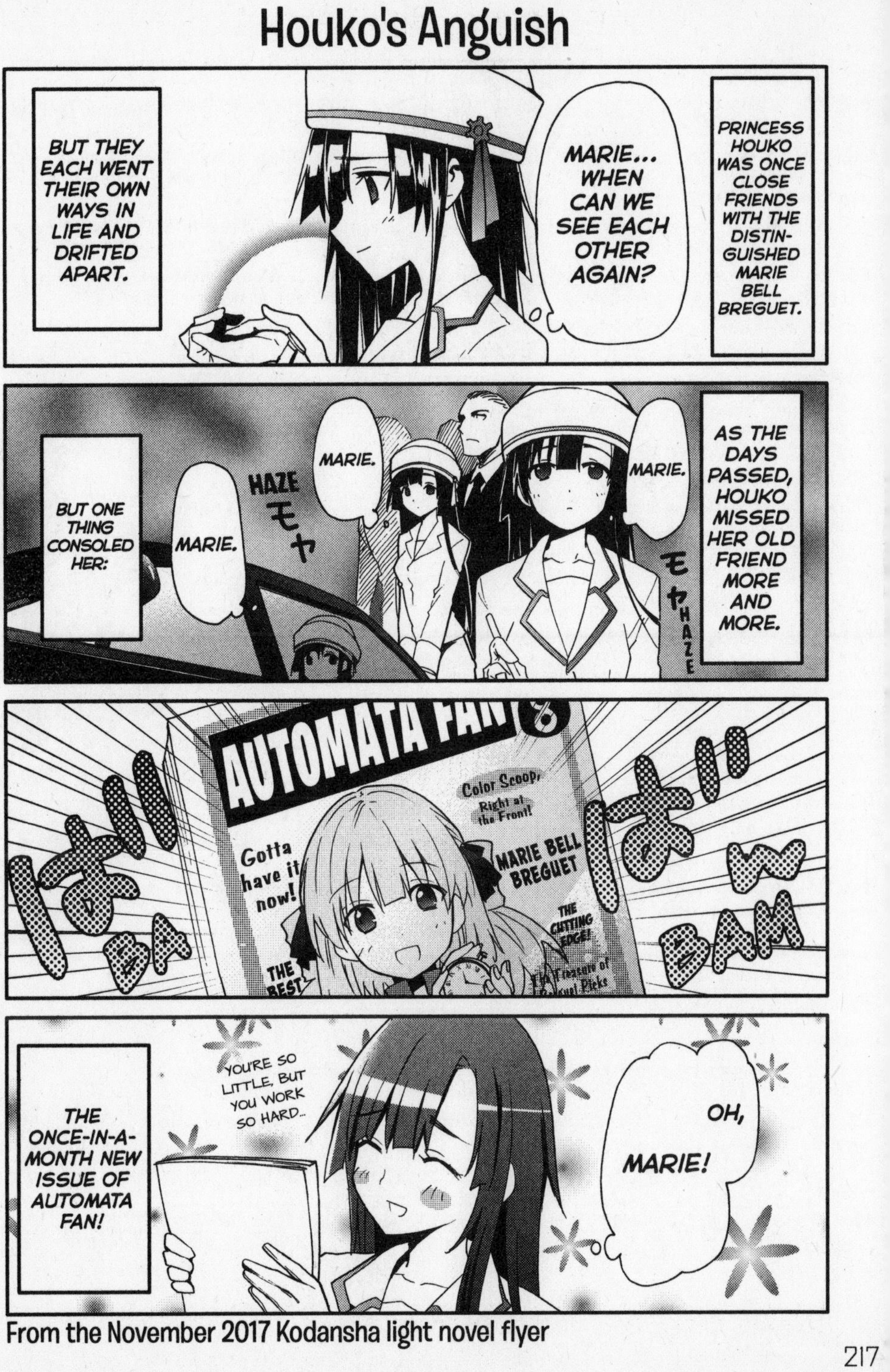
PRINCESS HOUKO WAS ONCE CLOSE FRIENDS WITH THE DISTIN-GUISHED MARIE BELL BREGUET.
MARIE... WHEN CAN WE SEE EACH OTHER AGAIN?
BUT THEY EACH WENT THEIR OWN WAYS IN LIFE AND DRIFTED APART.
AS THE DAYS PASSED, HOUKO MISSED HER OLD FRIEND MORE AND MORE.
モヤ HAZE
MARIE.
MARIE.
HAZE モヤ
MARIE.
BUT ONE THING CONSOLED HER:
BAM
AUTOMATA FAN 8
Color Scoop, Right at the Front!
MARIE BELL BREGUET
THE CUTTING EDGE!
Gotta have it now!
THE BEST
BA
OH, MARIE!
YOU'RE SO LITTLE, BUT YOU WORK SO HARD...
THE ONCE-IN-A-MONTH NEW ISSUE OF AUTOMATA FAN!

From the November 2017 Kodansha light novel flyer

YK: Hey, sorry this is out of the blue, but a friend pointed out to me, we can pretty much assume Naoto is doing it with RyuZU even though it's not shown.

TH: Uhh... This is not an 18+ book, you know. Well...whatever. Sure. Hit me with your theory of how Naoto isn't a virgin.

YK: So Naoto got a lot more assertive from Volume 2, right? In Volume 1, he was sure of what he felt, but even if Marie told him it was the others who were wrong and she needed his help, he didn't believe in himself enough to really buy into it, right?

TH: Oh... But isn't it because RyuZU told him he could and he actually did that from Volume 2 he started to speak up about what he felt?

YK: No, what my friend said is—things like that can't change people. Even if he's successful, even if he's recognized, fundamentally—there's only one thing that can make a man believe in himself.

TH: You mean...losing his virginity? (*Gulp.*)

YK: Yes, according to my friend, it's simple. A man's belief in his equipment is verily his belief in himself. (*Gulp.*)

YK: ...Think about it. Someone tells you you have talent. And then you've accomplished work with Marie and showed results. Could you then feel confident about yourself? Could you then be like Naoto?

TH: (*sincerely.*) ...Nah!

YK: Right?! So that's how it follows, Naoto got it on hot and heavy with RyuZU—and thereby, he found he was pretty good. And that's how he came to believe in himself! There is no other plausible explanation, my friend proclaimed!

TH: ...So what are you saying? That Marie's fragile aspects come from her virginity?

YK: Uh, no. This only applies to guys. My friend said:

> Listen. Men's anxiety and insecurity, confidence and self-esteem—when you get down to it, it all comes back to his weiner! Because we want women to want us! We want women's praise! We stake our lives so that pretty girls will tell us we're good! That, in the final analysis, is what men are!

So. Can you refute that? I couldn't...

TH: That argument is so rock-solid, you've brought me to my knees... But wait one second. If we assume that's true, does that mean that popularity can be achieved by losing one's virginity? Hypothetically.

YK: Oh. Nah, my friend said, "Doing it doesn't make you not a virgin."

TH: The hell is that paradox?! Hypothetically!

YK: Well, you see. What he's saying is, if just banging would give you confidence, you could just pay for it. But then there are still nonvirgins who don't have confidence. The real issue is whether there's an angel (girl) who will grant you (your thing) in an unconditional, positive way.

TH: Hey, wait. I'm asking you how to get popular so I'll be popular enough to have an angel like that, and you're saying to do that I have to first get the angel and have her comfortingly reassure my weiner? Where's the logic in that?! Hypothetically, of course!

YK: It's an infinite loop that maintains your state of unpopularity. Basically, a mysterious perpetual motion system to generate negentropy, you could say?

TH: A perpetual motion system to generate negative energy? (*Gasps.*) I have a new theory: Naoto suddenly became confident not because he lost his virginity, but because the negative energy of his virginity was reversed by RyuZU's imaginary gear and converted into positive energy—what do you think?!

YK: Uhh...sure, whatever works for you, man. =P Hypothetically!

TH: All of the above is fiction and has no relation to the novels, the comic, the anime, or my crappy, unpopular life!

Yuu
Kamiya
&
Tsubaki
Himana

1

Afterword

AFTERWORD

Here, with volume 9, we're nearing the end of the Shangri-La arc and of the comic. I enjoy that we're getting some serious violence such as we haven't seen since the beginning, along with a real hardcore psycho (Mr. Kiu). But he's not just a psycho. He's got a certain charisma and intelligence that makes him interesting.

By the way, my editor made me redraw the parts with Shirley and TemP a bunch of times to capture their cuteness.

I think I might have drawn TemP's breasts a little too big on the last page of Clock 45... At this point it's more of a joke than anything, right?

Editor: To guys, that's not a joke.

(Seriously?)

So yeah. I'll incorporate that feedback as I work on the next volume. I look forward to seeing you in Volume 10! ✩ Thank you for reading this far!

★ Special Thanks ★

Staff • Rin Nekoya
• Miho Miyanishi
• Kiyo Nekota
• Kanoto Ishikawa

Editor • Hiroshi Ogasawara

Designer • Ryo Hiiragi (I.S.W DESINGING)

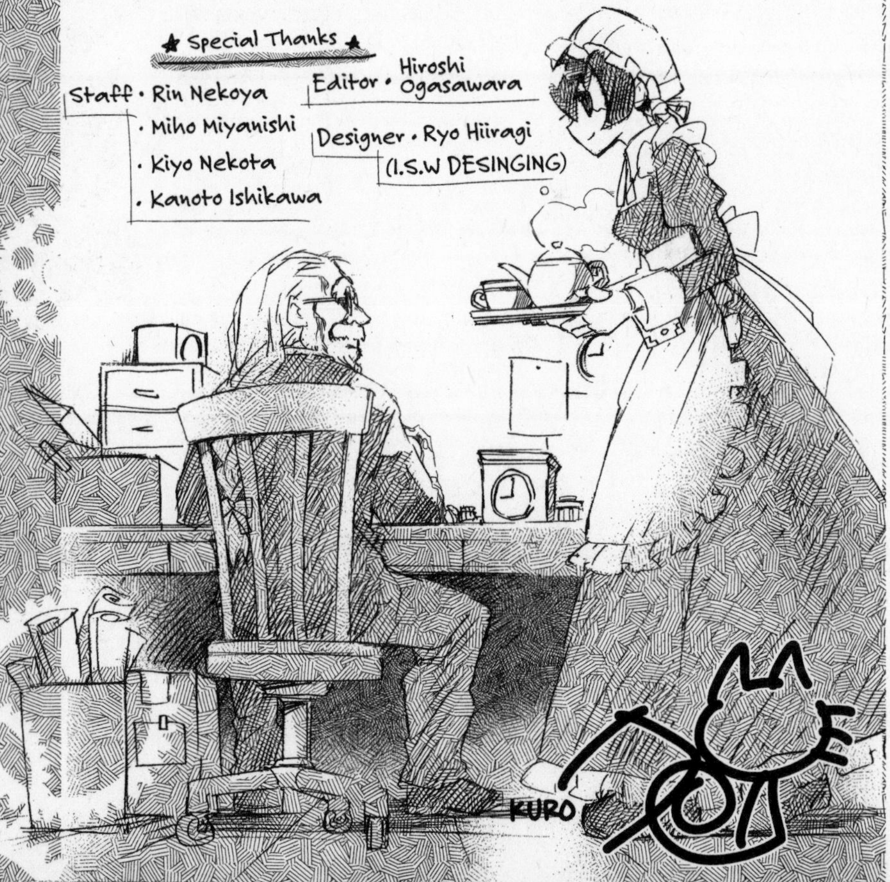

KURO

Translation Notes

TemP, page 200
TemP means "balance wheel."

Seal, page 211
In Japan, personal seals of a name are stamped in place of signatures.

Anego, page 212
Anego is a strict term for "elder sister," similar to *aniki*, a word for "elder brother" which yakuza use for immediate superiors.

Clockwork Planet

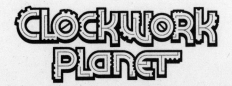

DELUXE EDITION

BATTLE ANGEL ALITA

After more than a decade out of print, the original cyberpunk action classic returns in glorious 400-page hardcover deluxe editions, featuring an all-new translation, color pages, and new cover designs!

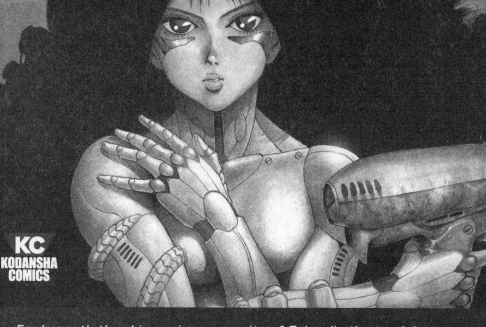

KC
KODANSHA
COMICS

Far beneath the shimmering space-city of Zalem lie the trash-heaps of The Scrapyard... Here, cyber-doctor and bounty hunter Daisuke Ido finds the head and torso of an amnesiac cyborg girl. He names her Alita and vows to fill her life with beauty, but in a moment of desperation, a fragment of Alita's mysterious past awakens in her. She discovers that she possesses uncanny prowess in the legendary martial art known as panzerkunst. With her newfound skills, Alita decides to become a hunter-warrior - tracking down and taking out those who prey on the weak. But can she hold onto her humanity in the dark and gritty world of The Scrapyard?

MARDOCK
マルドゥック・スクランブル
SCRAMBLE

Created by
Tow Ubukata

Manga by
Yoshitoki Oima

"I'd rather be dead."

Rune Balot was a lost girl with nothing to live for. A man named Shell took her in and cared for her...until he tried to murder her. Standing at the precipice of death, Rune is saved by Dr. Easter, a private investigator. He uses an experimental procedure known as "Mardock Scramble 09" on Rune, and it grants her extra-ordinary abilities. Now, Rune must decide whether or not to use her new powers to help Dr. Easter bring Shell to justice. But, does she even have the will to keep living a life that's been broken so badly?

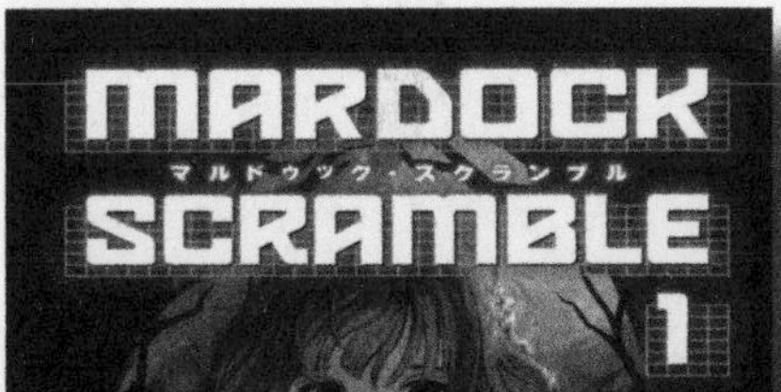
MARDOCK
マルドゥック・スクランブル
SCRAMBLE
1
created by
TOW UBUKATA
manga by
YOSHITOKI OIMA

Ages: 16+

KC
KODANSHA COMICS

VISIT KODANSHACOMICS.COM TO:

- View release date calendars for upcoming volumes
- Find out the latest about upcoming Kodansha Comics series

OWAC
2/19

A Kodansha Comics Trade Paperback Original
Clockwork Planet volume 9 copyright © 2018 Yuu Kamiya/Tsubaki Himana/Sino/Kuro
English translation copyright © 2018 Yuu Kamiya/Tsubaki Himana/Sino/Kuro
All rights reserved.

Published in the United States by Kodansha Comics, an imprint of
Kodansha USA Publishing, LLC, New York.

Publication rights for this English edition arranged through
Kodansha Ltd, Tokyo.

First published in Japan in 2018 by Kodansha Ltd., Tokyo

ISBN 978-1-63236-660-3

Printed in the United States of America.

www.kodanshacomics.com

9 8 7 6 5 4 3 2 1
Translation: Daniel Komen
Lettering: David Yoo
Editing: Haruko Hashimoto
Kodansha Comics edition cover design by Phil Balsman